D1342066

GENDER, PROPERTY AND POLITICS IN THE PACIFIC

Legal scholars, economists and international development practitioners often assume that the state is capable of 'securing' rights to land and addressing gender inequality in land tenure. In this innovative study of land tenure in Solomon Islands, Rebecca Monson challenges these assumptions. Monson demonstrates that territorial contests have given rise to a legal system characterised by state law, custom and Christianity, and shows that the legal construction and regulation of property has, in fact, deepened gender inequalities and other forms of social difference. These processes have concentrated formal land control in the hands of a small number of men leaders, and reproduced the state as a hypermasculine domain, with significant implications for public authority, political participation and state formation. Drawing insights from legal scholarship and political ecology in particular, this book offers a significant study of gender and legal pluralism in the Pacific, illuminating ongoing global debates about gender, land tenure, ethno-territorial struggles and the postcolonial state.

REBECCA MONSON is Associate Professor at the Australian National University College of Law. She has combined research and practice in the fields of social inequality, justice systems and resource governance for over fifteen years, with a particular focus on Australia and the Pacific Islands. She has held several Australian Research Council grants for socio-legal projects in the Pacific and regularly provides technical advice to aid donors, government agencies and international organisations.

Gender, Property and Politics in the Pacific

WHO SPEAKS FOR LAND?

REBECCA MONSON

Australian National University

CAMBRIDGE
UNIVERSITY PRESS

Shaftesbury Road, Cambridge CB2 8EA, United Kingdom

One Liberty Plaza, 20th Floor, New York, NY 10006, USA

477 Williamstown Road, Port Melbourne, VIC 3207, Australia

314–321, 3rd Floor, Plot 3, Splendor Forum, Jasola District Centre, New Delhi – 110025, India

103 Penang Road, #05–06/07, Visioncrest Commercial, Singapore 238467

Cambridge University Press is part of Cambridge University Press & Assessment,
a department of the University of Cambridge.

We share the University's mission to contribute to society through the pursuit of
education, learning and research at the highest international levels of excellence.

www.cambridge.org
Information on this title: www.cambridge.org/9781108844802

DOI: 10.1017/9781108953672

First published 2023

A catalogue record for this publication is available from the British Library.

Library of Congress Cataloging-in-Publication Data
NAMES: Monson, Rebecca, 1979– author.
TITLE: Gender, property and politics in the pacific : who speaks for land? / Rebecca Monson,
    Australian National University, Canberra.
DESCRIPTION: New York, NY : Cambridge University Press, 2022. | Includes bibliographical
    references and index.
IDENTIFIERS: LCCN 2022025803 (print) | LCCN 2022025804 (ebook) | ISBN 9781108844802
    (hardback) | ISBN 9781108953672 (paperback) | ISBN 9781108948876 (epub)
SUBJECTS: LCSH: Land tenure–Solomon Islands. | Women's rights–Solomon Islands. | Women
    and land use planning–Solomon Islands.
CLASSIFICATION: LCC HD1123 .M56 2022 (print) | LCC HD1123 (ebook) | DDC 333.3099593–dc23/
    eng/20220716
LC record available at https://lccn.loc.gov/2022025803
LC ebook record available at https://lccn.loc.gov/2022025804

ISBN 978-1-108-84480-2 Hardback

Contents

Maps

Acknowledgements

While it may sound trite, it is also true to say that this book would not have been possible without the support of family, friends, colleagues, institutions, networks and places. Mistakes and missteps in the pages that follow are absolutely my own. However this book emerges from learning from and with a great many people, not least of whom are the many Solomon Islanders who have taught me more than I could ever hope to capture in these pages. *Barava tangio tumas*! I am so enormously thankful for the friendship, collegiality and kinship that has been extended to me. I apologise in advance if I have forgotten to mention anyone.

I begin by acknowledging the Traditional Owners of the land I currently live and work on. Much of this book was written in what is now known as Canberra, on the unceded lands of the Ngunnawal and Ngambri people. I pay my respects to their Elders past and present, and thank them for their care of Country in the face of ongoing dispossession. I also acknowledge the custodians of the country I grew up on, the Gunaikurnai people. I thank them for their protection of Wurruk (land), Yarnda (waters), Watpootjan (air) and every living thing, and pay my respects to their Elders past and present. This land always was, always will be, Aboriginal land.

I am enormously thankful to Julie Anne Fakaia for permission to use the image, 'Spirits of the Solomons' that graces the cover of this book. The work denotes the many spirits of Solomon Islands and the interwoven cultures of its provinces. As Julie explained to me, 'the spirits of each province are different but equally important', and the work represents 'the connection with the spiritual world and our ancestors to protect our land and other resources, and also to protect our identity'. Julie's mother, Louisa Fakaia, explained to me that the work also conveys the talent of younger generations, and the modernisation of Solomon Islands' art – which is often under-represented on the global stage – by a woman. The mat in the background represents the interweaving of Solomon Islands' many people, and Kitchener Bird drew my attention to the fact that in Marovo, such mats would be made from vulu (discussed in Chapter 3).

My interest in Pacific legal systems was initially encouraged by Guy Powles and Melissa Castan at Monash University, and also by Philip Tagini over many cups of coffee and scribbled diagrams at Monash Wholefoods. John Handmer gave me confidence as a researcher and made my first trip to Solomon Islands possible, and Betty Luvusia invited me to travel with her to the Weather Coast.

When I embarked upon this particular project, Lincy Pendeverana suggested Kakabona as a field site and facilitated introductions. I offer my sincere thanks to the many people of Kolotoha, Verale, Verahoai, Vatukola, Kakabona, Tanavasa, Tangisalu, Mahu, Lumbu and Poha who welcomed me even when they already carried many research projects, consultations and workshops. Bruno Nana, Michael Tohina, Loretta Komikao Nana, Lorina Sekovani Nana, Vincent Kurilau, Francis Orodani, Paula Arahuri and Mary Borgia were especially generous with their time and knowledge and patiently taught me a great deal. I also learnt a great deal through a legal literacy workshop organised with Constance Hemmer, Julie Fakaia, Ruth Maetala and the Matana'ara Women's Association.

The extended Bird family and Buleani Community have given not only me but also my family more than I can put into words. I am immensely thankful for their ongoing generosity, guidance and friendship that stretches far beyond Buleani itself. Cliff Bird extended an initial invitation to work in Marovo, and Henry and Evelyn Bird hosted me and taught me a great deal – they are sorely missed. I thank the people of Sasaghana, Chea, Chubikopi, Cheara, Rukutu, Gepae, Patuseghe, Telina, Bisuana, Lolovuro and Batuna who welcomed me, shared their knowledge and gently nudged me when I was getting it wrong. *Leana vata ukala* and *leana vivia*.

The staff of a number of organisations in Solomon Islands have greatly assisted me by providing access to important documentation as well as space to work: the staff of the World Wildlife Fund and the National Resources Development Foundation in Gizo provided me with access to their collection of press clippings regarding the protests on Vella Lavella; the staff of the Magistrates' Courts in Gizo and Honiara provided me with access to court files; and the staff at the National Archives in Honiara have always gone above and beyond in assisting me to locate files relevant to this work. Permission and support for this work came from the Solomon Islands government, and I particularly thank the Ministry of Education and Human Resources Development and the provincial authorities of Guadalcanal and Western

Province. Without the permission and support of these institutions and their staff, this project would not have been possible.

The fieldwork that grounds this book was primarily undertaken during my doctorate at the ANU College of Law at the Australian National University, with financial support from an Australian Postgraduate Award and an Australian Federation of University Women Georgina Sweet Fellowship. Daniel Fitzpatrick, Chris Ballard, Margaret Jolly and Hilary Charlesworth provided insightful supervision and drew me into vibrant networks of scholars. I had the opportunity to extend my understanding during development consultancies and an Australian Research Council Discovery Grant (DP130104802) on property and climate change. An Australian Research Council Discovery Early Career Researcher Award (DE210100486) has provided me much-needed time to complete this book despite the exigencies associated with a global pandemic. I am enormously thankful for the ongoing support of my colleagues in the ANU College of Law under the deanships of Michael Coper, Stephen Bottomley, Sally Wheeler and Anthony Connolly.

Some of the ideas in this book have been published in 'Unsettled Exploration of Law's Archives: The Allure and Anxiety of Solomon Islands' Court Records' in *Australian Feminist Law Journal*; 'From *Taovia* to Trustee: Urbanisation, Land Disputes and Social Differentiation in Kakabona' in *The Journal of Pacific History*; and 'Vernacularising Political Participation: Strategies of Women Peacebuilders in Solomon Islands' in *Intersections*. I am grateful to the anonymous referees for their comments on those works, and to the editors of the journals for permission to draw on this material.

Teresia Teaiwa provided invaluable feedback on some of my very early ideas, and coincidentally with Bina D'Costa, provided important advice on feminist scholarship and solidarities. I am incredibly fortunate to wrestle with questions of land law and history alongside Joseph Foukona, and am thankful for ongoing collaborations with Kitchener Bird. In addition to those already mentioned, this book would not have been completed without the generosity, collegiality and friendship of Tarcisius Kabutaulaka, Gordon Nanau, Tammy Tabe, Patrick Pikacha, Jack Maebuta, Transform Aqorau, Paul Mae, Ali Tuhanuku, Kathleen Kohata, Carol Pitisopa, Philip Kanairara, Sophia Choniey, Florence Ramoni, Judith Foukona, Lucya Leong, Matthew and Louisa Fakaia, Angellina Fakaia, Judy and Johnson Fangalasu'u and Dianah and George Hoa'au. Siera Bird welcomed me when I arrived in Honiara, and Janet Mekaboti patiently coached me in Pijin during my first few months.

This work is also the product of thinking, talking, writing, teaching and conference-ing with Pyone Myat Thu, Tim Sharp, Matthew Allen, Sinclair Dinnen, Daniel Evans, Michelle Nayahamui Rooney, John Cox, Steffen

Dalsgaard, Brad Jessup, Caroline Compton, Sarah Milne, Miranda Forsyth, Melissa Demian, Louise Vella, and Debra McDougall, Bridget Fa'amatuainu and Dylan Asafo among others. I have benefitted from a vibrant network of ANU scholars concerned with critical and socio-legal approaches to the rule of law, including Jeremy Farrall, Nick Cheesman, Jolyon Ford, Moeen Cheema, Veronica Taylor, Jonathan Liljeblad and Desmond Manderson. Kylie Moloney and Kari James, also at ANU, helped me navigate the Pacific Manuscripts Bureau and secure permission to cite aspects of Ngatu's diaries, and I thank Jenny Sheehan at ANU CartoGIS Services for assistance with the maps. My thinking and practice around land, gender, development and 'expertise' has been nourished by Rea Abada Chiongson, Fiona Hukula and Ritu Verma, among others. Diti Bhattacharaya and Sarouche Razi provided valuable comments on specific aspects of this work, and Sam Rutherford provided exceptional research support and thoughtfully engaged with the text.

Asmi Wood has, from the time of my arrival at ANU, been an inspiring friend and colleague, and I have benefitted enormously from his sage advice. Sally Engle Merry and Christian Lund provided exceptional commentary on the doctoral work that formed the foundations of this book, and I am immensely appreciative of the insightful feedback from the two anonymous reviewers of the book manuscript. I thank Finola O'Sullivan, Marianne Nield and Rachel Imrie for guiding me through the publication process at Cambridge. I am also thankful for thoughtful engagement from Margaret Davies, Nicole Graham, Keith Camacho, Franz and Keebet von Benda Beckmann and Janine Ubink at various meetings and conferences.

The encouragement of Katerina Teaiwa and Nick Mortimer, Annie Kwai and Andrew Connelly and Alia Imtoual and José Luis Bobadilla Torres enabled me to get to the finish line despite all of us navigating various lockdowns and remote-schooling young children. Shakira Hussein's friend-ship and humour has sustained me for many years; Dru Marsh has an unparalleled ability to make me laugh until it hurts; and Grant Paulson and Kim Tuhaka-Paulson have long helped me wrestle with questions of imperi-alism and plurality.

I am incredibly thankful to my parents, Russell and Carol, who have always provided care and interest, as well as to my siblings and their partners – Katherine Monson and Mark Phelan, Andrew Monson and Anja Wondra. And last but certainly not least, my partner Charlie and our children Ruth and Chloe have provided me with the space, support, encouragement, joy, under-standing, hugs and love necessary for the book to be completed. They have borne the burdens of my absences of many kinds.

Ruthie and Coco: thank you for your patience. I hope you will find the pictures that you asked for in this book, even if they're not the kinds you anticipated.

Glossary

Bangara (Bareke, Marovo)	Man representative of the kokolo
Bangara male (Bareke)	A woman from a chiefly line responsible for placating the spirits, ensuring the security of influential men and the kokolo
Butubutu (Marovo)	Kin-based group
Chiama (Marovo)	Pre-Christian 'head priest'
Chupu (Ghari)	A variety of gift exchanges that may also have other names
Daki taovia (Ghari)	Influential woman, 'big' or chiefly woman
Dapi (Bareke)	Terraced pond fields cultivated by the kokolo under supervision of the bangara
Duli (Ghari)	Named matrilineage, often referred to as 'tribe'
Hope (Bareke, Marovo)	Sacred, prohibited, spiritually sanctioned place
Horevura (Bareke, Marovo)	The process of migration and resettlement from the bush to the coastal areas
Jif (Pijin)	Chief, a man representative of the group
Kastom (Pijin)	Custom, local or indigenous as distinct from foreign ways of doing things
Kokolo (Bareke)	Kin-based group
Kot (Pijin)	Court as well as other forms of dispute resolution by the state
Laens (Pijin)	Lines, lineage
Lotu (Pijin)	Church, Christianity, Christian beliefs, institutions and activities
Lukotu (Bareke)	A form of gift exchange
Malaghai (Ghari)	Leading warrior, specialised assassin

Pepesa (Bareke)	Named territory of land, sea or both
Puava (Marovo)	Named territory of land, sea or both
Ruta (Bareke)	Low-lying, swampy places for cultivating taro, associated with the women who cultivate them
Siama (Bareke)	Pre-Christian 'head priest'
Subtraeb (Pijin)	Sub-tribe
Taovia (Ghari)	Influential man, often referred to as jif (chief)
Tina (Ghari)	Often translated as 'family', a small, local matrilineage
Traeb (Pijin)	Tribe
Tutungu (Ghari)	Emplaced genealogical histories
Varane (Bareke, Marovo)	Leading warrior
Vele (Ghari)	Sorcerer
Vulu (Bareke, Marovo)	Leafy, pandanus-like shrub which grows in dense clumps and is very difficult to uproot
Vuluvulu (Bareke, Marovo)	'Blood core', lineal substance of the group, a woman of high standing
Vuvungu (Ghari)	Named matrilineages within the duli (tribe)

Grounding Debates about Land

Gender Inequality, Property and the Role of the State

Today, people everywhere around the world are fighting for land.[1]

> Andrew Te'e, commander of the Isatabu Freedom
> Movement, in the militia's newsletter,
> *Isatabu Tavuli*, March 2000

Olketa woman no save tok lo saed lo land.

Phrase commonly heard throughout Solomon Islands, which may be translated as women cannot, may not, or should not speak about land.

In his 2012 New Year's address to the nation, Solomon Islands' Governor General Sir Frank Kabui warned that land tenure was the issue most likely to spark conflict in the country. He expressed concern that Solomon Islanders were 'caught between our cultural way of life and the cash economy', and identified a number of key challenges including the need to register land held collectively by kin groups in order to make it 'marketable'; the inequitable distribution of resource revenue, not only within landholding groups but more significantly, between landholders and corporate investors; and the 'illegal occupation' of land in the vicinity of the national capital, Honiara, by migrants from other islands. He exhorted Solomon Islanders to 'adjust their mindset' in order to benefit from capitalist investment and move forward 'as one people and one nation'.[2]

This speech came in the aftermath of a period of land-related conflict known as 'the Ethnic Tension' (1998–2003) and in the midst of a multibillion

---

[1] Andrew Te'e, 'Land Is Sacred to Me', *Isatabu Tavuli* (2 March 2000).
[2] Previously discussed in Rebecca Monson, 'The Politics of Property: Gender, Land and Political Authority in Solomon Islands' in Siobhan McDonnell, Matthew Allen and Colin Filer (eds.), *Kastom, Property and Ideology: Land Transformations in Melanesia* (ANU Press, 2017) 383.

dollar state-building mission undertaken by Pacific Island Forum member countries (2003–2017). The core themes of the address occupy a prominent position in politics not only in Solomon Islands but many parts of the Pacific (Map 1.1), where the laws of independent states ensure that the vast majority of land is held under customary tenure. The merits of these arrangements are frequently discussed around cooking fires, market stalls and in churches; in the plush hotels in which logging deals are negotiated; and in the courts in which those transactions are subsequently contested. People bemoan the prevalence of land disputes, debate the advantages of customary tenure vis-à-vis state regulation, and discuss the ongoing reconfiguration of traditional notions of land, leadership and social relations in the face of colonisation, resource extractivism and increasingly, climate change. In Solomon Islands these matters have been a recurrent flashpoint for violence: in late 2021, protests against perceived political corruption and foreign control over natural resources once again led to rioting and looting, demands for increased provincial autonomy and the deployment of police and troops from across the region. However, these debates are certainly not unique to Solomon Islands – as observed by Andrew Te'e, an influential figure in the Solomon Islands' conflict, there are people across the world engaged in similar struggles and debates.

This book takes gender relations as a critical entry point for understanding debates about land and the ways in which seemingly 'local' property disputes are bound up with multiscalar struggles over natural resources and political ordering. I first visited Solomon Islands in 2004, in the immediate post-conflict period and largely on the invitation of Solomon Islander friends I had met through student and civil society networks in Melbourne, Australia. During that first visit, I was already aware that Solomon Islands was widely perceived to exemplify broader regional concerns regarding land tenure, economic development and 'weak states'. I quickly learnt, too, that it was impossible to understand any aspect of social life, including people's expectations of me as a young, white Australian woman, without paying serious attention to people's gendered, kin-based relationships with and through specific places – whether those places were the islands of their parents or grandparents, the village of a Member of Parliament or the swimming holes in which I bathed with other women while men did so further upstream. In this book I trace processes of negotiating claims to land across scales, particularly from the so-called 'local' through to the 'provincial' and 'national'. In so doing, I expose some of the ways in which struggles over legally defined property rights are bound up with the (re)production of gendered, racialised and territorialised identities, with

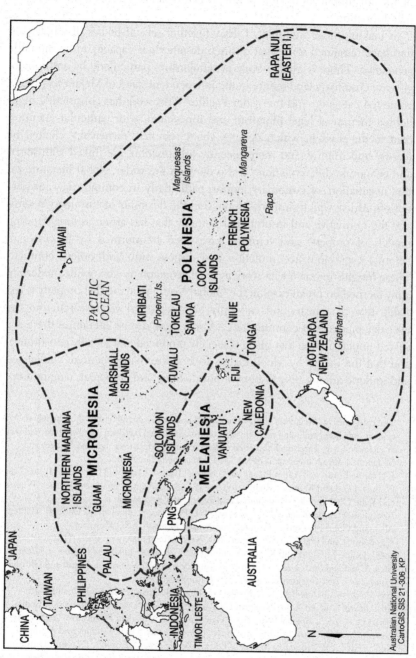

MAP 1.1. One view of the region showing Melanesia, Polynesia and Micronesia

significant implications for political participation, public authority and state formation.

In making these arguments I draw together several bodies of scholarship that have remained somewhat distinct, despite their capacity to be mutually generative. There is a large body of scholarship, particularly by anthropologists, on customary land tenure in the independent states of Melanesia (itself a contested category) and the wider Pacific.[3] This work has consistently highlighted themes of legal pluralism and innovation, with particular attention paid to the ways in which debates about resource 'ownership' elicited by forestry and mining, and more recently urbanisation, are linked with social and economic differentiation.[4] I also draw on the wider, global literature on the 'negotiation' of customary tenure, particularly in common law jurisdictions in Africa, which similarly emphasises the flexibility of customary systems and the normative and institutional plurality that has arisen as long-standing models of property and territory have been transformed by processes of colonial expansion, accumulation and dispossession and violent conflict.[5] These insights resonate with work by legal geographers who, while predominantly focused on urban cases in the Global North, contend that property is less stable than it appears and can only be understood via research into the everyday practices of communities.[6] Across these diverse literatures there is a shared understanding that space is socially produced and socially constitutive, and that the means by which claims to land are made, secured, challenged and undone are not only discursive but material and corporeal, ranging from

[3] The categories of 'Melanesia', 'Polynesia' and 'Micronesia' emerged from the nineteenth-century, racialised and often racist division of the islands that has been widely critiqued as well as reclaimed: e.g. Tarcisius Kabutaulaka, 'Re-Presenting Melanesia: Ignoble Savages and Melanesian Alter-Natives' (2015) 27(1) *The Contemporary Pacific* 110.

[4] E.g. Paula Brown and Anton Ploeg (eds.), 'Special Issue: Change and Conflict in Papua New Guinea: Land and Resource Rights' (1997) 7(4) *Anthropological Forum* 507; James F Weiner and Katie Glaskin (eds.), *Customary Land Tenure and Registration in Australia and Papua New Guinea: Anthropological Perspectives* (ANU Press, 2007); Siobhan McDonnell, Matthew Allen and Colin Filer (eds.), *Kastom, Property and Ideology* (ANU Press, 2017).

[5] E.g. Kristine Juul and Christian Lund (eds.), *Negotiating Property in Africa* (Heinemann, 2002); Janine M Ubink and Kojo S Amanor (eds), *Contesting Land and Custom in Ghana: State, Chief and the Citizen* (Leiden University Press, 2008); Nancy Lee Peluso and Christian Lund (eds.), *New Frontiers of Land Control* (Routledge, 2013).

[6] E.g. Franz von Benda-Beckman, Keebet von Benda-Beckmann and Anne Griffiths (eds.), *Spatializing Law: An Anthropological Geography of Law in Society* (Ashgate 2009); Robyn Bartel et al. (eds.), 'Special Issue: Legal Geography: An Australian Perspective' (2013) 51(4) *Geographical Research*; Irus Braverman, Nicholas Blomley, David Delaney and Alexandre Kedar (eds.), *The Expanding Spaces of Law: A Timely Legal Geography* (Stanford University Press, 2014); Sarah Keenan, *Subversive Property: Law and the Production of Spaces of Belonging* (Routledge, 2015).

everyday forms of territoriality such as the building of fences or clearing of land for gardens, to the use of violence such as the eviction of migrant settlers.

Questions of land, identity and development have been at the heart of conflict not only in Solomon Islands but also the Autonomous Region of Bougainville in Papua New Guinea, as well as a series of coups in Fiji, political instability in Vanuatu and struggles for freedom in East Timor, New Caledonia and West Papua. Much of the literature on the state in the southwest Pacific is therefore concerned with the relationship between struggles over natural resources and political instability and violent conflict.[7] A significant amount of attention has been paid to the legal recognition of territorially based 'tribes' and 'clans'. As we see throughout this book, these are not necessarily pregiven, static or inevitable identities, but are often fore-grounded and more clearly delineated as people seek to render themselves legible as 'customary landowners'. In the post-independence Melanesian states, where Indigenous custodianship of land is constitutionally enshrined and extractive industries the predominant form of 'development', these groups have emerged as a fundamental unit of political organisation.[8]

The relationship between land tenure, land conflict, and political authority and ordering has also received sustained attention in other contexts. In the literature on land tenure in Africa, there is widespread recognition that, as Sara Berry puts it, 'contests over land involve contests over authority as well as resources: they draw on and reshape relations of power as well as property'.[9] Christian Lund has extensively argued that property and political authority are in fact mutually constitutive, with processes of recognition trekking backwards and forwards between the two: that is, controlling access to a resource or adjudicating conflicts can produce legitimacy, and that in turn produces

[7] Chris Ballard and Glenn Banks, 'Resource Wars: The Anthropology of Mining' (2003) 32 *Annual Review of Anthropology* 287; Matthew G Allen, *Greed and Grievance: Ex-Militants' Perspectives on the Conflict in Solomon Islands, 1998–2003* (University of Hawaii Press, 2013).

[8] Colin Filer, 'Compensation, Rent and Power in Papua New Guinea' in Susan Toft (ed.), *Compensation for Resource Development in Papua New Guinea* (Law Reform Commission of Papua New Guinea, Monograph No. 6, Research School of Pacific and Asian Studies at The Australian National University, National Centre for Development Studies at The Australian National University, Pacific Policy Paper No. 24, 1997) 156, 6; Victoria Stead, *Becoming Landowners: Entanglements of Custom and Modernity in Papua New Guinea and Timor Leste* (University of Hawai'i Press, 2017); Tarcisius Kabutaulaka, 'Land Groups, Land Registration and Economic Development Projects on Guadalcanal, Solomon Islands' (2020) 42(3) *Pacific Studies* 107.

[9] Sara Berry, 'Debating the Land Question in Africa' (2002) 44(4) *Comparative Studies in Society and History* 638, 256.

authority, which then reinforces power to control access to land.[10] These processes are multiscalar, with Matthew Allen suggesting that in Melanesia, extractive industries have engendered three 'governable spaces' – that is, configurations of territory, identity and rule – namely, the space of customary landownership (or property), the space of island-based indigeneity (often understood in terms of regions or provinces) and the space of nationalism.[11]

These diverse bodies of scholarship demonstrate that property and political authority are crucially linked and multiscalar, but they have not yet paid sustained attention to the gendered aspects of these processes. I therefore draw on a related but somewhat distinct set of debates focused on gender inequality in customary land tenure systems. Yet here, in scholarly and policy debates regarding gender, land tenure and legal pluralism, I have often found voices, experiences and insights from the Pacific to be markedly absent. This cannot be attributed to a lack of interest on the part of Pacific Islanders, since the 1986 publication, *Land Rights of Pacific Women*, written by Pacific Islanders, was one of the earliest volumes on the subject anywhere in the world.[12] Rather, I suggest that it emerges from the geopolitical marginalisation of the Pacific Islands and Pacific feminists that has also been observed by Teresia Teaiwa and Claire Slatter in feminist security studies.[13] In this book I hope to bridge some of these empirical and analytical divides, bringing ongoing scholarly and policy debates about customary land in the Pacific, scholarship on property and political ordering and work on gender inequality and customary land tenure into closer dialogue. In so doing, I also respond to calls within legal geography to move beyond its current emphasis on contexts in the Global North and engage more deeply with legal pluralism, gender relations and political ecology.[14]

---

[10] Christian Lund, *Local Politics and the Dynamics of Property in Africa* (Cambridge University Press, 2008); Thomas Sikor and Christian Lund, 'Access and Property: A Question of Power and Authority' (2009) 40(1) *Development and Change* 1; Christian Lund, 'Rule and Rupture: State Formation through the Production of Property and Citizenship' (2016) 47(6) *Development and Change* 1199.

[11] Matthew G Allen, *Resource Extraction and Contentious States: Mining and the Politics of Scale in the Pacific Islands* (Palgrave Pivot, 2018), drawing in particular on Michael Watts, 'Violent Environments: Petroleum Conflict and the Political Ecology of Rule in the Niger Delta, Nigeria' in Richard Peet and Michael Watts (eds.), *Liberation Ecologies: Environment, Development and Social Movements* (Routledge, 2nd ed, 2004) 250.

[12] Cema Bolabola et al., *Land Rights of Pacific Women* (Institute of Pacific Studies of the University of the South Pacific, 1985).

[13] Teresia Teaiwa and Claire Slatter, 'Samting Nating: Pacific Waves at the Margins of Feminist Security Studies' (2013) 14(4) *International Studies Perspectives* 447.

[14] Franz von Benda Beckmann, Keebet von Benda-Beckmann and Anne Griffiths, 'Space and Legal Pluralism: An Introduction' in Franz von Benda-Beckmann, Keebet von Benda-

In the chapters that follow, I draw on colonial archives, court records and ethnographic work to track the ways in which Solomon Islanders have navigated imported legal models and pre-existing understandings of land and people to maintain and reorganise socio-spatial relations across more than a century of engagement with Christianity, Euro-American legalities, wage labour and extractive industries. Lawyers, economists and international development practitioners working in the Pacific have often demonstrated immense confidence in the ability of the state to 'secure' rights to land as a means to resolve land disputes, build peace, make land more 'marketable' and address socioeconomic inequality.[15] Yet by tracing struggles over land across sites, scales and time, we see that state intervention has overwhelmingly worked to generate social fragmentation and contestation, and consolidate control over land in the hands of a relatively small number of men while relegating many others to the sidelines of land deals. Moreover, these contests are not simply 'local' struggles; we see that they are multiscalar and entangled with wider issues of public authority, political participation and state formation. Indeed I argue that gendered processes of land disputing and gendered processes of authority formation are so intertwined as to be mutually constitutive, and they work to reproduce the state as a masculine, even hypermasculine, domain.

In the remainder of this chapter I introduce some key terms and debates that ground this book. Terms such as 'customary tenure' and 'land reform' may mean quite different things depending on the colonial and postcolonial history of the context in question, so I first introduce select aspects of land policy discourse in the Pacific, noting both global influences and regional particularities. In the second part, I highlight key features of ongoing scholarly and policy debates regarding gender relations and land tenure that I return to throughout this book, again grounding them in my understanding of debates in the Pacific. In the third section I explain my approach to property, and why

---

Beckmann and Anne Griffiths (eds.), *Spatializing Law: An Anthropological Geography of Law in Society* (Ashgate, 2009) 4; Irus Braverman et al., 'Introduction: Expanding the Spaces of Law' in Irus Braverman et al. (eds.), *The Expanding Spaces of Law: A Timely Legal Geography* (Stanford University Press, 2014) 1, 9; Daniel F Robinson and Nicole Graham, 'Legal Pluralisms, Justice and Spatial Conflicts: New Directions in Legal Geography' (2018) 184(1) *The Geographical Journal* 3, Dana Cuomo and Katherine Brickell, 'Feminist Legal Geographies' (2019) 51(5) *Environment and Planning A: Economy and Space* 1043; Josephine Gillespie and Nicola Perry 'Feminist Political Ecology and Legal Geography: A Case Study of the Tonle Sap Protected Westlands of Cambodia' (2019) 51(5) *EPA: Economy and Space* 1089.

[15] At the time of writing in late 2021, numerous donor-supported customary land recording programmes are underway in Solomon Islands, promoted as a means to ensure tenure security and reduce violent conflict.

I came to focus my attention on long-term processes of contesting land and the role of the state in legitimating claims to land. This possibly led me to foreground the ways in which gendered land relations are socially and discursively constructed, while potentially backgrounding (but never ignoring) everyday practices of land use and the materialities of land. In the fourth section I address the role of property scholars: throughout this book we see that 'ideas' about property and authority have implications 'on the ground', and this has shaped my writing in important ways. I conclude with a brief introduction to Solomon Islands and a chapter synopsis.

1.1 LAND, CUSTOM AND THE STATE: INEQUALITY AND THE (RE)TURN TO THE CUSTOMARY

Debates about land in Solomon Islands, as anywhere, are simultaneously global and structural, and situated in and particular to the communities in which they arise. The world's largest geographical region, the Pacific Ocean or Oceania, is often inscribed as 'small' and 'remote', yet Islanders and their places have long been part of a global flow of ideas and practices concerning law, property, gender and rights, channelled through networks of trade, government administration, education, development assistance and Indigenous political movements.[16] This was particularly clear when, from the 1950s onwards, colonial administrators in the Melanesian states of Solomon Islands (then the British Solomon Islands Protectorate), Papua New Guinea (administered by Australia) and Vanuatu (jointly administered by Britain and France) explicitly drew on ideas and technologies developed elsewhere as they sought to transform customary tenure systems by implementing a system of land registration developed in Sudan and Kenya.[17] This approach was influenced by modernisation theory's view of customary systems, which saw customary tenure as lacking clearly defined and enforceable rights, and therefore unable to provide the necessary 'security' to ensure agricultural investment and economic growth. These colonial attempts to codify and formalise customary tenure were extremely expensive, widely resisted and largely unsuccessful. Today, most land in the independent states

---

[16] Epeli Hau'ofa, 'Our Sea of Islands' (1994) 6(1) *The Contemporary Pacific* 148; Sally Engle Merry and Donald Brenneis, 'Introduction' in *Law and Empire in the Pacific* (SAR Press, 2004); Teresia Teaiwa, 'On Analogies: Rethinking the Pacific in a Global Context' (2006) 18(1) *The Contemporary Pacific* 71; Tracey Banivanua Mar, *Decolonisation and the Pacific: Indigenous Globalisation and the Ends of Empire* (Cambridge University Press, 2016).

[17] Peter Larmour, 'Policy Transfer and Reversal: Customary Land Registration from Africa to Melanesia' (2002) 22(2) *Public Administration and Development* 151.

in the Pacific remains unregistered, and more than 80 per cent of land in most countries is held under customary tenure.[18]

Solomon Islands became independent in 1978, preceded by Papua New Guinea in 1975 and followed by Vanuatu in 1980. These states, like others in the region, developed constitutional and statutory mechanisms affirming the importance of customary tenure (in fact the constitutions of many provide that custom is a general source of law). In general terms, this means that most people continue to gain access to land primarily through their association with groups that are understood to be collectively attached to the land (typically extended families and descent groups), rather than through freehold or leasehold. In Solomon Islands, customary land is held according to 'current customary usage',[19] a definition that explicitly acknowledges the possibility of innovation. In this sense the legal definition is consistent with popular understandings of kastom, a Pijin word that refers to local as opposed to foreign ways of doing things. Kastom is widely understood to emerge from both colonial and postcolonial experiences, and is certainly not limited to primordial or unchanging ideas and practices.[20]

During the 1980s and 1990s, debates about land tenure in Melanesia, as in many other parts of the world, became tied to economic liberalisation, and it is somewhat legendary that in 1995, the World Bank proposed a condition on a loan to the Papua New Guinean government that would require the registration of vast tracts of land. The proposal was leaked, there were large protests by students and non-governmental organisations, and both the government and the World Bank quickly backed down.[21]

---

[18] In all independent states aside from Kiribati, the Federated States of Micronesia and Tonga, more than 80 per cent of land is held under customary tenure. Available data indicates that approximately 45 per cent of land in Kiribati is customary land, with public and freehold land concentrated on the largest island, Kiritimati, while 95 per cent of land on other islands remains under customary tenure. In the Federated States of Micronesia, 65 per cent of land is held under customary tenure. Tonga came under the rule of King Tupou I in 1831, and the 1875 Constitution brought all land under the ownership of the king, who allocates access to men. This system is not commonly considered 'customary': AusAID, *Making Land Work*, Vols I and II (Commonwealth of Australia, 2008), 4, 29, 119.

[19] Land and Titles Act 1996 [Cap 133] (Solomon Islands), s 2 ('Land and Titles Act').

[20] For more detailed discussion focused on Solomon Islands see e.g. Debra L McDougall, *Engaging with Strangers: Love and Violence in the Rural Solomon Islands* (Berghahn Books, 2016), 37; Allen, *Greed and Grievance*, 15–17; David W Akin, *Colonialism, Maasina Rule, and the Origins of Malaitan Kastom* (University of Hawai'i Press, 2013). For discussion distinguishing custom and kastom in Papua New Guinea see Melissa Demian, 'Dislocating Custom' (2015) 38(1) *PoLAR: Political and Legal Anthropology Review* 91.

[21] Larmour, 'Policy Transfer'.

The protests in Papua New Guinea, and the subsequent abandonment of proposed registration, occurred as prevailing assumptions about customary tenure were beginning to shift. By the mid-1990s, there was a growing body of research that demonstrated that land titling programmes in many parts of the world had not only failed to deliver the security of tenure they promised, but played a role in exacerbating land-related conflicts, as well as deepening patterns of inequality linked to factors such as gender, class and ethnicity.[22] A related body of research drew attention to the existence of multiple, adaptable and overlapping claims to landscapes, which could not be adequately comprehended by the static, two-dimensional understandings of land inherent in land titling programmes. As noted by Dianne Rocheleau and David Edmunds in a landmark work on the gender dimensions of tree tenure, this led to the emergence of new approaches to property which emphasised that land and resource tenure is characterised by multidimensional niches in landscapes; that authority over resources is vested in multiple levels of social organisation, themselves adaptable and negotiated; and that land tenure systems must be understood as emerging from dynamic social relationships and processes of contestation.[23]

This scholarship has been relatively successful in challenging the once predominant view in development policy circles, namely, that replacing customary tenure with state-based systems of private freehold tenure is necessary to provide secure property rights, agricultural intensification and economic growth. When I commenced this work in the late-2000s, a new consensus had emerged among a range of influential policy institutions: now, there was a widespread perception that the role of the state was to provide the legal and administrative environment necessary to support the transformation of customary tenure in the 'right' direction. This was the view adopted by the World Bank in its 2003 report, *Land Policies for Growth and Poverty Reduction*, as well as AusAID's 2008 report, *Making Land Work*.[24]

---

[22] Jean-Philippe Platteau, 'The Evolutionary Theory of Land Rights as Applied to Sub-Saharan Africa: A Critical Assessment' (1996) 27(1) *Development and Change* 29; Ingrid Yngstrom, 'Women, Wives and Land Rights in Africa: Situating Gender beyond the Household in the Debate Over Land Policy and Changing Tenure Systems' (2002) 30(1) *Oxford Development Studies* 21.

[23] Dianne Rocheleau and David Edmunds, 'Women, Men and Trees: Gender, Power and Property in Forest and Agrarian Landscapes' (1997) 25(8) *World Development* 1351.

[24] Klaus Deininger, *Land Policies for Growth and Poverty Reduction* (World Bank and Oxford University Press, 11 June 2003), AusAID, *Making Land Work*. For discussion see further Platteau, 'The Evolutionary Theory of Land Rights'; Daniel Fitzpatrick, 'Evolution and Chaos in Property Rights Systems: The Third World Tragedy of Contested Access' (2005) 115(5) *Yale Law Journal* 996; Admos Chimhowu, 'The "New" African Customary Land Tenure:

As Ann Whitehead and Dzodzi Tsikata have demonstrated, this shift converged with the emphasis on 'participation', 'capacity-building' and local level land management taken by many non-governmental organisations.[25] Indeed the 're-turn to the customary' observed by Whitehead and Tsikata with respect to land occurred in the context of a wider turn within at least some parts of the international development community towards increased engagement with 'customary', 'informal' and 'hybrid' justice systems as a means to 'strengthen the rule of law'.[26]

Today, calls by neoliberal institutions for various forms of land registration or recording frequently coincide with the policy prescriptions of human rights advocates who, while drawing on different ideological premises, often promote similar reforms as a means to 'legally empower' women and Indigenous people against territorial encroachment and dispossession.[27] In the Pacific, there have been many efforts to map Indigenous territories, often through public hearings, and then legalise them by recording collective interests. For example, Vanuatu has experienced a 'land grab' in the last twenty years, largely as a result of political elites leasing commercially valuable land for their own benefit and that of investors. The response, with support from both neoliberal aid donors and Indigenous peoples' movements, has been legislative reform that provides that customary authorities are responsible for hearing competing claims to land ownership, and their decisions are recorded and not subject to any avenue of appeal or review.[28]

Characteristic, Features and Policy Implications of a New Paradigm' (2019) 81 *Land Use Policy* 897.

[25] Ann Whitehead and Dzodzi Tsikata, 'Policy Discourses on Women's Land Rights in Sub–Saharan Africa: The Implications of the Re–Turn to the Customary' (2003) 3(1–2) *Journal of Agrarian Change* 67.

[26] E.g. Deborah Isser (ed.), *Customary Justice and the Rule of Law in War-Torn Societies* (United States Institute of Peace Press, 2011), Brian Z Tamanaha, Caroline Sage and Michael Woolcock (eds.) *Legal Pluralism and Development: Scholars and Practitioners in Dialogue* (Cambridge University Press, 2012).

[27] Whitehead and Tsikata, 'Policy Discourses'; Aili Mari Tripp, 'Women's Movements, Customary Law, and Land Rights in Africa: The Case of Uganda' (2004) 7(4) *African Studies Quarterly* 1; Catherine Boone, 'Legal Empowerment of the Poor through Property Rights Reform: Tensions and Trade-Offs of Land Registration and Titling in Sub-Saharan Africa' (2018) 55(3) *Journal of Development Studies* 384.

[28] Siobhan McDonnell, 'Urban Land Grabbing by Political Elites: Exploring the Political Economy of Land and the Challenges of Regulation' in Siobhan McDonnell, Matthew G Allen and Colin Filer (eds.), *Kastom, Property and Ideology: Land Transformations in Melanesia* (ANU Press, 2017) 283; Sue Farran and Jennifer Corrin, 'Developing Legislation to Formalise Customary Land Management: Deep Legal Pluralism or a Shallow Veneer?' (2017) 10(1) *Law and Development Review* 1.

This shift towards affirming customary tenure systems is often viewed with a degree of caution by gender and development professionals, feminist legal scholars and women's rights advocates working in many parts of the world. Importantly, feminist scholars have often pointed out that while the flexibility of customary tenure systems may open up multiple pathways for negotiating access to land, not all of these pathways are equally accessible to all people. For example, anthropologist Margaret Rodman observed that in Vanuatu during the 1970s and 1980s, it was generally men who were 'masters of tradition' and able to manage contemporary interpretations of custom.[29] More recently, ni-Vanuatu development specialist Anna Naupa has warned that debates about the land grab in Vanuatu have focused on the role of foreigners in land deals, thereby neglecting the heterogeneity of customary groups, the role of local elites and the intimate, gendered exclusions of customary land practice.[30] In a related vein, Pauline Peters has cautioned against an overemphasis on 'negotiation' in Africa, urging us to pay closer attention to 'who benefits and who loses from instances of "negotiability" in access to land' and to the political and economic processes that 'limit or end negotiation and flexibility for certain social groups'.[31] These scholars highlight the need for accounts of land tenure that acknowledge the dynamism and negotiability of land relations, while also identifying the multiple norms, institutions and power asymmetries that enhance or constrain the ability of different people to succeed in contests over land. The challenge of acknowledging both the dynamism of land tenure and the structural conditions that may shape it is one that underpins many of the most persistent debates in scholarship on gender inequality and land tenure.

1.2 GENDER INEQUALITY IN LAND TENURE: GLOBAL AND REGIONAL DEBATES

The importance of women's rights to natural resources has been somewhat accepted by the international development community since the 1970s, and is recognised by the *Convention on the Elimination of all forms of*

---

[29] Margaret C Rodman, *Masters of Tradition: Consequences of Customary Land Tenure in Longana, Vanuatu* (University of British Columbia Press, 1987).

[30] Anna Naupa, 'Making the Invisible Seen: Putting Women's Rights on Vanuatu's Land Reform Agenda' in Siobhan McDonnell, Matthew G Allen and Colin Filer (eds.), *Kastom, Property and Ideology: Land Transformations in Melanesia* (ANU Press, 2017) 305, 313.

[31] Pauline E Peters, 'Inequality and Social Conflict Over Land in Africa' (2004) 4(3) *Journal of Agrarian Change* 314, 270.

Discrimination against Women (CEDAW).[32] However as Shahra Razavi observes, it was not until the 1990s that the field began to flourish, in part due to the increased interest in human rights-based approaches and democratisation in the aftermath of the Cold War.[33] Bina Agarwal's pioneering text, *A Field of One's Own: Gender and Land Rights in South Asia* was published in 1994,[34] and there is now a rich, varied and complex literature on gendered land relations, particularly with respect to common law jurisdictions in Africa and South Asia.[35]

The relationship between gender equality and land tenure has now emerged as a key concern for feminist scholars, development practitioners and civil society actors in many parts of the world, and there is relatively widespread agreement that women as a social group are often losing out as a result of land transformations occurring at various scales across the globe.[36] This perception is reflected in the Sustainable Development Goals, set by the UN General Assembly in 2015, which include the target of 'reform' to ensure access, ownership and control over land and other forms of property in order to achieve gender equality and empower women and girls.[37] However, there is significant debate as to how exactly women are 'losing out', why it matters and

---

[32] CEDAW contains specific clauses on equality in agrarian reforms, and in the ownership, management and disposition of property: *Convention on the Elimination on All Forms of Discrimination Against Women*, opened for signature 18 December 1979 (entry into force 3 September 1981), 1248 UNTS 13, Arts 14(2)(d), 15(2), 16(1)(h).

[33] Shahra Razavi, 'Introduction: Agrarian Change, Gender and Land Rights' (2003) 3(1–2) *Journal of Agrarian Change* 2, 4; Shahra Razavi, 'Liberalisation and the Debates on Women's Access to Land' (2007) 28(8) *Third World Quarterly* 1479.

[34] Bina Agarwal, *A Field of One's Own: Gender and Land Rights in South Asia* (Cambridge University Press, 1994).

[35] For similar observations see Caitlin Kieran, Kathryn Sproule, Sheryl Doss, Agnes Quisumbing and Sung Mi Kim, 'Examining Gender Inequalities in Land Rights Indicators in Asia' (2015) 46 (S1) *Agricultural Economics* 119; Sonia Akter, Pieter Rutsaert, Joyce Luis, Nyo Me Htwe, Su Su Ban, Budi Raharjo and Arlyna Pustika, 'Women's Empowerment and Gender Equity in Agriculture: A Different Perspective from Southeast Asia' (2017) 69 *Food Policy* 270. Radcliffe observes that with the notable exception of the work of Deere and León, gender has often been a secondary concern in scholarship on Latin America: Sarah A. Radcliffe, 'Gendered Frontiers of Land Control: Indigenous Territory, Women and Contests over Land in Latin America' (2014) 21(7) *Gender, Place and Culture* 854; Carmen Diana Deere and Magdalena León, *Empowering Women: Land and Property Rights in Latin America* (University of Pittsburgh Press, 2001).

[36] Michael Levien, 'Gender and Land Dispossession: A Comparative Analysis' (2017) 44(6) *Journal of Peasant Studies* 1113.

[37] United Nations General Assembly, *Transforming Our World: The 2030 Agenda for Sustainable Development*, 70th sess, Agenda items 15 and 116, UN Doc A/RES/70/1 (21 October 2015), Goal 5, Target 5.A.

what kinds of 'reforms' might engender greater equality in contexts characterised by a high degree of legal pluralism.

As feminist perspectives and gender analyses of land tenure have proliferated, a wide range of implicit and explicit conceptual differences and debates have emerged in scholarship as well as policy discourses. There have been major (and sometimes heated) disagreements about the nature of people's interests under customary tenure, the effect of economic, political and legal transformations of customary systems, and the advantages and disadvantages of customary tenure as compared to state regulation of land. One of the most enduring analytical differences arises between those who perceive land tenure primarily in terms of a hierarchical and gendered 'bundle of rights' and focus on the content of norms and the institutions that adjudicate those rights; and those who emphasise gendered knowledges, subjectivities and processes of negotiation, interaction and contestation.[38]

For the purpose of my discussion here, I refer to these different starting points or analytical emphases as 'rights-based approaches' on the one hand and 'feminist political ecology' approaches on the other.[39] These approaches are certainly not distinct in feminist scholarship and I risk simplifying and essentialising very complex debates and movements, however I hold them apart momentarily for heuristic reasons, as they enable me to highlight some of the key contours of global debates regarding gendered land relations and debates in the Pacific, at least as I understand them. Scholars of both approaches share a concern with understanding the ways in which transformations in customary tenure engendered by colonisation and commodification have affected gender relations and women in particular, however they differ in important respects, including in their understanding of the dynamism of legal systems and the role of the state in addressing gender inequality.

The paradigmatic rights-based approach, which is predominant in global policy dialogues, in the reports produced by international organisations, and in my own discipline of law, typically starts by 'mapping out' the key laws, norms and institutions affecting land relations and assessing them by reference

---

[38] This distinction is also observed by Razavi, and Whitehead and Tsikata: Razavi, 'Introduction: Agrarian Change', 23; Whitehead and Tsikata, 'Policy Discourses', 77. On the persistence of this tension in debates regarding gender and legal pluralism more broadly see Rachel Sieder and John Andrew McNeish, 'Introduction' in John Andrew McNeish and Rachel Sieder (eds.), *Gender Justice and Legal Pluralities: Latin American and African Perspectives* (Taylor & Francis, 2013) 1, 14.

[39] In a similar vein Doss et al. identify feminist human rights, feminist liberal economics and feminist political economy: Cheryl Doss, Gale Summerfield and Dzodzi Tsikata, 'Land, Gender and Food Security' (2014) 20(1) *Feminist Economics* 1.

to human rights frameworks, notably CEDAW.[40] These approaches are often influenced by Amartya Sen's entitlement model and emphasise that people's control over land is central to their capacity to 'lead the kinds of lives they value'.[41] Studies in this tradition acknowledge that people's experiences of legal pluralism are diverse and vary according to factors including gender, class, race and marital status. However it is important to note that gender is still conceived of primarily in terms of a binary of women/men. To date, very little attention has been paid to more diverse gender identities, gender identities and gender expression, or to sexual orientations.[42]

Rights-based accounts understand land tenure as comprised of multiple, socially embedded claims to land or 'a bundle of rights', which are organised in a gendered hierarchy. Studies drawing on this approach often conclude that women's land rights lack the characteristics of 'ownership' and are therefore 'usufructuary' and 'secondary' because they are dependent on relations with others, whereas men are often found to hold 'primary' rights. However, these concepts and distinctions emerge from Euro-American jurisprudence and liberal thought, and as Ann Whitehead and Dzodzi Tsikata have noted, their application to customary systems is often highly contested.[43] I return to this issue further below, but at this juncture note that these concepts are remarkably persistent not only in development policy and legal

---

[40] E.g. Sue Farran, 'Land Rights and Gender Equality in the Pacific Region' (2005) 11 *Australian Property Law Journal* 131.

[41] Amartya Sen, *Development as Freedom* (Oxford University Press, 1999); for one discussion see Ambreena Manji, '"Her Name Is Kamundage": Rethinking Women and Property among the Haya of Tanzania' (2000) 70(3) *Africa* 482, 491–5.

[42] Susie Jacobs observes that the question of sexuality remains 'largely unexplored', and Saunoamaali'i Karanina Sumeo notes with respect to gender identities and expression that she was 'unable to find any literature on the voices of *fa'afafine* and *fakaleitī* in the land discourses or in urban planning in the Pacific': Susie Jacobs, 'Gender, Land and Sexuality: Exploring Connections' (2014) 27(2) *International Journal of Politics, Culture, and Society* 173, 173; Karanina Sumeo, 'Land Rights and Empowerment of Urban Women, Fa'afafine and Fakaleitī in Samoa and Tonga' (PhD thesis, Auckland University of Technology, 2016) 3. There is however a rapidly growing body of work by Indigenous scholars drawing on critical traditions to address heteropatriarchy in property regimes in settler colonial contexts: see for example Sarah Hunt and Cindy Holmes, 'Everyday Decolonization: Living a Decolonizing Queer Politics' (2015) 19(2) *Journal of Lesbian Studies* 154; J Kēhaulani Kauanui, *Paradoxes of Hawaiian Sovereignty: Land, Sex and the Colonial Politics of State Nationalism* (Duke University Press, 2018), Kim TallBear, 'Identity Is a Poor Substitute for Relating: Genetic Ancestry, Critical Polyamory, Property, and Relations' in Brendan Hokowhitu et al. (eds.), *Routledge Handbook of Critical Indigenous Studies* (Routledge, 2021); Hōkūlani K Aikau, 'Mana Wahine and Mothering at the Lo'i: A Two-Spirit/Queer Analysis' (2021) *Australian Feminist Studies*, DOI: 10.1080/08164649.2020.1902272.

[43] See e.g. Whitehead and Tsikata, 'Policy Discourses', 78.

practice, but also in scholarship. Scholars of Melanesia often deploy this language to describe customary arrangements, even as they simultaneously critique the imposition of Euro-American conceptions of property upon those systems. Furthermore, as we see throughout this book, these concepts have enduring effects 'on the ground', and are crucial to ongoing debates about land in Solomons Islands.

Rights-based accounts of gendered land relations frequently trace contemporary inequalities to customary principles of inheritance (particularly when patrilineal) and the division of labour, as well as to transformation of customary systems wrought by colonialism, capitalism and neoliberalism.[44] Numerous studies have exposed the negative effects of land titling programmes, which have often undermined the customary rights that historically protected women, while simultaneously enabling male household heads to strengthen their control over land by registering their customary claims as 'ownership'. There is also widespread recognition that even when statutory law assures women the same rights as men (for example, through gender equitable titling), women may lack effective control over land due to discriminatory social norms and practices, weak implementation, insufficient enforcement capacity, lack of political will and poor access to legal services.[45] Rights-based accounts are therefore not entirely static; however, as Ambreena Manji observes, they are non-discursive – a rights-based account typically 'looks at the rule, notes the gap between rule and practice, and puts it down as a failure of implementation'.[46] That is to say, they recognise the importance of both de jure and de facto entitlements, but their starting point is usually the former and they regard behaviour as either following or deviating from these rules. These approaches tend not to acknowledge or address the diverse ways in which new norms may be generated, and they often see 'social practice' primarily in terms of *challenges* for gender equality. They are unable to fully acknowledge the non-legal, extralegal and illegal means by which people may gain, maintain and control access to land and importantly, generate new norms.

Movements of scholars and advocates emphasising a rights-based approach differ immensely in the extent to which they believe the state can address inequality, but their analytical emphasis on norms and institutions and the

---

44 See e.g. Perpetua W Karanja, 'Women's Land Ownership Rights in Kenya' (1991) 1991 *Third World Legal Studies* 109; Susan Farran, 'Land Rights and Gender Equality in the Pacific Region' (2005) 11 *Australian Property Law Journal* 131; Faustin Kalabamu, 'Patriarchy and Women's Land Rights in Botswana' (2006) 23(3) *Land Use Policy* 237.

45 See e.g. Agarwal, *A Field of One's Own*, Whitehead and Tsikata, 'Policy Discourses'.

46 Ambreena Manji, '"Her Name is Kamundage": Rethinking Women and Property Among the Haya of Tanzania', (2000) 70(3) *Africa* 482, 494.

'failures of implementation', often leads them to demonstrate greater confidence in the state than in customary regimes. Whitehead and Tsikata have observed that although feminist lawyers in Africa hold many reservations about state law, law reform to 'secure' women's rights to land is often seen as preferable to 'simply allowing customary law to evolve'.[47] Nitya Rao has similarly concluded that collectives in India have 'put greater faith in legal and policy reform than in changing customary value systems'.[48] Movements of feminist lawyers, NGO collectives and civil society groups in many parts of the world have embraced rights-based discourse and invested significant amounts of energy into bringing test cases, seeking reform of state law to amend inheritance practices and secure women's rights to land and improving legal literacy. These strategies may be appropriate in some contexts, but they also reinforce the legal positivist assumption that privileges the authority of state law – as Manji has argued, rights-based approaches assume that gender inequality is most likely to be remedied by ensuring women have formal legal ownership of land, then taking steps to ensure that normativity catches up afterwards.[49]

These rights-based accounts of gendered land relations and social change often sit uneasily with debates in Solomon Islands and the wider Pacific, at least as I understand them as a non-Indigenous scholar and occasional development consultant. This is particularly obvious with respect to the role of the state. As I have noted, people of the Pacific have long been concerned with questions of gender inequality and land relations, as exemplified by the lively contributions to *Sustainable Development or Malignant Growth*, a landmark collection edited by 'Atu Emberson Bain.[50] However, within existing scholarship and civil society commentary, there is often a marked reluctance to recommend state intervention in land matters, even among those who have embraced rights-based approaches and advocated law reform with respect to other matters such as gender-based violence.[51] I understand this reluctance as

[47] Whitehead and Tsikata, 'Policy Discourses', 92.

[48] Nitya Rao, 'Custom and the Courts: Ensuring Women's Rights to Land, Jharkhand, India' (2007) 38(2) *Development and Change* 299, 301.

[49] Manji, "Her Name is Kamundage", 494. See also Wendy Olsen, *Moral Political Economy and Poverty: Four Theoretical Schools Compared* (Department of Economics, University of Oxford, Economics Working Paper Series No. GPRG-WPS-031, 2005) 28.

[50] 'Atu Emberson-Bain (ed.), *Sustainable Development or Malignant Growth? Perspectives of Pacific Island Women* (Marama Press, 1994).

[51] For discussion of Papua New Guinean women's engagement with human rights discourses see Martha Macintyre, "'Hear Us, Women of Papua New Guinea': Melanesian Women and Human Rights' in Anne-Marie Hilsdon, Martha Macintyre, Vera Mackie and Maila Stivens (eds.), *Human Rights and Gender Politics: Asia-Pacific Perspectives* (Routledge, 2000), 143.

grounded in the widespread commitment to maintaining customary tenure –
that is, not only Indigenous control over land, but Indigenous ontologies,
values, practices and *kinship* with land – which is seen as essential to the
maintenance of uniquely Pacific forms of governance, sovereignty and the
capacity of Islanders to exert any power vis-à-vis national, regional and international institutions and structural asymmetries.[52]

The commitment to maintaining customary tenure means, as Kristina
Stege observes for Marshall Islands, that state involvement in land matters is
often regarded with scepticism and suspicion, including by governments
themselves.[53] Where relatively clear calls for state involvement do exist, they
generally relate to remedying perceived deficiencies in existing legislative
recognition of custom, rather than advocating further legislative interference
with, or codification of, custom. To give an example, in Kiribati there is
support for legislative reform to ensure that daughters can inherit the same
share of land as sons – but this targets the colonial Native Lands Ordinance
1956, which purported to codify customary tenure, and did so by vesting
individual title in the most senior male in the kin group, thereby entrenching
patrilineal inheritance.[54] Calls for legislative reform have typically been far
more reserved in contexts where the principles of customary tenure have not
been codified, as is the case in Solomon Islands, Vanuatu and Papua New
Guinea. In general terms, in these contexts, calls for state intervention have
often been framed in terms of the need to 'protect' custom and devolve further
authority to the local level, for example through recording territorial boundaries and the names of landholding groups, and affirming the role of chiefs in
resolving disputes.

I stress that this widespread caution with respect to state intervention in land
matters should not be assumed to be an endorsement of current practice nor a
romanticisation of customary tenure (although in some instances it may be).

[52] See e.g. Melanesian Indigenous Land Defence Alliance, 'Declaration of the 3rd Meeting of
the Melanesian Indigenous Land Defence Alliance (MILDA) Held at Natapao Village on the
Island of Lelepa, Vanuatu, 10–11 March 2014' (2014), available at http://milda.aidwatch.org.au;
Spike Boydell, 'The "Pacific Way": Customary Land Use, Indigenous Values and
Globalization in the South Pacific' in Alan Tidwell and Barry Scott Zellen (eds.), *Land,
Indigenous Peoples and Conflict* (Routledge, 2015) 108.
[53] Kristina E Stege, 'An Kōrā Aelōñ Kein (These Islands Belong to Women): A Study of Women
and Land in the Republic of the Marshall Islands' in Elise Huffer (ed.), *Land and Women: The
Matrilineal Factor: The Cases of the Republic of the Marshall Islands, Solomon Islands and
Vanuatu* (Pacific Islands Forum Secretariat, 2008) 1, 21.
[54] Secretariat of the Pacific Community, *Stocktake of the Gender Mainstreaming Capacity of
Pacific Island Governments: Kiribati* (2015); Claire Slatter, 'Gender and Custom in the South
Pacific' (2012) 13–14 *Yearbook of New Zealand Jurisprudence* 89, 97–8.

Anna Naupa and Joel Simo, who have been key figures in land policy debates in Vanuatu, emphasise the importance of maintaining kastom but are clear that contemporary decision-making is marked by inequality and exclusion, particularly as between men and women, and local political elites and 'other' landowners. They observe that in one of their sites, Raga, there has been 'a gradual shift in attitude towards women's involvement in land matters; increasingly, it is being perceived as a male-only domain', while in Mele, 'contemporary interpretation of kastom (traditional values and customs) . . . has further marginalised women from land decision-making processes'.[55] In the same volume, Ruth Maetala, a leading expert on gender and natural resource management in Solomon Islands, concludes that on Guadalcanal, Isabel and Makira, 'men always want to head the negotiations' regarding extractive industries and tourism, and they do so by disregarding 'matrilineal protocols' that should accord women a role.[56]

I have often found it difficult to reconcile these accounts by Pacific writers with the rights-based, hierarchical understandings of tenure that predominate in aid policy discourses and the global dialogues led by international organisations. I suggest that they share far more in common with the kinds of analytical approaches developed within feminist political ecology – approaches which, like the work of Pacific feminist scholars, remain largely neglected in both legal scholarship and policy debates concerned with gender, land and property rights.[57] The accounts I have highlighted here emphasise relational and

---

[55] Anna Naupa and Joel Simo, 'Matrilineal Land Tenure in Vanuatu: "Hu i Kakae Long Basket?" Case Studies of Raga and Mele' in Kristina E Stege (ed.), *Land and Women: The Matrilineal Factor: The Cases of the Republic of the Marshall Islands, Solomon Islands and Vanuatu* (Pacific Islands Forum Secretariat, 2008) 74, 77.

[56] Ruth Maetala, 'Matrilineal Land Tenure Systems in Solomon Islands: The Cases of Guadalcanal, Makira and Isabel Provinces' in Elise Huffer (ed.), *Land and Women: The Matrilineal Factor: The Cases of the Republic of the Marshall Islands, Solomon Islands and Vanuatu* (Pacific Islands Forum Secretariat, 2008) 35, 51. See also Martha Macintyre, 'Petztorme Women: Responding to Change in Lihir, Papua New Guinea' (2003) 74(1–2) *Oceania* 120.

[57] For key discussions, see e.g. Ritu Verma, *Gender, Land and Livelihoods in East Africa: Through Farmers' Eyes* (International Development Research Centre, 2001); Rie Odgaard, 'Scrambling for Land in Tanzania: Processes of Formalisation and Legitimisation of Land Rights' (2002) 14(2) *European Journal of Development Research* 71; Farhana Sultana, 'Fluid Lives: Subjectivities, Gender, and Water in Rural Bangladesh' (2009) 16(4) *Gender, Place and Culture* 427; Fiona A Mackenzie, 'Gender, Land Tenure and Globalisation: Exploring the Conceptual Ground' in Dzodzi Tsikata and Pamela Golah (eds.), *Land Tenure, Gender, and Globalisation: Research and Analysis from Africa, Asia and Latin America* (International Development Research Centre, 2010) 35; Rebecca Elmhirst, 'Introducing New Feminist Political Ecologies' (2011) 42(2) *Geoforum* 129, Sharlene Mollett and Caroline Faria 'Messing With Gender in Feminist Political Ecology' (2013) 45 *Geoforum* 116.

processual understandings of identity, place and custom, and they situate gendered land relations within wider political economic processes such as globalisation, neoliberalism, resource extractivism and agrarian change. They stress that kastom is 'interpreted' and cultural protocols may be 'disregarded'; they highlight that both claims to land and the discourses through which they are constituted are dynamic, multiple and contested. Importantly, these accounts consistently understand land tenure in terms of fluid, negotiable and reciprocal relationships. For example, Naupa and Simo identify differences in men's and women's customary claims but resist assessing these in terms of a 'traditional' hierarchy, emphasising instead the symbolic and embodied entanglement of people with each other and the land, notably with respect to reproduction of the kin group that collectively holds the land. They ultimately conclude that 'women's [customary] land rights and relationships to land are as important as those of men, yet manifested differently'.[58]

My observations here will be familiar to scholars of the Pacific, who will recognise that this aspect of Naupa and Simo's analysis resonates with – indeed they seem to refer to – the so-called Melanesian model of sociality associated with anthropologist Marilyn Strathern among others.[59] This model emphasises that understandings of personhood and kinship in Melanesia are relational, contingent and elicited through social and material exchanges. Strathern suggests that whereas Westerners tend to 'regard the sexes in a permanent relation of asymmetry', in Melanesia, 'the asymmetry is always there, but men's and women's occupation of these respective positions is always transient'.[60] On this view, Melanesian understandings contrast with the Western models of property and personhood, which perceive the individual as an ontologically privileged category, and assume clear boundaries between subject and object, self and other, male and female. The Melanesian model therefore challenges rights-based accounts of customary tenure, and both socialist and liberal ideas of rights-based development more

---

[58] Naupa and Simo, 'Matrilineal Land Tenure', 85.

[59] Naupa and Simo link their analysis to Lissant Bolton's work, which expressly draws on Strathern: see Naupa and Simo, 'Matrilineal Land Tenure', 85 citing Lissant Bolton, *Unfolding the Moon: Enacting Women's Kastom in Vanuatu* (University of Hawai'i Press, 2003), 95.

[60] Marilyn Strathern, *The Gender of the Gift: Problems with Women and Problems with Society in Melanesia* (University of California Press, 1988) 330–32. See also Marilyn Strathern, *Kinship, Law and the Unexpected: Relatives Are Always a Surprise* (Cambridge University Press, 2005).

broadly, that assume a polarised, asymmetrical gender structure in which most men have land and most women do not.[61]

Strathern has described the 'Melanesian model of sociality' as 'a kind of convenient or controlled fiction',[62] and it has been enormously valuable in exposing the fraught relationship between Euro-American and Melanesian understandings of gender and property. Throughout this book we see that Euro-American juridical conceptions of property have been inadequate for understanding the fluidity of Melanesian socio-spatial relations, and also central to their disruption and erosion, by asserting and naturalising particular boundaries and hierarchical binaries, including men/women, owners/users and autochthons/migrants. However as Michael Scott observes, the 'Melanesian model' is also sometimes treated as 'common knowledge about the way Melanesians think and act';[63] indeed I have encountered its deployment as 'common knowledge' about Pacific Islanders generally. When mobilised *in this way*, the model essentialises both Melanesian and Western ontologies; it fails to address questions of social change and the transformative effects of Euro-American property on Indigenous subjectivities and aspirations; and it tends to emphasise dynamism and reciprocity at the expense of acknowledging social inequality within customary tenure systems. Such use of the model encourages the conclusion that the political elites who sequester logging royalties, or the lawyers who invoke the language of individual rights on a daily basis, are abandoning their supposedly 'traditional' and 'Melanesian' relationality and egalitarianism for a 'modern' and 'Western' individualism.[64]

One corrective to these dichotomies lies in approaches to legal pluralism that depart from attempts to 'map' multiple, somewhat distinct 'systems' – for example, adopting a rights-based approach that would treat 'Melanesian' and

---

[61] Rocheleau and Edmunds, writing in 1997, suggest that the assumption of a polarised gender structure, held in both liberal and socialist feminist circles, was challenged by the emergence of new constructs of property that emphasise negotiation, contestation and complementarity. This is certainly true of much scholarship (such as that by feminist political ecologists), but I suggest that the assumption of a polarised gender structure persists in global policy debates and may have been strengthened with the rise of more legalistic, rights-based approaches: cf Rocheleau and Edmunds, 'Women, Men and Trees', 1352.

[62] Strathern, *The Gender of the Gift*, 6.

[63] Michael W Scott, 'Neither "New Melanesian History" nor "New Melanesian Ethnography": Recovering Emplaced Matrilineages in Southeast Solomon Islands' (2007) 77(3) *Oceania* 337, 351.

[64] In a related vein Riles has argued that anthropological accounts of property often depend on 'critical distance' from lawyers and essentialisations of legal theory: Annelise Riles, 'Property as Legal Knowledge: Means and Ends' (2004) 10(4) *Journal of the Royal Anthropological Institute* 775.

'Western' property systems as semi-autonomous and even irreconcilable spheres – and instead emphasise that social actors navigate dynamic, interacting and mutually constitutive moral-normative orders. Boaventura de Sousa Santos' influential concept of 'interlegality' emphasises that 'socio-legal life is constituted by different legal spaces operating simultaneously on different scales and from different interpretive standpoints'. Santos directs our attention to the ways in which social actors mobilise, resist, appropriate and (re)arrange 'multiple networks of legal orders', in 'the dull routine of eventless everyday life' as much as 'sweeping crises'.[65] As Rachel Sieder and John-Andrew McNeish observe, the concept of interlegality 'encourages us to explore the ways in which contemporary legal constellations are constituted diachronically through complex historical trajectories and sedimentations'.[66] In this book I draw on Sieder and McNeish's use of the term 'legal pluralities' and similarly advocate an approach that emphasises 'analyzing context, historical trajectories and local agency and understandings'.[67] While I employ the language of 'state', 'kastom' and 'Christianity' to refer to the moral-normative and institutional fields that people navigate while contesting and reconfiguring the terms of land tenure, we see that people navigate these domains of efficacious action in diverse ways and at multiple, interlaced and shifting scales, sometimes holding them apart and contrasting them, and at other times collapsing distinctions. Moreover, people do not simply 'access', 'use' or 'consume' law but actively produce it, and Solomon Islands' legal pluralities are constantly being made, unravelled and reconfigured.

In highlighting particular traditions in social theory, and feminist political ecology in particular, I am not suggesting that Indigenous accounts of land should be treated primarily as empirical materials to be read through these traditions. As Linda Tuhiwai Smith has extensively demonstrated in *Decolonizing Methodologies*, and as I highlight throughout this book, Western social theory has been and remains central to the dispossession of Indigenous peoples from their land and the land of its people.[68] However, Smith does not advocate a total rejection of Western theory, but rather an approach that centres Indigenous concerns and world views, and then comes

---

[65] Boaventura De Sousa Santos, 'Law: A Map of Misreading: Toward a Postmodern Conception of Law' (1987) 14(3) *Journal of Law and Society* 279.

[66] Sieder and McNeish, 'Introduction', 1, 8.

[67] Ibid, 23.

[68] Linda Tuhiwai Smith, *Decolonizing Methodologies: Research and Indigenous Peoples* (Zed Books 2006), 78ff.

to understand and employ theory from those perspectives.[69] Just as scholars of legal pluralism have emphasised that people navigate 'legal constellations', so too does Smith emphasise that all scholars must have an awareness of the multiple theoretical traditions they navigate in order to expose those that are problematic and weave new ones.

The approach that I advocate here therefore starts with local concerns and understandings. In the section that follows I sketch my approach to the analysis of gendered legal pluralities, and explain how it enabled me to acknowledge themes of relationality, agency and contestation in land tenure, while also exposing some of the norms, rules and institutions that narrow or enhance the opportunities for contestation by different people and groups, and in so doing, sediment particular legal forms, inequalities and exclusions. In particular, I explain why, when seeking to understand what Solomon Islanders were teaching me and the concerns they were emphasising, I turned to property as an organising category, and drew on the diverse threads of scholarship I have highlighted here – that is feminist scholarship on gender and customary land tenure; literature on property and political institutions; and legal geography's emphasis on the co-constitutive relationship of law, space and people.

1.3 'DON'T SIGN THOSE DOCUMENTS!': ACCESS AND PROPERTY

In 2008, my hosts and friends Kitchener and Natalie Bird, both from the Bareke Peninsula in central Marovo Lagoon, took me to a nearby village in order to meet with a branch of the Solomon Islands' United Church Women's Fellowship. I had started my doctoral fieldwork with an interest in learning more about gendered land relations, and Kitchener and Natalie suggested that one of the ways I could pursue these interests would be by visiting the church women's groups that regularly meet in almost every village across Solomon Islands. These groups are a crucial part of the social landscape – in fact as Solomon Islanders will quickly explain to any newcomer to their country, the churches are the only system of governance that stretches from the national (and often international) level through to villages across the country. Churches play an important role in organising and governing social life, and

---

[69] Ibid, 39. Teresia Teaiwa similarly suggested approaching theory as 'a key, a plow, a sail, an oar' that can 'get you where you want to go' in advancing Pacific interests: Teresia Teaiwa 'The Ancestors We Get to Choose: White Influences I Won't Deny' in Katerina Teaiwa, April K. Henderson and Terence Wesley-Smith (eds) *Sweat and Salt Water: Selected Works* (University of Hawai'i Press, 2021), 223ff.

church women's groups provide an avenue for women to share skills, ideas and resources for initiatives ranging from soap-making to micro-credit, logging protests and peacebuilding during conflict.[70]

I sat at the front of the church at Rukutu, hesitantly explained myself and my research, and the women and I began to tok stori – a conversational process and Indigenous research methodology explained by Kabini Sanga and others that entails sharing stories, co-creating knowledge and acknowledging, establishing and developing social relations.[71] Importantly, tok stori often entails identification and discussion of shared connections to people and places; it is a method and methodology that reiterates emplaced identities and simultaneously establishes the norms that govern the conversation. These positionalities and protocols are expressed corporeally as much as discursively – certain people may sit at the centre or front of a room or a mat, while others may sit just outside, and these locations may vary depending on the conversation. At some point in this particular conversation, I decided to broach the subject of the intensive industrial logging that occurs throughout Marovo and asked, 'what do you all think about logging?' (All of my discussions were in Solomon Islands Pijin, so to be more precise, I asked 'wannem iufala tingting lo saed lo logging?') The discussion, which had been fairly sedate until that point, erupted, with people speaking loudly over the top of each other and some standing up and waving their hands to make their point. Finally, Joyce Ngini, a recognised leader in the village and in national church networks, managed to command everyone's attention. She turned to me and said (in Pijin),

> Foreigners want to talk with the men. We women are excluded from these discussions and negotiations. When it comes to logging, we're victims, the men dominate us, we're oppressed! This is because historically, women could not talk. It was a sign of respect. The men had to talk about everything. So today, *olketa woman no save tok*. If a woman talks, the axe will come!

Joyce then sat down, making it clear she had finished, and the other women in the room erupted into laughter.

---

[70] See in particular the special issue of *Oceania* edited by Douglas: (2003) *Oceania* 74(1–2).

[71] Kabini Sanga, Martyn Reynolds, Irene Paulsen, Rebecca Spratt and Joash Maneipuri, 'A Tok Stori about Tok Stori: Melanesian Relationality in Action as Research, Leadership and Scholarship' (2018) 2(1) *Global Comparative Education* 3. Tok stori is not simply 'a chat' or an 'open ended conversation'. As Farrelly and Nabobo-Baba argue for the closely related methodology of talanoa, it should be understood as an 'empathic apprenticeship': Trisia Farrelly and Unaisi Nabobo-Baba, 'Talanoa As Empathic Apprenticeship' (2014) 55(3) *Asia Pacific Viewpoint* 319

Joyce's impassioned statement could be interpreted in several ways. She used the phrase 'olketa woman no save tok' – a phrase I have now heard in many parts of Solomon Islands and return to throughout this book – which may be variously translated as women may not, cannot or do not talk. Adopting a rights-based approach, this could easily be read as a description of a gendered hierarchy of customary entitlements, in particular the idea that according to kastom, the role of 'speaking for land' is reserved for men of the landholding lineage, and women should not generally 'talk' about land matters in public arenas such as community meetings, negotiations of timber rights or court hearings. Joyce's subsequent statement that 'the axe will come' is multivalenced – it is a reference to the weapon historically used in head-hunting raids, and Joyce uses it as a metaphor for both the social conflict and the silencing that might arise if a woman 'speaks up' in contravention of social norms, especially in the context of timber rights' negotiations which are themselves generative of enormous tension.

This is precisely the kind of analysis that is frequently adopted in the reports produced by development banks and non-governmental organisations, and it portrays women as a specific category of people who are essentially trapped between the patriarchy of customary norms and the practices of multinational logging companies. It is not entirely inaccurate, for throughout this book we see that kastom is often reconfigured in ways that sideline women and many other members of landholding communities. However, it is important to acknowledge that the role of 'speaking for land' is not only shaped by gender, but by a range of emplaced relationships and processes, such as extent of residence on the land and genealogical proximity to founding lineages. The role is not typically associated with women, but nor is it generally associated with people who 'come in' to the land via other means such as migration – although it might also be associated with any of these people if they are known to be highly efficacious in their negotiations with courts or the representatives of logging companies. Rights-based approaches are largely unable to compre-hend the complexity and instability of these categories, the immensely vari-able ways in which people are situated with respect to land, or the ways in which social, economic and spatial relations are mutually generative.

Importantly, as I have noted in Section 1.2, rights-based approaches are largely non-discursive, and they often fail to acknowledge that women draw on a range of strategies to navigate culturally situated, historically transforming legal repertoires. Joyce was not only describing kastom, but actively contesting it. Her references to 'who may talk' about land matters and the possible use of a weapon associated with a form of warfare that locals understand to be firmly in the past was largely tongue-in-cheek. Her statement was met with *laughter* from every other woman in the room. Joyce employed humour as a strategy for describing, critiquing and challenging a common practice that is often justified as 'the way we have always done things'. She was not only commenting on the very real obstacles that women face when they attempt to participate in negotiations with logging companies, but also making a strategic choice about how she would challenge those norms and practices.

A rights-based approach that is focused on identifying the content of a set of interests, rather than understanding processes of contestation, is not likely to fully comprehend Joyce's statement and potential influence here. Rather, it is likely to highlight only the ways in which women are constrained, contributing to the widespread and persistent portrayal of Melanesian women as silenced, and as victims of a culture in which they are relegated to a subordinate role. It is therefore crucial to pay attention to the ways in which claims are made, challenged and legitimated, particularly over time. Moreover, as Cecile Jackson has argued,[72] attention must be paid not only to highly visible, dramatic struggles, but also to the 'quiet' everyday contests over land – such as those that might occur when a group of women meet with a foreign researcher in a village church.

Focusing on everyday negotiations and contestations, and understanding land claims as material and corporeal as well as discursive, requires attention to the actual practices of land use and management. Local level studies of land use and management often reveal that people have more extensive access – what Jesse Ribot and Nancy Peluso have referred to as 'the ability to benefit from things' – than de jure accounts would suggest.[73] For example, people from Malaita often assert that 'women cannot be landowners', yet Alice Pollard emphasises that gardens are managed by women.[74] In Marovo, women may be excluded from logging negotiations, but they are generally woven into vast social networks that enable multiple claims to a variety of resources and places. Some women may, for example, paddle a canoe for several hours to harvest nuts from a specific tree that was planted and cultivated by an ancestor. It is clear, as Ribot and Peluso have put it in their influential essay *A Theory of Access*, that a very large array of institutions, social

---

[72] Cecile Jackson, 'Gender Analysis of Land: Beyond Land Rights for Women?' (2003) 3(4) *Journal of Agrarian Change* 453, 461.

[73] Jesse C Ribot and Nancy Lee Peluso, 'A Theory of Access' (2003) 68(2) *Rural Sociology* 153, 155; see also Michael Kevane and Leslie C Gray, 'A Woman's Field Is Made at Night: Gendered Land Rights and Norms in Burkina Faso' (1999) 5(3) *Feminist Economics* 1, 3.

[74] Alice Aruhe'eta Pollard, *Givers of Wisdom, Labourers without Gain: Essays on Women in the Solomon Islands*, edited by Anthony R Walker (Institute of Pacific Studies, University of the South Pacific, 2000), 32.

and political-economic relations and discursive strategies shape the ability of actors to benefit from things.[75] Yet in speaking of 'domination', 'oppression' and 'exclusion' – strong, confronting words in Pijin – Joyce was emphasising that not all forms of access to all resources are equally available to all people. Furthermore, she was drawing my attention to the role of both foreign-owned logging companies and the state in recognising, validating and consolidating some claims to land and trees rather than others.

Joyce's passionate statement stuck with me because it was made in 2008, at the height of aid and security policy discourses emphasising the 'fragility', 'weakness' and 'remoteness' of state norms and institutions in Solomon Islands and elsewhere in the south-west Pacific, particularly as against the 'strength' of customary norms and institutions. Yet 'the state' did not feel particularly 'distant' or 'remote' in my discussions with women in Rukutu, nor with people in many other parts of Solomon Islands. It felt profoundly *present*, for time and time again, people drew my attention to norms, institutions, practices and props associated with the state. To give another example, two years after the meeting at Rukutu, I was in Honiara at a large workshop regarding gender mainstreaming in government departments. Another woman from Marovo, who I will call Naomi, was also in attendance. Naomi usually lives in Honiara, but returns home regularly to visit her elderly father. Like many people of Marovo, she pays close attention to the activities of logging companies and their negotiations with local landholders. Over morning tea, Naomi told me that she'd recently been home. At the end of her visit, as she was about to board her return flight to Honiara, she saw her brother disembarking, having just arrived from the capital. Naomi explained that this concerned her, as she had heard rumours that her brother had been attending meetings with representatives of a logging company. She ran back to her father and pleaded with him:

> Do NOT sign any documents. You must NOT sign any documents. No matter what he says, I do not want you to sign ANYTHING until I come back home and we talk about it.

Naomi's concern about her father signing documents, like Joyce's emphasis on 'discussions and negotiations' with foreign logging companies, suggests that some claims to land and trees are rather more 'sticky' – or as legal geographer Nicholas Blomley aptly puts it, 'sedimented' – than others.[76] As we shall see

---

[75] Ribot and Peluso, 'A Theory of Access'.
[76] Nicholas Blomley, 'Performing Property: Making the World' (2013) 26(1) *Canadian Journal of Law & Jurisprudence* 23.

throughout this book, and perhaps most strikingly in the case of the Tension, the material rearrangement of space does not necessarily flow from legal documents, yet their power is simultaneously revealed by the fact that land records 'disappear' from the archives as frequently as survey pegs do from the land. While framing my inquiries in terms of a broad interest in 'hao na pipol lukluk and tok aboutem land' (how people see and talk about land), Solomon Islanders repeatedly and passionately relayed their concerns that logging, mining and the sale or leasing of land were occurring to the benefit of a small number of men who are able to become trustees, signatories and beneficiaries of royalties, while most other members of communities are left bearing the burden of the negative impacts of transactions.[77] Notably, all of these arrangements involve some claims to land rather than others being sanctioned, validated and consolidated, particularly – but certainly not exclusively – by state authorities.

My efforts to understand the things people were showing, telling and teaching me about land, and the issues they were expressing concern about, drew my attention to processes of *making* or *forming* property – that is, to the ways in which people attempt 'to secure rights to natural resources by having their access claims recognised as legitimate property by a politico-legal institution', and the ways in which institutions sanction and legitimise some claims as property rather than others.[78] Here I draw on Thomas Sikor and Christian Lund's definition of property as 'legitimised claims, in the sense that the state or some other form of socio-political authority sanctions them', whether that authority is associated with law, custom or convention;[79] as distinct from all the ways in which people may benefit from things, including extralegal or illegal means.[80]

Property is, of course, notoriously difficult to define. The definition I have adopted here arose from my attempts to understand the concerns that people were sharing with me, and to reconcile the fluidity and 'negotiability' of customary land tenure with the impact of the formal legal and political arena

---

[77] See also the following detailed works: Tarcisius Kabutaulaka, 'Paths in the Jungle: Landowners and the Struggle for Control of Solomon Islands' Logging Industry' (PhD thesis, Australian National University, 2001); Gordon Leua Nanau, 'Can a Theory of Insecure Globalisation Provide Better Explanations for Instability in the South Pacific? The Case of Solomon Islands' (PhD thesis, University of East Anglia, 2008); Lincy Pendeverana, 'Pursuing Livelihoods and Re-Imagining Development in the Oil Palm Regions of the Guadalcanal Plains, Solomon Islands' (PhD thesis, Australian National University, 2021).

[78] Sikor and Lund, 'Access and Property', 1.

[79] Ibid.

[80] Ribot and Peluso, 'A Theory of Access'.

that they were highlighting.[81] In the chapters that follow I demonstrate that by focusing on the ways in which people seek to transform more general 'access' to land into 'property' sanctioned by politico-legal institutions – whether those institutions are associated with kastom, religion or the state – I was able to acknowledge and begin to understand agency and contestation, as well as the processes and factors that have constrained the space for negotiation and legitimation by different people, social groups and institutions. Importantly, this approach also enabled me to attend to questions of scale. Implicit in Joyce's reference to warfare was the understanding that struggles over logging licences and the distribution of royalties have long been implicated in a range of multiscalar conflicts, including struggles for provincial autonomy. In a few, brief, passionate words, Joyce immediately drew my attention to the relationship between seemingly 'local' struggles over property and wider territorialising projects and state formation.

1.4 PROPERTY SCHOLARS AND PROPERTY FORMATION

Property is not simply inscribed onto land and bodies, it emerges from them; indeed as legal geographers have often emphasised, law, place and people are co-constituted. For example, gardening is a key means for establishing and maintaining land claims in Solomon Islands, and Alice Pollard emphasises for the'Are'Are people, 'if a woman has a large and productive garden, she will be identified as *keni putinitae*, industrious and capable; on the other hand, if her garden is small and unproductive she will be identified as lazy and ignorant, even a thief'.[82] Gendered land relations are therefore performed, in the sense of subjects performing gendered presentations such as industrious gardening, or observing protocols about speaking (or not speaking) in certain social gatherings. They are also performative, in the sense of everyday, material iterations of ideas and abstractions about gender and property that reproduce that normativity and are so routinised as to appear natural.[83]

Property may be made, reiterated, sedimented and sometimes unsettled, through everyday practices such as women and children collecting shellfish from tidal zones while men fish in the open ocean; men felling trees and clearing land for gardens predominantly cultivated by women; closely related

---

[81] In a related vein see Eleanor Andrews and James McCarthy, 'Scale, Shale and the State: Political Ecologies and Legal Geographies of Shale Gas Development in Pennsylvania' (2014) 4(1) *Journal of Environmental Studies and Sciences* 7.

[82] Pollard, *Givers of Wisdom*, 32.

[83] Blomley, 'Performing Property', drawing particularly on Judith Butler, *Bodies That Matter: On the Discursive Limits of 'Sex'* (Routledge, 1993).

kin utilising a particular path through the bush; an elderly woman paddling across the lagoon to harvest nuts from a tree; or foreign researchers ensuring they seek permission from the appropriate leaders when they first make contact with a community. All of these practices create and recreate specific socio-spatial relations, and all entail processes of legitimation by socio-political institutions. Furthermore, they are informed by the land and the non-human world – by unusual rock formations or mountains housing spirits, the quality of the soil for planting and seasons to harvest, the availability of the plants necessary to calm waves or the presence of a crocodile in the vicinity of a path through the bush. The land itself is not static but active – tidal zones are highly gendered places in which land and water come and go, gardens may be left fallow and return to bush, rivers frequently flood and change course, new land may emerge from the ocean due to tectonic uplift, and many Solomon Islanders are deeply concerned with the prospect of ground for gardens and houses being lost due to climate-induced sea level rise.

If we understand property as made, uplifted, renegotiated and eroded, we should also direct attention to the role of scholars and scholarship in these processes. As legal theorist Margaret Davies observes, once we accept that property is an effect produced by ideas, physical-environmental factors and social behaviours or performances, then we must also acknowledge that we 'have choices over our abstractions' and can prefigure and test alternative conceptualisations that might ultimately lead to new 'performances' and 'facts on the ground'.[84] Scholars of property are often relatively silent as to their own role in making and unmaking property, yet as Joseph Foukona has demonstrated, they have long been influential in the development of land policy in Solomon Islands, as well as the vocabularies of people debating the terms of land tenure in their villages.[85] The gap between scholarly 'abstractions' and new 'facts on the ground' can therefore be quite small, and it is important to acknowledge the potential for scholarship to have unintended consequences, and even deepen the very inequalities we claim to unsettle and address.

In writing this book I have endeavoured to trace the ways in which land relations have been reconfigured over time, while being mindful of the implications of my arguments for future performances of property. This work will be read, debated and used in ways that I can anticipate, as well as many that I cannot. Academic literature is regularly utilised in land claims in the

---

[84] Margaret Davies, 'Material Subjects and Vital Objects: Prefiguring Property and Rights for an Entangled World' (2016) 22(2) *Australian Journal of Human Rights* 37, 39.

[85] Joseph Foukona, 'Land, Law and History: Actors, Networks and Land Reform in Solomon Islands' (PhD thesis, Australian National University, 2017).

Pacific,[86] and in Solomon Islands the *Land and Titles Act 1996* ('Land and Titles Act') specifically provides that such literature is prima facie evidence of custom, 'unless and until the contrary is proved'.[87] Here, state law quite clearly 'sediments' not only specific 'facts' about land claimed by academics but their 'expertise' more broadly, and my understanding of this has shaped this book in multiple ways. I have attempted to be alert to the possibility that scholarship may be counter-normative and contribute to ongoing, collaborative efforts to shift existing parameters of property and authority, just as it might reinforce dominant understandings of law, place and people.

I have also tried to be aware that my own emplacement as a white Australian has implications for how I should 'speak' about land according to kastom – that is, the grounded, culturally particular understandings of how different kinds of people should communicate and relate to the human and non-human world.[88] Foreigners are often positioned as the 'experts' on Solomon Islands, a positioning I understand to both emerge from and repro-duce representations of Solomon Islands and Solomon Islanders as somehow outside cosmopolitan modernity and the rule of law. As Paige West has recently demonstrated at length for Papua New Guinea, such representations are central to ongoing, multiple, material and non-material forms of accumu-lation and dispossession.[89] This book is sole-authored but it emerges from my ongoing conversations and collaborations with people who are mentioned throughout its pages, as well as many others, and we are all situated differently, and understand our responsibilities differently, in ongoing discussions about land in Solomon Islands and the wider region. I have come to understand that for 'outsiders' such as myself, forming, maintaining and when necessary restoring, 'right relations' – that is, being 'good kin' rather than 'experts' –

---

[86] For examples see Gerhard Schneider, 'Land Dispute and Tradition in Munda, Roviana Lagoon, New Georgia Island, Solomon Islands: From Headhunting to the Quest for Control of Land' (PhD thesis, University of Cambridge, 1996); Ian Scales, 'The Social Forest: Landowners, Development Conflict and the State in Solomon Islands' (PhD thesis, Australian National University, 2003); Greg Rawlings, '"Once There Was a Garden, Now There Is a Swimming Pool": Inequality, Labour and Land in Pango, a Peri-Urban Village in Vanuatu' (PhD thesis, Australian National University, 2002). This is of course not unique to Melanesian states; as Aileen Moreton-Robinson observes for Australia, 'patriarchal whiteness sets the criteria for proof and the standards of credibility': Aileen Moreton-Robinson, *The White Possessive: Property, Power and Indigenous Sovereignty* (University of Minnesota Press, 2015), 69.

[87] Land and Titles Act 1996 [Cap 133] (Solomon Islands), s 239(2).

[88] See also Rebecca Monson and George Hoa'au, '(Em)Placing Law: Migration, Belonging and Place in Solomon Islands' in Fiona Jenkins, Mark Nolan and Kim Rubenstein (eds.), *Allegiance and Identity in a Globalised World* (Cambridge University Press, 2014) 117.

[89] Paige West, *Dispossession and the Environment: Rhetoric and Inequality in Papua New Guinea* (Columbia University Press, 2016).

requires a capacity not only to listen and observe but to discern between that which we are invited to know and that which we are encouraged to reproduce in writing or otherwise; between that which is shared with us on the understanding that we will hold it closely and that which we may redistribute widely.[90]

There are many aspects of land – stories concerning the emergence of humans from the cosmos, the paths the ancestors travelled, precolonial warfare, interactions between humans and non-humans and details of gift exchanges between groups – that are vital to contemporary land relations, but which I have decided not to reproduce in the pages that follow because they may be 'dangerous' in at least two interrelated senses. First, such details are crucial to legal contests and their reproduction may entail forms of violence and dispossession I have explored in detail elsewhere,[91] and second, 'thick description' of these aspects of land tenure has often worked to deepen the racist objectification and exoticisation of Pacific Islanders.[92] For reasons of both kastom and state law – which I hold apart here as they entail different understandings of emplaced relationships and conduct – in the pages that follow I sometimes use pseudonyms for historical and contemporary people and social groups; I leave some aspects of disputes and socio-spatial boundaries rather 'fuzzy'; I refer to cosmologies and aspects of oral histories in broad rather than detailed terms; and I endeavour to expose not only the impacts of hegemonic models but also the diversity of debates and practices from which alternatives might emerge.

1.5 SOLOMON ISLANDS AND CHAPTER OVERVIEW

From 1998 to 2003, Solomon Islands was plunged into a period of violent, land-related conflict that resulted in many deaths, widespread displacement

---

[90] See also Anja Kanngieser and Zoe Todd, 'From Environmental Case Study to Environmental Kin Study' (2020) 59(3) *History and Theory* 385.

[91] Rebecca Monson, 'Unsettled Explorations of Law's Archives: The Allure and Anxiety of Solomon Islands' Court Records' (2014) 40(1) *Australian Feminist Law Journal* 35.

[92] As a white Australian woman working in Solomon Islands I am situated in fundamentally different ways, but similar comments are made by Irene Watson and Audra Simpson. Watson refers to her reluctance to provide specific examples of relationships to ruwi, 'because of the dangers of mistranslation, appropriation, and commodification': Irene Watson, 'Sovereign Spaces, Caring for Country, and the Homeless Position of Aboriginal Peoples' (2009) 108(1) *South Atlantic Quarterly* 27, 38. Simpson refers to her discomfort with the role of 'thick description prose-master': Audra Simpson, 'The Ruse of Consent and the Anatomy of "Refusal": Cases from Indigenous North America and Australia' (2017) 20(1) *Postcolonial Studies* 18, 23. See also Paige West's commentary on the slippage between the 'ontological turn' and primitivising traditions: Paige West, *Dispossession and the Environment: Rhetoric and Inequality in Papua New Guinea* (Columbia University Press, 2016), 30.

and in many senses the collapse of state-based systems of law and order. At the heart of the conflict – commonly referred to as 'the Ethnic Tension' or simply the Tension – were long-standing concerns among the people of Guadalcanal, the most economically 'developed' island in the country, that their privileged status as the Indigenous custodians of the land was being eroded, and the concerns of migrants from other islands who had moved to Guadalcanal in search of education and employment. By 2003, Solomon Islands was routinely described as a 'failed state' and the government repeatedly sought assistance from countries in the South Pacific. This eventually resulted in the mobilisation of the thirteen-year Regional Assistance Mission to Solomon Islands (RAMSI), comprised of personnel drawn from across the Pacific Island Forum member countries.

In the years immediately following the conflict, transitional justice efforts included a Commission of Inquiry into Land Dealings and Abandoned Properties on Guadalcanal, and a Truth and Reconciliation Commission (TRC). The latter was formally launched by Archbishop Desmond Tutu in 2009, modelled on the South African TRC and the first of its kind in the region. It was chaired by Reverend Sam Ata and presented a final report to the parliament in 2012. The parliament resisted calls to release the report, citing its size and sensitivity, but it became widely available in April 2013 after its editor, Reverend Terry Brown – a retired bishop of the Anglican Church of Melanesia, Canadian national and long-time resident of Solomon Islands – released it online.[93] The prominence of church leaders in these processes and debates underscores their importance in contemporary politics, and as we see throughout this book, it emerges from a long history of both collaboration and struggle between church leaders and government officials.

Solomon Islands emerged as a distinct political and territorial unit as a result of imperial expansion and colonisation, and now comprises more than 900 mountainous volcanic islands and low-lying coral atolls stretching between Bougainville, an autonomous region of Papua New Guinea, and Vanuatu. The people who call these islands home are culturally and linguistically diverse – more than 95 per cent of the population identifies as Indigenous to Solomon Islands, and approximately eighty languages are

---

[93] Louise Vella, '"What Will You Do with Our Stories?" Truth and Reconciliation in the Solomon Islands' (2014) 8(1) *International Journal of Conflict and Violence* 91; Terry Brown, 'The Solomon Islands "Ethnic Tension" Conflict and the Solomon Islands Truth and Reconciliation Commission: A Personal Reflection' in David Webster (ed), *Flowers in the Wall: Truth and Reconciliation in Timor-Leste, Indonesia and Melanesia* (University of Calgary Press, 2018), 279.

spoken, with Solomon Islands Pijin as a lingua franca.[94] The largest islands are dominated by central mountain ranges that descend rapidly towards the ocean, and with the exception of extensive plains on north-east Guadalcanal, there is little coastal plain. Most islands are covered in dense rainforest or open grasslands, and contemporary settlement is concentrated in coastal areas that are fringed by mangroves and coral-reef lagoons, or a beach and open ocean.

The European powers were largely uninterested in formally colonising the southwest Pacific until the 1850s, when tropical commodities became increasingly valuable and a regional labour trade emerged. Thousands of Pacific Islanders, including an estimated 30,000 people from Solomon Islands, were taken, often by force or deception, for indentured labour in Queensland and the Pacific Island colonies. As I explain in the following chapter, missionaries, administrators and publics in Britain and Australia became increasingly concerned with the supposed lawlessness of the region, and this contributed to the islands coming within the loose jurisdiction of the High Commissioner of the Western Pacific from 1877. Britain then annexed the islands and declared the British Solomon Islands Protectorate in 1893.[95] A colonial system of government was established and new external and internal boundaries were drawn up that variously reinforced or conflicted with pre-existing polities and often prompted new forms of political expression. When Solomon Islands became independent in 1978, the constitution established a unitary system of government, and today there are nine provinces (Map 1.2). In the chapters that follow we see that there are ongoing debates about the merits of these arrangements as compared with a federal system.

The economy has, since the colonial period, been heavily dependent on agricultural development and the exploitation of natural resources, in particular copra, fishing, logging and oil palm. Solomon Islands attracts significant attention from aid donors, as it is often understood to be one of the 'least developed countries' in the world, ranking 152 out of 189 countries and territories in the 2018 Human Development Index.[96] Most people (75 per cent of the population in 2019) live in dispersed rural settlements and are very

94 Solomon Islands National Statistics Office, *Report on the 2009 Population and Housing Census – National Report (Volume 2)* (Solomon Islands Government, 2009).
95 Western Pacific Order in Council 1877 (UK); Pacific Order in Council 1893 (UK). Germany established a protectorate over New Guinea in 1884, which extended to include Bougainville, Shortland Islands, Choiseul and Isabel. Authority over the Shortlands, Choiseul, Isabel and Ontong Java was transferred to the British in 1899: Deryck Scarr, *Fragments of Empire: A History of the Western Pacific High Commission, 1877–1914* (ANU Press, 1967).
96 United Nations Development Programme, *Briefing Note for Countries on the 2020 Human Development Report: Solomon Islands* (UNDP, 2020).

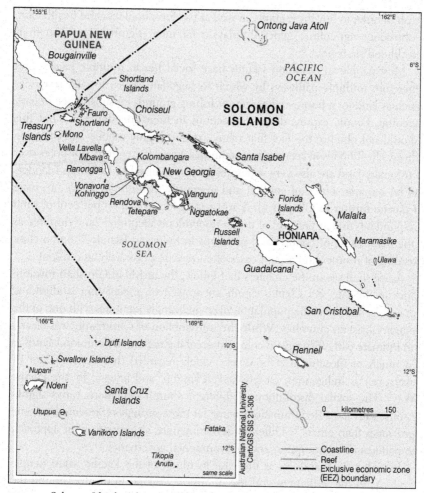

MAP 1.2. Solomon Islands and provincial boundaries

dependent on subsistence agriculture and fishing. The remainder of the population live in Honiara (18 per cent) and other urban centres (7 per cent),[97] where many people are more reliant on cash but still depend on gardens in which they grow a range of root crops, vegetables and leafy greens. Urban and rural areas are dotted with small trade stores that sell a narrow range of essential goods including rice and 'two-minute noodles'; tinned fish and pork; sugar, salt, tea and coffee; soy sauce and vegetable oil; kerosene, matches, fish hooks and soap. While most people need and want access to

---

[97] Solomon Islands National Statistics Office, 2019 *National Population and Housing Census Project – Provisional Count* (16 November 2020).

cash in order to buy these goods, as well as pay for school fees and health care, subsistence agriculture generally plays a far more significant role in their livelihood strategies.

Most people in Solomon Islands have social ties to multiple places, and therefore multiple pathways by which to negotiate access to vital resources such as land for a house and garden or fishing grounds for subsistence or cash income. People express deep connections to their ancestral lands but this should not obscure the fact that many are also highly mobile and pursuing diverse livelihoods in seemingly distant sites across the country. Disputes over customary land are also very widespread and perceived by Solomon Islanders to be a major source of conflict and insecurity in multiple senses (an issue I pursue further in Chapter 4). A 2011 survey found that 65 per cent of rural respondents and 41 per cent of urban respondents identified 'land disputes' as 'the main cause of conflict and problems in Solomon Islands',[98] and a close reading of murder and assault cases often reveals a link with land disputes.

As we shall see in the chapters that follow, the arrival of Christian missionaries in the late 1800s had a significant impact on pre-existing landholding practices, and today the population overwhelmingly identifies with one of the major Christian churches. While the introduction of Christianity was clearly an intimate part of European colonisation of the region, in Solomon Islands as in much of Oceania it is now very widely regarded (but certainly not by everyone) as Indigenous, closely tied to kastom, and integral to 'the Pacific Way'. The spatial distribution of different church affiliations varies significantly, with some denominations being far more strongly represented in some provinces than others.[99] Different denominations also vary in their approach to patterns of consumption and environmental governance.

In Solomon Islands, as is the case in much of the Pacific, most people understand the settlement and use of customary land to revolve around the cohabitation or shared use of a named place, by a named kin group, which traces descent to an apical ancestor (or ancestors). The extent to which lineages have 'always' held land, and/or whether contemporary understandings have emerged in the context of colonial legal struggles, is debated and cannot be avoided in any critical examination of predominant stories of property. However, it is also clear that these groups are vitally important to

---

[98] Regional Assistance Mission to Solomon Islands, 2011 *People's Survey: Full Report* (RAMSI 2012), 91–92.

[99] A total of 92 per cent identify with one of the major Christian churches, 7 per cent belong to other religions and 1 per cent identified as having 'no religion' in the last census: Solomon Islands National Statistics Office, *Report on the 2009 Population and Housing Census – National Report (Volume 2)* (Solomon Islands Government, 2009).

and deeply valued by Solomon Islanders today.[100] Societies in the western islands are generally understood to be cognatic, and people will often explicitly describe themselves as belonging to both the kin group of their mother and that of their father. The people of Guadalcanal (with the exception of Malaitan communities at Marau Sound), Isabel, Central Province and Makira are often described as following matrilineal descent systems, and people in these areas will often foreground membership of a kin group and claims to land traced through women. On Malaita there is an emphasis on patrilineal descent, but here people will trace some claims through, and to, women. Societies on the Polynesian islands of Rennell, Bellona, Tikopia, Anuta and Ontong Java also emphasise patrilineal descent.

While systems of landholding and social ordering are highly diverse, people generally lay claim to both land- and kin-based allegiances by drawing on histories of ancestral origin and migration, the establishment of boundaries and sacred sites, ritual exchange and intermarriage between groups and the birth of descendants. These stories are embedded in landscapes and seascapes, punctuated by important sites such as sacred sites, existing or abandoned villages, old gardens and trees. This gives rise to what James Fox refers to as 'topogenies' that tie people to place,[101] and in this sense the storied landscapes of Solomon Islanders often share similarities with those of other Austronesian-speaking people, whose places stretch from Taiwan to Timor and Madagascar to Easter Island.[102] Narratives of belonging based on histories of ancestral origins and migration are a key feature of these systems, as are 'founder-focused ideologies' according to which greater status is allocated to those who descend from earlier, rather than later kin group founders. These emplaced histories construct a complex web of relationships that stretch through centuries and across islands, regions and the borders of contemporary nation states.

In the chapters that follow we see that contemporary landholding arrangements emerge from these emplaced histories and culturally persistent understandings of people and place, as well as processes of renegotiation generated by capitalist trade, the colonial legal system, Christian missions, extractive

---

[100] See e.g. Scott, 'Neither "New Melanesian History" nor "New Melanesian Ethnography"'; McDougall, *Engaging with Strangers*, 185–186.

[101] James J Fox, 'Place and Landscape in Comparative Austronesian Perspective' in James J Fox (ed.), *The Poetic Power of Place: Comparative Perspectives on Austronesian Ideas of Locality* (ANU Press, 2006) 1, 8–12.

[102] Peter Bellwood, James J Fox and Darrell Tryon, 'The Austronesians in History: Common Origins and Diverse Transformations' in Peter Bellwood, James J Fox and Darrell Tryon (eds.), *The Austronesians: Historical and Comparative Perspectives* (ANU Press, 2006) 1.

industries and ubanisation. In Chapter 2, I trace the ways in which questions of land tenure, property rights and territorial boundaries have been contested and debated at the national level since colonisation. We see first, that struggles over state-sanctioned property rights were bound up with a range of territorialising projects and were simultaneously struggles over political authority. Christian missionaries, colonial authorities and Indigenous leaders all sought to establish their authority through the delimitation, enclosure and control of geographical space.[103] Second, whereas existing scholarship on legal pluralism in the Pacific foregrounds the domains of kastom and state law,[104] my focus on land struggles reveals the emergence of legal pluralities and forms of authority associated not only with kastom and the state, but also Christianity. I demonstrate that Christianity has been central to the legal worlding of Solomon Islands and Solomon Islanders, and that multiscalar, interlocking territorialising projects have constituted the legal pluralities we observe today. Third, Solomon Islanders' experiences during this period were diverse, with some people becoming relatively effective legal actors, very quickly. These processes have been highly gendered, not least because different people encountered the new social worlds established by the state, colonial plantations and the churches in quite different ways.

In Chapter 3, I focus on the (re)negotiation of land tenure and authority on the Bareke Peninsula and its surrounds in central Marovo Lagoon, Western Province (Map 1.3 and Map 1.4). This region has become known for its unique lagoon and biodiversity, as well as the widespread ecological destruction and social inequalities wrought by forestry. This chapter considers the extent to which contemporary gender inequalities can be traced to a flawed legislative framework, to patriarchal kastom and/or to the erosion of women's customary rights by colonialism. Drawing on archival and ethnographic work, I show that missionaries and colonial administrators recognised some masculine aspects

---

[103] Robert David Sack, *Human Territoriality: Its Theory and History* (Cambridge University Press 1986), Peter Vandergeest and Nancy Lee Peluso, 'Territorialization and State Power in Thailand' (1995) 24(3) *Theory and Society* 385.

[104] Most legal scholars mention Christianity or religion only in passing, see e.g.: Miranda Forsyth, *A Bird That Flies with Two Wings: Kastom and State Justice Systems in Vanuatu* (ANU Press, 2009), Jennifer Corrin, 'Plurality and Punishment: Competition between State and Customary Authorities in Solomon Islands' (2020) 51(1) *The Journal of Legal Pluralism and Unofficial Law* 29, Miranda Forsyth and Thomas Dick, 'Liquid Regulation: The (Men's) Business of Women's Water Music?' (2021) *International Journal of Law in Context*, https://dx.doi.org/10.1017/s1744552321000574 cf John Barker, 'All Sides Now: The Postcolonial Triangle in Uiaku' in John Barker (ed.), *The Anthropology of Morality in Melanesia and beyond* (Ashgate, 2008) 75; John cox, 'Israeli Technicians and the Post-Colonial Racial Triangle in Papua New Guinea' (2015) 85(3) *Oceania* 342.

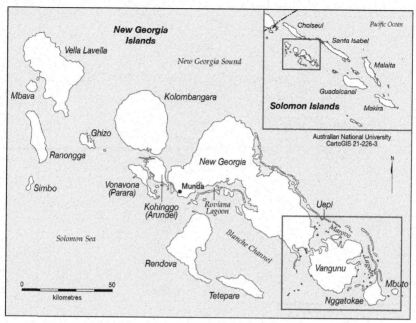

MAP 1.3. New Georgia group

of the local polity and disregarded others, in particular the feminine aspects, facilitating a simplification and sedimentation of both authority and land tenure that enabled some men leaders to consolidate their control over land. These processes of (mis)recognition and simplification are reproduced today, with control over logging being concentrated in the hands of a small number of men leaders and entrepreneurs, to the exclusion of most other members of landholding groups. The chapter demonstrates that first, contests over property and the establishment of chiefly efficacy are mutually constitutive. Second, while the contemporary inequalities that characterise these processes can be partially traced to the structural features of property systems, they also emerge from long-term processes of colonial intrusion and capitalist development. I therefore suggest, along with Claire Slatter among others, that at least some contemporary inequalities emerge not from 'custom' but from the simplification of the multiplicity of authority that may exist in customary practice, and the persistent failure or refusal to acknowledge important aspects of gendered influence with respect to land.[105]

---

[105] Slatter, 'Gender and Custom' at 92–93, noting similar comments from Jocelyn Linnekin and Jean Zorn. For the longevity of such arguments see also Vanessa Griffen, 'The Pacific Islands:

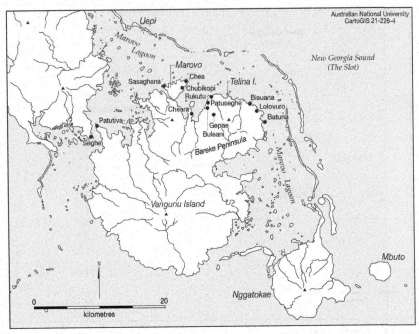

MAP 1.4. Bareke Peninsula and Central Marovo Lagoon

Chapter 4 focuses on the historical development of Kakabona, a series of peri-urban villages that lie to the immediate west of Honiara (Map 1.5 and Map 1.6) and one of the focal points of violence during the Tension. Drawing on a series of land disputes that came before the chiefs and courts during the 1980s and 1990s, triggered in part by rapid urbanisation and land sales, I demonstrate that land disputes entail the delineation of boundaries between people and on the ground, sometimes in palpably exclusionary ways. In Kakabona as in Marovo, these processes have enabled a small number of men to consolidate control over land and political authority more broadly. However, these processes are also distinct and fundamentally emplaced, informed by culturally specific identities and meanings attached to the land. Taking the emotional or affective dimensions of land disputes as my starting point, and particularly the multifaceted 'danger' of disputes and the sense of precarity they generate, I explain how land disputes have emerged as a key

All It Requires Is Ourselves' in Robin Morgan (ed.), *Sisterhood is Global* (Anchor Press and Doubleday, 1984), 517 and more recently J Kēhaulani Kauanui, *Paradoxes of Hawaiian Sovereignty: Land, Sex and the Colonial Politics of State Nationalism* (Duke University Press, 2018) 29–30.

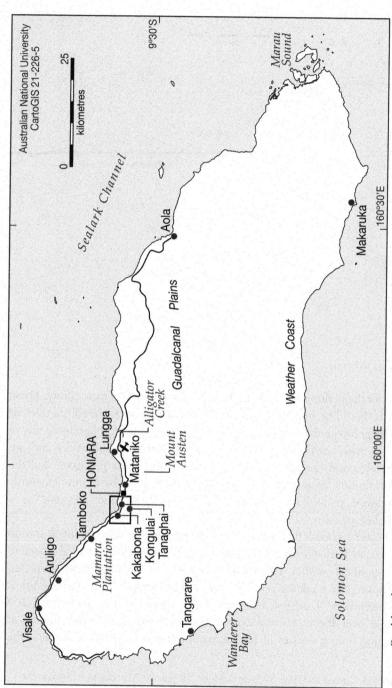

MAP 1.5. Guadalcanal

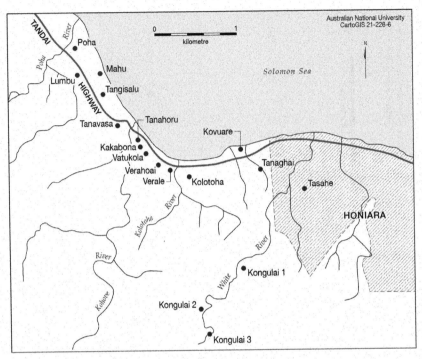

MAP 1.6. Kakabona

arena for the performance of particular idealised models of masculinity. These models should be understood in terms of what Raewyn Connell has referred to as 'hegemonic masculinities', they are 'the currently most honoured way of being a man' as opposed to other, 'subordinated masculinities', and are contestable and open to change.[106] I suggest that these processes, and the co-constitution of property and masculine authority, have simultaneously reproduced peri-urban areas as sites of insecurity, and the state as a masculine domain.

Chapter 5 extends the existing literature on property rights, political author-ity and state formation by adopting an explicit focus on the gendered aspects of ethno-political conflict. The conflict of 1998–2003 has often been interpreted as exposing the weaknesses of the state and the tenacity of customary norms and institutions. I suggest, however, that it should also be understood as a struggle over the scope and constitution of political authority, that is, as emerging from processes of state formation rather than failure. During the

---

[106] See RW Connell and James W Messerschmidt, 'Hegemonic Masculinity: Rethinking the Concept' (2005) 19(6) *Gender and Society* 829, 832.

conflict, militants made territorial claims that were grounded in highly gendered notions of culture, ethnicity and space, and in the aftermath, significant attention has been devoted to consolidating particular socio-spatial distinctions via a new constitution. Fuelled in part by ongoing tensions over land, the conflict demonstrates that seemingly 'local' struggles over property have significant implications for political participation and state formation. In Solomon Islands, these processes are highly gendered and work to reproduce state norms and institutions as a masculine, even *hypermasculine* domain. This is perhaps most profoundly highlighted by the widespread gender-based violence perpetrated during the conflict, which was not merely an effect of territorial claims but constituted them, with devastating consequences.

I conclude in Chapter 6 by reconsidering the assertion that women may not, cannot and/or do not speak about land matters, and do so through an explicit focus on the strategies used by women to contest property, territory and authority. Rather than focusing on processes of exclusion, I turn my attention to collaborative efforts to disrupt dominant, exclusionary and frequently violent understandings of property, territory and political authority, and craft more expansive practices that acknowledge a multiplicity of relationships with land. The strategies that emerge, which appear to resonate with at least some struggles elsewhere in the region, suggest that when people challenge hypermasculinist assertions of property and authority, it is not generally the language and institutions of the state that they turn to, but rather the resources offered by custom and Christianity. An emphasis on state laws and institutions as the primary mechanism for addressing inequality not only detracts attention from these strategies, but constrains them, undermining the efforts of Solomon Islanders to reconfigure law, property, authority and their nation.

2

Navigating Custom, Church and State

Property, Territory and Authority in the Protectorate Era

People across the Pacific have long been woven into complex networks of warfare, alliance and exchange; however, those in the southwest Pacific began to encounter a new kind of visitor during the 1500s, as European explorers and merchants began travelling through the islands. The European powers were initially uninterested in formally colonising the southwest Pacific, but this changed when plantation economies and an associated labour trade began to develop during the nineteenth century. Britain established the Western Pacific Territories in 1877, thereby extending the jurisdiction of the High Commissioner for the Western Pacific (based in Fiji) to the British Solomon Islands Protectorate, the New Hebrides (now Vanuatu, which was jointly administered with France) and the Gilbert and Ellice Islands Colony (now Kiribati and Tuvalu, respectively), among others.

This chapter exposes the centrality of law to the ways in which colonialism was conceived, enacted, legitimated and, for some people at least, normalised. Euro-American property law formed a vital part of the arsenal of technologies used by British administrators to organise and govern people and space, but it was also resisted, appropriated, reconfigured and often simply ignored by Islanders. Extant colonial records and oral histories demonstrate that Solomon Islanders defended their lands by adopting 'legal' language and form; however, they also insisted on the recognition of vernacular forms of place-making, authority formation and conflict management – now often referred to as kastom. Furthermore, colonial administrators had to contend with another novel set of people, institutions and norms: those of the Christian missions. While colonial administrators and Christian missionaries undoubtedly collaborated, they were often in conflict, and struggles over land and the delineation of territorial boundaries were bound up with contests over political authority. European traders, Christian missionaries, Indigenous leaders and Protectorate officials all sought to establish and assert their authority in territorial terms, drawing on multiple discursive and material genres associated with kastom, Christianity and the British administration in order to delineate space and manage people and resources within that space.

The intimate relationship between land control and state power is now well documented in many parts of the world,[1] and in this chapter, I demonstrate that contests over state-sanctioned property form part of a suite of interlocking territorialising projects in which a range of actors compete to delimit and assert control over a geographic area. These projects have been constitutive of not only state power but also the authority of the Christian missions, and contests over land ownership during the early colonial period were often entangled with the emergence of new political subjectivities based around churches. Furthermore, whereas legal pluralities in the Pacific have often been understood in terms of the categories of 'custom' and 'law', colonial struggles over land engendered a normative and institutional plurality in which claims to land are legitimised by reference to the domains of not only kastom and state law but also Christianity. However, the interweaving of these domains varies across Solomon Islands. While undertaking this research, I reviewed hundreds of pages of court records covering disputes stretching from the colonial period to the present and noted that references to Christian idioms were a far more prominent feature of land disputes in Western Province than in Guadalcanal, and perhaps anywhere else in the country. In this chapter I begin to unravel the reasons for these differences.

The renegotiation of land and leadership has also been highly gendered. Differently positioned people – including women and men, chiefs and land-owners, Malaitans and the people of the western islands – have encountered the social worlds of the state, plantations and churches in very different ways. In particular, from the outset of the colonial period, the language of state law and the practices of British administrators tended to privilege a small number of influential men, enabling them to extend their authority while remaining largely inaccessible to the majority of the population.

2.1 NEW KINDS OF VISITORS AND NEW KINDS OF EXCHANGE: TRADERS, BLACKBIRDERS, MISSIONARIES

The people of the islands now known as Solomon Islands have always travelled and engaged with visitors to their shores, and prior to colonisation,

---

[1] The literature is vast, but I draw particularly on Robert David Sack, *Human Territoriality: Its Theory and History* (Cambridge University Press, 1986); Peter Vandergeest and Nancy Lee Peluso, 'Territorialization and State Power in Thailand' (1995) 24(3) *Theory and Society* 385; Lund, 'Rule and Rupture'; Neil Loughlin and Sarah Milne, 'After the Grab? Land Control and Regime Survival in Cambodia since 2012' (2021) 51(3) *Journal of Contemporary Asia* 375.

there were extensive networks of warfare, alliance and exchange that ensured a flow of people, goods and ideas within and between different islands. In many societies there was a system of bush–coastal barter, where people from bush communities living in the interior met people from coastal areas on the beaches to exchange taro, betelnut, pigs and other bush products for fish, shellfish and lime made from coral. In the islands in the east, such as Guadalcanal and Malaita, warfare appears to have taken the form of fairly localised confrontations between bush and coastal groups, whereas in the western islands such as Ranongga and New Georgia, it often involved large war parties mounted for the purpose of travelling to other islands to acquire heads and captives. Such warfare was closely connected to cosmological and ritual cycles, and while some captives were destined for ritual death, many were incorporated into local social systems through marriage and adoption.[2] As Debra McDougall has shown for Ranongga, women were actively involved in these networks, and oral histories record the work of women in making productive connections and drawing outsiders into their own groups.[3] However, as we shall see, their role in these processes shifted with the arrival of European traders and missionaries and became increasingly constrained with the expansion of plantation agriculture and the deepening of state authority during the twentieth century.

The first recorded European visitors to the islands were a group of Spanish explorers led by Alvara de Mendaña, who landed on Santa Isabel in 1568. They were followed by naval captains, merchants and whalers, who tended to stay on their ships and occasionally met with locals on the beaches. Interactions between locals and European visitors intensified during the nineteenth century, and trading stations were established at several sites, including Simbo and Mono in New Georgia, Santa Catalina and Makira Harbour in Makira, and the atoll of Sikaiana.[4] Here, locals provided traders with access to copra, bêche-de-mer, tortoiseshell, sandalwood and land, in return for goods such as fish hooks, nails, iron axes and firearms, which were often used for warfare. These exchanges established new patterns of

---

[2] For further discussion see eg Shankar Aswani (ed.), 'Special Issue: Essays on Head-Hunting in the Western Solomon Islands' (2000) 109 *Journal of the Polynesian Society*.

[3] Debra McDougall, 'Fellowship and Citizenship as Models of National Community: United Church Women's Fellowship in Ranongga, Solomon Islands' (2003) 74(1/2) *Oceania* 61. Marovo oral histories record the central role of women in specific rituals surrounding headhunting, notably with respect to very young captives.

[4] Set out in detail in Judith A Bennett, *Wealth of the Solomons: A History of a Pacific Archipelago, 1800–1978* (University of Hawai'i Press, 1987) 20–44.

negotiation over natural products and brought about fundamental and inter-connected changes within Solomon Islander societies.

People in readily accessible coastal areas were the first to engage in trade with Europeans, and oral histories and scholarly accounts attest to the fact that this enabled some men in coastal areas to extend their influence in new ways.[5] Scholarship discussing this period tends to highlight specific, named men and emphasise two key features of political organisation that are critical for under-standing the reconfiguration of land tenure and masculine prestige that occurred from the mid-1800s onwards. First, in many parts of Solomon Islands, there appears to have been a triumvirate of idealised leadership functions involving a leader in warfare, an entrepreneurial feast-giver and a religious leader.[6] These models of masculinity have also often been under-stood in terms of 'men of war' and 'men of peace'.[7] Second, on most islands, political authority appears to have been fractured and diffuse, achieved more than ascribed, and characterised by a high degree of negotiation and contest-ation. Leadership in Solomon Islands is often described in terms of the much-debated distinction, initially proposed by Marshall Sahlins, between the Melanesian 'big man system' based on competition and the Polynesian 'chiefly system' in which leadership is inherited.[8] For example, the taovia of Guadalcanal were not assured of their status but rose to prominence by mobilising people (warriors, dancers, bamboo panpipers) and goods (pigs, betelnut, shell money) in warfare, feast-giving and ceremonial occasions (see Chapter 4). Leadership in Marovo may have been more influenced by hereditary preference, with the role of the bangara depending upon a

[5] See further Bennett, *Wealth of the Solomons*; Geoffrey M White, *Identity through History: Living Stories in a Solomon Islands Society* (Cambridge University Press, 1991); Edvard Hviding, *Guardians of Marovo Lagoon: Practice, Place, and Politics in Maritime Melanesia* (University of Hawai'i Press, 1996).

[6] WG Ivens, *Melanesians of the South-East Solomon Islands* (Kegan Paul, Trench, Trubner, 1927); H Ian Hogbin, *Experiments in Civilization: The Effects of European Culture on a Native Community of the Solomon Islands* (Routledge & Kegan Paul, 1969); Roger M Keesing, *Elota's Story: The Life and Times of a Solomon Islands Big Man* (University of Queensland Press, 1978); Hviding, *Guardians of Marovo Lagoon*.

[7] Margaret Jolly, 'Men of War, Men of Peace: Changing Masculinities in Vanuatu' (2016) 17(3/4) *Asia Pacific Journal of Anthropology* 305.

[8] Marshall D Sahlins, 'Poor Man, Rich Man, Big-Man, Chief: Political Types in Melanesia and Polynesia' (1963) 5(3) *Comparative Studies in Society and History* 285. Cf. Maurice Godelier and Marilyn Strathern (eds.), *Big Men and Great Men: Personifications of Power in Melanesia* (Cambridge University Press, 2008); Geoffrey Miles White and Lamont Lindstrom, *Chiefs Today: Traditional Pacific Leadership and the Postcolonial State* (Stanford University Press, 1997).

combination of male primogeniture, alliances through marriage and recognised leadership ability (Chapter 3).

Trading with Europeans destabilised existing paths to masculine status while also providing avenues for some men to extend their authority in unprecedented ways. European traders tended to seek out male 'chiefs', who they perceived to be individualised centres of authority over collectively held resources, and then establish long-term trading relations with them. This allowed some men in coastal areas to continually deepen their influence in trade, warfare and feast-giving. As Judith Bennett has emphasised, influential men, such as Soga on Isabel, Maghratulo of Vella Lavella and Hingava in Roviana, were able to build their prestige and extend their influence over larger areas – and many more people – than may have previously been possible, by managing access to resources that were valued by Europeans and locals alike and by arming formidable war parties with iron axes and guns.[9]

The intensification of trade also laid the foundations for important economic and socio-spatial distinctions between the islands in the west and those in the east that persist to date. By the late 1800s, people in the western islands, Savo and Makira were sufficiently engaged in trading that some European traders had installed agents there. However, people in the eastern islands, particularly Malaita, were generally perceived by the Europeans to be more difficult to engage with and perhaps more importantly, have fewer products of interest. These islands initially remained on the periphery of European trading networks, but this quickly changed when labour recruiters began to tour the islands in search of cheap and coercible labour for agricultural production and extractive industries in Queensland, Fiji, Samoa and elsewhere.[10]

Thirty years after the abolition of the slave trade elsewhere in the British Empire,[11] and with high commodity prices driving the emergence of plantation economies in the South Pacific, a new labour trade developed. Recruiting vessels began visiting islands in the eastern Solomons – Isabel, Makira, Nggela, Guadalcanal and Malaita – during the 1860s, and between 1870 and 1910, at least 30,000 Solomon Islander men were taken overseas as indentured labourers. Only very small numbers of women were recruited, and the majority of labourers were young, unmarried men.[12]

---

9   Bennett, *Wealth of the Solomons*, 88–93.
10   Ibid, 31, 46–49.
11   Here I refer to the Slavery Abolition Act 1833 (3 & 4 Will IV c 73).
12   See, e.g., Peter Corris, *Passage, Port and Plantation: A History of Solomon Islands Labour Migration, 1870–1914* (Melbourne University Press, 1973); Clive Moore, *Kanaka: A History of Melanesian Mackay* (Institute of Papua New Guinea Studies and University of Papua New Guinea Press, 1985).

Labouring exposed men from the eastern islands to new languages, objects, ideas and economic practices as they encountered Europeans as well as other Pacific Islanders, and it is likely that some men deliberately sought employment. However, it is also clear that many thousands were 'blackbirded' and taken against their will or under false pretences. Once on the ships and plantations, Islanders were subjected to brutal treatment from Europeans.[13] Tracey Banivanua Mar has meticulously exposed the ways in which this violence both emerged from and reproduced popular imagery of the Western Pacific as home to black, savage, physically strong and inherently lawless cannibals occupying spaces beyond the reach of 'civilisation' and 'law'. These racialised stereotypes were central not only to this period of the Pacific labour trade but also to the founding of the colonial property regime, the introduction of the White Australia Policy and the mass deportation of Islanders from Australia at the turn of the twentieth century.[14]

Another group of foreign men began to tour the islands at around the same time as the labour recruiters, namely Christian missionaries. Roman Catholic missionaries arrived in the 1840s but abandoned their work due to illness and conflict with local groups, which included fatal attacks on Bishop Epalle and a priest on Makira.[15] The Church of England's Melanesian Mission also faced resistance, and in 1871, Bishop Patteson, a key figure in the Christianisation of the Western Pacific, was killed at Nukapu in the Reef Islands. His murder was widely interpreted overseas as an act of revenge for the blackbirding of five young men.[16] This reinforced colonial portrayals of the region as inherently lawless and violent and fuelled the growing concern among the public in Australia and Britain that the labour trade was little more than thinly disguised slavery. The following year, the Pacific Islanders Protection Act 1872 was passed to regulate the trade and to extend jurisdiction over British subjects

---

[13] For a careful discussion of both coercion and agency, see Victoria Stead, 'Money Trees, Development Dreams and Colonial Legacies in Contemporary Pasifika Horticultural Labour', in Victoria Stead and Jon C Altman (eds.), *Labour Lines and Colonial Power: Indigenous and Pacific Island Labour Mobility in Australia* (ANU Press, 2019) 312.

[14] Tracey Banivanua Mar, 'Consolidating Violence and Colonial Rule: Discipline and Protection in Colonial Queensland' (2005) 8(3) *Postcolonial Studies* 303; Tracey Banivanua Mar, *Violence and Colonial Dialogue: The Australian-Pacific Indentured Labor Trade* (University of Hawai'i Press, 2007).

[15] J Boutilier, 'A Bibliographic Review of Solomon Islands History' (1979) 12 *Transactions and Proceedings* (Fiji Society, Suva) 25, 30; Paul Sillitoe, *Social Change in Melanesia: Development and History* (Cambridge University Press, 2000) 22.

[16] Charles E Fox, *The Story of the Solomons* (DOM Publications, 1967) 31. Kolshus and Hovdhaugen argue that it was more likely a response to Patteson's insistence on taking young men for training: Thorgeir Kolshus and Even Hovdhaugen, 'Reassessing the Death of Bishop John Coleridge Patteson' (2010) 45(3) *Journal of Pacific History* 331.

on islands not under 'civilised' jurisdiction. Thus, as Banivanua Mar has demonstrated for Fiji (where, in many respects, the colonial acquisition of land and labour proceeded quite differently), racialised narratives of the savagery of Islanders and the violence of the labour trade were intrinsic to the production of the colonial frontier and the legal order that flowed from it; they not only enabled but compelled Britain to bring the disorderly people and places of Solomon Islands within the realm of the Rule of Law.[17]

While Solomon Islands came under the jurisdiction of the British High Commissioner based in Fiji from 1877 onwards,[18] this was only intermittently felt within the islands. The Colonial Office was reluctant to assume the economic burden of another colony, and the High Commissioner's authority was intended to protect British interests in the Western Pacific rather than extend to the local people or other European nationals. British authority tended to manifest episodically and often extremely violently, most notably when the Royal Navy toured the islands to police the labour trade or respond to attacks against British subjects. The latter were regarded as 'acts of war' and sufficient to justify the execution of Indigenous men and the ransacking and shelling of sacred sites and villages unfortunate enough to be accessible to the British. As Judith Bennett notes, this strategic extension and withdrawal of European power legitimated the periodic display of brute force against Indigenous people and ensured British access to raw materials and labour, without incurring the cost of direct, ongoing political control.[19]

Existing scholarly accounts have, with a few notable exceptions such as postgraduate theses written by Solomon Islander women,[20] paid relatively little attention to the impact of colonial expansion on the authority or influence of local women. There is also little mention of the names let alone experiences or influences of expatriate women, such as European and Islander

---

[17] Tracey Banivanua Mar, 'Frontier Space and the Reification of the Rule of Law: Colonial Negotiations in the Western Pacific' (2009) 30(1) *Australian Feminist Law Journal* 23.

[18] Western Pacific Order in Council 1877 (United Kingdom).

[19] Bennett, *Wealth of the Solomons*, 104–105; Joseph Foukona, 'Land, Law and History: Actors, Networks and Land Reform in Solomon Islands' (PhD thesis, Australian National University, 2017) 105–112. See also Antony Anghie, *Imperialism, Sovereignty and the Making of International Law* (Cambridge University Press, 1st ed., 2004) 90.

[20] Alice Aruhe'eta Pollard, 'Painaha: Gender and Leadership in 'Are'Are Society, the South Sea Evangelical Church and Parliamentary Leadership – Solomon Islands' (PhD thesis, Victoria University of Wellington, 2006); Siona Diana Koti, 'A Historical Analysis on Gender Inequality in Solomon Islands: Solomon Islands Women under Pre-Colonial, Colonial and Post-Colonial State' (Master's thesis, Seoul National University, 2014). See also Debra McDougall, '"Tired for Nothing?" Women, Chiefs, and the Domestication of Customary Authority in Solomon Islands', in Hyaeweol Choi and Margaret Jolly (eds.), *Divine Domesticities: Christian Paradoxes in Asia and the Pacific* (ANU Press, 2014).

missionaries. Colonial records similarly provide very few glimpses of women and their lives, and those that exist are refracted through a lens that is male and predominantly European.[21] The accounts produced by expatriate women during the colonial period exhibit an almost total lack of interest in local women, their views and experiences,[22] and I am yet to encounter any records produced by local women during this period. However a critical, ethnographically-informed engagement with existing texts and oral histories strongly suggests that the opportunities presented by traders were relatively more available to local men than women.[23] For example, whereas the institutionalised barter between bush and coastal people had historically involved women exchanging goods on the beach with men standing armed in the background, a small number of influential men were now at the forefront of negotiations with European whalers and traders (who were also overwhelmingly men). When local women were directly involved in this trade, their agency may have been severely constrained.

The 'civilising' mission of Christianity had double-edged and transformative effects. Colonial administrators appear to have largely ignored local women, but the missionaries did not. They established health clinics as well as schools that provided a relatively rare opportunity for women to learn about the language and practices of Europeans, and skills that they could use for income generation.[24] However, Alice Pollard has observed that whereas men were provided with leadership training and equipped to leave their communities on mission work, women were trained in domestic schools and emerged lacking confidence and assertiveness.[25] Women were therefore trained primarily as wives and mothers, and as Anne Dickson-Waiko has demonstrated for Papua New Guinea, Christianity contributed to the emergence of separate spheres for men and women, and ultimately ensured a weakened position for women within the arena of the nation-state.[26]

---

[21] Goodwin finds that this lens is male; however, I emphasise that it is also overwhelmingly English or Australian. Bryonny Goodwin, '"Supposed Figure of a Woman?" Homosociality in the British Solomon Islands, 1880–1940' (MA thesis, University of Auckland, 2006).

[22] See Caroline Mytinger, *Headhunting in the Solomon Islands around the Coral Sea* (Macmillan, 1942); Osa Johnson, *Bride in the Solomons* (Garden City, 1946); Charmian Kittredge London, *Voyaging in Wild Seas, Or a Woman among the Head Hunters (A Narrative of the Voyage of the 'Snark' in the Years 1907–1909)* (Mills & Boon, 1915).

[23] For discussion of colonial archives and Melanesian women's agency see Bronwen Douglas 'Provocative Readings in Intransigent Archives: Finding Aneitymese Women' (1999) 70 *Oceania* 111

[24] Pollard, *Givers of Wisdom*.

[25] Ibid.

[26] Anne Dickson-Waiko, 'Women, Individual Human Rights, Community Rights: Tensions within the Papua New Guinea State' in P Grimshaw et al. (eds.), *Women's Rights and Human Rights* (Palgrave, 2001).

Increased engagements with traders, blackbirders and missionaries prompted the reworking of relationships between local people and their environments during this period, but the general absence of imperial authorities in Solomon Islands left a great deal of influence in the hands of locals. Given the robust trade in arms within the islands, European traders and missionaries were dependent on the maintenance of good relationships with locals for their physical safety as well as the success of their economic and spiritual endeavours. There were numerous instances of intermarriage between Solomon Islander women and European traders, and the experiences of the former were clearly very mixed – some traders stayed long term and ensured the wellbeing of their families, while others deserted them. However, at least some of the trader's wives, and certainly their relatives, were able to exert significant influence over the fortunes of their European husbands. For example Judith Bennett explains that Lelenduri of Roviana married British trader T. G. Kelly, and when Kelly's main trading rival, Peter Pratt came to establish a trading post nearby (on land claimed by the family of his wife, Simaema from Vonavona), Lelenduri's people, led by Hingava (the chief at Munda, and the most powerful man in Roviana Lagoon) successfully opposed the land acquisition in the colonial courts.[27] Nuatali (referred to elsewhere as Niutali) was the eldest daughter of Kiti, a woman of the Lambete people of Munda, and Poto from Kusaghe in north New Georgia, who married the influential trader Norman Wheatley (her second husband).[28] I return to Nuatali further below, but at this point note that oral and written accounts strongly suggest she played a significant role in Wheatley's success as a trader, including through facilitating his land purchases.[29]

2.2 COLONIAL VIOLENCE AND THE APPROPRIATION OF LAND AND LABOUR

Colonial intrusion accelerated towards the end of the century, as colonial desires for Pacific land and labour intensified in the context of rising prices for tropical commodities such as copra. Violence, both threatened and realised, was central to these processes – it was critical to the foundation, legitimation

---

[27] Bennett, *Wealth of the Solomons* 71
[28] I have previously referred to 'Frances Niutali', following GG Carter. However I have since corresponded with descendants who have emphasised that her name is Nuatali.
[29] GG Carter, *Tiè Varanè: Stories about People of Courage from Solomon Islands* (Unichurch, 1981) 11–12.

and operation of the colonial frontier and the socio-spatial reordering that flowed from it. In Solomon Islands as in Banivanua Mar's account of Fiji, racialised constructions of the islands as the home of black headhunters, and frequented by anarchic labour recruiters who were now arming the locals with guns, were central to the 'spatio-legalities' underpinning colonial expansion and the imposition of British law and order upon Indigenous peoples and places.[30] In 1892, the Griffiths ministry in Queensland publicly reversed its decision to abandon the labour trade, and did so against a backdrop of intensifying Anglo-German competition and differing approaches to the supply of arms to Islanders – Britain prohibited it while Germany did not, providing a competitive advantage to German interests.[31] This enabled Britain's 1893 declaration of a Protectorate over Solomon Islands to be readily framed as a 'protective' and 'humanitarian' intervention.

Antony Anghie has argued that the 'civilising mission' drove the development of international law, with the protectorate 'a wonderfully flexible legal instrument' that allowed sovereignty to remain 'undefined in order that it could be extended or withdrawn according to the requirements of British interests'.[32] This was certainly the case in the Solomons, where there was no treaty. Rather, the High Commissioner in Fiji recommended that a resident Deputy Commissioner be appointed to administer the islands, and locals were supposedly notified of the new arrangements when the Royal Navy began to bombard villages and raise flags before disappearing once again.[33] The first Resident Commissioner, Charles Woodford, arrived in the islands two years later, tasked with developing a plantation economy to fund the Protectorate. From the turn of the century until World War II, the colonial administration was largely preoccupied with firstly, 'pacifying' Islanders and bringing them within the realm of 'law', notably through the suppression of Indigenous warfare; and secondly, appropriating Indigenous land and labour through a series of Native Land Regulations, Native Tax Regulations and Labour Regulations. While trading and missionisation had altered negotiations within

---

[30] Banivanua Mar, 'Frontier Space' citing David Delaney, Richard T Ford and Nicholas Blomley 'Preface: Where is Law' in Nicholas Blomley, David Delaney and Richard T Ford (eds.), *The Legal Geographies Reader: Law, Power and Space* (Oxford Wiley Blackwell 2001) xiii.

[31] Doug Munro and Stewart Firth, 'German Labour Policy and the Partition of the Western Pacific: The View from Samoa' (2008) 25(1) *Journal of Pacific History* 85; Scarr, *Fragments of Empire*; Bennett, *Wealth of the Solomons*, 105.

[32] Anghie, *Imperialism, Sovereignty and the Making of International Law*, 89.

[33] David Russell Lawrence, *The Naturalist and His 'Beautiful Islands': Charles Morris Woodford in the Western Pacific* (ANU Press, 2014) 169–170; Scarr, *Fragments of Empire*, 261; Foukona, 'Land, Law and History', 119–124.

and between the people of Solomon Islands, the colonial legality and planta-tion agriculture destabilised them even further, engendering profound socio-spatial transformations and sedimenting particular distinctions that persist today.

2.2.1 'Pacification' and Missionisation: Transforming Socio-spatial Relations

'Pacification' was central to colonial expansion, as enforcing the cessation of Indigenous warfare was integral to meeting the moral demands of publics in Britain, Australia and New Zealand; establishing the authority of British intervention; and attracting foreign investment to the Protectorate. However, the selective enforcement of such policies belied the humanitarian claims made by the British: pacification policies tended to be enforced only when European interests were threatened, and violence against British subjects was deemed an act of war, justifying an extreme response.[34] In 1908, for example, a group of young men attacked and killed Oliver Burns, who was Norman Wheatley's agent in Marovo Lagoon. The local people fled the area, fearing the response of Protectorate officials, and some sought the protection of the Methodist missionaries, Reverend John Francis and Helena Goldie, in nearby Roviana Lagoon. A series of punitive expeditions followed, consisting of white traders, government officers and men from other islands who sailed along the coastline in gunboats, firing at villages and leaving a trail of burned homes and canoes, raided gardens and wounded villagers.[35]

Similar incidents occurred elsewhere in the islands, and although colonial administrators and the media in Britain and Australia portrayed Indigenous violence as extreme, this was precisely the kind of violence meted out by the Royal Navy.[36] At least some British subjects recognised this, and on numerous occasions missionaries in New Georgia assisted Islanders who sought refuge during punitive expeditions. This contributed to the emergence of powerful alliances between New Georgians and some missionaries vis-à-vis Protectorate officials, and laid the foundations for future relationships between the people of New Georgia, church leaders and the government. It also laid the

---

[34] See generally W P Morrell, *Britain in the Pacific Islands* (Clarendon Press, 1969), 184–186; A M Healy, 'Administration in the British Solomon Islands' (1966) 5 *Journal of Administration Overseas* 194, 196.

[35] K B Jackson, 'Tie Hokara, Tie Vaka: Black Man, White Man: A Study of the New Georgia Group to 1925' (PhD thesis, Australian National University, 1978) 177–181; Carter, *Tiè Varanè*, 53ff; Bennett, *Wealth of the Solomons*, 61–63.

[36] For discussion of newspaper accounts see e.g. David Russell Lawrence, *The Naturalist and His 'Beautiful Islands': Charles Morris Woodford in the Western Pacific* (ANU Press, 2014) 217ff

foundations for the legal pluralities of the western islands, in which Christian idioms are especially prominent. There were, of course, many instances in which foreign missionaries, planters and government administrators represented a more united front against locals, such as when missionaries and planters sought assistance from the government for repeated attacks by locals on their enterprises, or when colonial administrators approved a land transfer with the hope that it would encourage settlement in strategic areas.[37]

Nineteenth-century trading with Europeans had destabilised relationships within and between communities, but the increased presence of colonial authorities deepened this and channelled socio-spatial reorganisation in quite particular directions. The cessation of warfare and the growing influence of Christianity altered ritual cycles and the means by which men achieved prestige, but new opportunities to pursue rivalries and build alliances were simultaneously opening up. In the western islands it was common for influential men and their networks to align themselves with either the Methodist Mission or the Seventh Day Adventists (SDA).[38] Foreign traders also formed alliances with missionaries, and trading rivalries such as those between Norman Wheatley (Nuatali's husband) and Frank Wickham (a great friend of Hingava) influenced the course of Christian evangelisation of the western islands, establishing patterns of denominational allegiances, specifically with respect to the Uniting Church and Seventh Day Adventists, which persist today.[39]

By the early 1900s, the coastlines were largely safe from headhunting raids, and people living in the interior of larger islands began to move down to the coast, often with the encouragement of missionaries and drawn by the opportunities for trade, education and training. As we see throughout this chapter, becoming a Christian and taking up residence in coastal areas were intrinsically linked, and the spatial reorganisation of the population was central to the emergence of Christian subjectivities and contemporary legal pluralities.

The reorganisation of the population also contributed to a general intensification of land use in coastal areas as villages, missions and plantations

---

[37] See Bennett, *Wealth of the Solomons*, 108–109; Foukona, 'Land, Law and History', 153–159; Clive Moore, *Making Mala: Malaita in Solomon Islands, 1870s–1930s* (ANU Press, 2017), 345ff.

[38] Darrell Whiteman, 'Melanesians and Missionaries: An Ethnohistorical Study of Socio-Religious Change in the Southwest Pacific' (PhD thesis, Southern Illinois University, 1981) 292.

[39] Wickham and Wheatley encouraged the Methodists to come to Roviana in 1902, but when Wheatley fell out with both Wickham and Goldie, he then invited other Christian missions into the district, and was ultimately successful in encouraging the Seventh Day Adventists to settle in Viru Harbour in 1916: Bennett, *Wealth of the Solomons*, 61–63.

expanded. Land sales to Europeans increased, as did commercial exploitation of resources in coastal areas. The residents of Solomon Islands – both foreign and local – became increasingly occupied with debates regarding who controlled access to marine and terrestrial products, as well as the economic wealth obtained from their sale. Products that had once been regarded as crucial to the sustenance of the entire kin group – including trochus shells, sacred objects and land – were now more likely to be treated as alienable commodities. The legitimacy of these transactions is the subject of significant debate today, and oral histories emphasise that land and goods were often sold to Europeans by local men who had questionable rights to do so. Europeans, carrying their own cultural biases with them, perceived land and its products to be objects managed by either an individual or a single corporate descent group; assumed that only men could enter into contracts; and dealt with people they perceived to be the male representatives (or 'chiefs') of those groups. While local wives and in-laws of traders may have been active 'behind the scenes' in these transactions, I have not encountered a single instance of a woman's name appearing in the records of colonial land sales, and women as a group were generally less likely than men to speak or understand the plantation Pijin used in negotiations.[40]

2.2.2 *Acquiring 'Waste' Lands and Eroding Indigenous Places*

Colonial officials in Solomon Islands (as in neighbouring Papua) did not assume that the underlying title in the territory vested in the Crown,[41] and the precise basis for land acquisition and recognition of Europeans' land rights was the matter of significant debate among colonial officials in Fiji, Solomon Islands and elsewhere. From the turn of the century, the acquisition of vast tracts of land required for a plantation economy was largely facilitated by a series of 'Waste Land Regulations'. These regulations legitimated the acquisition of land by British subjects, by two methods. The first provided that land that was used by its 'native owners' could be sold by those owners directly to British subjects, as either freehold or leasehold. The second, which was the

---

[40] See also Bennett, *Wealth of the Solomons*, xvii, 118.
[41] See further Sue Farran and Don Paterson, *South Pacific Property Law* (Cavendish, 2004) 38–39; John Mugambwa, 'A Comparative Analysis of Land Tenure Law Reform in Uganda and Papua New Guinea' (2007) 11(1) *Journal of South Pacific Law* 39; Daniel Fitzpatrick, Caroline Compton and Joseph Foukona, 'Property and the State or "The Folly of Torrens": A Comparative Perspective' (2019) 42(3) *University of New South Wales Law Journal* 953.

means by which most alienation occurred, provided that land that was deemed 'waste' or 'vacant' could be acquired with the approval of colonial administrators.[42]

The Waste Land Regulations acknowledged the legitimacy of Solomon Islanders' claims to land – these claims were not submerged through the legal fiction of *terra nullius* as in nearby Australia. However, the regulations ensured that any land that was not currently and very obviously occupied could be readily acquired. As Nicholas Blomley has argued, the imagined world of the savage is not only disordered and violent, but an 'anomic world without property',[43] and the Foreign Office was firmly of the view that 'the natives' of Solomon Islands were 'practically savages without any proper conceptions of ownership of land'.[44] The definitions of native 'ownership' in the regulations emerged from and reproduced legal and popular discourses that erased Solomon Islander claims, places and production, representing land as empty, 'wasted' space that could be legitimately brought within the realm of European law and occupation. In fact these narratives *demanded* the creation and enforcement of private property as a civilising and even humanitarian measure. The 'emptying out' of land and invisibilisation of its custodians accumulated over time – the 1896 regulations provided that 'vacant' land meant 'vacant by reason of extinction of the original owners and their descendants', apparently acknowledging that all land had once been occupied but might now be 'empty', but by 1900, the existence of such land was so widely accepted that it required no definition or indeed any explanation as to how it came to be 'vacant'.[45]

By 1914, colonial authorities were increasingly concerned with speculative dealings between Europeans and purported chiefs, and the implications for Indigenous production and the health of the population. They also needed to

---

[42] Solomon Islands (Land) Regulation 1896) (Queen's Regulation No. 4 of 1896), s 10, followed by Solomons (Waste Lands) Regulation of 1900 (Queen's Regulation No 3 of 1900) which provided for a Certificate of Occupation to be issued. For detailed discussion see further Joseph D Foukona, 'Legal Aspects of Customary Land Administration in Solomon Islands' (2007) 11(1) *Journal of South Pacific Law* 64; Foukona 'Land, Law and History', 112ff.

[43] Nicholas Blomley, 'Law, Property, and the Geography of Violence: The Frontier, the Survey, and the Grid' (2003) 93(1) *Annals of the Association of American Geographers* 121, 209. See also Aileen Moreton-Robinson, *The White Possessive: Property, Power and Indigenous Sovereignty* (University of Minnesota Press, 2015), 109–122.

[44] Ian C Heath, 'Land Policy in Solomon Islands' (PhD thesis, LaTrobe University, 1979) 105, quoting Foreign Office to Law Officers 18 November 1899 and Law Office to Foreign Office 13 December 1899 FO 834/19.

[45] Solomons (Waste Land) Regulation 1900 (Queen's Regulation No. 3 of 1900), Solomons (Waste Land) Regulation 1904 (King's Regulation No. 1 of 1904).

raise revenue, which had dropped due to the end of the labour trade and the associated decline in shipping licence fees following the introduction of the White Australia Policy. New regulations were passed that abolished the freehold sale of land and established a leasehold system in which the government was the sole purchaser of land.[46] Under these new regulations, rights to land acquired under the previous regulations were retained, and such land redefined as 'private land'. 'Native land' could only be acquired by the government, which it could then lease to non-natives provided the administration formed the view that first, the natives had consented, and second, that the land was not under cultivation or required for the future support of the natives.[47]

The 1914 regulations constituted a vital territorialising practice and extended state power over land, for Protectorate officials were now even more crucial intermediaries in the mapping, allocation and realisation of resource rights for foreigners. Further, while purportedly protecting Islanders from undue land loss. Protectorate officials often exploited discourses of 'waste', 'vacant' and 'uncultivated' land, taking vast tracts of the most arable land out of Indigenous control, often after minimal, if any, investigation into its use or the Indigenous claims that might exist over it.[48] Some land was recognised as being occupied, and was obtained by traders, planters or the government after negotiations with particular individuals, invariably men.

From the perspective of Solomon Islanders, the people selling land often had questionable entitlements to do so, and it is likely that many had little understanding of how Europeans viewed these transactions, at least initially.[49] From the perspective of traders and planters, land sales demarcated discrete, bounded parcels of land, and disentangled and detached them from disordered, ungoverned native space. Local people who entered these parcels were then perceived as interlopers, and court records for this period reveal that they were frequently evicted – with threatened or actual violence – from what they must surely have regarded as their own lands. Locals were often chased out of plantations by traders and planters armed with guns, and were then

---

[46] Solomons Land Regulation 1914 (Kings Regulation No. 3 of 1914).

[47] Ibid.

[48] Isireli Qalo Lasaqa, 'Melanesians' Choice: A Geographical Study of Tasimboko Participation in the Cash Economy, Guadalcanal, British Solomon Islands' (PhD thesis, Australian National University, 1968); John Houainamo Naitoro, 'Solomon Islands Conflict: Demands for Historical Rectification and Restorative Justice' (Paper presented at the Pacific Updates on Solomon Islands, Fiji and Vanuatu. Hosted by the National Centre for Development Studies, Asia Pacific School of Economics and Management, Australian National University, 2000).

[49] Bennett, *Wealth of the Solomons*, 119.

prosecuted and sometimes imprisoned for trespass.[50] As was the case with the brutality that constituted 'pacification', the violence of land appropriation was legitimated by, and sedimented, state law. This gave the British colonial enterprise an air of moral authority, at least to European audiences, despite the fact that there was often very little compliance with the letter of that same law.

2.2.3 *Acquiring Indigenous Labour, Establishing New Social Worlds*

The development of a plantation economy required not only land but also labour, and as land was remade as a legal object so too did people emerge as legal subjects with various entitlements and obligations: diverse groups speaking hundreds of languages were now homogenised in legal instruments as 'the natives' while also being treated as belonging to distinct 'districts', some men became known as 'chiefs' and 'landowners', and many periodically became 'labourers'. Prior to 1920, there was very little legislation affecting 'the natives' aside from land regulations, but in that year, the administration passed the Native Tax Regulation 1920, which imposed a head tax on all males between the ages of sixteen and sixty.[51] This constructed men of a particular age as the productive agents within the commodity economy, reinforcing the gendered division of labour encouraged by the missions and entrenching unpaid, 'private' caring and domestic work as feminised tasks. The Labour Regulation 1922 established minimum conditions for the recruitment of labourers and their employment by European planters, and while this may have reassured concerned publics in London, Sydney or Auckland as to the humanity of employment conditions on plantations, in practice the regulations were rarely enforced and conditions were often extremely difficult for workers.[52]

As with the overseas labour trade, the bulk of labourers working on the plantations were from the central and eastern islands – Guadalcanal, Makira and particularly Malaita – with the concentration of plantations in the western islands allowing people from those islands to pursue other activities closer to home.[53] While small numbers of women travelled to missions and plantations

---

[50] Trespass is one of the most common charges listed in the court books from the colonial period held in Gizo. Some of the parties to land disputes in Kakabona have told the courts of their ancestors being 'chased out' of their territories by white planters.

[51] Solomons Land Registration (Amendment) Regulation 1922 (King's Regulation No. 10 of 1920).

[52] Solomons Labour Regulation 1922 (King's Regulation No. 15 of 1922); Bennett, *Wealth of the Solomons*, 153–160.

[53] Christine Dureau, 'Decreed Affinities: Nationhood and the Western Solomon Islands' (1998) 33(2) *Journal of Pacific History* 197, 210.

in Solomon Islands, as was the case elsewhere in the colonies of the southwest Pacific, migrant labour overwhelmingly took men away and left women rooted in their villages.[54]

Plantation life facilitated novel forms of social interaction and, as we shall see, supported the emergence of socio-spatial distinctions that became central to the anti-colonial movements that rose to prominence in the aftermath of World War II. Young men who laboured in the plantations in Solomon Islands or overseas often returned home with new skills and knowledge acquired from other Islanders as well as Europeans. Roger Keesing argued that this had implications for intergenerational relationships, as young men could deploy new forms of knowledge and practice as a means to gain a measure of influence vis-à-vis their elders.[55] Returned labourers were also among those who benefited from the new property regime: Jimmy Sura appears to have been the first Solomon Islander to register land in the Protectorate when he returned from labouring in Queensland with a Scottish wife, Agnes Brown.[56] Thus from the earliest days of the Protectorate era, Solomon Islanders were drawn into the new economy in different ways, and although there were notable exceptions such as Agnes Brown or Nuatali, it was typically men who were first equipped with the language – both literal and conceptual – necessary to negotiate with Europeans.

2.3 THE FIRST LANDS COMMISSION: CONSTITUTING LEGAL PLURALITIES

By 1914, land disputes were a source of growing concern for Protectorate officials, and a Lands Commissioner was appointed to settle land claims made by Solomon Islanders against Europeans and the government.[57] Debra McDougall observes that the first Lands Commission, held from 1919 to 1923, appears to have been critical to establishing the forms of political authority and land tenure that are often taken for granted today.[58] However, its records are now scattered, incomplete and inaccessible to most people. Solomon Islanders are well aware of the legal significance of the records for

54 Margaret Jolly, 'The Forgotten Women: A History of Migrant Labour and Gender Relations in Vanuatu' (1987) 58(2) *Oceania* 119.
55 Roger Keesing, 'Plantation Networks, Plantation Culture: The Hidden Side of Colonial Melanesia' (1986) 82–83 *Journal de la Société des Océanistes* 163, 166.
56 Bennett, *Wealth of the Solomons*, 195.
57 Solomons and Gilbert and Ellice Islands (Commission of Inquiry) Regulation 1914 (King's Regulation No. 4 of 1914).
58 McDougall, *Engaging with Strangers*, 166.

contemporary claims, and I have become accustomed to excitedly opening boxes of land-related records in the National Archives in Honiara, only to find them empty. While some people hold records of relevance to them, there appears to be only one surviving public collection, which was transferred to Auckland by the Foreign Office in the 1980s. This occurred despite opposition from the government of the newly independent Solomon Islands.[59] Efforts to repatriate these records have so far been unsuccessful, and when legal histor-ian Joseph Foukona examined them in 2014, he found many missing.[60] In the absence of a relatively complete collection of publicly available records, it is challenging to trace the ongoing effects of specific determinations, as well as the wider conceptual reformulations of land tenure, kinship and authority the Phillips Land Commission may have prompted.

For the first few years of its existence, the Lands Commission was highly ineffective, constrained by logistical difficulties, as well as what appears to have been a lack of interest on the part of Commissioner GG Alexander. Foukona observes that while Alexander had gained significant understanding of land issues during his previous posting in Fiji, he held the post of commis-sioner in Solomon Islands for just eight months before going to Tanganyika, and most of his time was spent outside the Protectorate.[61] Alexander left few records for his successor, and when Australian judge Frederick Beaumont Phillips took over as Lands Commissioner in 1920, he had to rehear many claims.[62] The Land Commission held inquiries in the areas under dispute, and sought to identify the boundaries of the land, the owners, and the legitimacy of alienation under the relevant regulations. Many of the claims concerned land held by the foreign-owned companies, including the Malayta Company (later Fairymead Company) and Levers Pacific Plantation Limited (the Levers Brothers' Pacific subsidiary), while others concerned land acquired by the missions. Commissioner Phillips found that about half of the area granted had not in fact been 'vacant, unowned or unoccupied'; however, most of the land that was actually returned to Solomon Islanders had not been developed, and many of the complaints against European companies were not investigated at all.[63]

---

[59] Monica Wehner and Ewan Maidment, 'Ancestral Voices: Aspects of Archives Administration in Oceania' (1999) 27(1) *Archives and Manuscripts* 23, 31.

[60] J Foukona, personal communication, 15 June 2021.

[61] Foukona, 'Land, Law and History', 159–191.

[62] Colin H Allan, *Customary Land Tenure in the British Solomon Islands Protectorate* (Western Pacific High Commission, 1957) Chapter X.

[63] Heath, 'Land Policy', 204–210.

One of the most striking features of the Phillips Land Commission, which I suggest is central to understanding its enduring legacies including contemporary legal pluralities, is the extent to which it became the site of intense struggle between Protectorate officials, traders, missionaries and local leaders. The Reverend John Frances Goldie was a prominent figure in these struggles, and had arrived in the islands in 1902, when he went to Roviana as a member of the first group of Methodist missionaries sent from Sydney. Goldie went on to become the chairman of the Solomon Islands District of the Methodist Mission until his retirement almost fifty years later, and was extremely influential in the affairs of the Protectorate. In 1921, he wrote to Commissioner Phillips, enclosing a petition from 'the Chiefs and Land-Owners' of the western islands which requested, among other things, that Goldie himself be permitted to take the place of the officer appointed by the colonial administration to represent the Indigenous claimants.[64] Goldie's letter was polite and, on the face of it, respectful of the authority of Protectorate officials. Indeed he claimed he had advised the chiefs *not* to challenge the authority of the commission. However by this time, Goldie had spent almost twenty years in the Protectorate and he had a well-established reputation for 'causing trouble' and appropriating the role of government. Goldie was a formidable figure for Methodist converts in the western islands and almost certainly had some involvement in writing the petition, but the language of the petition is quite different from his own correspondence, suggesting that it was not his work alone. The petition consists of four pages of closely typed, numbered paragraphs:

Sir,

At a meeting of Chiefs and land-owners of the Western Sols at which Reps were present from [illegible] (in the Shortlands), Choiseul, V. Lavella, Simbo, Rendova, Marovo, [illegible] and all the district of N. Georgia, it was reported that information had come from the D.O at Gizo, that the S/S had refused our very reasonable request for repstn on the proposed Lds Cmsn. Regret was expressed that the S/S had not thought it worthwhile to reply to our letter.

1   Surprise and regret was also expressed [by the chiefs at the meeting] at the statement in paragraph 3 of your letter, that the King is responsible for all actions of the officers of the Govt in Solomon Islands. We have

---

[64] J F Goldie to the Acting Resident Commissioner of the British Solomon Islands (Solomon Islands National Archives, BSIP 18/IV/25/24, 19 November 1921).

been taught for many years to honour the King, and we cannot believe that many of the actions of the officials have the approval of his Majesty.

2   It is quite true, as you say, that we have failed to understand perhaps that these officers have been appointed to protect our interests. We are children in these matters, and we cannot yet understand,

3   How our interests were protected in the seizure and sale without our knowledge and consent of the great isld of Kulambangara (Duki) or

4   How our interests were protected by the seizure and sale of the whole of the coast-line of New Georgia, from Nauro (Diamond Narrows) to Marovo – a distance of nearly 50 miles, or by giving the white man the right to hunt us from our own land.

5   We fail to understand also how our interests have been protected by the forcible alienation of practically the whole island of Rarare Wona Wona. This great wrong – done by Govt officials without even our knowledge – leave us without land suffct in this locality to grow our food.[65]

The petition was signed by forty-two men who are described as 'Chiefs of the Western Solomon Islands'. Three of these people were from Choiseul, two from Mono (near the Shortland Islands) and the remainder were from the New Georgia group. The petition reveals the emergence of particular identities in political parlance, notably the masculine 'chiefs' and 'land-owners' of 'the Western Solomon Islands'. It contains numerous references to honouring the King; invokes the obligation of Protectorate officials to 'protect' the interests of supposedly 'childlike' natives who depend on land for subsistence; opposes the 'seizure', 'sale' and 'forcible alienation' of land; and pits the actions of Protectorate officials against the reputation of the monarchy. The 'Chiefs and Land-owners' had clearly grasped the symbolic repertoires of the British administration and were intent on using them to challenge the appropriation of land by Europeans. As Christian Lund observes, the language and paraphernalia of the state are not the preserve of government institutions alone,[66] and the chiefs in the western islands had observed and adopted the racialised juridical foundations of the colonial state (most notably in the ironic reference to being 'children in these [legal] matters') as well as its instruments (such as a petition). The Phillips Land Commission in general, and its

---

[65]   Petition from the Chiefs and Land-Owners of the Western Sols, 21 June 1921, J F Goldie to the Acting Resident Commissioner of the British Solomon Islands (Solomon Islands National Archives, BSIP 18/IV/25/24, 19 November 1921).

[66]   Cf Christian Lund, 'Twilight Institutions: Public Authority and Local Politics in Africa' (2006) 37(4) *Development and Change* 685.

hearings in particular, provided a highly public arena in which the Protectorate's own symbolic repertoire could be adopted by other institutions (here, 'chiefs' and 'landowners') and mobilised against Protectorate officials to contest their authority and legitimacy and in so doing, assert their own.

Protectorate officials were willing to accommodate some of the requests in the petition but refused others, simultaneously reasserting their authority in relation to Goldie as much as the 'Chiefs and land-owners'. Goldie and other 'friends of the natives' were allowed to give evidence before the Lands Commissioner, but they were not permitted to take the place of the officer appointed by the colonial administration to represent the natives.[67] The significance of the struggle to the Protectorate administration is revealed by the words of Resident Commissioner Kane, who was of the view that 'both natives and Europeans' perceived the debate as 'a final test of strength between the Government and Mr Goldie'.[68]

2.3.1 *Sectarian Territoriality*

If Goldie was known among Protectorate officials for 'causing trouble', he was probably of even more concern to other missionaries. Across the Protectorate a range of missions were competing to establish their authority, and the records of the Phillips Commission reveal the territoriality of these struggles in vivid detail. Most of the claims that came before the commission concerned land alienated to planters, but four concerned land in the New Georgia Group that had been alienated to the Seventh Day Adventist Mission.[69] This was big business, as borne out by the fact that the Seventh Day Adventists secured the law firm of choice for the Australian establishment, Allen, Allen and Hemsley, to act on their behalf.[70] In a letter to Commissioner Kane, the Secretary to the SDA Mission asserted that they had made 'strong representations' to Phillips' predecessor concerning

---

[67] Letter from the Resident Commissioner (Solomon Islands National Archives, BSIP 18/IV/25/24, 22 May 1922); Letter from the Resident Commissioner (Solomon Islands National Archives, BSIP 18/IV/25/24, 23 August 1922).

[68] Kane to High Commissioner (Solomon Islands National Archives, WPHC 2671 of 1922, 26 August 1922).

[69] Claims number 25, 26, 27 and 60 against the landholdings of the Australasian Conference Association Ltd. of Sydney at Ugeli (in Rendova), Telina (central Marovo Lagoon), Rava (Viru Harbour) and Kudu Point, Maulu (Ranongga), respectively.

[70] Allen, Allen and Hemsley to F Beaumont Phillips (Solomon Islands National Archives, BSIP 18/IV/25/24, 28 May 1921).

the adverse attitude of the Methodist Missionary towards our operations, which attitude expressed itself in the form of raids by Methodist natives on the lands of our adherents, which lands they would proceed to clear and plant, declaring when interrogated, that they were but emissaries of their white missionaries who had sent them to dispute the ownership of the lands in question.[71]

Such territorialising strategies were crucial to the assertion of authority by both European missionaries and Solomon Islanders. Missionaries aimed to build a common sense of identity among converts, and the organisation of activities was expressed in terms of space – through the construction of church build-ings; the development of new villages and plantations associated with specific missions; and the definition of parishes, districts and regions. The coexistence of multiple, overlapping missions therefore produced multiple, overlapping territories, and the missions' desire for exclusive authority produced heated contests over the boundaries of those territories. Territorialisation provides a potent language for the legitimation of authority, and it is entirely plausible that Goldie 'sent' Methodist converts to dispute land ownership in order to assert the religious authority of the Methodist Mission vis-à-vis the Adventist mission. Indeed, the Secretary for the Adventist missions complained to Commissioner Kane that Goldie 'has been known to openly boast that he would "drive us from the group"'.[72]

Goldie may have been an influential agent of political ferment, but the idea that Solomon Islander converts to Methodism 'were but emissaries' of white missionaries is far less plausible. In fact it grossly underestimates the interests and capacities of Islanders. Denominational affiliation provided Solomon Islanders with a novel and potent means for expressing socio-spatial differ-ences, and I suspect that Indigenous converts to Christianity were no less concerned than foreign missionaries with establishing and exerting control over space. Oral histories suggest that coastal areas on large islands had often been accessed by multiple groups, for example by bush groups living in the interior as well as coastal groups from smaller, outlying islands. However as traders plied the coastline, plantations were established, and growing numbers of people converted to Christianity and relocated to large villages in coastal areas, demand for access to land and other resources intensified. Converts to Methodism – and perhaps particularly those local men seeking to expand their

[71] H M Blunden, Seventh Day Adventist Islands Missions Secretary to R R Kane Esquire, Resident Commissioner of the British Solomon Islands (Solomon Islands National Archives, BSIP 18/IV/25/24, 12 July 1922).
[72] Ibid.

influence – probably needed very little encouragement from white missionaries to clear and plant the land that was also being cultivated by Adventists.

These processes are clearly evident in the records of *Native Claim No 26*, regarding Telina Island, which had been leased to the Adventists by Jorovo (also known as Kanijama), a warrior of Vangunu and Gatokai (Map 4). The island was also claimed by the Busimati, a Bareke (bush) group, who were represented by the Bareke bangara (now often translated as 'chief'), Sagende. The transcripts of hearings suggest that by 1924, the men who came before the commission were already experienced in land transactions with foreigners, and had encountered various forms of 'court'. While the records contain notes from expatriates that 'the natives do not understand legal matters', I suggest that the transcripts of hearings reveal the opposite. Local men went to significant lengths to explain the intricacies of their land tenure systems – they recounted genealogies, the transmission of the role of bangara to men and sometimes women and details of warfare, feasts and exchange. They also sought to articulate the differences between Indigenous and European understandings of the world in terms that the British administrators might recognise. Where there was a lack of understanding, it was often on the part of the Europeans. It is clear from the transcripts that colonial officials could not (or would not) conceive of land being occupied and used by many, entangled people, and were instead focused on identifying a specific, unilineal lineage attached to a specific, clearly demarcated territory.

The emphasis on unilineal descent groups was to become a common feature of the judicial interpretation of customary tenure throughout the Protectorate era. Reflecting widespread assumptions within British social anthropology at the time, and models of unilineal descent and primogeniture originally developed with reference to African societies, Protectorate officials fairly consistently assumed that land tenure revolved around discrete, bounded groups linked to an equally defined territory, with those groups defined by either patrilineal or matrilineal descent.[73] These heteronormative, biological and gender-binary understandings of kinship, and equally static views of place, meant that as Protectorate officials sought to delineate interwoven places and legitimate them as property, they were confronted with claims that appeared to 'compete'. Furthermore, in the case of *Native Claim No 26*, this 'conflict' appeared to be a sectarian one, with the parties and their witnesses firmly divided along sectarian lines. This led the Deputy for the Natives to perceive

---

[73] See further Sharon W Tiffany, 'Customary Land Disputes, Courts and African Models in the Solomon Islands' (1983) 53(3) *Oceania* 277

an 'extraordinary conflict of evidence',[74] where I suspect the parties were in fact recounting the shared use of land and coexistence of claims. Commissioner Phillips noted the 'manifestation of a certain sectarian keenness among the natives at the Inquiry',[75] but nevertheless felt able to conclude that:

> This evidence shows that the [Bareke] people were formerly, at any rate, bush people, and that have only 'come down' to the saltwater in comparatively recent times. From Sagendi's evidence it also seems clear that when his people came down to the beach they encountered opposition from the beach people who claimed the land.[76]

Arriving at determinations based on 'fact' rather than 'politics' was critical to the justification and legitimation of the Protectorate administration, based as it was on the introduction of rationality, law and order where there had supposedly been none. However, the records of *Native Claim No 26* reveal that whatever Commissioner Phillips purported to 'find', the only conclusion that could reasonably be reached based on the evidence presented by the claimants was that territorial conflicts were now tightly woven with the new religion.

2.3.2 *Big Men and Struggles over Property*

It is difficult to find any trace of women's voices in the records of the Phillips Commission that remain publicly available. Extant correspondence concerning the commission is consistently written by, and to, expatriate missionaries, colonial officials and lawyers, all of whom appear to have been men. Transcripts of hearings indicate that the parties and witnesses who came before the commission were not only consistently men, but those who were regarded by locals and colonial administrators alike as important 'chiefs' and 'warriors'. This does not mean that other Indigenous people were passive observers rather than active participants in colonial struggles. There was at least one woman who appeared before the Lands Commission – Nuatali. By the early 1900s, Nuatali had left Norman Wheatley and was living with a man named Lai, who was from Sabana on Isabel. One of their children, Jacob Zinihite, told George Carter:

---

[74] *Report of the Lands Commission: Native Claim No. 26 respecting land at Telina Island, Marovo Lagoon, claimed by the Australian Conference Association Ltd*, 18 June 1924, Annexure II (copy on file with the author).
[75] Ibid.
[76] Ibid.

A Melbourne lawyer, J. Beaumont Phillips, was brought to the Solomons. Many people came to give evidence, and some of the noted leaders of the people spoke. There was only one woman – Niutali [*sic*].

. . .

She told the court that she had been born at Munda, that she was descended from the Kazukuru people...She said that she was surprised and angry at the amount of land that was claimed by Levers and other companies. She had waited a long time for the men to speak up and say something about it. They had not, so she herself had come to court.

'Now all of the black men will die because his ground has been taken from him, and he has none...We want the land back we are not allowed to take things from the white man's ground...We want a place to live on, to walk about on. We want the land back because by and by we got no place to live.'[77]

In Zinihite's retelling, Nuatali's claims were grounded primarily in her concerns about the future sustenance of her community, an observation that Katerina Teaiwa also makes of the Banaban women who clung to their trees and opposed phosphate mining in the Gilbert and Ellice Island Colony during the same period.[78] Nuatali appears to have been the only woman to appear before the Phillips Commission, and she did so not only because of her own individual interest in the land, but importantly, because 'the men' who were obliged to 'speak up' to defend collective interests had failed to do so. This suggests that while some women played a role in constructing what Carol Rose refers to as the 'narratives, stories, and rhetorical devices'[79] that make up claims to property, there was a degree of acceptance that it should generally be men who performed those narratives in the arenas established and recognised by the colonial system. If the 'vernacular' of colonial regimes was 'the language of law',[80] it was a language that, like English and Pijin, was most readily mobilised by a relatively small number of men, many of whom were regarded as 'chiefs' and 'warriors'.

---

[77] Quoted in Carter, *Tiè Varanè*, 12–13. Carter refers to Nuatali as 'Niutali', but as noted previously, the descendants I have met refer to her as Nuatali, and this is certainly the name that is common among Solomon Islanders today.

[78] Katerina Martina Teaiwa, *Consuming Ocean Island: Stories of People and Phosphate from Banaba* (Indiana University Press, 2014) 132.

[79] Carol M Rose, *Property and Persuasion: Essays on the History, Theory and Rhetoric of Ownership* (Westview Press, 1994), 6.

[80] J Comaroff, 'Governmentality, Materiality, Legality, Modernity: On the Colonial State in Africa' in Jan-Georg Deutsch, Heike Schmidt and Peter Probst (eds.), *African Modernities: Entangled Meanings in Current Debate* (James Currey, 2002).

2.4 NATIVE ADMINISTRATION AND NATIVE COURTS: SEDIMENTING GENDERED PUBLIC AUTHORITY

During the 1920s, the association between expressions of state authority and specific models of masculine influence was tightened even further. British colonial administrators increasingly turned their attention to incorporating 'the natives' into systems of governance through the establishment of a version of indirect rule. These efforts were motivated by growing concern regarding the perceived depopulation and decline of native society[81] as well as the expanding authority of the missions on some islands. Until this point, the colonial government had, with the notable exceptions of regulating land and masculine labour, been largely disinterested in the affairs of 'the natives'. However, in many places the authority of particular missions and missionaries – such as Reverend Goldie of the Methodist Mission in the western islands, and Bishop Wood of the Melanesian Mission in the central islands – was now well established and more influential than the government.[82]

In Solomon Islands, indirect rule involved the demarcation of territorial boundaries that were believed to correspond with 'natural ethnological divisions',[83] and the appointment of village constables, village headmen and subdistrict headmen who were answerable to the expatriate district officer for each of the districts.[84] Many of Mahmood Mamdani's observations regarding indirect rule in Africa hold true for Melanesia also: while British administrators in Solomon Islands did not go to the same extent to develop 'native codes', indirect rule was similarly premised on the inclusion of a colonised majority in a regime of 'customary' power, it was grounded in ethnically defined identities, and it privileged a particular authority (the 'chief') who was defined in terms of masculinity.[85] Protectorate officials' search for 'traditional chiefs' not only overlooked the contested nature of leadership and the ambiguity of social boundaries, but also the possibility of

---

[81] For recent analysis of the influence of ideas of depopulation on colonial land policy and indirect rule see Foukona, 'Land, Law and History'; Akin, *Colonialism, Maasina Rule and the Origins of Malaitan Kastom*, 94–131.

[82] Hugh Laracy and Eugénie Laracy, 'Custom, Conjugality and Colonial Rule in the Solomon Islands' (1980) 51(2) *Oceania* 133.

[83] Memorandum: Native Administration Officers (Solomon Islands National Archives, BSIP I/III/F/13/23, 14 October 1943). The memorandum sets out attempts to give effect to indirect rule in the District of Guadalcanal.

[84] Native Administration (Solomons) Regulation 1922 (King's Regulation No. 17 of 1922).

[85] Mahmood Mamdani, *Citizen and Subject: Contemporary Africa and the Legacy of Late Colonialism* (Princeton University Press, 1996).

women exercising various forms of authority. It invariably led them to men who had knowledge of the government, English and Pijin.[86]

Sara Berry has argued that indirect rule in Africa did not so much consolidate state authority or rigidify the social order as 'provoke a series of debates' regarding custom that continue to shape power, meaning and access to resources.[87] In many respects this was also the case in Solomon Islands, where indirect rule frequently destabilised pre-existing political geographies and established the grounds for new ones, with diverse and ongoing implications for local authority and the conditions of access to land and other resources. In some places, such as Malu'u on the north coast of Malaita, indirect rule created a proliferation of claims to authority as the men appointed as government headmen were in open competition with church-appointed leaders.[88] In other instances, it enabled some men to extend and consolidate their authority over both land and people, a theme I develop in Chapter 3. In a vein similar to Berry, I suggest that in both cases, indirect rule did not define the Indigenous order, but established the grounds for ongoing debates regarding the nature of 'traditional' leadership and the territorial division of lineages and ethnic groups. Importantly, as we see here and in the chapters that follow, it sedimented both land control and public authority as masculine domains, and channelled ongoing debates regarding property, territory and political authority along thoroughly gendered terrain.

Once the Native Administration Regulation 1922 came into effect, Protectorate officials were increasingly confronted with questions relating to kastom, and district officers made various attempts to document the social organisation and practices of different districts.[89] As is now well-recognised in the literature on indirect rule, these ethnographic endeavours sought to

---

[86] Eg Ivens observed that administrators tended to appoint men with experience of government and knowledge of English as village police: Walter George Ivens, *The Island Builders of the Pacific: How and Why the People of Mala Construct Their Artificial Islands, the Antiquity and Doubtful Origin of the Practice, with a Description of the Social Organization, Magic and Religion of Their Inhabitants* (Seely, Service & Co, 1930), 86.

[87] Sara Berry, 'Hegemony on a Shoestring: Indirect Rule and Access to Agricultural Land' (1992) 62(3) *Africa* 327; Berry, 'Debating the Land Question in Africa'.

[88] David Hilliard, 'The South Sea Evangelical Mission in the Solomon Islands: The Foundation Years' (1969) 4(1) *Journal of Pacific History* 41; Roger M Keesing, 'Politico-Religious Movements and Anticolonialism on Malaita: Maasina Rule in Historical Perspective (Part I)' (1978) 48(4) *Oceania* 241; Ralph R Premdas and Jeffrey Steeves, 'The Solomon Islands: An Experiment in Decentralization' (Working Paper Series, Pacific Islands Studies Program, Center for Asian and Pacific Studies, University of Hawaii at Manoa, 1985).

[89] This was encouraged by Resident Commissioner Ashley despite opposition from Suva, and advocated by anthropologist Ian Hogbin: H Ian Hogbin, 'Culture Change in the Solomon Islands: Report of Field Work in Guadalcanal and Malaita' (1934) 4(3) *Oceania* 233; Laracy and

impose or restore order on societies that were perceived to be chaotic or vulnerable, and to reinforce the autonomous rationality of the colonial state.[90] However, the ethnographic descriptions produced by district officers in Solomon Islands are extremely thin, often limited to a few pages setting out a list of key matters. As David Akin has observed, 'one finds fewer claims to or attributes of "ethnographic acuity" in the BSIP archives than in those for other colonies'.[91] The records I have reviewed are brief and do not provide sources, but it is likely that the assumptions about gendered leadership and expertise prevailing among Protectorate officials, as well as local norms circumscribing close contact between genders, not only led male officials to appoint male 'headmen', but to take their perspectives on custom as authoritative. Thus while indirect rule in Solomon Islands certainly did not rigidify 'custom', I suggest that it sedimented state-sanctioned authority as a masculine domain.

When Native Courts were established in various forms from 1939, they were presided over by elders who were 'men of standing in native life' appointed by the district headman.[92] These courts, like the Phillips Land Commission, regularly threw sectarian and kin-based contests over authority into sharp relief. When reporting on the establishment of the courts in the western islands, the District Commissioner was at pains to emphasise that 'the Court at present should not be given wide powers in land matters' because of the risk of bias:

> There will always be among the elders a personal interest in the outcome of such cases, and this together with the strong line of demarcation which exists between the different Mission adherents may lead, probably will lead, to decisions not entirely in accordance with the facts.[93]

Laracy, 'Custom, Conjugality and Colonial Rule'; Sharon W Tiffany, 'Customary Land Disputes, Courts and African Models'.

[90] See e.g. Peter Pels, 'The Anthropology of Colonialism: Culture, History, and the Emergence of Western Governmentality' (1997) 26 *Annual Review of Anthropology* 163; U Kalpagam, 'Colonial Governmentality and the Public Sphere in India' (2002) 15(1) *Journal of Historical Sociology* 35.

[91] Akin, *Colonialism*, 5.

[92] Letter from the District Officer of Gizo to the Secretary of the Government re: Native Courts (Solomon Islands National Archives, BSIP I/III/49/19 October 1941). See further Laracy and Laracy, 'Custom, Conjugality and Colonial Rule'; Healy, 'Administration'; T M Talasasa, 'Settlement of Disputes in Customary Land in British Solomon Islands Protectorate' (1970) 11 *Melanesian Law Journal*; Sharon W Tiffany, 'Disputing in Customary Land Courts: Case Studies from Solomon Islands' (1979) 7 *Melanesian Law Journal* 99.

[93] Letter from the District Officer of Gizo to the Secretary of the Government re: Native Courts (Solomon Islands National Archives, BSIP I/III/49/19 October 1941).

It is clear that from the perspective of the government, the role of the archetypal rational implementer of state law remained confined not only to men, but to white men, the only people deemed capable of reaching dispassionate, objective determinations, 'particularly in land matters'.

2.5 WORLD WAR II AND AFTERMATH: CONTESTED TERRITORIES AND DIVERSE LEGAL PLURALITIES

World War II left an indelible mark on the physical and social worlds of Solomon Islanders. It reshaped the development trajectories of different islands, and also contributed to the emergence of a number of highly organised movements against European hegemony that consolidated particular expressions of territoriality and legal plurality that endure today.

The war arrived decisively in Solomon Islands when, in January 1942, the Japanese began to repeatedly bomb the capital of the Protectorate at Tulagi. Protectorate officials withdrew to the bush on nearby Malaita, and expatriate plantation owners fled, leaving Islander workers stranded on the plantations. Many of the missionaries also left. When American forces arrived in August, Guadalcanal quickly became the scene of one of the bloodiest battles in the Pacific. By March 1943, that battle had been won by the Allies and the conflict moved northwest. New Georgia then became a major battleground, until the Allied forces took control of most of the Protectorate.[94]

A large portion of colonial records were destroyed during the war, including most of the land records,[95] and this created the kind of 'Ground Zero' in legal positivist terms that has been observed in the aftermath of conflict and disasters elsewhere.[96] It unravelled previous attempts by colonial administrators to 'discover custom' and create legal certainty in property relations, and allowed for the reopening of claims that had apparently been 'settled'. The physical landscape was irrevocably changed, with many of the roads and airports built during the war remaining critical infrastructure to date. Following the war, the capital of the Protectorate and the Western Pacific High Commission was

---

[94] Judith A Bennett, *Natives and Exotics: World War II and Environment in the Southern Pacific* (University of Hawaii Press, 2009); Anna Annie Kwai, *Solomon Islanders in World War II: An Indigenous Perspective* (ANU Press, 2017).

[95] Policy on Leasing and Renting of Crown and Native Land (Solomon Islands National Archives, BSIP 7/VIII/SS5/1, n.d.); Lands Commission (Solomon Islands National Archives, BSIP I/III/F35/49; n.d.).

[96] Daniel Fitzpatrick, 'Ontologies of Property: Land Titling after the Indian Ocean Tsunami Disaster' (2018) 11(2) *Global Environment* 294.

moved to Honiara, from Tulagi and Suva, respectively, partly to take advantage of this infrastructure.[97]

World War II irrevocably changed the social as well as physical landscape. It amplified pre-existing resistance to European hegemony, and fuelled resentment towards the British in particular. The rapid evacuation of most Europeans had not gone unnoticed by locals, who often had positive encounters with American troops. Solomon Islanders in the Labour Corp and African American troops also shared their experiences of and struggles against white supremacy and racial subordination, and this served to strengthen existing anti-colonial ideals and movements.[98]

Similar encounters between Islanders and Americans profoundly shaped the attitudes, perspectives and expectations of people in many parts of the region, and when colonial officials began to reassert their authority at the end of the war, they faced numerous challenges.[99] In Solomon Islands, the economy was decimated, and a number of movements resisting European hegemony emerged in various parts of the Protectorate, employing different vocabularies depending on the political contests they were enmeshed in.

2.5.1 *Malaita: Maasina Rule*

One of the best known post-war movements was Maasina Rule, a predominantly Malaitan movement whose key demands included improvements in the terms of plantation employment; the codification of kastom; the establishment of native councils and courts with leaders appointed by communities rather than the government; and the establishment of a Malaita-wide council. Members of the movement did not simply wait for the government to respond, they organised themselves to implement the changes they demanded – they relocated into larger communities in coastal areas, where they worked in cooperative plantations and refused to pay the government head tax, instead paying it to their leaders. They also sought to codify custom, particularly by documenting the aspects of land tenure now central to property disputes, such as land boundaries, genealogies and sacred sites. By 1947, the movement had instituted a pan-Malaita government with a hierarchical system of chiefs at

---

[97] M E P Bellam, 'The Colonial City: Honiara, a Pacific Islands' Case Study' (1970) 11(1) *Pacific Viewpoint* 66, 70.

[98] See e.g. Keesing, 'Politico-Religious Movements' (Part I); Whiteman, 'Melanesians and Missionaries'; White, *Identity through History*, 43; Kwai, *Solomon Islanders in World War II*; Allen, *Greed and Grievance*, 73ff.

[99] Geoffrey M White and Lamont Lindstrom (eds.), *The Pacific Theater: Island Representations of World War II* (University of Hawaii Press, 1989).

village, subdistrict and district levels, and a 'Federal Council' at the peak. The government's response was initially conciliatory, but from around mid-1947, colonial officials moved to a policy of suppression and eradication that was strikingly reminiscent of 'pacification', with intimidation by British aircraft and warships, the destruction of villages and the arrest of thousands of adherents.[100]

Maasina Rule has been extensively discussed, most recently by David Akin, who emphasises its origins as a labour movement and sees it as a a struggle for civil and political rights similar to those in America and elsewhere during the same period.[101] One of the striking features of the movement was the extent to which it developed a culture of legality that was not only mobilised against the colonial government but was *the* privileged mode of resisting the colonial administration's incursions into Indigenous lives. If Protectorate officials had used the legal construction and regulation of property as a means to acquire land, the head tax to force people into plantation labour, and indirect rule to establish social and administrative order, they now found those structures turned against them. Moreover, kastom was expanded far beyond a 'source of law' maintained at the whim of the government to consolidate its rule – it became, as Akin observes, 'a realm that the government was to leave fully to Malaitans, and that furthermore would include almost everything'.[102]

Importantly, the movement marked the emergence of a pan-Malaitan identity that united previously diverse groups into a single political community delimited by the boundaries of the island. The people of the eastern islands had borne the brunt of the brutality of plantation labour, and it was now the language (Pijin) and social networks of the plantations that provided the avenues through which the movement's message could be communicated and a regional identity emerge.[103] Maasina Rule invoked the 'natural' solidarity of Malaitans to legitimise their demands, including their demand for the replacement of the government's multiple, subdistrict councils with a single, all-Malaita district council. In so doing, the movement elided distinctions

---

[100] See further Keesing, 'Politico-Religious Movements', (Part I), 241–261; Roger M Keesing, 'Politico-Religious Movements and Anticolonialism on Malaita: Maasina Rule in Historical Perspective (Part II)' (1978) 49(1) *Oceania* 46, 46–73; Roger M Keesing, 'Kastom and Anticolonialism on Malaita: "Culture" as Political Symbol' (1982) 13(4) *Mankind* 357; Hugh Laracy, *Pacific Protest: The Maasina Rule Movement, Solomon Islands, 1944–1952* (University of the South Pacific, 1983).

[101] Akin, *Colonialism, Maasina Rule and the Origins of Malaitan Kastom*.

[102] Ibid, 7.

[103] Cyril Belshaw, 'Native Politics in the Solomon Islands' (1947) 20(2) *Pacific Affairs* 187; Allen, *Greed and Grievance*, 61ff; Akin, *Colonialism, Maasina Rule and the Origins of Malaitan Kastom*, 165–213.

between subdistricts and *enlarged* the ethno-territorial distinctions central to the colonial administration's system of indirect rule, rather than resisting the state's territorialising strategies entirely. This approach appears to have been effective – in 1953, a New Native Administration Regulation was passed, based on a Kenyan ordinance, providing for the introduction of a native council for each district.[104] The first council to be established was Malaita's (replacing Maasina Rule's 'Federal Council'), and it took another ten years before the five local councils of the Western District (Shortlands, Choiseul, Vella, Roviana and Marovo) were amalgamated into a single Western Council.[105]

2.5.2 *Guadalcanal: The Society for the Development of Native Races and the Moro Movement*

While Protectorate officials' attentions were focused on Maasina Rule, anti-colonial movements were also emerging elsewhere in the Protectorate. Matthew Belamatanga of Guadalcanal had a reputation among Protectorate officials for 'standing up to the Europeans' and collaborating with Maasina Rule,[106] and founded the 'Society for the Development of the Native Races' that was active on north-west Guadalcanal from 1947. This movement mobilised a combination of international law, national law and kastom, invoking the language of the United Nations Charter to demand greater economic development and better access to formal education, as well as the codification of kastom and the establishment of kastom courts.[107] While this was not a long-lasting movement, it provides an early example of the interweaving of discourses of universal rights with profoundly emplaced and particular kastom, a theme I return to in the chapters that follow.

A far more influential movement emerged on the Weather Coast (Map 5) several years later, triggered in part by divisions that emerged from the very same 1953 regulation that sought to placate demands for greater autonomy in neighbouring Malaita. The Moro Movement centred on Pelise Moro of

---

[104] Native Administration Regulation 1953. According to Healy, the Kenyan African District Councils Ordinance No. 12 of 1950 was circulated to all district commissioners for comment, and 'headmen' were also consulted: Healy, 'Administration', 202.

[105] See further Ralph R Premdas and Jeffrey S Steeves, 'Decentralization and Development in Melanesia: Papua New Guinea and the Solomon Islands' (1985) 51(2) *International Review of Administrative Sciences* 120, 125–126; Ralph Premdas, Jeff Steeves and Peter Larmour, 'The Western Breakaway Movement in the Solomon Islands' (1984) 7(2) *Pacific Studies* 34, 37; Bennett, *Wealth of the Solomons*, 105.

[106] Tour Report – Visale Subdistrict – April 1–5, 1957 (Solomon Islands National Archives, BSIP II/F3/9/1/1, 1957).

[107] Bennett, *Wealth of the Solomons*, 299.

Makaruka on the Weather Coast, who advocated self-sufficient economic development and a return to kastom. Three written versions of Moro's teachings were published by William Davenport and Gülbün Çoker,[108] and each asserted that the creator Ironggali appointed a Paramount Chief, Tuimauri, and then divided and allocated named territories that were marked out by 'peck' – a Pijin term for survey peg – to named chiefs. These teachings identified Moro as the current paramount chief, and rejected the concepts of 'waste lands' and 'public lands'.[109] By the end of 1957, the movement had a structure of leaders, clerks and their duties, with taxes and levies being collected and retained by a central authority.[110] The Moro Movement, like Maasina Rule, adopted the language and instruments of the colonial administrators, submerging the diversity of communities on Guadalcanal and foregrounding an island-wide political community. In so doing, it posed a challenge not only to the colonial administration's constructions of Indigenous territory and authority, but the authority of the colonial regime and its exploitation of Guadalcanal's resources more broadly.[111] While the movement never achieved the level of influence Maasina Rule did vis-à-vis colonial authorities, we shall see in Chapter 5 that its influence reverberated during the 1998–2003 conflict.

2.5.3 *The Western Solomons and the Christian Fellowship Church*

The movements that arose on Malaita and Guadalcanal might be understood as a contest between Solomon Islanders foregrounding idioms of kastom as against Protectorate officials representing the colonial state. By contrast, political contests in the western islands took an entirely different form. Here, the missions were a far more significant influence than the government, and people were sharply divided by their allegiance to either the Methodist Mission (led by the obstinate Reverend Goldie) or the Seventh Day Adventist missions.[112]

As Judith Bennett explains, Reverend Goldie was outside Solomon Islands when the Japanese invaded, and the government did not allow him to return until 1945. When Goldie did return, he found that the mission had suffered

---

[108] William Davenport and Gülbün Çoker, 'The Moro Movement of Guadalcanal, British Solomon Islands Protectorate' (1967) 76(2) *Journal of the Polynesian Society* 123, 136.

[109] Cited ibid 146–147.

[110] Ibid 130–134.

[111] Matthew G Allen, 'Resisting RAMSI: Intervention, Identity and Symbolism in Solomon Islands' (2009) 79(1) *Oceania* 1, 6, Naitoro, 'Articulating Kin Groups and Mines', 147.

[112] Cf Dureau, 'Decreed Affinities', 213.

significant material losses and, perhaps more significantly, that a new movement had emerged under the leadership of one of the men he had trained, Silas Eto. Like many Solomon Islanders, Eto believed the Americans had a more respectful approach to Islanders than the British, and in the aftermath of the war he wrote a letter to President Roosevelt requesting that America take over Solomon Islands. Ishmael Ngatu, who had established the Methodist Mission in Marovo and was now the Marovo District Headman, reported the matter to the colonial authorities, Eto was imprisoned for treason, and then released when Goldie threatened legal action.[113] While this chain of events continued the tradition of several missionaries, including Goldie, of asserting their political influence and shielding Solomon Islanders from some of the excesses of colonial administrators, it also revealed tensions within the denomination.

Any loyalties that tied Eto to the Methodists broke down after Goldie's death in 1954 (followed by Ngatu in 1955), and the Christian Fellowship Church emerged as a distinct movement led by Eto.[114] In this movement it was Christianity rather than state law that was reappropriated to extend Indigenous self-expression against European hegemony, and the missionaries rather than the colonial administrators that moved to repress it. Goldie's successor, the Reverend Carter, reportedly told people that the government would throw them in jail if they followed Holy Mama Silas Eto (Mama meaning 'father', 'mother' or 'God'). The Christian Fellowship Church became influential across the western islands and importantly, more amicable relations developed as growing numbers of Solomon Islander men took over leadership of the Methodist churches.[115]

The Christian Fellowship Church, the Moro Movement and Maasina Rule all remain influential in Solomon Islands in various ways today, and all emerged from and reproduced particular legal pluralities, with Christianity particularly prominent in territorial struggles in the western islands. Each movement grappled with the vocabularies and institutions that European authorities sought to impose – 'customary law' in the case of Maasina Rule and the Moro Movement, Christianity in the case of the Christian Fellowship Church – and imbued them with explicitly political, anti-hegemonic meanings. It is difficult, however, to track Solomon Islander women's participation in these movements, as there are few traces of their voices in either the

[113] Bennett, *Wealth of the Solomons*, 300; Esau Tuza, 'The Solomon Islands' Response to the Gospel' (Paper presented to the South Pacific Regional Conference on the World Methodist Historical Society, Wesley College, Auckland, New Zealand, 18–23 May 1987).

[114] Alan Richard Tippett, *Solomon Islands Christianity* (Lutterworth Press, 1967), 212–226.

[115] G Bartlet, 'Holy Mama Again', *Pacific Islands Monthly* (January 1979); E Tuza, 'Paternal Acidity', *Pacific Islands Monthly* (January 1979).

Protectorate's records or the scholarly literature. Alice Pollard, who to my knowledge is the only Malaitan woman to have written about Maasina Rule, emphasises that it was 'driven by men and from men's perspectives', but also stresses that women were present in key discussions, worked on cooperative plantations and 'cooked and fed' the crowds that gathered. According to Pollard, there were efforts to establish a system of women's leadership parallel to the system of male chiefs.[116] Akin argues that the exclusion of women from the Protectorate's records was not mere oversight, but quite calculated – he suggests that if colonial administrators had acknowledged the role of women in Maasina Rule, it would have 'undercut the claim that one reason the movement had to be repressed was that it oppressed women'.[117]

2.6 TOWARDS INDEPENDENCE: DEBATING THE TERRITORIAL STRUCTURE OF THE STATE

The global push towards decolonisation in the aftermath of World War II prompted a flurry of activity as Protectorate officials sought to develop the political, legal and economic infrastructure they believed necessary for independence. The 1960s and 1970s saw the progressive expansion of district administration, local councils and native courts.[118] Customary Land Appeal Courts were established in each district, and tasked with hearing appeals against determinations of native courts (later replaced by local courts) dealing with customary land.[119] Land issues generally, and land law and administration in particular, received significant attention from Protectorate officials. Until this time land policy had been largely ad hoc, and government involvement in land disputes between Solomon Islanders typically occurred through the intervention of expatriate district officers who operated with minimal guidance from higher authorities.[120]

This approach was no longer seen as viable in the aftermath of the war. Old claims had been reopened and reinvigorated when expatriates abandoned the

---

[116] Pollard is mildly critical of women who she perceives were 'ill-prepared' and 'failed to seize' the opportunities presented to them; however, she emphasises that resistance movements were 'driven by men and from men's perspectives': Pollard, 'Painaha', 104. Roger Keesing's account cautions against the assumption of a unity of interest among women, highlighting differences of opinion between women in Kwaio pagan communities and those in coastal Christian communities: Roger M Keesing, *Custom and Confrontation: The Kwaio Struggle for Cultural Autonomy* (University of Chicago Press, 1992), 142–144.

[117] Akin, *Colonialism, Maasina Rule and the Origins of Malaitan Kastom*, 280.

[118] Premdas and Steeves, 'The Solomon Islands: An Experiment in Decentralization'.

[119] Lands (Amendment) Act 1972 [Cap 98] (Solomon Islands).

[120] Tiffany, 'Disputing in Customary Land Courts', 99–100.

plantations, enabling Solomon Islanders to enter them, harvest fruit and hunt cattle. The colonial administration also determined that the future economy would depend upon forests and fisheries, and from a legal perspective, these remained largely within the control of Solomon Islanders.[121] In 1951, a second land commission, the Allan Land Commission, was established to examine 'the whole system of customary tenure and its course of evolution, against the general background of pre-war, post-war and future development'.[122] Commissioner Colin Allan toured the islands to conduct public consultations covering matters such as the social organisation of communities, land boundaries and the genealogical histories of landholding groups.[123] The final report, published in 1957, is an extensive document worthy of the detailed examination that has been undertaken by other scholars,[124] but I highlight three points here.

First, the report emphasised that attempts by Protectorate officials to define the Indigenous social and spatial order had in fact led to further complexity:

> As time has gone by, and sub-district and district boundaries have undergone many changes, these have been overlaid by changes in jurisdiction of headmen, Local Councils, and Native Courts. The position has become very confusing. Thus 'Rovianas' might mean the people of the Roviana sub-district, which is a Council area; the people who live in the lagoon of that name situated east of Dude; the people of Roviana islands, or descendants of migrants from that island now living on Parara island in the Wana Wana lagoon; or indeed anyone whose skin is black and speaks the Roviana language...[125]

Thus rather than clarifying, stabilising or rigidifying Indigenous institutions and the territorial structure of the state, colonial efforts to codify custom had led to a proliferation of understandings of community membership, leadership and territory. This had led to increased 'confusion', at least for colonial administrators.

---

[121] Colin H Allan, 'The Post-War Scene in the Western Solomons and Marching Rule: A Memoir' (1989) 24(1) *Journal of Pacific History* 89, 93; Judith A Bennett, 'Forestry, Public Land, and the Colonial Legacy in Solomon Islands' (1995) 7(2) *The Contemporary Pacific* 243.

[122] Allan, 'Customary Land Tenure', ii.

[123] Ibid, iii.

[124] See e.g. Heath,'Land Policy'; P Larmour, 'Land Policy and Decolonisation in Melanesia: A Comparative Study of Land Policymaking and Implementation before and after Independence in Papua New Guinea, Solomon Islands and Vanuatu' (PhD thesis, Macquarie University, 1987); Foukona, 'Land, Law and History'.

[125] Allan, 'Customary Land Tenure', 62.

Second, Commissioner Allan stressed the importance of considering 'sectarian differences' and approaching the churches as major beneficiaries of resource revenues and authorities in resource governance:

> Sectarian differences obtrude themselves no more than elsewhere in Colonial territories, but feeling runs highest when conflict occurs over land matters. . .Local revenues [of churches] are still linked directly or indirectly to the produce of land or sea. It would be unwise when putting into effect any overall policy which might be decided on in consequence of the submission of this report, to discount the strength of any sectarian feeling which it might stimulate.[126]

Third, the report of the Allan Commission provides a clear example of the evolutionary and modernising discourses regarding customary tenure, agricultural intensification and economic growth that prevailed at the time. According to Allan, there was a shift underway in many areas, from communal to individual tenure, and from matrilineal or cognatic systems towards primogeniture.[127] He 'foresaw the ultimate extinction of custom in its present form' and recommended 'a policy which takes into account the present continuing need for the customary system, but which at the same time guides it along progressive lines towards the emergence of a modern tenure system, based on adjudication and registration of individual title'.[128] He recommended that the government take steps to adjudicate and register land, and replace customary tenure with private, freehold tenure in order to encourage development 'where the conditions [were] ripe for it'.[129]

Allan's recommendations for the establishment of a land register were implemented, and freehold estates were registered as perpetual estates, while Crown leases were registered as fixed-term estates.[130] Solomon Islanders later regained control over some of these lands through a government redress scheme that established cooperatives, and provided loans for the purchase of plantations. The remaining land owned by non-Solomon Islanders was converted into leases from the national government.[131] However, Allan's proposals with respect to customary land never gained traction – more than 90 per cent of available land remains under customary tenure today, and is generally

---

[126] Ibid, 81.
[127] Ibid, 267–269.
[128] Ibid, 277.
[129] Ibid, 269, 278.
[130] Peter Larmour, 'Alienated Land and Independence in Melanesia' (1984) 8(1) *Pacific Studies* 1.
[131] Larmour, 'Alienated Land'; Premdas and Steeves, 'The Solomon Islands: An Experiment in Decentralization'.

unregistered.[132] Moreover in the chapters that follow, we see that any shift towards individualisation and patriliny has hardly been as complete as Allan predicted.

2.6.1 The Debate about Federalism

The entangled and ongoing reconfiguration of community membership, political authority and territoriality highlighted by the Allan Commission became even more pronounced as Independence drew near. A Constitutional Committee was established to consider the form of the post-independence state, and a major divide emerged between those who supported a federal system of government that would give more autonomy to regions founded on island-wide identities, and those who were in favour of a unitary system.[133] Understanding debates about the territorial structure of the state during this period is critical to understanding the 1998–2003 conflict, discussed further in Chapter 5, and ongoing debates about federalism.[134]

Debates about federalism and decentralisation emerged from and reproduced ongoing debates about political authority, community membership and natural resource rights. These dynamics were particularly obvious in the Western District, which encompassed the Shortland Islands, Choiseul and the New Georgia group. The colonial administration had treated a chain of diffuse polities as a single district, and this politico-legal geography was embraced by local leaders for some purposes but not others. As we have seen, a 'western' identity was asserted by the 'chiefs and land-owners' during the 1923 Phillips Commission, and in 1972, male leaders across the western islands initiated the amalgamation of local councils into the Western District Council.[135] Allegiances forged in the context of property disputes in the 1920s now emerged in the 'Western Breakaway Movement', which demanded a federal structure and more autonomy for the provinces.

By the 1970s, the Western District's economy was the most monetised in Solomon Islands, and provided significant employment in plantation agriculture, forestry and fishing. Many people in the western islands expressed frustration about the contribution made by local industries and resource

---

[132] Commonwealth of Australia, Making Land Work (AusAID, 2008), 4.
[133] Yash Ghai, 'The Making of the Independence Constitution' in Peter Larmour (ed), Solomon Islands Politics (Institute of Pacific Studies of the University of the South Pacific, 1983); Premdas and Steeves, 'The Solomon Islands: An Experiment in Decentralization'.
[134] Monson and Hoa'au, '(Em)Placing Law'.
[135] Ian Scales, 'The Coup Nobody Noticed: The Solomon Islands Western State Movement in 2000' (2007) 42(2) Journal of Pacific History 187.

extraction on their own lands to government coffers in Honiara, particularly given the lack of visible returns in the form of services and infrastructure. There were also complaints about the alienation of land for plantations and timber, and the use of Wagina (near Choiseul) and Titiana (on Ghizo) for the resettlement of the Micronesian Gilbertese (i-Kiribati) from the Gilbert and Ellice Island Colony.[136]

These concerns contributed to growing opposition to migration, which was heard not only in the western islands but in many parts of the country, and directed towards Malaitans in particular. The socio-economic differences established during the early colonial period had persisted and contributed to the perception that Malaitans dominated the economy: of all of the provinces, Malaita was the most populous, with the fewest cash-income opportunities, so Malaitans typically migrated elsewhere in order to access these opportunities. Malaitan men made up the most significant proportion of migrant labour across the Protectorate, and were concentrated on Guadalcanal, the Central Islands and in the Western District, where they often married local women. There was (and is) a widespread understanding that these societies emphasise matrilineal or cognatic descent and inheritance, and some people expressed the view that men from densely populated, patrilineal Malaita were deliberately seeking wives from matrilineal societies in order to obtain land.[137]

These concerns regarding land, migration and intermarriage both emerged from and reinscribed long-standing colonial discourses about land and people. The colonial division of labour, coupled with colonial discourses of social organisation and customary tenure, had inscribed Malaita in particular as a place of patrilineal and patriarchal ideology and practice, populated by people who were hard workers, but competitive and aggressive, as against the matrilineal spaces and peoples of other islands, who were feminised as weak and docile.[138] Understandings of 'matrilineal', 'patrilineal' and 'bilateral' kinship that had been utilised by both the Phillips Commission and the Allan Commission were now firmly embedded in the lexicons of expatriates and

[136] Premdas et al., 'The Western Breakaway Movement'; Premdas and Steeves, 'The Solomon Islands: An Experiment in Decentralization'; Larmour, 'Alienated Land', 105–6; Dureau, 'Decreed Affinities'; Tammy Tabe, 'Climate Migration and Displacement: Learning from Past Relocations in the Pacific' (2019) 8(7) *Social Sciences* 218.

[137] Premdas and Steeves, 'The Solomon Islands: An Experiment in Decentralization'; Premdas, Steeves and Larmour, 'The Western Breakaway Movement'; Dureau, 'Decreed Affinities'.

[138] Premdas et al., 'The Western Breakaway Movement', 46; Dureau, 'Decreed Affinities', 215; Michael W Scott, 'The Matter of Makira: Colonialism, Competition, and the Production of Gendered Peoples in Contemporary Solomon Islands and Medieval Britain' (2012) 23(1) *History and Anthropology* 115.

Solomon Islanders alike, and gave rise to gendered and territorialised notions of culture and ethnicity which, as we shall see in Chapter 5, not only persist but may contribute to political instability and violence today.

When the 'Western Breakaway Movement' emerged, it invoked the 'natural' solidarity of the political community it purported to represent, and asserted a 'Western' identity based on the widespread use of the Methodist lingua franca Roviana, as well as the darker skin of many people in the western islands. In August 1977, MP Geoffrey Beti asked:

> Is it because we are black as compared to other people in Solomon Islands that the government does not want to meet our wishes?[139]

The assertion of a 'Western' identity therefore became an assertion not only of territorialised culture, language and citizenship, but also race. In its 1975 submission to the Kausimae Committee considering the constitution, the council for the Western District asserted:

> ...the way our islands have been arranged by the creator has...determined how far and with which island groupings the majority of our people have identified themselves and have a growing emotional attachment.[140]

As with Maasina Rule, territory did not merely 'spatialise' an existing regional identity, putting a pre-existing classification 'on the ground'; it was a vital constituent of it. In contrast to Maasina Rule, however, the Western Breakaway Movement could not demarcate a regional identity based on a single island. By invoking the arrangement of islands 'by the creator' as well as skin colour (presumably also determined by the creator), the Western Breakaway Movement constructed and naturalised a primordial Western identity in opposition to 'other' Solomon Islanders, even while simultaneously recognising the dynamism of this 'growing attachment'. This de-emphasised long histories of intermarriage and adoption with people from other islands and regions such as Isabel and Guadalcanal. It also downplayed internal distinctions such as those between 'bush' and 'coastal' people, and between the members of different missions.[141]

---

[139] Premdas et al., 'The Western Breakaway Movement', 205, citing the *National Drum*, 28 August 1977.

[140] Premdas et al., 'The Western Breakaway Movement', 38, citing Submission of the Western Council, August 1975, Special Committee on Provincial Government Background Paper No. 28.

[141] Edward LiPuma, 'The Formation of Nation-States and National Cultures in Oceania' in Robert J Foster (ed.), *Nation Making: Emergent Identities in Postcolonial Melanesia* (University of Michigan Press, 1997) 33, 55; Dureau, 'Decreed Affinities', 205.

The political geography asserted by the Western Breakaway Movement emphasised 'the West' as both a people and a place, suffering the incursion of 'other' Islanders, particularly Malaitans, with the West's natural resources being plundered by a central government that provided little in return. While this movement posed the most significant threat to the colonial administration's territorialisation of the islands, leaders in other districts also called for greater autonomy through the adoption of a federal system. Their arguments typically focused on the need to recognise the distinct traditions of regions that were noticeably based on the colonial delineation of administrative districts, as well as the risk of discrimination by a central government that was widely assumed to be dominated by Malaitans. When the Constitutional Committee reported, it 'noted a growing interest among the people in a form of quasi-federal constitution', but it recommended against the adoption of a federal system due to cost. Instead, it recommended a unitary constitution, with substantial devolution of power and responsibility to the district level.[142]

When Solomon Islands became independent on 7 July 1978, a unitary system of government was adopted, and the eight existing district councils were transformed into provinces.[143] Official Independence celebrations did not occur in Western Province, and Western members of the council boycotted festivities in Honiara.[144] While Western Province did join the rest of the country in celebrating Independence Day the following year, scholars Ralph Premdas, Jeffrey Steeves and Peter Larmour cautioned that this should not be assumed to be the end of debates about decentralisation and federalism.[145] Indeed as Chapter 5 will demonstrate, issues of regional autonomy were prominent during the conflict of 1998–2003, as well as its aftermath.

2.7 CONCLUSION

In Solomon Islands as elsewhere in the British Western Pacific Territories, the strategic presence and absence of state law, in both its representational and material sense, was central to the ways in which colonialism was conceived,

---

[142] Solomon Islands Legislative Assembly, *Report of the Constitutional Committee, 1975* (1976), 2 para [12].

[143] Ghai, 'The Making of the Independence Constitution', 9; Sam Alasia, *Party Politics and Government in Solomon Islands* (State, Society and Governance in Melanesia (SSGM) Program Discussion Paper No 97/7, The Australian National University, 1997).

[144] Dureau, 'Decreed Affinities'.

[145] Premdas et al., 'The Western Breakaway Movement', 55. See further Bennett, *Wealth of the Solomons*, 329; Dureau, 'Decreed Affinities', 217.

enacted and legitimated. Representations of the world of Solomon Islanders as savage, violent, and without law and property, produced the colonial frontier and not only legitimated but demanded the use of law backed by military force to achieve 'pacification', to delineate boundaries and direct people's relations with land-based resources and to mobilise the labour necessary to sustain the plantation economy. These racialised stereotypes persist and continue to legitimate multiple forms of discursive, economic and physical violence today.[146]

The transformations underway during the nineteenth and twentieth centuries were not, however, merely driven by British administrators. They were consciously and strategically navigated by Solomon Islanders, not always entirely within the terms laid down by British officials, and often in collaboration with Christian missionaries. The legal pluralities forged in these struggles must be understood not only in terms of the repertoires of custom and law, but also Christianity. This normative and institutional plurality has provided a range of opportunities for contesting the terms of property, territory and political authority, and this chapter has demonstrated that Solomon Islanders have been quick to mobilise around questions of access to and control over land and other resources. Issues of land rights, citizenship and the distribution of authority in space occupied a central position on the agenda of local politicians and Protectorate officials in the lead-up to Independence, and they have remained on the agenda of every government since.

Islanders' encounters with the new social worlds established by the state and churches were immensely varied, but trading, missionisation and colonisation all tended to enable a small number of men to extend their influence, while new opportunities for economic and political influence remained largely inaccessible – at least directly – to other people. While women undoubtedly had diverse roles and experiences in the negotiations and contests underway during the Protectorate era, it is difficult to find any trace of them in archival records and court records. Once claims to property, territory and authority were made in the forms recognisable by colonial administrators, it was primarily men – male European missionaries, local men of prestige and colonial administrators – who performed, endorsed and rejected those claims, and in so doing, bolstered their authority further. Indeed as Anne Dickson-Waiko has demonstrated for Papua New Guinea, we see that in Solomon Islands too,

---

[146] See Stead, 'Money Trees'; Rebecca Monson, Keith Camacho and Joseph Foukona, 'The Pacific' in Sundhya Pahuja, Luis Eslava and Ruth Buchanan (eds.), *Oxford Handbook of International Law and Development* (Oxford University Press, forthcoming, 2022).

colonial policies on land, labour and indirect rule facilitated the participation of (at least some) Indigenous men in the economic and political life of the new state, while women remained grounded in their villages, now reconfigured as a private realm.[147]

Yet as the differences between Indigenous resistance movements on Guadalcanal, Malaita and in the western islands demonstrate, the transformations occurring during the Protectorate era were not only global and structural, but also situated and particular, with contests over property, territory and authority occurring in diverse ways and at many levels simultaneously. Furthermore, scholarship that emphasises the authority of named men, while failing to expose the views, roles, expertise and influence of (at least some) other people may reinforce the erasures and inequalities that emerged during the colonial period. Thus in the chapters that follow I pay closer attention to the gendered aspects of struggles over property and authority in two specific places: the Bareke Peninsula on Vangunu Island in central Marovo Lagoon, a region famed for both its biodiversity and the devastation wrought by industrial logging; and Kakabona, a string of peri-urban villages to the immediate west of the national capital Honiara, on the island of Guadalcanal.

---

[147] A Dickson-Waiko, 'Colonial Enclaves and Domestic Spaces in British New Guinea' in K Darian-Smith, P Grimshaw, S Macintyre (eds.), *Britishness Abroad: Transnational Movements and Imperial Cultures* (Melbourne University Press, 2007) 205.

3

Chiefs, Priests and Vuluvulu

Selective Recognition and the Simplification of Authority in Marovo Lagoon

Every good thing that was practised before, has gone! Lots of people have come inside, and jealousy and hatred have changed every good thing! The love of money has changed every good thing. Love of money, hatred, jealousy have come inside! You white people have spoiled every good thing!

Elderly woman, Bareke village, 2008

Colonial expansion destabilised the ways in which land tenure and authority were constructed, performed and exercised across Solomon Islands, altering the opportunities for their negotiation and rearrangement. As the previous chapter demonstrated, Solomon Islanders were drawn into these processes in different ways, with implications for their participation in ongoing struggles over the terms of property, territory and political authority. This chapter explores these themes with greater specificity, focusing on the (re)configuration of land tenure and authority on the Bareke Peninsula and surrounding areas in Marovo Lagoon (Map 1.3 and Map 1.4).

Marovo is the largest lagoon of its type in the world, fringed by a unique double chain of raised barrier reefs. It is well known as a biodiversity hotspot, a hub for tourism and a proposed World Heritage Site. It is also known for its forests, which have become global commodities, Solomon Islands' main export and the target of rapacious industrial logging on customary land. As highlighted by Joyce Ngini in Chapter 1, women as a social group are largely excluded from negotiations regarding logging deals, especially when debates enter public fora such as village meetings and timber rights hearings.[1] As a

---

[1] See also Michelle Dyer, 'Transforming Communicative Spaces: The Rhythm of Gender in Meetings in Rural Solomon Islands' (2018) 23(1) *Ecology and Society* 17; Michelle Dyer, 'Eating Money: Narratives of Equality on Customary Land in the Context of Natural Resource Extraction in the Solomon Islands' (2017) 28(1) *Australian Journal of Anthropology* 88.

result, they are largely unable to have their claims to land and trees recognised as property by state institutions, and are limited to indirect rather than direct receipt of logging royalties. In conversations with people in villages across central Marovo, as well as in Honiara, Suva and Canberra, I have heard these forms of exclusion attributed to new kinds of interactions with 'lots of people', 'the love of money', and a decline in the 'good things' that historically affirmed the authority of women and collectivities with respect to both land and people. These local accounts contrast somewhat with the tendency of donor agencies and non-governmental organisations to highlight the experiences of women abstracted from those of the wider group; emphasise the structural features of property systems; and trace contemporary inequalities to patriarchal kastom, as well as to flawed legislative frameworks and weak law enforcement.[2]

This chapter demonstrates that contemporary inequalities in land and forest governance, and state-sanctioned property rights in particular, must be understood as relational, dynamic, and situated within ongoing processes of social and economic change and the transformative effects of missionisation, legal imperialism and the commodification of natural resources. It shows that the people of Marovo have adeptly navigated the symbolic, institutional and material repertoires of kastom, church and state to renegotiate the terms of property, territory and authority in the face of the many dispossessions wrought by colonial expansion, but that the reconfiguration of landholding and key political institutions has worked to benefit some segments of the local polity far more than others. I particularly highlight the ways in which the selective and iterative recognition of specific idealisations of masculine authority – by missionaries, state bureaucrats and the 'middle men' of transnational corporations, among others – has contributed to a simplification of customary tenure, erosion of multiplicity in kinship and gendered authority and the emergence of far greater inequality in political institutions than I suspect was historically the case. This is highlighted by contemporary practices regarding logging, where social actors are differently positioned to be legible to the state and receive legitimation of their claims to property, thereby reproducing their authority (or lack of it). I therefore contribute to a growing and very diverse stream of scholarship on Pacific Islander women and gender to suggest – as Claire Slatter and J Kēhaulani Kauanui among others have – that at least some forms of contemporary gender inequality emerge from the

---

[2] For just one example, Minter et al. find that women on Malaita are excluded as they have 'secondary' rather than 'primary' rights under custom (which are held by men), and there is no mention of change over time: Tessa Minter et al., *From Happy Hour to Hungry Hour: Logging, Fisheries and Food Security in Malaita, Solomon Islands* (Penang: Worldfish, 2018).

ongoing, colonial flattening and simplification of multifaceted forms of gendered authority that exist in customary or Indigenous norms and practices, and the persistent failure and refusal to acknowledge important aspects of women's influence.[3]

3.1 PEOPLE OF THE BUSH, PEOPLE OF THE SEA

On a wet winter day in Canberra, 2007, Solomon Islander theologian Cliff Bird and I sat contemplating a map of Solomon Islands, discussing forestry in various parts of the country and the many inequalities it elicits. Reverend Bird suggested that I might pursue my research by living with his family on the Bareke Peninsula, and he traced his finger across the map, explaining that the name 'Bareke' refers to a people, a language and a place woven into the cultural complex that stretches across the western Solomon Islands. As a geographic location, the Bareke Peninsula is located on north-east Vangunu, one of the three large volcanic islands that fringe Marovo, and is surrounded by hundreds of smaller islands, including Marovo Island. Vangunu's steep caldera slopes are densely forested, and with the exception of a large tract of land in the southeast, the island is largely unregistered customary land. The Bareke Peninsula is the most densely populated part of the island, with villages of various sizes concentrated along the coastline and the islands offshore. There is a noticeable absence of inland settlement; however, the remains of old settlements, terraces, *Canarium* nut trees and sacred sites serve as a reminder that this was not always the case.

In Marovo, as in many other parts of Island Melanesia, there is a historical distinction between the 'bush people' and 'coastal people', with the former previously living in the hills of Vangunu and the latter occupying smaller, surrounding islands. While aspects of these distinctions have transformed since the nineteenth century, they remain evident in differences in language, political organisation, territorial holdings and ecological orientation. The Bareke people are 'of the bush' and historically spoke Bareke, while the groups associated with Marovo Islands and other surrounding islands are 'of the sea', and spoke Marovo. These categories are very prominent in the socio-spatial landscape, especially in the context of debates over resource control; however, they are also traversed by emplaced genealogical histories that affirm that

---

[3] Slatter, 'Gender and Custom' at 92–93, J Kēhaulani Kauanui, *Paradoxes of Hawaiian Sovereignty*, particularly Chapter 3. See also (among many others) Vanessa Griffen, 'The Pacific Islands: All It Requires Is Ourselves; Noenoe K Silva, *Aloha Betrayed: Native Hawaiian Resistance to American Colonialism* (Duke University Press, 2004).

many people and groups have strong associations with both bush and coastal groups.

Denominational distinctions are also prominent, and as we saw in the previous chapter, they have been tightly woven with territorial conflicts. Village churches provide a focal point for social life and are crucial to the organisation of space, ritual practice and material production. In central Marovo, the vast majority of people identify with either the United Church of Solomon Islands, which emerged from the Methodist Mission, or with the Seventh Day Adventist Church. The United Church holds major church services on Sundays, and tends to encourage cooperative economic activity, whereas the Seventh Day Adventist Church observes the Sabbath on Saturdays, is characterised by a more individualistic approach to economic activity and prohibits consumption of betelnut, alcohol, shellfish, crustaceans and pigs. These denominational distinctions both complement and cross-cut bush-coastal differences. Today, most villages on the Bareke Peninsula are recognised as being 'of the bush' and associated with the United Church, while most villages on the surrounding islands are recognised as being 'of the sea' and Seventh Day Adventist adherents. The Repi people of Telina have strong historical ties to both bush and coastal groups, but belong to the Seventh Day Adventist Church, which tends to bring their 'coastal' affinities to the fore, while the people of Chubikopi are 'coastal' people and United Church adherents, which foreground their ties with 'bush' communities.

In contemporary discussions, bush and coastal people describe the landscapes and seascapes they depend upon in terms of named pepesa (territories, or puava in Marovo) held by particular kokolo (a kin-based group, referred to as butubutu in Marovo). These groups – often referred to as 'lines' or 'tribes' in Pijin – are generally said to comprise a number of families that claim descent, through women and men, from the first settler of the land.[4] Bush people explain that their pepesa stretch from old inland settlements in the mountains, often bearing the same names as the group, down to coastal areas. This land is known by oral histories that link living people and their ancestors to specific features in the landscape such as ridges, caves, rivers, shrines and trees. The claims of coastal people stretch across similarly vast areas, particularly marine.

These groups and places are not distinct, but overlap and interweave. When early colonial administrators sought to identify distinct, bounded corporate groups associated with distinct, delineated territories, they were instead

---

[4] See e.g. Wilson Gia Liligeto, *Babata: Our Land, Our Tribe, Our People: A Historical Account and Cultural Materials of Butubutu Babata, Morovo* (Institute of Pacific Studies, University of the South Pacific, 2006) 21.

confronted with competing claimants who explained their attachments to land by reference to myriad overlapping genealogical connections, prominent people who were associated with numerous groups and places across the lagoon, and specific sites that appeared to establish overlapping territories. Cliff Bird's discussion of the internal organisation of these territories suggests that they might be best understood in terms of focal points in the landscape rather than rigid outer boundaries, with the association between the people and their pepesa most intimate and exclusive at the centres of ritual activity furthest inland, and becoming progressively more diffuse as the territory stretches towards the coastal areas.[5] I understand the kokolo in similar terms – as I explain further in Section 3.2.2, it appears to have been most clearly defined around core institutions of masculine and feminine authority. However, as we shall see, this socio-spatial landscape was reconfigured and became understood in new ways as trading with Europeans intensified during the course of the nineteenth century.

3.2 TRANSFORMING TRADITIONS

The nineteenth century was a time of significant transformation in the political ecologies of Marovo Lagoon. Oral histories, colonial records and archaeological evidence all point to a rapid decline in large-scale, irrigated taro cultivation in the interior of Vangunu, and the reorganisation of bush populations in coastal areas. The precise drivers of these transformations remain the subject of debate among bush and coastal people, but they were undoubtedly linked with an increase in trading with Europeans, the cessation of Indigenous warfare and conversion to Christianity.

In the period immediately prior to colonisation, the people of Marovo were woven into extensive intra- and inter-island systems of raiding and trading, which revolved around ritual cycles of headhunting and the exchange of specialist products from different regions. These networks extended throughout the western islands, and raids from Marovo often reached Santa Isabel, the

---

[5] According to Bird, the lose (room) is furthest inland, where the kokolo's valuables are stored and the bush people are safest from raiding parties; the palavanua (verandah) is the place for interaction with 'the other', which may lead to an openness or withdrawal to the lose; the coastal areas, estuaries and offshore fishing grounds were the maurunuani (covering) that 'encloses both the [lose] and [palavanua] – the covering that seals the Bareke people': Cliff Bird, 'Pepesa – The Household of Life: A Theological Exploration of Land in the Context of Change in Solomon Islands' (PhD thesis, Charles Sturt University, 2008) 49–52. See also Scales, 'The Social Forest', 95ff.

Russell Islands and Guadalcanal.[6] Within Marovo, bush and coastal people often viewed each other as enemies in warfare, but they also met on the beaches to exchange products from their respective domains – meat, betelnut and taro from inland areas were necessary for ceremonial feasts, and exchanged for fish, lime made from coral and shell valuables. The local accounts of land tenure provided to the Lands Commissioner Phillips (discussed in Chapter 2 and Section 3.4) clearly refer to the movement of named men across significant distances during the 1800s, as they built alliances, cultivated gardens and held residences in multiple sites between southern New Georgia and Nggatokae.

By the 1880s, these exchange networks had incorporated European traders, and European goods were being traded throughout the western islands, moving along exchange routes to arrive in bush villages in the interior of Vangunu. This generated fundamental and interconnected adjustments in the relationships between bush and coastal groups in Marovo that have been the subject of previous scholarship.[7] In this chapter I extend these accounts by situating the contemporary gendered political ecology of logging within this historical reconfiguration of relations within bush and coastal groups. In particular, I suggest that whereas the precolonial political ecology of bush and coastal people appears to have been characterised by a degree of complementarity and exchange between gendered domains of land use, labour and ritual and political authority, the twentieth century saw some forms of attachment to and authority over place progressively eroded, while other forms were recognised, extended and sedimented.

3.2.1 *Gendered Places and Labour*

Growing numbers of European traders began plying the waters of Marovo and Roviana in the mid-1800s, and initially traded with coastal people who lived in relatively accessible areas. Very few Europeans ventured inland until well into

---

6   Peter Sheppard, 'Four Hundred Years of Niche Construction in the Western Solomons' in Mathieu Leclerc and James Flexner (eds.), *Archaeologies of Island Melanesia: Current Approaches to Landscapes, Exchange and Practice* (ANU Press, 2019) 117.

7   Tim Bayliss-Smith, Matthew Prebble and Stephen Manebosa, 'Saltwater and Bush in New Georgia, Solomon Islands: Exchange Relations, Agricultural Intensification and Limits to Social Complexity' in Mathieu Leclerc and James Flexner (eds.), *Archaeologies of Island Melanesia: Current Approaches to Landscapes, Exchange and Practice* (ANU Press, 2019) 35; Tim Bayliss-Smith and Edvard Hviding, 'Taro Terraces, Chiefdoms and Malaria: Explaining Landesque Capital Formation in Solomon Islands' in Thomas N Håkansson and Mats Widgren (eds.), *Landesque Capital: The Historical Ecology of Enduring Landscape Modifications* (Routledge, 2014) 75.

the twentieth century, although Lieutenant BT Somerville led a surveying party into north Vangunu in 1893.[8] Bareke oral histories and archaeological evidence suggest that at this time, bush people lived in large, stable settlements as well as in smaller ones that were periodically relocated due to warfare and the demands of shifting agriculture.[9] As explained to me by Kitchener Bird (Cliff Bird's brother),

> Before, the bush people didn't go to the sea. They fished in the rivers and climbed trees to get possums and geckos. The men did this. Because of the headhunting, it was dangerous for women. So the women stayed in the village and did the cooking. Some warriors would stay behind as security for the village. Women also did the gardening. There were two places for planting: one was dapi, a place beside streams, small waters and big rivers. Men prepared this by laying stones beside the water – they built a wall for stopping a flood. Then, a woman would plant it. The man also made a place for when there was a drought, for irrigation – the man would divert the water so that the ground was irrigated. The second place for planting was ruta. This was a place prepared by men, but women had the skills to prepare them if necessary. Women planted and picked these gardens.

This highlights a number of critical aspects of precolonial resource use and labour by the Bareke people. Kitchener emphasised the cultivation of the main root crop, taro, in two particular kinds of irrigated pond fields. This was a common feature of precolonial agricultural systems in Marovo, and while similar forms of agriculture have been reported elsewhere in the Solomons and the Pacific, the implications for gender relations remain relatively unexplored.[10] As Kitchener highlighted, Bareke people regularly distinguish between two forms of taro cultivation, dapi and ruta. Dapi consisted of large, complex systems of irrigated terraces that oral histories suggest were cultivated by a group of people under the supervision of a senior man, often referred to as the bangara (chief). According to Bareke oral traditions, taro produced in this manner was pivotal in the ceremonial life of the bush people, in the

---

[8] Scales, 'The Social Forest', 35–54.

[9] Bareke oral traditions and archaeological evidence suggest that there were relatively small settlements, as well as much larger ones: Tim Bayliss-Smith, Edvard Hviding and Tim Whitmore, 'Rainforest Composition and Histories of Human Disturbance in Solomon Islands' (2003) 32(5) *Ambio* 346.

[10] The extensive literature includes Bayliss-Smith et al., 'Rainforest Composition'; Bayliss-Smith and Hviding, 'Taro Terraces'; Margaret M Tedder, 'Old Kusaghe' (1976) 4 *Journal of the Cultural Association of the Solomon Islands* 41; Patrick Vinton Kirch, *The Evolution of the Polynesian Chiefdoms* (Cambridge University Press, 1984); Matthew Spriggs, 'Taro Irrigation Techniques in the Pacific' in Satish Chandra (ed.), *Edible Aroids* (Clarendon Press, 1984).

institutionalised barter that occurred on the beach as women from the bush exchanged products with women from coastal areas and in wider regional exchange systems. Ruta were quite different: they were low-lying, swampy places that were often established by diverting water from a stream with rather simple arrangements of wood, rocks or other materials. Taro harvested in these places was central to ritual life, including specific ceremonies associated with headhunting, but they differ from dapi in that Bareke people consistently describe a strong association between particular women and ruta. Indeed they often referred (in Pijin) to ruta as being 'owned' by or 'belonging' to women.[11] As Kitchener explained,

> Ruta is special because it is mixed with water, water flows down through that place. It is a small place but a rich place. If a man went and abused that place, he would be killed that day. Women own ruta. There isn't any man who owned ruta. Men just follow the women there.

Kitchener's account points to the importance of gender as an organising principle in the construction of place and labour more broadly. For both bush and coastal people, what is now described in Pijin as 'women's work' was focused in the interior or 'core' areas of the pepesa such as villages and gardens, while the forest and sea further afield were associated with masculinity. It was generally men who transformed 'wild' land and rivers into 'domestic', by felling trees, diverting streams and burning debris in preparation for cultivation, while planting and cultivating was undertaken primarily by women. There was also a spatialised division of labour with respect to riparian and marine places: as in many (but not all) societies in the Pacific Islands, it was generally (but not exclusively) men who went fishing in the rivers, lagoon and open sea, while women and children often stayed closer to the shore, collecting the shellfish and fish that hid in the reef flats. These socio-spatial distinctions should not be understood in terms of clear-cut binaries, as all of these places were permeable and unstable: wild forests could be cleared, streams could be diverted, gardens could be allowed to return to forest and tides would invariably return to cover the reef flats.

Kitchener also mentions the ever-present risk of headhunting raids in precolonial Marovo, and refers to its influence on the gendered division of space and labour. Headhunting was closely linked with ritual cycles, and

---

[11] Cf Hess' description of gender in relation to taro cultivation on Vanua Levu (Vanuatu), where taro gardens are maintained by both female and male labour, but only men may go near the water source: Sabine C Hess, *Person and Place: Ideas, Ideals and the Practice of Sociality on Vanua Lava, Vanuatu* (Berghahn Books, 2009) 118–119.

foreign captives played an important role in the reproduction of lineage relationships.[12] The question of whether women organised raids remains open,[13] but women certainly played a significant role in the flow of things, people and ideas associated with headhunting. AM Hocart observed women on Simbo performing rituals over captives taken in raids, apparently introducing them to local spirits so that those spirits would not harm them.[14] Debra McDougall has argued that historical narratives on on Ranongga suggest that women had an important role in rituals and sometimes claimed captives as their adopted children in order to prevent them being killed.[15] In describing some of the responsibilities of women in Bareke practices, Natalie Bird told me of 'the chief's woman, the menoha, who came from the vuluvulu (blood core of the tribe)' who had special responsibilities for caring for captives from other places, who were regarded as sacred and 'set apart' from the rest of the community. Bareke and Ilumu (bush) traditions also refer to occasions when the bangara male – a woman from a chiefly line – would be asked by the bangara (chief) and varane (warrior) to call on the spirits when they were angry, placate them and ask that they refrain from striking the men when they entered the hope (a sacred site).[16] Thus in ritual life as in agriculture and trade there were gendered domains, with men and women having complementary roles in mediating production, exchange and ritual. Furthermore, women clearly had vital roles in engaging with 'outsiders', whether human or non-human, captives or people who came by other means.

---

[12] The substantial literature includes John F Goldie, 'The People of New Georgia, Their Manners and Customs and Religious Beliefs' (1909) 22 *Proceedings of the Royal Geographical Society* 23; Jackson, 'Tie Hokara, Tie Vaka' and more recent works cited throughout this chapter.

[13] McDougall refers a 'female chief named Ajapaqo who had recruited war canoes and warriors from several other lineages by paying each shell valuables': Debra McDougall, 'Paths of Pinauzu: Captivity and Social Reproduction in Ranongga' (2000) 109(1) *Journal of the Polynesian Society* 99, 109. Dureau refers to a female warrior, Lipuriki on Simbo, stating that 'whether or not she existed, her legend arises precisely out of her being female': Christine Dureau, 'Skulls, Mana and Causality' (2000) 109(1) *Journal of the Polynesian Society* 71, notes 5, 7.

[14] A M Hocart, 'Warfare in Eddystone of the Solomon Islands' (1931) 61 *The Journal of the Royal Anthropological Institute of Great Britain and Ireland* 324.

[15] McDougall, 'Paths of Pinauzu', 109.

[16] Liligeto states that coastal Babata women on Marovo Island were prohibited from participating in the ceremony involving the sacrifice of a child, and also from going to places skulls were kept, but notes that there were ceremonies (such as praying to the gods and eating particular foods) that only women could perform: Liligeto, *Babata*, 55–57, 68. White's interlocutors on Isabel advised him that it was strictly *tabu* for women to enter the altar area, with the exception of the wife of a chief: White, *Identity through History*, 38.

3.2.2 *Chiefs, Priests and Vuluvulu*

When I first questioned people in Marovo about land matters, they were generally quick to describe land as being held by a kokolo or butubutu, and explain that 'people in Marovo follow both sides', with people belonging to the kokolo/butubutu of both parents. As Edvard Hviding observes, these terms refer to 'a diverse set of groups and categories of people related through some source of "sameness" and commonality, be it descent, filiation, or residence'.[17] Kokolo/butubutu are often understood by Marovo people as a named category derived from distant founding ancestors (what anthropologists might refer to as 'clan'), but they may also be defined by descent from more proximate ancestors (what might be referred to as 'lineage'), particularly in the context of legal disputes. It is important to emphasise that even when defined in terms of descent, these categories are not confined to biological kinship: lineage narratives frequently refer to the adoption of captives taken from elsewhere, with captives and their descendants considered part of the kokolo. However, as scholars working across the western islands have demonstrated, these categories appear to have become a far more prominent feature of social life, acquired new valences and emerged as corporate landholding groups in the context of legal struggles over land from the early 1900s onwards.[18]

For the purposes of my discussion here, I suggest that one way of understanding kokolo/bubutu is in terms of focal points – as is the case for the places that constitute them, these groups may have been most clearly defined around a number of core institutions. While kokolo/bubutu certainly were explained to me by reference to a specific place (or places) where the ancestors – sometimes distant, sometimes proximate – emerged, arrived or experienced some transformative event, they were far more commonly explained to me by reference to key political institutions. These institutions, I was told, constitute the kokolo as much as the land does – without them, the group cannot exist. Bush and coastal people repeatedly drew my attention to these institutions in explaining social organisation, land relations and how they perceived them to have changed over time. Put simply, these institutions were central to people's accounts of the decline of 'good things', and I suggest that understanding the

---

[17] Hviding, *Guardians of Marovo Lagoon*, 136.

[18] See e.g. Edvard Hviding, 'Indigenous Essentialism? "Simplifying" Customary Land Ownership in New Georgia, Solomon Islands' (1993) 149 *Bijdragen tot de Taal-, Land- en Volkenkunde/ Politics, Tradition and Change in the Pacific* 802; Edvard Hviding, 'Disentangling the Butubutu of New Georgia: Cognatic Kinship in Thought and Action' in Ingjerd Hoëm et al. (eds.), *Oceanic Socialities and Cultural Forms: Ethnographies of Experience* (Berghahn Books, 2003) 71; Scales, 'The Social Forest', 95–126.

reconfiguration of these institutions is crucial to understanding gendered property relations today.

Anthropologist Edvard Hviding, who has produced a large body of work on Marovo, suggests an historical distinction in the organisation of bush and coastal settlements, with the bush people residing in small patrilineages that belonged to a clan organised around matrilineal substance, referred to as vuluvulu, and coastal people living in larger, centralised settlements with an emphasis on patrilineal descent and patrilineally derived leadership.[19] Hviding understands this in terms of a 'men-leadership-puava' complex among coastal groups, and a 'women-blood-pepesa' complex among bush groups.[20] In my own discussions with people from Marovo, both bush and coastal people frequently mentioned the concept of vuluvulu, but it was certainly a more prominent feature in my discussions with bush people. Soon after I first arrived in Marovo, Kitchener took me aside, ensured I had a pen and notebook ready, and explained the precolonial bush polity:

> The number three is very important in Bareke culture. We had three important people: the vuluvulu, the chief or bangara, and the warrior or priest, who was called the varane. The bangara was to talk about land, to fight, and for witchcraft. These are the chiefs' responsibilities. The vuluvulu was a woman. The bangara must consult with the vuluvulu, the chief must consult the woman. The chief is spokesperson, then has two senior people, one man and one woman. My grandmother taught me about this. The varane were Bareke warriors. They did lots of things. They did the priestly activities.[21]

---

[19] Hviding, *Guardians of Marovo Lagoon*, 147–149. Cf T Russell, 'The Culture of Marovo, British Solomon Islands' (1948) 57(4) *Journal of the Polynesian Society* 306, 307.

[20] Hviding, *Guardians of Marovo Lagoon*, 147–149. Hviding uses the Marovo term puava, I use the Bareke term pepesa.

[21] This quote has been amended from an earlier published version, which referred to the siama (priests, responsible for sorcery and sacrifices): Rebecca Monson, 'Negotiating Land Tenure: Women, Men and the Transformation of Land Tenure in Solomon Islands' in Janine Ubink and Thomas McInerney (eds.), *Customary Justice: Perspectives on Legal Empowerment* (International Development Law Organization, 2011) 169. It has been amended following further discussion and review by Kitchener. The differences in the two versions point to the complexity of leadership and the simplification that occurs as Indigenous concepts are made legible to outsiders. The models of masculinity discussed by Kitchener are not distinct, and his identification of three institutions is not exclusive for there were also many other titles. Aswani similarly highlights a range of titles for Roviana: Shankar Aswani, 'Forms of Leadership and Violence in Malaita and in the New Georgia Group, Solomon Islands' in Pamela J Stewart and Andrew Strathern (eds.), *Exchange and Sacrifice* (Carolina Academic Press, 2008) 171.

Kitchener's account of leadership among the Bareke draws attention to his grandmother's knowledge and expertise, and her role in the transmission of cultural knowledge, as well as the multiplicity of authority and the critical role of women in the precolonial bush polity. The term vuluvulu has multiple meanings in both Bareke and Marovo. One meaning refers to the people who constitute the 'blood core' of the kokolo, with an emphasis on matrilineal descent or cumulative matrilateral filiation. As Cliff Bird explains, the term deploys a botanical idiom to describe the intertwining of people, their kokolo and the land, as the vulu is a shrub which 'if it grows as a part of a whole – which by its very nature should be the case – is extremely difficult to be uprooted'.[22]

The term vuluvulu is also used to refer to specific women of high standing. In our discussions, bush and coastal people often translated vuluvulu as 'the oldest female', 'the first-born girl', 'a princess', or 'the queen of the tribe', and frequently pointed me to specific, named women – often ancestors, but also women who are alive today – just as they did when explaining the bangara (chiefs). In the past, these women had a vital role in ceremonial matters, 'advising the chief', and providing hospitality to visitors to the land. As one elderly woman from a coastal Adventist village explained,

> The vuluvulu is the right hand of the chief. Whatever the chief tells her, she must cause to carry out. For example, she looks after people and prepares food for visitors.

Wilson Liligeto, also from a coastal group, names individual vuluvulu and similarly explains that '[a] vuluvulu is the queen of the tribe and presides over many tribal ceremonies'.[23]

The term vuluvulu therefore refers to the collective 'blood core' of the tribe, and also to individual women with particular responsibilities and forms of influence. Bareke oral traditions recall 'special women' who, in a manner very similar to the bangara, wore shell valuables on their arms and legs demonstrating their status. These shell rings were carved from the fossil shells of giant clam (*Tridacna* sp.), a well-known feature of the New Georgia islands. While there is little trace of these influential women in colonial records or existing scholarship, there may have been parallels elsewhere in the western islands. Shankar Aswani and Christine Dureau both refer to an influential woman known as the bangara magota in Roviana and Simbo, respectively, with Aswani quoting a senior man who described the wearing of shell valuables

[22]   Bird, 'Pepesa', 43–44.
[23]   Liligeto, *Babata*, 50.

and a ceremony to appoint the 'female chief', and Dureau suggesting in a footnote that they achieved their status due to their skill in organising feasting.[24]

Contemporary discussions demonstrate that vuluvulu has an array of meanings – as people explained, 'lots of words go back to vuluvulu, almost everything relates to vuluvulu'. As shared lineal substance or the 'blood core' of the group, as well as significant woman leaders who are 'first born girls', vuluvulu embodies the mutually constitutive relationship between a group and its territory, and the transmission of those relations primarily through women. In explaining this connection, people in Marovo, and bush people in particular, often emphasised to me that land in general is feminised – 'land is mother' and 'the womb of life' – and many highlighted the precolonial practice of burying the placenta and umbilical cord in the ground. This practice remains widespread among many Pacific peoples today, and enacts the mutually constitutive relationship between women, the group and the land, not only discursively but materially and corporeally.[25]

The other institutionalised positions of leadership named by Kitchener are that of the bangara and varane, and oral traditions underscore a close relationship between the vuluvulu and bangara. Cliff Bird describes the role of the bangara as including the protection of members of the kokolo; custodianship of the pepesa; building the prestige of the kokolo through the accumulation and redistribution of wealth; and providing a link to the 'divine other' along with the *siama* (priest).[26] For both bush and coastal people, leadership was both ascribed and achieved by a combination of hereditary preference and ability. A man who could influence people and mobilise great resources for feasting, exchange and warfare might become a bangara. Equally, a young man with a hereditary claim to the position might, if he lacked the requisite skills, be passed over in favour of a more capable uncle, brother or cousin.[27]

[24] Aswani, 'Forms of Leadership', 183–184; Dureau, 'Skulls, Mana and Causality', note 9. Queensland-based artist Tania Tonuika Taylor references similar traditions in her works 'Bakiha' and 'Santa Isabel'.

[25] For discussion see for example Vicki Lukere 'Conclusion: Wider Reflections and Survey of the Literature' in V Lukere and M Jolly (eds.) *Birthing in the Pacific: Beyond Tradition and Modernity?* (University of Hawai'i Press, 2001) 178, Naomi Simmonds 'Mana Wahine: Decolonising Politics' (2011) 25(2) *Women's Studies Journal* 11, Christine Taitano DeLisle *Placental Politics: CHamoru Women, White Womanhood, and Indigeneity under U.S. Colonialism in Guam* (University of North Carolina Press, 2021), 28, 35-36.

[26] Bird, 'Pepesa', 44; Hviding, *Guardians of Marovo Lagoon*, 86.

[27] Boyle T Somerville, 'Ethnographical Notes in New Georgia, Solomon Islands' (1897) 26 *The Journal of the Anthropological Institute of Great Britain and Ireland* 412; Hviding, *Guardians of Marovo Lagoon*, 88.

Today the term is generally translated into Pijin as jif ('chief'), while the hymns and liturgies of both United Church and Seventh Day Adventist churches use it to translate the term 'lord' (in reference to God).

Bush and coastal people alike often assert that 'the vuluvulu and bangara could not be separated, they belonged together', and oral histories bear out the complementary – indeed mutually constitutive – relationship of these institutions in determining both roles and lineage. The bush people say the role 'passes through women', and during the Phillips Commission in 1923, the Bareke bangara Sagende stated that 'a chief...might be a man, might be a woman'.[28] The coastal people appear to have emphasised patrilineal descent, with women being appointed bangara if there were no suitable men.[29] The responsibilities of the vuluvulu and bangara were also complementary – Liligeto explains that the vuluvulu 'was responsible for performing ceremonies that the bangara could not perform', but had 'no authority to talk about puava butubutu (tribal land) and no leadership role in the tribe'.[30] This suggests that while the vuluvulu expressed and embodied feminine and matrilineal connections to land, the role of 'speaking for the land' was a masculine domain.

The third role mentioned by Kitchener, the varane, could be described as both a leader in warfare and a priest. The varane conducted divination rituals at the oru (burial site) to 'see' the likely outcome of an intended raid or headhunting expedition. It is clear from the oral histories explained to the Phillips Commission (discussed further below) that varane were often associated with numerous places and groups scattered across the lagoon, and that the idealised functions of varane and bangara could find expression in a single person.

These accounts all underscore the mutually constitutive relationship between people and place, and the personification of these relationships by influential men and women, chosen through both male and female primogeniture. There was also a degree of complementarity between distinct sociospatial domains, with reciprocal configurations of places and people – vuluvulu and bangara, men and women, bush and sea. These categories were not static binaries but negotiable dualisms; however, trading with Europeans had profoundly uneven effects that enabled some people far more than others to negotiate a new set of relations more to their interest.

---

[28] Report of the Lands Commission: Native Claim No. 26.
[29] Hviding, *Guardians of Marovo Lagoon*, 86; Edvard Hviding and Tim Bayliss-Smith, *Islands of Rainforest: Agroforestry, Logging, and Eco-Tourism in Solomon Islands* (Ashgate, 1st ed, 2000) 39–40.
[30] Liligeto, *Babata*, 50.

3.2.3 *Early Encounters with White Men*

Trade between Europeans and the people of New Georgia intensified from the mid-1800s onwards, as a growing number of traders visited Roviana and Marovo Lagoons seeking their abundant, and valuable, tortoiseshell and bêche-de-mer. This had multiple implications for relationships within bush and coastal groups, as well as between them.[31] Europeans did not venture inland, but engaged with coastal groups who lived in locations readily accessible to Europeans and managed access to the resources traders desired. This destabilised the political economy since coastal groups were the first to receive iron goods such as axes, which were then used for a range of purposes including gardening, building canoes and warfare. As we saw in the previous chapter it was typically men who were already influential – men who are today recalled as bangara – who were at the forefront of these negotiations. Coastal men who built strong trading relations with foreigners were able to acquire guns and iron tools that they could use to deepen their control over the marine resources sought by European traders, thereby increasing their capacity to acquire yet more European goods. These processes appear to have been associated with an escalation in the intensity and geographical spread of headhunting, and while the causal relationship is debated, it is clear that control over maritime trading networks and expanding cycles of headhunting offered coastal men new opportunities to demonstrate their efficacy, build prestige and extend their influence.[32]

These processes altered relationships between people, their environment and sacred objects in multiple ways. In the late 1800s, Lieutenant Somerville recorded,

> One day I found...an exceedingly large and well carved tomahawk, which I promptly began to bargain for with my friend Raku, who was king of the place. I had nearly tempted him to surrender by three *kalo* (whale's teeth) when a little old white-haired man dashed over at me from the other side of the house, seized the tomahawk out of my hands, in great excitement, and declared that it was *Hope Ngeténa*, 'very sacred', did not belong to the king to sell, but to the whole village; that he was the sacred man, and it was his

---

[31] See Bennett, *Wealth of the Solomons*, 83–87, 305–355; Hviding, *Guardians of Marovo Lagoon*, 101ff.

[32] See eg J M McKinnon, 'Tomahawks, Turtles and Traders' (1975) 45(4) *Oceania* 290; Hviding, *Guardians of Marovo Lagoon*; Liligeto, *Babata*, 13–14; Bayliss-Smith et al., 'Saltwater and Bush'; Tim Thomas, 'Axes of Entanglement in the New Georgia Group, Solomon Islands' in M Leclerc and J Flexner (eds.), *Archaeologies of Island Melanesia: Current Approaches to Landscapes, Exchange and Practice* (ANU Press, 2019) 103.

business to take care of it, and then disappeared in a great state of mind to hide it more securely. Raku laughed a bit foolishly, but quite gave in, and the other men standing around did the same.[33]

As products acquired a commercial value, they became understood and dealt with in new and different ways by Solomon Islanders – Somerville's account suggests that the tomahawk was sacred and entrusted to the care of another, but Raku was nevertheless tempted to sell it to a foreigner. Importantly, Raku was provided with an opportunity to do so due to Somerville's perception of him as 'the king of the place'. The possibility of wealth accumulation led to the revaluation and reorganisation of relationships between people and things – including sacred objects such as axes, which were crucial to the gift economies of the western islands – as particular people sought to consolidate their control over those things valued by Europeans.

3.3 LOTU: COLONIAL 'PACIFICATION', THE ESTABLISHMENT OF MISSIONS AND SOCIO-SPATIAL REORGANISATION

While trading with Europeans altered previous patterns of resource use, social organisation and leadership, the reconfiguration of relations between people and their places deepened with the establishment of Christian missions and the British Solomon Islands Protectorate, and often became sedimented in forms that persist into the present. Colonial 'pacification' and lotu – a Pijin term that refers to Christian beliefs, institutions and activities – contributed to the spatial reorganisation of bush and coastal groups and the reconfiguration of gendered constructions of place and resource use. It also consolidated the authority of the bangara at a time when the bush and coastal polities were being rapidly renegotiated.

3.3.1 *The Suppression of Indigenous Warfare and the Destabilisation of Authority*

In Marovo, as is the case elsewhere in the western islands, local accounts of missionisation are intimately entwined with accounts of the suppression of Indigenous warfare, and a transition from war to peace.[34] As we saw in the

---

33 Somerville, 'Ethnographical Notes', 392.

34 In Marovo as in Ranongga, people refer to the pre-pacification period as 'the time before' and 'a time of darkness', and their stories of this period are marked by an oscillation between brutality against strangers and kindness as captives are absorbed into local groups (although notably, the two 'poles' can also be difficult to distinguish for the contemporary, Western listener,

previous chapter, European desires for Pacific land and labour (re)produced European assumptions of Indigenous lawlessness and savagery, and in the western islands this entailed a sustained campaign to eradicate all practices associated with headhunting. The people of New Georgia were actively targeted by naval bombardments, attacks by native police and vigilantism by planters. Colonial authorities sought out sacred sites and destroyed them, with the desecration of Indigenous places also constituting an assault on Indigenous knowledges, histories, kinships and access to ancestral power. Foreign missionaries often protected locals, and in so doing extended their influence. In Marovo, the killing of Oliver Burns is often recalled as a watershed marking the 'beginning of the end' of this period.

As noted in the previous chapter, in 1908 a group of young warriors killed white trader Oliver Burns. This was apparently in response to the imprisonment and death of Ara, the brother of a local chief, Lela.[35] The people involved in the attack, as well as others living in the area, rapidly dispersed, anticipating the brutality of the British response that would follow. One of the men involved in the attack was Ishmael Ngatu, a young man from Patutiva, who belonged to a chiefly line via his mother (that is, vuluvulu). Ngatu fled to Munda in Roviana Lagoon, where he was sheltered by the Methodist Mission's Reverend Goldie.[36] While there, Ngatu converted to Christianity and the two men established a relationship that was to become crucial to the evangelisation and governance of Marovo.

The attack on Burns received wide coverage in the press in Australia and New Zealand, and this probably fuelled the response that followed. European traders, government officials and Islanders recruited and armed elsewhere in the Protectorate undertook several punitive expeditions, during which they raided gardens, burned houses and shelled coastal areas. High Commissioner Charles Woodford reported that 'the lesson inflicted [was] a severe one',[37] and while small-scale feuding continued, oral traditions recall these events as marking the end of headhunting in Marovo.

Colonial 'pacification' had a significant impact on the idealised masculine models of the bangara and varane, as colonial officials enforced laws against the acquisition of firearms, destroyed canoes and suppressed any practices they saw as connected to headhunting. Trading had already destabilised bush and

---

particularly with respect to narratives regarding child captives): cf McDougall, *Engaging with Strangers*, 64–90.

[35] K B Jackson, 'Tie Hokara, Tie Vaka', 175.

[36] Hviding, *Guardians of Marovo Lagoon*, 119.

[37] Bennett, *Wealth of the Solomons*, 107, quoting Woodford to Major (11 January 1909 WPHC 4/ IV/261/1908).

coastal polities, and while this enabled some men to extend their influence, colonial pacification now removed their capacity to build prestige through warfare and practices such as divining the likely outcome of raids.[38] The implications for feminine models of ritual and political authority have received very little attention from scholars, but it seems likely that pacification destabilised and weakened institutions such as the bangara male, a woman from a chiefly line who was responsible for placating the spirits, ensuring the security of influential men, and enabling them to enter the hope (sacred site) where they undertook rituals on behalf of the kokolo (group).

3.3.2 *The Spatial Reorganisation of Bush and Coastal Groups*

In 1912, Ngatu left Roviana and returned to Marovo with a Tongan missionary, Paul Havea. The pair established a Methodist mission station at Patutiva and continued using Roviana as the church's lingua franca. The mission quickly established a following among the bush people of Marovo, but were repeatedly rejected by the coastal people. Hviding explains that the coastal Repi and Babata people, including bangara Tatagu, wanted the Church of England since its missionaries were known to use English, the language of commerce and colonial administration. Coastal leaders eventually allowed Griffith and Marion Jones of the Australian Seventh Day Adventist Mission to establish a school and a mission at Sasaghana in 1915, but only after the missionaries assured them that they would teach their children English.[39]

Missionaries encouraged their converts to move into consolidated villages in accessible areas, and this process is now known as horevura, literally, 'descend and emerge', referring to the bush people's descent and emergence from the forest into the coastal areas. The exact drivers and period of horevura are debated,[40] and are critical to contemporary land disputes, a reminder that to adjudicate on history is to adjudicate on land claims. It is undisputed, however, that the contemporary political geography, in which settlements are

---

[38] Hviding, *Guardians of Marovo Lagoon*, 115–118; see also White, *Identity through History*, Chapter 5; Hocart, 'Warfare'.

[39] Hviding, *Guardians of Marovo Lagoon*, 118–120. McDougall notes the same motivation for Ranonggans embracing Adventism: McDougall, 'Fellowship and Citizenship', 65.

[40] Cliff Bird emphasises the influence of pacification, conversion to Christianity and the agency of bush groups, while others have emphasised the diminished populations and political power of bush groups vis-à-vis coastal groups, the relative isolation of bush groups from trade and the formation of new alliances between relocated coastal groups and bush people: Bird, 'Pepesa', 50; cf Hviding and Bayliss-Smith, *Islands of Rainforest*, 149–152; Bayliss-Smith et al., 'Saltwater and Bush'.

concentrated in coastal areas and divided into Adventist villages and United Church villages, emerged from this period. Migration and resettlement entailed adaptation of socio-spatial distinctions between 'bush' and 'coastal' people, as coastal people took up gardening in coastal swiddens, while bush people settled on the coast and started fishing further away from the coastline than they may have previously done. In some instances this entailed a more flexible integration of pre-existing categories of people, land and labour. However, as we see further in Section 3.4, it was also a period in which both landholding groups and their territories became demarcated by outer boundaries (rather than emanating from culturally significant social and spatial 'focal points') and rather more sedimented through legal processes.

3.3.3 *Transformations in Gendered Domains of Land Use and Authority*

The suppression of warfare, missionisation and reorganisation of the population in coastal areas destabilised existing gender relations, often weakening the discursive and material connection between women and the land. In discussing these shifts, bush people often pointed me to the fact that they no longer bury the placenta in the soil, a practice that is understood to corporeally connect women, children and land. According to Cliff Bird, this practice ceased with the arrival of the Methodist Mission and the establishment of health services (based on biomedical models that treated the placenta as clinical waste) by Reverend Goldie's wife, Helena.[41] Many people also noted the decline in ruta, the taro terraces associated with women, as people moved into coastal areas, took up Christian rituals in place of older ones and increasingly focused on commercial copra production.[42] Very few (if any) ruta are under cultivation today, and bush people often expressed concern that younger people lack the knowledge necessary for this form of taro cultivation. In our discussions, a number of people specifically advocated the reinvigoration of both the knowledge and practice of these forms of agriculture as a means of strengthening the status of women with respect to land.

Conversion to Christianity and the suppression of practices associated with Indigenous warfare also led to a decline in aspects of pre-Christian feasting,

---

[41] Bird, 'Pepesa', 87; cf C T J Luxton, *Isles of Solomon: A Tale of Missionary Adventure* (Methodist Foreign Ministry, 2nd ed, 1955).

[42] See Somerville, 'Ethnographical Notes'; John Connell, 'The Death of Taro: Local Response to a Change of Subsistence Crops in the Northern Solomon Islands' (1978) 11(4) *Mankind* 445; Matthew G Allen, 'The Evidence for Sweet Potato in Island Melanesia' in C Ballard et al. (eds.), *The Sweet Potato in Oceania: A Reappraisal* (2005) 99.

dancing and ritual,[43] with diverse implications for gendered subjectivities and social institutions. As Debra McDougall observes for Ranongga, the cessation of warfare may have enabled women to move around more freely, and it appears to have affirmed and even increased their historical role in drawing in 'foreign others' and 'welcoming strangers' (including missionaries).[44] In Marovo, ritual authority and a connection with divine others had previously been the domain of a number of influential women such as the bangara male, and it is possible that many more women could now access spiritual power directly, and enter the new sacred sites established by missionaries. At the same time, missionisation reinforced particular idealisations of masculine authority at a time when local polities were already in flux, and this contributed to the erosion of at least some forms of influence historically associated with women.

Some missionary couples, such as Methodist John F Goldie and Helena Goldie, and Adventist Griffith Jones and Marion Jones, worked together. However, both oral histories and scholarly accounts suggest that men – whether English, Australian, from elsewhere in Solomon Islands or the Pacific – typically went ahead into a new area without their wives but with men colleagues, and established a presence following negotiations with the bangara. These negotiations over access to land and the establishment of a new church were therefore a highly masculine domain. Furthermore, the new, formal positions of ritual leadership within the churches were predominantly available to men, and typically taken up by aspiring or existing bangara. The model of land control and church leadership promulgated by the missionaries was therefore predominantly masculine, and often white. It wasn't until the 1960s, when the Methodist Women's Fellowship was founded, that formal, clearly defined leadership roles were widely held by local women. Perhaps most strikingly, the Methodist Mission used the term bangara to translate 'lord', not only incorporating the institution of bangara into the liturgical life of the church and encoding particular figures of masculinity, but tightly weaving the figure of Jesus as messiah, saviour and redeemer with the role of influential local men. Other conceptions of authority, such as varane and vuluvulu, were not incorporated into these new institutions and

---

[43] See Bird, 'Pepesa', 81. While old rituals and ceremonial activities continued away from the eyes of expatriate missionaries and colonial administrators in many parts of Solomon Islands, this does not appear to have been the case in Marovo, apparently due to Ngatu's influence. One woman explained to me that 'we stopped all that when the missionaries came. We had to stop everything. We couldn't continue these things in secret because Ngatu would find out, and then he would chop off our heads!'

[44] McDougall, 'Fellowship and Citizenship', 67.

practices in similar ways. Rather, they appear to have been overlooked or
actively excluded.

3.4 KOT: PROPERTY, PUBLIC AUTHORITY AND LEGAL PLURALITY

The turn of the twentieth century was a period of intense negotiation,
contestation and reorganisation of previous patterns of resource use and
settlement. It was also a period in which new vocabularies and understandings
of land tenure and leadership emerged and became sedimented in forms that
persist in the present. Commissioner Phillips observed that Solomon Islanders
used the term kot (court) to refer to 'practically any conversation *ex parte* or
otherwise' with a government official,[45] including district officers, land commissions and courts. Examining these interactions provides vital insights into
the ways in which the people of Marovo navigated the new vocabularies,
concepts and institutions associated with the Christian churches and colonial
administration, with implications for contemporary land tenure, leadership
and legal pluralities.

3.4.1 *Survey Pegs and Land Sales: Property and Prestige*

If the end of warfare and the acceptance of Christianity had ambivalent
implications for gender relations, this could hardly be said of the expansion
of the colonial legal system, which consistently reinforced specific idealisations of masculine authority. Colonial administrators carried with them
assumptions about property and authority that provided an array of opportunities for at least some local men to retain and even expand their influence over
both land and people. Europeans expected to find male 'chiefs' who were
individualised centres of authority over a corporate landholding group and its
associated territory, and these assumptions enabled some bangara – those with
the knowledge and skills necessary to negotiate with Protectorate officials – to
collaborate with officials to mark land boundaries, consolidate their authority
over land and have it recognised as 'ownership'.[46] This facilitated a simplification of land tenure whereby some expressions of authority over land could be
foregrounded, disentangled from a wider web of socio-spatial relations and
consolidated; while other understandings of the relationship between people
and place were repeatedly submerged.

---

[45] Report of the Lands Commission: Native Claim No. 26, Annexure II, 8.
[46] See also White, *Identity through History*, at 88 regarding Isabel.

One example of this process revolves around a boundary marker on Marovo Island, which was established in 1913 by the bangara Tatagu with the assistance of District Officer Barley. While Tatagu's influence had waned in some respects with the end of inter-island raiding and prestige-goods trading, he retained significant influence among his kin, traders and Protectorate officials alike. In 1911, for example, he travelled throughout the lagoon and successfully collected rifles in support of colonial pacification policies.[47] Tatagu's collaborations with colonial administrators appear to have served him well, for as one of his descendants recounts:

> Tatagu's relationship with Protectorate officials was strong, and because of this, he was able to gain the assistance of District Officer Barley in marking the boundary of Babata Land in 1913...They did this by cutting a distinctive mark in the trunk of a coconut tree, which was later replaced by a cement post.[48]

The establishment of the cut in the tree, and subsequently the cement post – 'peck' in Pijin – had ongoing effects, and became crucial in a boundary dispute that came before the district commissioner decades later, in 1950. In *Okeni v. Ragoso*,[49] the defendant Ragoso (one of Tatagu's sons) indexed his claim to the boundary marker and recalled how it was established by his father in the presence of a number of police officers who came from other islands. According to Ragoso, 'Okeni and the [other claimants] did nothing when they were there because Tataku [sic] owned the land and nobody else did'. Okeni disputed this, arguing that his failure to speak was not indicative of his lack of rights to the land, but arose from his lack of understanding of the implications of the event:

> Q. [...] Do you know that the D.O. and Tataku put a spearline [boundary] across the point?
> A. Yes I know but it was done when we did not understand such things.
>
>   [...]
>
> Q. Why did you say nothing when they were there at the time and could have straightened it out?
> A. When they did it we did not understand what was going on.

[47] Liligeto, *Babata* 14.
[48] Ibid, 24.
[49] *Okeni v Ragoso*, WP 29/8/1950.

One of the witnesses for the plaintiff, Lupeni, similarly suggested that his own lack of familiarity with white men and their laws prevented him from speaking up.[50] This is entirely plausible, since in 1913 the post would have been unfamiliar technology to many people, and it marked an outer boundary, whereas a group's association with the land had historically been strongest at the core of the territory. Tatagu's familiarity with colonial administrators' own strategies for enacting property, and possibly his understanding of the concepts underpinning these strategies, enabled him to have his claims legitimated as property by the state, and consolidated by the peg. While this did not extinguish alternative claims, it did foreground some understandings of land tenure while submerging others, as courts have continually recognised the claims asserted by the peg. Other understandings of land tenure do persist, but to my knowledge they have not been materially asserted for several decades.

Tatagu is just one of several bangara of central Marovo who persuaded district officers to legitimate their claims and construct fixed cement markers in strategic locations during this period. According to Hviding and Bayliss-Smith, it was the 'fuzziness' of overlapping territories that allowed individuals and small groups of people to sell land to white planters and traders, and they suggest that the bangara saw the demarcation of land boundaries as essential to counteract this.[51] Liligeto similarly describes Tatagu's motivation as being the need to retain the land for the benefit of the tribe.[52] I suggest that it was not so much the ambiguity of territorial boundaries that allowed the sale of land but rather colonial conceptions of and desires for Indigenous land. When the bangara clarified boundaries they may have 'secured' particular places for particular people through processes of state recognition, but they did so in response to colonial encroachment, and their efforts remade both land and people in new ways.

Whatever the intention of the bangara, the demarcation of boundaries entailed numerous forms of 'cutting', not only on the trunks of trees, but in the overlapping socio-spatial landscapes of Marovo. Whereas both territories and groups had previously been defined in terms of focal points, they were now increasingly defined in terms of outer boundaries. As territorial boundaries were clarified, the interwoven, relational spaces of Marovo were carved up

---

[50] In cross-examination, Lupeni was asked whether he knew that the district officer and Tatagu had marked the place, and if so, why he didn't speak up. He responded that he did now, but that he didn't say anything about it because 'we were frightened of the white man then'.

[51] Hviding and Bayliss-Smith, *Islands of Rainforest*, 79.

[52] Liligeto, *Babata*, 25.

into discrete parcels legible (and therefore alienable) to white administrators, traders, planters and missionaries; and so too were the many entangled people who had shared these places differentiated from each other, with some people and not others emerging as 'landowners'. Furthermore, the marking of boundaries not only asserted a group's claims to land, but also chiefly efficacy, and this served to expand the influence of senior men. Property formation thus became tied to chiefly authority, not only in the eyes of traders, colonial administrators and foreign missionaries, but also locals.

This meant that as space was conceptually revalued and reorganised, so too were the relationships within and between the kokolo and butubutu, with ongoing effects. While people in central Marovo explain that historically, the role of the bangara was to 'look after' the land and the group,[53] they increasingly emerged as individualised centres of authority over land if not people. When Adventist missionaries arrived at Marovo Island in 1915, locals and missionaries alike appeared to accept that it was Tatagu's permission they needed to establish a presence on the island.[54] Similarly, Ngatu's reputation as a 'traditional chief' and his leadership within the Methodist Mission enabled him to sell 800 acres of land at Seghe to the government in 1913.[55] Land records demonstrate that when disputes came before the courts, influential men often cited their sale of the land as evidence of both their chiefly status and ownership of the land – a logic that was regularly accepted by the courts, making property and public authority quite literally two sides of the same coin.[56] The colonial legal system therefore facilitated, in multiple and mutually reinforcing ways, a simplification of the politico-legal geography, enabling a small number of influential men to mark boundaries and disentangle both the land and their authority from a wider web of pre-existing relationships.

3.4.2 *Legal Pluralities of Kastom, Church and State*

Contemporary legal pluralities have histories, and in the previous chapter I noted that Christian idioms are a prominent feature of court records for the western islands. The expansion of missions and colonial administration

---

[53] This is the language used by Sagende before the Phillips Commission: Report of the Lands Commission: Native Claim No. 26.

[54] Hviding, *Guardians of Marovo Lagoon*, 117–118, Liligeto, *Babata*, 16–17.

[55] C H Allan, *Memoir of the Solomon Islands, 1948–1957* (Pacific Manuscripts Bureau, PMB 1189/16, 1979); Bennett, *Wealth of the Solomons*, 116.

[56] In one matter, Letipiko referred to at least five senior men involved in different transactions, and the court accepts this as evidence of their 'ownership': *Letipiko v Ruben Ngatu*, Marovo Native Court 3/1976.

disrupted previous understandings of people and place, and both the churches and colonial administration introduced a range of discursive, institutional and material opportunities to renegotiate the terms of landholding and leadership. In the western islands, territorial struggles were deeply entangled with schisms between Methodists and Adventists, and this generated legal pluralities in which Christian moral-normative orders were invoked in courts and in villages (including through signs, gardens, church buildings) as frequently and prominently as kastom and law.

As we saw in Chapter 2, the Phillips Commission (1919–1923) became the site of intense contestation between members of rival missions, whether they were foreign missionaries or converts. Australian missionaries and colonial administrators clearly perceived these disputes as emerging from sectarian conflict. However, I suggest that rather than introducing schisms, in some instances at least, Methodism and Adventism provided new vocabularies, rituals, institutions and sites by which people could differentiate themselves, at a time when socio-spatial relations within and between bush and coastal groups were already being renegotiated. One such example is *Native Claim No 26* concerning Telina Island, which the Australian Adventist mission leased from Jorovo (also known as Kanijama), a warrior of Nggatokae and Vangunu. This lease was challenged in the commission by bush groups represented by the bangara Sagende.

The records of *Native Claim No 26* identify the claimants as the Busimati (a Bareke group), who by that time were associated with the Methodist Mission. However, the dispute clearly concerns people from several bush groups, including the Ilumu, with a variety of Ilumu claims made before the commission – some in support of the Busimati, some in support of the Adventists and others that were different again. According to contemporary accounts, the Busimati and Ilumu are genealogically related; however, the Ilumu appear to have developed affinities with coastal people as a result of increased interaction and intermarriage during the nineteenth century, well before missionisation.[57] Socio-spatial distinctions were therefore already being renegotiated when missionaries arrived in Marovo. Where colonial administrators saw schisms and perceived them to be *caused* by missionisation, I suggest that it is more likely that conversion to either Methodism or Adventism provided the Ilumu with new pathways for asserting social and spatial distinctions at a time when these were already in flux. Today, the Ilumu people are predominantly Adventist, with the exception of the people at Rukutu village, who some say

---

[57] Cf Hviding, *Guardians of Marovo Lagoon*, 100.

converted to Methodism largely as a result of the territorial dispute over Telina – a dispute that was still repeatedly coming before the courts fifty years later.[58]

When reading colonial court records for Marovo, it is clear that Christianity, as much as colonial law, was implicated in both the material rearrangement of space and in the reorganisation of concepts, vocabularies and arguments that could be put to work renegotiating land tenure and leadership. *Koni* v. *Rebi*,[59] heard during the 1970s, turned on competing histories of occupation, migration, resettlement and alliance, notably during the *horevura* years, and the Marovo Court found that although Koni's line were the original occupants of the land, Rebi's line now held it due to long occupation. The High Court of the Western Pacific upheld this decision, with both courts concluding that when Koni's group 'left the land following the call of the missionaries', they intended to abandon it.[60]

These findings exemplify Eurocentric understandings of land as space emptied of meaning and a commodity capable of being relinquished by one group, acquired by another and commercially transacted. They refuse to acknowledge the historical mobility of the people of Marovo or the enduring ties to land that persist for Pacific peoples many generations after relocation.[61] My emphasis here, however, is less on Eurocentric perceptions of place and more on the efforts of parties and witnesses – all of whom were Methodists – to navigate these perceptions and solicit the courts' recognition of their relationships with land. All of the parties and witnesses grounded their claims to the land in extensive accounts of Indigenous history, knowledge and practices, and they explicitly wove these accounts with the moral-normative orders

---

[58] *Oreli of Telina v John Kera and Tuti of Rukutu*, Marovo Local Court Case 8/1978. Similar disputes have been observed elsewhere in Western Province: D McDougall, 'The Unintended Consequences of Clarification: Development, Disputing and the Dynamics of Community in Ranongga, Solomon Islands' (2005) 52 *Ethnohistory* 81, 99ff.

[59] *Timothy Koni v Rebi from New Michi*, Native Court, Marovo Civil Case No 4/1971 (*Koni v Rebi 1971*), also *Timothy Koni of Gepae v Rebi of New Michi*, Native Court Civil Case 11/1969 (*Koni v Rebi 1969*).

[60] The Marovo Native Court found although the people of Koni's line were the original occupants, they relinquished their claim during the *horevura* years, and Rebi's line now held it due to long occupation. The High Court of the Western High Pacific upheld this decision. Both courts determined that when Koni's group 'left the land following the call of the missionaries', they intended to abandon it: *Koni v Rebi 1971*; *T Koni v J Repi*, High Court of the Western Pacific, Native Land Appeal No 5 of 1972. Note that Repi is also rendered Rebi.

[61] For example Teaiwa explains in detail the multigenerational circulation of people between islands within the Gilbert and Ellice Island Colony, as well as the enduring connections Banabans displaced to Fiji during the 1940s have to present-day Kiribati: Teaiwa, *Consuming Ocean Island*.

promulgated by the missionaries as well as the colonial administration. One of the appellants, Napitalae Aleve, told the court:

> We are under the custom and the Law but Rebi said that descent or tribe is nothing but why the Bible tells us about the descent mention in the Gospel according to St Matthew? Is it nothing? Is the Law against custom? And the custom against the Law?[62]

Here Aleve resisted any attempt to pit 'custom', 'law' and 'the Bible' against each other, and responded to Rebi's claim that the appellants had 'left the land' by suggesting that such arguments were unbiblical. While Aleve's arguments clearly did not succeed, they appealed to multiple sources of authority (custom, Christianity and law) and must have been somewhat provocative and persuasive in a context where colonial administrators and locals alike equated being 'Christian' with being both 'law abiding' and 'morally good'. Another witness for the appellants, Alovini, asserted,

> I am one of the Busimati's witnesses, I didn't come [from] other Islands or places and I come to stand before you and before God to tell you how we came to own this land at Ghoanahai.

Alovini's assertion that he was a 'man of the place' needs to be understood in the context of the widespread understanding, common across Solomon Islands, that the people who 'belong' to the land are the ones with the greatest authority and knowledge to speak about it. In introducing himself, Alovini asserted such authority, and then acknowledged the authority not only of the court but also the Christian God.

The court records for *Koni v. Rebi* are more extensive than most, but they demonstrate an argumentative pattern – that is, an interlacing of vocabularies associated with custom, Christianity and state law – that may be seen in many other records for land claims in Marovo, including very recent ones.[63] The semantic formulae sanctioned by the churches, as well as the state, have therefore been crucial to the ways in which people have framed their claims to land. Furthermore, when Indigenous claimants wove claims grounded in Indigenous knowledge and practice with Christianity and state law, and sought recognition of their claims by missionaries and colonial administrators,

---

[62] *Koni v Rebi* 1971, per Napitalae Aleve.
[63] In a dispute heard in 2006, the defendant commenced his testimony with: 'Justice and all the member and servant of God, I was coming and sit down before you at present. For the accusation, and our father in heaven will show us the truth. These are my first words for those of you my important man. Now I am going to tell you my story...' *Deni v Metu*, Local Court Land Case 2/2006.

they simultaneously imbued the new understandings, vocabularies and institutions associated with those domains with at least a degree of legitimacy.

If these strategies recognised and therefore facilitated an extension of European authority over Indigenous lives, they also ensured its fragmentation, for conflict between competing missions had a fundamental impact on the influence of the colonial administration at the local level. In 1949, the district commissioner reported on the Marovo Native Council, which was meeting regularly under the leadership of Ngatu, now the District Headman:

> At present Government influence is secondary to that of the Missions which dominate every village. There is a sharp cleavage between the natives of the Seventh Day Adventist and Methodist faiths and everything possible was done to break down the barrier. Even in the Council meeting there was an objection to the new President of the Native Court on the grounds that he represents a different religious sect to his own. The power of mission teachers has already been mentioned as derogatory to the authority of the headman.[64]

Thus from the perspective of Protectorate officials, religious schisms posed a threat to the authority of the state, contesting and threatening to fragment the territorial boundaries and political structures demarcated as part of indirect rule. Colonial administrators sought to draw 'custom' into the arena of the 'state', and keep 'the church' at a distance, but these distinctions proved impossible to sustain, with narratives and forms of authority from one arena frequently slipping into others.

3.5 MASTERS OF PLURALITY: SEDIMENTING PROPERTY AND AUTHORITY

As we have seen, trading with Europeans, conversion to Christianity and the expansion of the colonial state – however slow, unsteady and fragmented – destabilised pre-existing understandings of land tenure and leadership, and the effects of this were very uneven. Processes of recognition worked to simplify and consolidate authority over land and people in the hands of a relatively small number of men who were typically 'masters of plurality'[65] – that is, men

---

[64] Report on a tour of Marovo Subdistrict by the District Commissioner, 1 June 1949 (Solomon Islands National Archives, BSIP 7/III/33/4).

[65] This phrase draws on Rodman's 'Masters of Tradition' and see also McDonnell's 'Masters of Modernity'. I prefer a term that avoids potential binaries (including the nature/culture divide associated with modernism) and emphasises dynamism and interaction: Rodman, *Masters of Tradition*; Siobhan McDonnell, 'Exploring the Cultural Power of Land Law in Vanuatu: Law as a Performance That Creates Meaning and Identities' (2013) 33 *Intersections: Gender and Sexuality in Asia and the Pacific*.

who were able to navigate multiple networks or constellations of legal order and emerge as key actors within each of the spheres of kastom, church and state.

3.5.1 *Ngatu: Chief, Church Leader and Government Headman*

Ishmael Ngatu exemplifies those men who were able to navigate the new sources of power that were opening up as a result of missionisation and colonial administration. Ngatu held a position of leadership within the Methodist Mission, his reputation as a chief enabled him to sell land to the government, and he generated cash through business ventures. He is remembered not only for establishing Methodism in Marovo, but for his related leadership in establishing the first cooperative copra venture by villages. With historian Judith Bennett, I suspect that his role in developing this large-scale scheme of copra production, transport and marketing was an expression of the precolonial role of the bangara in supervising the production of taro on dapi.[66]

The development of a system of indirect rule was crucial to the consolidation and expansion of Ngatu's authority, and as we shall see, his legacies. Ngatu was appointed district headman for Marovo, and held the post until it was abolished in the 1940s, at which point he became a member of the Native Court instead. Court records, oral histories and written histories all indicate that he was heavily involved in determining land disputes as well as other native court matters. Ngatu's assertion of his position as bangara and his appointment by the Protectorate administration must have had a recursive effect, for in the process of legitimating some claims and not others, his authority was simultaneously reinforced: as people sought to secure their rights to land by having those claims legitimised by Ngatu, and therefore by 'traditional', 'church' and 'state' authorities, that process simultaneously consolidated Ngatu's authority in the eyes of local people, foreign missionaries and Protectorate officials alike.

Ngatu's success in negotiating all three arenas of church, state and kastom meant he became widely regarded as the chief over a large area – by the 1920s, he was already regarded by at least some people as 'the chief from Nggatokae to Ramata'.[67] This negotiation of new avenues to prestige could hardly be

---

[66] Bennett, *Wealth of the Solomons*, 116, 244.

[67] *Report of the Lands Commission: Native Claim No 26* per Sagende; see also John Garrett, *Where Nets Were Cast: Christianity in Oceania since World War II* (Institute of Pacific Studies in association with World Council of Churches, 1997) 53–55.

regarded as capitulating to European authority, for Ngatu was well known for his willingness to oppose state authorities as well as his colleague, Reverend Goldie.

Ngatu and Goldie were both strong personalities, and while they collaborated on mission work, there were also public confrontations between the two men. One such instance arose in the 1920s, when Goldie decided to establish a mission station at Patutiva, a proposal that was resisted by the people occupying the area. The land was nevertheless acquired in 1928, apparently as a result of numerous misunderstandings among locals regarding the acquisition process and the extent of the land acquired; misunderstandings which were convenient to Goldie and not corrected by Protectorate officials. Ngatu was among the men who purportedly agreed to the acquisition, but according to Goldie's successor, expatriate missionary George Carter, he was unaware of the contents of the document he had signed until a district officer explained it to him. Ngatu's own account suggests that he was furious when he discovered that a larger area had been acquired, and confronted Goldie:

> Mr. Goldie spoke again, "This ground is sacred now, from here to the banyan tree." No one spoke until I said, "you white people think that we native people are like dogs or pigs that have no thoughts of their own." Then I spoke to Nika and Viulu "you accuse me of stealing the land at Patutiva," but I was only talking. We got up and went. I was very upset and angry and went down to Kanoko.[68]

Ngatu was also known for his willingness to confront state officials, highlight their logics of discrimination and contest their authority. He is said to have angrily opposed the attempts by the District Officer in New Georgia, Major Clemens, to influence the appointment and operation of the local council (of which Ngatu was the head):

> You want to make the Council a farce. You want to apparently transfer certain powers and authority to us, and yet are unwilling to trust and relinquish such powers yourself.[69]

Ngatu is just one of a number of men who, while finding their old forms of influence slipping away, were able to navigate the new economic and institutional orders that were simultaneously opening up during the first few decades of the Protectorate. However, he is of particular interest here because

---

[68] Ishmael Ngatu, *Diaries, 1927–1954* (Ms English translation) 8 December 1928 (Pacific Manuscripts Bureau PMB MS 1109, Reel 1), see also Carter, *Tiè Varanè*, 59.

[69] G C: Goldie to Scrivener 14 Jan 1946 cited in Bennett, *Wealth of the Solomons*, 294.

by tracing his legacy, we see the critical influence of the state legal system in sedimenting some versions of land tenure far beyond the actions of any particular individual.

3.5.2 *Sedimenting Kastom*

Majoria v. *Jino*[70] provides a salient example of the ways in which the semantic and institutional structures of the state were mobilised during the early colonial period to consolidate some versions of land tenure and authority while eroding others, with implications that reverberate for generations. In 1914, just two years after returning to Marovo to establish the Methodist Mission, Ngatu heard a land dispute that arose from the attempted purchase of land on Vangunu by the English trader Norman Wheatley. Decades before the introduction of native courts and their harnessing by more high profile forms of resistance such as Maasina Rule, people were already bringing their disagreements to Ngatu, who was holding relatively formal hearings. He was also recording the details of disputes and his decisions in an exercise book titled *Buka Kot Koa Ri tie Muho* ('This book is the record of court cases of native people'). Ngatu concluded that the land belonged to Rikana, and that Luze therefore needed to repay the money he received from Wheatley:

> July 26 1914
>
> This is a court case between Rikana, Huba on one side. Whereas Luze and Kilasa on the other. And the Court decided that the land at RODO belongs to Rikana. But you Kilasa you were only adopted said the court. And the Court asked Luze as to where is the source of your genealogy.
>
> And Luze said he came from Bareke. Alright, you baked 3,000 thousand and you repaid the money you got from Norman because the land belongs to Rikana from which you get money from Norman.
>
> This is what the court said on this day and that is all.[71]

That Ngatu produced this document, a paradigmatic artefact of legal knowledge practices, raises a host of questions that cannot be fully pursued here. I suspect that by 1914 he had already encountered records of leases, and it is clear that by the time of the Phillips Commission, his colleague Goldie had a strong interest in the 'proper' settlement of disputes. Ngatu's book also reveals

---

[70] *Majoria v Jino* [2003] SBHC 29, HC-CC 261-2002 (8 April 2003) (*Majoria v Jino* 2003); *Majoria v Jino* [2008] SBHC 54, HCSI-CC 225 of 2005 (16 May 2008) (*Majoria v Jino* 2008).

[71] Translated version in *Majoria v Jino* 2003.

an emphasis on biological kinship rather than the more diverse webs of relations that have always existed in Marovo – the court questioned the claims of those who were 'only adopted', and this remains a common feature of land disputes today. What is especially interesting to me here is the way in which subsequent courts, comprised of both foreign and Indigenous judges, have wrestled with the implications of the records and – somewhat contrary to policy discourses emphasising 'weak' state institutions with little influence over 'customary land' – have sedimented some versions of customary tenure while eroding others.

In some senses Ngatu's attempts to 'settle' the dispute over Rodo land failed, for more than a century later, the descendants of Rikana and Luze are still embroiled in protracted litigation concerning the land.[72] However, Ngatu's determination, and his production of the record in particular, has nevertheless made some claims more 'sticky' than they might otherwise have been. In 2003, the descendants of Rikana sought a declaration from the High Court that Ngatu's written decision was binding. Justice Brown considered whether Ngatu had the authority to adjudicate the Rodo land dispute, and determined that he did, since he was both a 'traditional chief' and a 'government representative'. Justice Brown reached this conclusion partly because there was no debate among the parties about whether Ngatu 'stood high among his people'. However, he placed much greater weight on the account of Ngatu published by missionary George Carter, and on Land Commissioner Colin Allan's findings regarding the definition of the bangara in nearby Roviana Lagoon in the 1950s.[73] Justice Brown also stressed the significance of Protectorate officials' appointing Ngatu as a headman:

> I am further satisfied that Ishmael Ngatu of Patutiva was a customary leader in Marovo for that was a prerequisite to his appointment as a District Headman during the administration of the British Solomon Islands by the High Commissioner Charles Morris Woodford.[74]

In determining whether or not Ngatu was in fact a 'traditional chief' or 'customary leader', Justice Brown did not ignore the views of Solomon Islanders, but he appeared to place much greater weight on the perceptions of expatriates – Carter, Allan and other colonial officials. He also reasoned that Ngatu's appointment as a district headman would not have been possible *unless* he was a 'customary leader' – that is to say, Justice Brown was clear that

---

72 Recent matters include *Koina v Clerk to Local Court (Western)* [2013] SBHC 69; HCSI-CC 155 of 2013 (21 June 2013); *Lada v Majoria* [2016] SBHC 65; HCSI-CC 134 of 2016 (17 May 2016); *Estate of Oliver Jino v Majoria* [2017] SBCA 1; SICOA-CAC 15 of 2016 (5 May 2017).

73 Carter, *Tiè Varanè*; Allan, *Customary Land Tenure*.

74 *Majoria v Jino* 2003.

he saw Ngatu's appointment as district headman as evidence of him being a bangara. This circular reasoning with respect to Ngatu's 'traditional' and 'state' authority led Justice Brown to conclude that Ngatu's decision was in fact binding, because it was akin to 'best evidence':

> A written record, such as this, lays to rest the risk inherent in the oral traditional story, from mouth to mouth, from generation to generation.[75]

Justice Brown's reasoning overlooked the immense contestation that often surrounded the role of both district headman and 'traditional' leader (discussed in Chapter 2). It also denied the possibility that written accounts of history and territoriality might be contested, and it privileged particular classifications of experts (male expatriates, chiefs, headmen) and knowledge production (notably written). This reasoning reinforced the capacity of some men to speak authoritatively and to 'know' land, custom and its people. It also provides a paradigmatic example of the repeated objectification of customary tenure effected by the state legal system. According to Justice Brown, Ngatu must have been a bangara because Protectorate officials saw him as such, and Ngatu's *Buka* is merely a record of 'facts' that were 'collected' by Ngatu, because Ngatu asserted that they were so. This recursive reification of customary tenure was furthered in a subsequent appeal, where Justice Faukona remarked:

> In Solomon Islands history and genealogy connected to ownership of customary land and its boundaries, is normally one. There cannot be two. And these histories are passed down from one generation to another in perfection and accuracy, without being swayed whatsoever. One cannot collect histories from others. It is something [which] belongs to a tribe and they treasure as sacred and only members of the tribe will learn and know.[76]

This view of kastom led Justice Faukona to doubt the sincerity of the claimant, who had 'swayed' in his evidence concerning the boundary of Rodo land.[77] In reaching his conclusion, Justice Faukona, like Justice Brown, prioritised written accounts of customary tenure, and also emphasised the importance of precedent and the doctrine of *res judicata*.

In the decisions of Ngatu, Justice Brown and Justice Faukona – all clearly influential legal actors – we can see the consolidation of particular forms of land tenure, authority and knowledge with respect to land. We see that the

---

[75] Ibid.
[76] *Majoria v Jino 2008*.
[77] Ibid.

explanations of property and authority provided by Rikana and Ngatu, and subsequently Justice Brown and Justice Faukona, became naturalised, objectified and dehistoricised; some versions of kastom were sedimented while others eroded or submerged. Ngatu's record, and the subsequent determinations, may therefore be understood in terms of what Annelise Riles' refers to as the 'instrumental genre' of law – the records of chiefs and courts do not merely represent particular versions of custom, but instantiate them.[78] While Ngatu's *Buka* and Tatagu's peck did not rigidify kastom to such an extent that they expunged alternative interpretations, they set in motion a series of material iterations of specific ideas and abstractions about property that endure far beyond these men themselves.

3.5.3 *Women, Men and Kot*

Women's voices are noticeably absent from the records of Lands Commissions, chiefs' hearings and High Court sessions. I examined dozens of court books concerning land disputes in Marovo Lagoon and elsewhere in Western Province, some of which contained records of hundreds of matters, and stretching from the colonial period until 2012. I found only one involving a woman as either a key witness or party. That matter, heard in 1985, concerned Lighuru land, which the plaintiff Patson Dioni said had been purchased through a form of gift exchange, *lukotu*, from the defendant Miriam Achi.[79] People in central Marovo cite Achi as an example of a 'strong woman who fought about land', and while the court found in favour of the plaintiff, the records attest to her confident and detailed explanation of kastom, as well as her skilled cross-examination of the plaintiff.

The relative absence of women and the predominance of senior men in these highly formalised modes of dispute resolution is often explained by people in central Marovo in terms of the idea that 'olketa no save tok' – a reference to the gender norms that suggest it is inappropriate gendered behaviour for women to speak about land matters in public arenas such as courts, as well as the assumption that women often lack the customary knowledge and oratorical skills necessary to speak persuasively in these arenas. I was frequently told that custodianship of the land centres on the vuluvulu, who must be consulted in each and every decision with respect to land, but that it is ultimately the bangara who may, and should, 'speak for' the land.

---

[78] A Riles, 'Law as Object' in Donald Brenneis and Sally Engle Merry (eds.), *Law and Empire in the Pacific: Fiji and Hawai'i* (SAR Press, 2004) 187.

[79] *Patson Dioni v Miriam Achi* Marovo Local Court, 7/1985.

While people often assert that 'olketa woman no save tok' (women may not, cannot or should not speak) and court records tend to confirm this observation, a close reading of those records and existing histories sometimes provides glimpses of women who not only 'talked', but did so in a highly persuasive way. I came across one such instance in the records of a land dispute that came before the Marovo Local Court in 1974. That record contained references to another, earlier dispute held in 1928, which is said to have involved a named woman. According to claimants in the 1974 matter, the woman in the 1928 dispute was so persuasive that she 'nearly won the case'. The other side won, but the claimants in the 1974 dispute attributed this to the intervention of a local leader who, they alleged, coached the parties and witnesses in genealogical matters.[80] A further example is provided by Liligeto, who refers to Talivuru, who was Tatagu's niece and 'a recognised source of the (coastal Babata) tribe's traditional history and knowledge'. During the Allan Commission in the 1950s, Jorovo – the leader who leased Telina to the Adventists – left a hearing in Patutiva and paddled back to Marovo Island to confirm with Talivuru and others that the statements he had made were correct.[81] This suggests that Talivuru was not only a recognised source of knowledge and expertise in such matters, but that she had vital opportunities to influence contests over land.

Furthermore, women as a social group undoubtedly contributed to the process of adaptation, contestation and recognition of claims in a variety of ways not revealed by the written records of chiefs' hearings, Land Commissions and courts; not least of which would have been through conversations within the household, and decisions about the abandonment of old practices in favour of new ones. Women must have made decisions, although constrained by the powerful conjunction of European medicine and Christianity, about whether they would continue burying the placenta on the land. Similarly, they must have made decisions about whether they would continue the time-intensive cultivation of ruta following the introduction of sweet potato, the expansion of copra production, the rise of Christian practice and the reorganisation of communities in coastal areas.

By tracking contests over time we see that as Land Commissions and courts have investigated, 'discovered' and recorded custom, the material iteration of their findings has sedimented some expressions of landholding and authority

---

[80] *Concerning Luqa Land*, Marovo Native Court Civil Case No 6/1974. I could not find a copy of the 1928 determination (which is not surprising, since many records were destroyed during World War II).

[81] Liligeto, *Babata*, 1, 25-6.

while eroding others. The records of Land Commissions and courts, like the liturgies of churches, make no reference to the role of vuluvulu, despite containing numerous references to the role of the bangara, who were clearly perceived to be authoritative in land matters.[82] Colonial administrators and missionaries alike recognised some segments of the bush polity and disregarded others, consistently reinforcing the role of bangara while failing to accord any recognition to the concept of vuluvulu, whether as 'blood core' or 'a senior woman'. This channelled the reconfiguration of the connections between women and land, and the kokolo and land, in quite particular directions, at least within the arena of the state, with important implications for contemporary resource control.

3.6 LOGGING, JIFS AND ENTREPRENEURS: THE ONGOING SIMPLIFICATION OF AUTHORITY TODAY

Since the 1990s, people of the Bareke Peninsula and the surrounding islands have entered into an ever-growing range of negotiations, transactions and conflicts with extra-local parties, particularly with respect to logging. The Forest Resources and Timber Utilisation Act 1978 (FRTU Act) provides that any person who is interested in logging customary land must apply to the Commissioner of Forest Resources for consent to negotiate with the relevant government authorities and the 'owners' of land and timber rights.[83] In theory, the Provincial government then holds a 'timber rights hearing', at which it determines a range of issues, including whether the people who propose to grant the timber rights represent all those who are entitled to grant such rights; who the customary landholders are; and how any profits are to be shared. This information is then recorded in a 'Certificate of Customary Ownership', more commonly known as 'Form Two'. The individuals listed in the Form Two are deemed to be entitled to negotiate with the logging company. There is a right of appeal to the Customary Land Appeal Court, the decision of which is final and conclusive, subject only to the original jurisdiction of the High Court.[84]

---

[82] See, e.g., *Majoria v Jino* 2003.

[83] Forest Resources and Timber Utilisation Act 1978 [Cap 40] (Solomon Islands), s 7(1) (FRTU Act). This Act has been the subject of frequent amendments that are not always readily available. I have used the version that is available (as at September 2019) on the Pacific Islands Legal Information Institute, at www.paclii.org, which is the version that is most commonly used by legal practitioners in Solomon Islands. This of course raises a range of interesting questions about what the law 'is'.

[84] This process is set out in the FRTU Act, Part III.

The regulation of forestry in Solomon Islands is notoriously complex and there is now a large literature documenting collusion between foreign – mostly Malaysian and Chinese – logging companies and local politicians, irregularities in the timber rights hearing process, poor monitoring and enforcement and the inequitable distribution of logging royalties.[85] Even if ideally implemented, the FRTU Act presupposes that it is possible to identify bounded corporate 'landowning' groups, representatives of those groups and bounded territories to which both groups and their representatives hold various rights. As a result, debates about the 'ownership' of land and trees in timber rights hearings and before courts often revolve around competing unilineal constructions of descent groups.[86] This process of making and legitimating claims to land and trees as property results in relationships between people bound by generations of shared descent, occupation, and use of the land being fractured or 'cut'.[87] In at least one instance, it has precipitated protracted litigation between a father and his son.[88] The emotional toll of these conflicts is high. One sunny day, I walked with a group of friends to the top of a ridge, where we stood quietly surveying the brown scars across the landscape, and the run-off that locals note stains the rivers and lagoon the colour of 'Milo'. In rather typical Marovo style, one of the members of our group interrupted our sad ruminations by joking that he wished that the loggers would hurry up and destroy everything so that people could live peaceably once again.

[85] See e.g. Ian Frazer, 'The Struggle for Control of Solomon Island Forests' (1997) 9(1) *The Contemporary Pacific* 39; Judith A Bennett, *Pacific Forest: A History of Resource Control and Contest in Solomon Islands, c 1800–1997* (Brill, 2000); Tarcisius Kabutaulaka, 'Rumble in the Jungle: Land, Culture and (Un)Sustainable Logging in Solomon Islands' in Antony Hooper (ed.), *Culture and Sustainable Development in the Pacific* (ANU E Press, 2000) 88; Matthew G Allen, 'The Political Economy of Logging in Solomon Islands' in Ron Duncan (ed.), *The Political Economy of Economic Reform in the Pacific* (Asian Development Bank, 2011) 277; Debra McDougall, 'Church, Company, Committee, Chief: Emergent Collectivities in Rural Solomon Islands' in Mary Patterson and Martha Macintyre (eds.), *Managing Modernity in the Western Pacific* (University of Queensland Press, 2011) 121, Dyer, 'Eating Money', Transform Aqorau 'Solomon Islands' Foreign Policy Dilemma and the Switch from Taiwan to China' in G Smith and T Wesley-Smith (eds) *The China Alternative: Changing Regional Order in the Pacific Islands* (ANU Press, 2021) 319.

[86] Hviding, 'Indigenous Essentialism?'; Hviding, 'Disentangling the Butubutu'. Cf Simon Foale and Martha Macintyre, 'Dynamic and Flexible Aspects of Land and Marine Tenure at West Nggela: Implications for Marine Resource Management' (2000) 71(1) *Oceania* 30.

[87] Marilyn Strathern, 'Cutting the Network' (1996) 2(3) *Journal of the Royal Anthropological Institute* 517.

[88] An ongoing dispute between these two people and their lineages has resulted in at least twelve determinations in the High Court and Court of Appeal between 2003 and 2017.

There is a widespread perception within Solomon Islands that women bear a disproportionate burden of both the social fragmentation and ecological destruction associated with logging, yet simultaneously have limited capacity to influence debates regarding timber rights.[89] In our discussions regarding logging, people in Marovo constantly pointed me to vuluvulu, and I suggest that they did so precisely because they perceive the contemporary marginalisation of women from negotiations and decision-making to be linked with long-standing assumptions among colonial administrators, expatriate missionaries and other 'outsiders' regarding gendered authority over land. Indeed I suggest that the concept of vuluvulu is central to the ways in which many people debate, theorise and propose solutions to the challenges of propertisation and resource extraction they now confront.

The FRTU Act sets out a process whereby landholders should be identified *before* negotiations start. However, in practice, logging companies and people claiming to be landowners are typically engaged in discussions long before the commissioner of forests is approached and a timber rights hearing held. Furthermore, while forested land is widely understood to be the collective territory of a kokolo, representatives of logging companies often engage with a very small number of individuals rather a wider group.[90] It is these people who then become the signatories to agreements, and they are generally (if not always) men – some are bangara and other older, influential men, while others are younger, entrepreneurial men who may become bangara in the future. While some of these people are of influential descent, many have become powerful through a relatively high level of formal education and literacy; their understanding of the regulatory frameworks governing forestry; and their ability to persuade elderly, sometimes illiterate bangara to endorse and promote logging.

The simplification and erasure of the multiplicity of authority with respect to land minimises the extent to which companies are required to engage with groups and ensures that industrial logging remains economically viable and profitable. However it also generates intense contestation and undermines the moral authority of the introduced legal system even as Solomon Islanders simultaneously turn towards it. The proponents of logging are widely believed

---

[89] This was also extensively documented by Kabutaulaka for Guadalcanal, Isabel and Choiseul more than twenty years ago: Kabutaulaka, 'Paths in the Jungle'.

[90] Scales, 'The Social Forest', 97–105; Tarcisius Kabutaulaka, 'Global Capital and Local Ownership in Solomon Islands' Forestry Industry' in Stewart Firth (ed.), *Globalisation and Governance in the Pacific Islands* (ANU Press, 2006) 252; Morgan Wairiu and Gordon Nanau, *Logging and Conflict in Birao Ward of Guadalcanal, Solomon Islands* (Islands Knowledge Institute, IKI Working Paper No. 1, 2010).

to receive financial and other forms of support from logging companies when they appear in timber rights hearings and court appeals. Many landholders also believe that logging companies may influence the outcome of hearings through the provision of funding to the members of those fora. The High Court has acknowledged these perceptions and emphasised the government's obligation to provide the funds necessary for Customary Land Appeal Courts to hear appeals, but in the context of extremely constrained funding for the justice system, has reluctantly allowed the parties in some matters to share the costs of having their case heard.[91] This understandably contributes to the perception – if not the fact – that companies are able to influence the outcomes of hearings, and it fuels a general sense of cynicism and exhaustion that discourages people from pursuing the legal avenues that might otherwise provide a measure of accountability.

The representatives listed in logging agreements are legally (as both a matter of state law and kastom) obliged to share royalties with other members of the groups listed on those agreements. However, it is widely acknowledged that there is a general lack of transparency and accountability as to how this occurs. People complain that they do not know when royalties are distributed, or how much money they are entitled to. As highlighted by my conversation with Naomi, introduced in Chapter 1, licence negotiations and royalty distributions often occur in the urban centres of Honiara or Gizo, which are located hundreds of kilometres away from the site of logging operations and the villages affected by them, thus involving expensive and time-consuming travel for members of the affected groups. This makes it extremely difficult for potential claimants to access information and hold signatories accountable. As was the case with traders, missionaries and the Protectorate administrators before them, representatives of logging companies find it cheap and convenient to engage with a small number of individuals they perceive to represent the group, rather than the entire kokolo, let alone multiple people from multiple kokolo, and this is facilitated by the requirements of the state legal system. This enables a small number of men to carve out a 'big man' status and strengthen their power base within their kokolo and beyond by obtaining and distributing logging revenue.

Women as a social group are particularly likely to be excluded from access to these negotiations and the financial benefits that flow from them. When I asked women how their kokolo made decisions about logging, a typical response was to laugh sarcastically, or to declare with either anger or

---

[91] *Clerk to Western Customary Land Appeal Court v Attorney-General* [2003] SBHC 106; HC-CC 070 of 2003 (6 June 2003).

resignation: 'Mi no save, olketa no talem mifala any samting' ('I don't know, they don't tell us anything'). It is likely that at least some women have a greater role in negotiations than these responses suggest, and women are often very vocal in discussions and debates over logging within households and church groups. However, government records such as court transcripts and logging licences support people's perceptions of the exclusion of women from the highly public decision-making fora established by the state legal system. In the logging files I reviewed, each file for Marovo Lagoon had a Form Two which listed between one and fifteen names of men as those 'lawfully able and entitled to grant timber rights'. Of the dozens of court records I reviewed, not one listed women as parties or witnesses in timber rights hearings or court appeals.[92] Some women told me that they have attempted to attend hearings and have waited on the beach for hours for this purpose, only to be told when a boat arrives that 'there is only room for men'. These processes result in an almost total absence of women's names from the official documents and agreements produced by state legal processes. This confirms and constructs women's role in decision-making as marginal, *at least within the arena of the state*, while simultaneously reinforcing the influence of a small number of people who manage decision-making for the entire landowning group.

The predominance of a small number of men leaders within state-based decision-making fora, and the almost total absence of women is often explained by reference to the idea that it is senior men, and not women, who have the socially sanctioned ability to 'talk' about land matters. Yet as we saw in Chapter 1, this view of kastom is also contested. People may explain the absence of women from state-based decision-making processes by reference to the phrase 'olketa woman no save tok' (women may not/do not/cannot talk), but many simultaneously critique this norm and current practices – and importantly, they do so by drawing attention to the concept of vuluvulu.

As we have seen, vuluvulu is multivalenced and may refer to an individual woman, a group of women or the 'blood core' of the kokolo. Many people drew my attention to the complexity of the term and described it as 'unclear'. This might be attributed to the problems of translation across languages and cultures (especially since I do not speak any of the local languages), but some people also suggested that the concept is changing, or not as well understood

---

[92] In 2009, the Magistrates Court in Gizo allowed me to review more than twenty large court files regarding logging, all of which contained transcripts and judgments arising from repeated appeals, often over many decades (the distinction between files is not always clear because of the complex interlocking disputes). I reviewed all of the Form Twos relevant to Marovo that I could retrieve from the Ministry of Forestry in both 2009 and 2011. I conducted a further extensive review of decisions on PacLII, which refer to the details in Form Twos, in 2021.

as it once was. What is 'clear', however, is that the feminine vuluvulu has not been simplified and incorporated into the arenas of church and state – or indeed into the discourses of development consultants, logging companies or environmental NGOs – whereas the masculine bangara has been. The fact that Bareke people regularly translate the role of bangara simply as 'jif' (chief) but do not do likewise for the role of vuluvulu, may not tell us anything about the historical role of these institutions. It does, however, point to a multiplicity of forms of authority with respect to land, and their uneven recognition and incorporation into state-sanctioned authority. It suggests that some segments of the bush polity have been strategically simplified and foregrounded, while others remain salient in some contexts but are obscured in the Pijin- and English-dominated arenas of government ministries, courts, logging companies and international development agencies.

The concentration of control over logging in the hands of a small number of masculine bangara and entrepreneurs, and the almost total exclusion of women as a social group, needs to be understood partly in terms of the semantic, institutional and procedural structures established by the FRTU Act. However, placing too great an emphasis on the legislative frameworks governing logging obscures long-term processes of social and economic differentiation. Missionaries and colonial officials did not necessarily intend to 'rewrite' kastom, but by repeatedly recognising and empowering some Indigenous institutions while overlooking others, they ensured that land control and political authority became concentrated in the hands of a small number of influential men. This process continues today, with logging companies and the courts treating a relatively small number of men as the most legitimate representatives of both the population and the customs that govern the land.[93]

3.7 CONCLUSION

Discussions about logging in Marovo provide a sharp reminder, if ever one were needed, that customary groups are not homogeneous, and that 'the local' is not necessarily a site of equality. Many people are angry about the extent to which control over decision-making processes and royalties have been concentrated in the hands of a small number of men, to the exclusion of other people. They argue that these practices are at odds with kastom, particularly values of ecological stewardship, collective management of land and the

---

[93] Cf Lund, *Local Politics*, 46.

concept of vuluvulu, which emphasizes both the entanglement of many people with the land *and* the authority of particular women. Such statements could be interpreted as an appeal to a romanticised vision of kastom and a more egalitarian past that never existed. However, the long-term renegotiation of land tenure and leadership, and the consolidation and erosion gendered social institutions with respect to land, suggest that references to the 'good things' of the past cannot be so easily dismissed.

As we have seen, trade, missionisation, the establishment of the colonial state and the plantation economy all served to destabilise the ways in which property, territory and authority were performed and reproduced, altering the possibilities for their rearrangement. Many of the discursive, material and corporeal connections between women and the land were undermined while particular models of masculinity, specifically the bangara, were recognised and reinforced by Christian missionaries and Protectorate officials. The role of the bangara was transformed into that of 'chief' and 'landowner', and this strengthened the authority of some men over both land and people at a time when the customary polity was being rapidly renegotiated. The reproduction of particular idealisations of masculine leadership, and the simultaneous failure of the church and state to accord any kind of recognition to the concept of vuluvulu – whether as 'blood core' or 'a senior woman' – has contributed to the production and reproduction of legal control over land and trees as a masculine domain.

Today most, if not all, people in Marovo have access to land for subsistence. However, they are differently positioned to gain endorsement of their claims to resources as property rights, and this reproduces their exclusion from decision-making as well as the financial benefits associated with logging. These inequalities – the concentration of control over logging in the hands of a small number of men, and the exclusion of many other people – cannot be understood merely as the product of a flawed legislative framework, or patriarchal customs silencing women and privileging chiefs. Rather, they emerge from long-term, reiterative processes of socio-spatial differentiation and, crucially, the strategic simplification of socio-spatial relations through processes of state recognition. Even if missionaries, colonial administrators and local bangara did not intend to 'change' customary systems, in the process of recognising some aspects of customary practice and disregarding others, they inevitably influenced and enabled particular interpretations into the future.

4

From Taovia to Trustee

Land Disputes, Insecurity and Authority in Kakabona

God made Adam and Eve, and it is a Christian principle that women should be included in decision-making regarding land. It is a *sin* not to include women! When we sin, there will be consequences...and now we've seen what those consequences are.

Mary Borgia, Mahu village, 2008

Previous chapters have shown that colonial expansion established new kinds of negotiations over land, and people competed not only to have their claims to land recognised as property, but also for recognition of their political authority to organise access to land. These processes reproduced particular idealisations of masculine authority at a time when pre-existing polities were being rapidly renegotiated. Today, land control has emerged as a pre-eminently masculine domain, with de jure if not de facto control over land strongly tied to the idea of 'chiefs'. The men who are regarded as current or future chiefs are those who predominate as claimants and witnesses in the courts, they are the people most likely to be the signatories of logging contracts and the trustees of land registered on behalf of groups, and they are also most likely to be the direct recipients of revenue flowing from resource commodification.[1] These trends may be observed across the country; however, in this chapter I demonstrate that they emerge in culturally specific and fundamentally emplaced ways. My focus here is on the historical development of Kakabona, a series of peri-urban settlements that stretch along the coastline to the immediate west of the Honiara town boundary (Maps 1.5 and Map 1.6).

---

[1] For similar observations see for example John Naitoro, 'Articulating Kin Groups and Mines: The Case of the Gold Ridge Mining Project in the Solomon Islands' (PhD thesis, Australian National University, 2002); Kabutaulaka, 'Paths in the Jungle'.

Pacific Island cities have some of the highest growth rates in the world, and Honiara is one of the most rapidly growing cities in the region. This has contributed to intense contestation over alienated land inside the town boundary, as well as the customary land that lies beyond.[2] It is well known that in the years preceding the Tension, some Guadalcanal people, generally men, were selling land to migrants from other parts of Guadalcanal and from other islands, without consulting other members of their landholding groups and in contravention of widely held understandings of kastom.[3] This is widely perceived to have contributed to the grievances underlying the Tension, but land sales appear to have continued unabated in the aftermath of the conflict. On a typically hot, sunny day, Mary Borgia, a resident of Kakabona, explained to me that she saw such practices, and the exclusion of women in particular, as a 'sin', since Guadalcanal is a matrilineal society in which land is collectively held and women are regarded as the custodians. Mary was also hopeful that these practices might be transformed; she thought that in the wake of the Tension, people realised that the consequences of such sin could be grave and extend from intimate contests among kin to wider political instability and conflict.

This chapter situates the consolidation of particular forms of masculine authority within processes of labour migration and urbanisation. It demonstrates that these processes have been mediated through long-standing models of matrilineal kinship, masculine prestige and gift exchange, and have also contributed to the active, self-conscious reassessment of these models. Thus as feminist political ecologists have often emphasised – and as Mary's arguments regarding matriliny, collectivity and sin demonstrate – contests over land are not only about material needs and access to resources, but also about regimes of cultural meaning and the vocabularies and discourses through which claims to land are constructed, recognised and denied.[4] This insight leads me to question the predominant assumptions among major development institutions that first, land disputes are largely attributable to increased

---

[2] Cf Michelle Nayahamui Rooney, '"There's Nothing Better than Land": A Migrant Group's Strategies for Accessing Informal Settlement Land in Port Moresby' in Siobhan McDonnell, Matthew Allen and Colin Filer (eds.), *Kastom, Property and Ideology* (ANU Press, 2017) 111.

[3] Tarcisius Kabutaulaka, 'Beyond Ethnicity: The Political Economy of the Guadalcanal Crisis in Solomon Islands' (No 01/1, Canberra, ACT: State, Society and Governance in Melanesia (SSGM) Program, Australian National University, 2001).

[4] Eg Fiona Mackenzie 'Gender, Land Tenure and Globalization: Exploring the Conceptual Ground' in D Tsikata and P Golah (eds.), *Land Tenure, Gender and Globalisation: Research and Analysis from Africa, Asia and Latin America* (International Development Research Centre, 2010), 47; Sharlene Mollett and Caroline Faria 'Messing with Gender in Feminist Political Ecology' (2013) 45 *Geoforum* 116

competition for access to urban land, and second, the identification and recording of boundaries and 'owners' of land can 'secure' people's rights and reduce the potential for conflict.[5] In Kakabona, we see that processes of legitimising claims to land as property – and particularly the juridical construction and regulation of property – have generated enormous uncertainty; deepened social fragmentation and stratification; and reproduced land disputes as 'dangerous' matters. These processes, which I emphasise must be understood in both material and moral terms, have underpinned the emergence of land disputes as an important arena for the performance of hegemonic models of masculine authority and consolidated land control in the hands of a relatively small number of men. Moreover, they have (re)produced state-based forums as a masculine domain and 'dangerous' for women.

4.1 'WE DON'T KNOW WHO THE MAIN FLOWER IS': URBANISATION AND INSECURITY

The first time I walked along the road that stretches through Kakabona, it was to introduce myself to people and begin seeking permission to undertake research there. Lincy Pendeverana, a fellow geographer who is from the Weather Coast, had suggested it as an appropriate place for me to explore questions of urbanisation, and while I initially understood 'Kakabona' to refer to a string of villages along the coastline, I quickly learnt that it refers to a number of places – a hamlet, a larger village and a wider area encompassing numerous villages. All of the place names discussed in this chapter operate at multiple scales and invoke a complex layering of territories, and the boundaries, ownership and leadership of each is contested. In this chapter, I use the name 'Kakabona' to refer to the customary land that stretches between White River on the town boundary and Poha River some 5 kilometres further west.

As I discuss further throughout this chapter, the existence of multiple, overlapping and interwoven territories emerges in part from histories of mobility and reorganisation of the population of Guadalcanal. The people of northwest Guadalcanal had already experienced a period of significant socio-spatial reorganisation prior to increased engagement with Europeans in the 1800s. Spanish accounts from the 1500s record numerous large villages along the

---

[5] For a paradigmatic example of immediate relevance to the case under consideration, see United Nations Secretary-General's Peacebuilding Fund *Project Document Template: Inclusive Governance of Natural Resources for Greater Social Cohesion in Solomon Islands* November 2019

coastline;[6] however, by the 1800s these populations had moved inland, possibly in response to an increase in raiding from Nggela, Savo and the western islands prompted by trading with Europeans. When the Protectorate was declared in 1893, the population was concentrated in small hamlets situated on hilltops.[7]

During the early 1900s, the population was reorganised again, as large villages developed in the vicinity of missions and plantations along the northern coastline. However, the areas surrounding Kakabona and Honiara continued to be only sparsely populated, and oral histories suggest that people in this area were highly mobile and concentrated in small hamlets in the bush.[8] This changed when, in the aftermath of World War II, the capitals of the Protectorate and the Western Pacific High Commission were relocated to Honiara, and housing and infrastructure along the coastal strip rapidly expanded. Today, the area between White River and Poha River has an estimated population of 2,500 people and houses jostle for space in the narrow strip of flat land that lies between the ocean and the steep hills behind the villages.[9] On the eastern side, close to the Honiara town boundary, numerous land parcels have been registered under the Land and Titles Act,[10] with titles bearing the names of trustees who represent a named landowning group (or groups). Land further west is generally unregistered, and widely understood to be divided into large blocks associated with different matrilineages.

The majority of people living in Kakabona belong to these matrilineages, which have oral histories linking them to a variety of places in the vicinity of Honiara. Many other residents of Kakabona have lineage narratives that

---

6   Lord Amherst and Basil Thomson, *The Discovery of the Solomon Islands by Alvaro de Mendaña in 1568: Translated from the Original Spanish Manuscripts* (Hakluyt Society, 1st ed, 1901).

7   For further discussion see e.g. David Roe, 'Prehistory without Pots: Prehistoric Settlement and Economy of North-West Guadalcanal, Solomon Islands' (PhD thesis, Australian National University, 1993), 17–18; Murray Bathgate, 'From Precontact to Contemporary Times: The Ndi-Nggai, West Guadalcanal, Solomon Islands', in Murray Chapman and R Mansell Prothero (eds.), *Circulation in Population Movement: Substance and Concepts from the Melanesian Case* (Routledge & Kegan Paul, 1985), 2; Lasaqa, 'Melanesians' Choice', 100.

8   Paravicini observed a village of eighty houses as a place he called 'Kakabona': Eugen Paravicini, *Reisen in Den Britischen Salomonen* (Huber and Company, 1931), 23. However, Bathgate refers to just one family living at Vatukola around the turn of the century, and this accords with the accounts provided to me: Murray A Bathgate, *Fight for the Dollar: Economic and Social Change in Western Guadalcanal, Solomon Islands* (Alexander Enterprise, 1993), 797.

9   Fred Siho Patison and Steve Ereinao, *Mamara New Capital City Development Phase 1 Environment Impact Statement (EIS): Chapter 11: Social and Cultural Assessment Report* (Metropolis Pacific and Telios Corporate and Consultancy Services, 2020).

10 Land and Titles Act 1996 [Cap 133].

connect them to other places on Guadalcanal, notably the areas around Tangarare and Visale. There are smaller but still substantial numbers of people who identify with other places throughout Solomon Islands, many of whom have settled in Kakabona after marrying someone from a local lineage, and others who have accessed land through other relationships, such as employment in local schools or Catholic church at Tanaghai.

Residents of Kakabona generally rely on a combination of subsistence gardening, income from tourism operations along the local beaches and enterprises such as floriculture and trade stores. Some people have employment in Honiara, and others have small plantations (cocoa and copra) nearby. As is common in urbanising Melanesia, many people experience a sense of insecurity and precarity, and this may be understood partly in material terms: many residents comment on their limited access to affordable land, poor infrastructure, low incomes and high costs of living. I suggest, however, that material scarcity provides only a partial explanation for this sense of insecurity and precarity, which also needs to be understood in terms of the culturally particular meanings attached to land, and to struggles over land.

Soon after my initial visit to Kakabona, I met with a senior man who is widely regarded as a local expert on land matters. This man, who I call James here, belongs to a relatively small network of male leaders whose names consistently appear as trustees for numerous parcels of land in the vicinity of Honiara and who frequently appear in the courts on behalf of recognised landholding groups. Despite James' knowledge of land matters, and his well-established capacity to successfully persuade panels of chiefs and courts of the truth and certainty of his claims, he emphasised the 'confusion' surrounding land tenure in Kakabona:

> This is how ownership should be: imagine a bunch of bananas. The main flower is the main owner. Then we have many other tribes in the bunch, surrounding the main flower. However we don't have that here – we don't know who the main flower is. To be an owner, they must prove which is the big, strong banana...then they have next rights. The banana at the bottom is small and loses rights.

James drew on the metaphor of a bunch of bananas to explain common understandings of social organisation, which hold that a group with a common ancestor may grow into separate branches.[11] According to James, at least some of the lineages jostling to be recognised as landowners in Kakabona

---

[11] Bainton reports a similar use of the metaphor for Lihir in Papua New Guinea: Nicholas Bainton, *Lihir Destiny: Cultural Responses to Mining in Melanesia* (ANU Press, 2010), 74.

share a common ancestry, and have divided into separate branches which – if people understood their histories in more detail – would be clearly organised within a hierarchy of land rights. In the most general terms, Guadalcanal is understood to be a matrilineal society divided into exogamous moieties, with people accessing land through named matrilineages that vary across the island. Kakabona and other areas around Honiara are broadly understood to comprise large territories associated with named groups including Haubata, Kakau, Kidipale, Simbo and Lakuili.[12] These groups are often referred to in Pijin as traebs, with further subdivisions of subtraebs or laens (tribes, subtribes, lines). In our conversations people less commonly referred to them in the local language, Ghari, as duli, vuvungu and tina (typically translated as tribes, subtribes and family). The names of subtraebs reflect their belonging to a large group – for example, land in the Kongulai catchment, which provides most of Honiara's water supply, is registered in the names of two recognised subtribes of Haubata, namely Haubata Taonavua and Haubata Ganiqoana.[13]

James' use of the metaphor of the bunch of bananas emphasised that in the context of the rapid relocation of the population to coastal areas in the aftermath of World War II, significant debates have arisen regarding the boundaries of local lineages, their relationship with each other and their associated territories. Disputes over urbanised customary land frequently turn on which ancestor or 'big flower' occupied Kakabona first, how different lineages or 'bananas' are linked to those ancestors (whether through cognatic descent, affinal links or gift exchange) and the extent of their territories. These matters are intensely socially fragmenting and generate enormous anxiety, and to some extent this can be understood by reference to the well-known effects of the juridical construction and regulation of liberal property. As Nicholas Blomley and other progressive property scholars have shown for a variety of contexts, the legal construction and regulation of liberal property entails constructing, 'cutting' and disentangling discrete, bounded parcels of land, and similarly discrete, bounded 'landowners', from multiple, fluid and always-unfolding socio-spatial relationships.[14] We see these processes quite clearly in land disputes concerning Kakabona; however, I suggest that the sense of

---

[12] Haubata is often spelled Ghaubata and Gaubata, Simbo may be Thimbo.

[13] Land in the Kongulai catchment, Perpetual Estate No 191-06-1, is registered in the names of these two groups that are generally said to be 'tribes' or 'subtribes' of Haubata.

[14] E.g. Nicholas Blomley, 'Cuts, Flows, and the Geographies of Property' (2010) 7(2) *Law, Culture and the Humanities* 203; Davina Cooper 'Opening Up Ownership: Community Belonging, Belongings, and the Productive Life of Property' (2007) 32(3) *Law & Social Inquiry* 625; Alain Pottage, 'The Measure of Land' (1994) 57(3) *Modern Law Review* 361; Strathern, 'Cutting the Network'.

insecurity they generate and importantly, the gender implications that flow from this can only be properly understood by reference to long-standing vocabularies and discourses through which claims to identity, land and belonging are constructed, reorganised, legitimated and denied.

4.2 KAKABONA BEFORE WORLD WAR II: RENEGOTIATING PLACE, PRESTIGE AND GIFT EXCHANGE

Claims to land are claims to belonging, to both people and place. When the people who belong to Kakabona's lineages explain their claims to land, they typically draw on highly complex and emplaced genealogical histories that connect them to a variety of people, groups and places. These histories are sometimes referred to as tutungu, and they recount, often in great detail, the ways in which people moved through the landscape; specific interactions between named people, spirits, birds and other creatures at named sites; the details of intermarriage and gift exchange between groups; and sometimes, the emergence of a new group from a larger one and their relocation to a new place. These histories are linked to specific sites, some of which are clearly established by humans, such as hamlets, ancestral shrines or gardens, while others may be hills or pools in a river where significant events such as encounters with spirits are known to have occurred. The names of these sites do not simply identify a place or people: as Tarcisius Kabutaulaka has emphasised, names tell stories, and they are mnemonics for historical movement, significant actions and events and the relationships between people and places.[15] Moreover these stories are not simply etched across landscapes but informed by them, with Guadalcanal known for its active landscapes; steep, unstable slopes; and rivers prone to flash flooding.[16]

Existing scholarship suggests that when contact between locals and Europeans intensified in the 1800s, people typically lived in small hamlets pursuing swidden agriculture and arboriculture, with the landscape comprising an integrated network of places associated with different groups. Residential groups appear to have been highly mobile, moving through well-defined paths in the landscape as part of a regular pattern of migration associated with swidden agriculture and their attachments to land. When

---

[15] Tarcisius Kabutaulaka has said, with respect to debates regarding place names in Honiara, 'names are not just identities of places or people, names also tell stories': Evan Wasuka, 'Push for Return to Indigenous Names for Honiara Streets and Landmarks', *Pacific Beat* (ABC Radio Australia, 6 August 2020). Cf Bainton, *Lihir Destiny*, 78.
[16] Roe, 'Prehistory without Pots', 11–38.

people moved into a new area, important trees and gardens would be established in allotments associated with a smaller family unit (often referred to as tina by residents of Kakabona), while the mature bush surrounding hamlets and gardens would be associated with the larger group (the vuvungu or subtraeb). According to Murray Bathgate, who worked on plantations to the west of Kakabona during the 1970s, hamlets, gardens and altars constituted the centre of activity in a territory, while the outer areas were left uncultivated, partly because neighbouring groups could be hostile towards each other.[17] This suggests that on north-west Guadalcanal as in Marovo, space was known and turned into place through paths and focal points of human and non-human activity, rather than the demarcation and communication of outer boundaries.

Residence within these landscapes was generally patrilocal, with men typically living in their father's district until early adulthood, marriage or the death of their father, at which time they would often return to their mother's district (that is, their own matrilineage) and establish themselves with the support of their maternal uncle. Guadalcanal people sometimes explain patrilocal residential groups as comprising a more stable lineage and another in-marrying lineage (or several). This gendered geography was subtle and fluid, as matrilineages were more 'grounded' in some places and more mobile in others; shifting cultivation fostered mobility and the ebb and flow of focal points in the landscape; neighbouring hamlets were densely interwoven by birth and marriage; and people often lived in close proximity to their own matrilineage, even if they lived in the hamlet of their spouse. Different groups were also woven together by a degree of complementarity, exchange and interdependence, exemplified by what appears to have been a system of dual shrines on north-west Guadalcanal. Archaeologist David Roe has suggested that these shrines may have been 'paired', with lineages prohibited from entering their own shrines, and men from one lineage and moiety performing rituals at the shrine belonging to men from another lineage and moiety and vice versa.[18]

From the 1900s onwards, these flexible and integrated relationships between people and the places they depended upon were destabilised and reorganised, with three processes especially salient for understanding contemporary debates regarding land in Kakabona. First, the establishment of large

[17] M. Bathgate, *Fight for the Dollar*; M.A. Bathgate, *Matriliny and Coconut Palms: The Control and Inheritance of a Major Capital Resource among the Ndi-Nggai Speakers of Western Guadalcanal in the Solomon Islands* (Alexander Enterprise, 1993), see also Ian Hogbin, *A Guadalcanal Society: The Kaoka Speakers* (Holt, Rinehart and Winston, 1964); Roe, 'Prehistory without Pots', 147.

[18] Roe, 'Prehistory without Pots', 33.

coconut plantations and missions, and the requirement to pay the head tax, drove a major reorganisation of socio-spatial relations. Second, as discussed in previous chapters, avenues to masculine prestige were reconfigured, with missionisation, the expansion of plantation agriculture and legalisation of land tenure facilitating the extension of particular forms of masculine authority. Third, gift exchange acquired new valences in the context of increased migration and the commoditisation of land. In many senses these transformations were similar to those underway in other parts of Guadalcanal and across the Protectorate more broadly; however, they were also profoundly emplaced, with inflections specific to the communities in which they arose.

4.2.1 *Religious Unity, Legal Pluralities and Socio-spatial Reorganisation*

The people of north-west Guadalcanal engaged with European traders and missionaries as early as the 1830s; however, this engagement was initially sporadic because the coastal areas were frequented by raiding parties from other islands and the majority of the population lived in the bush, in areas that were inaccessible to raiding parties and certainly to Europeans.[19] By the turn of the century, British suppression of Indigenous warfare had made the coastlines relatively safe, and expatriate planters, the Melanesian Mission (Church of England) and Marist Brothers (Roman Catholic) quickly established plantations and stations in accessible coastal sites, typically on land that they acquired directly from men they perceived to have the authority to sell it.[20]

By 1910, both the Melanesian Mission and the Marists had established a significant presence on Guadalcanal, particularly on the far north-west coast, and the struggle that followed has been described by historian Hugh Laracy as 'an unabashed contest for the possession of souls'.[21] This process destabilised relationships within and between groups, not least because missionaries actively discouraged the feasts that were central to the reciprocal exchange between groups and the prestige of men, perceiving them to be a waste of resources. It also shifted relationships between people and the places they depended upon. At Visale, for example, there was a fairly rapid decline in the

---

[19] M.A. Bathgate, *Matriliny and Coconut Palms*, 7.

[20] A 'head man', Bili, appears to have been influential in the purchase of land at Tangarare, while Kokobi, an 'old chief' and 'high priest' influenced the establishment of the station at Visale: Bathgate, *Fight for the Dollar*; Claire O'Brien, *A Greater than Solomon Here: A Story of Catholic Church in Solomon Islands 1567–1967* (Catholic Church Solomon Islands, 1995), 123.

[21] Hugh Laracy, *Marists and Melanesians: A History of Catholic Missions in the Solomon Islands* (ANU Press, 1976), 44.

feasts honouring the spirit who inhabited the peak behind the mission station. The last feast was held in 1905, and in 1910, the peak collapsed, portentously at Easter. By the end of that year, the Marists had not only built the first large stone church in the Protectorate, but also marked its opening by hosting an extraordinary feast for over a thousand people.[22]

These events altered the trajectory of missionisation on north-west Guadalcanal and swung the struggle firmly in favour of the Marists. Viewed from the twenty-first century, this seems relatively unsurprising, given the impressive display of territorial and ritual power by the Marists. Indeed, it is easy to perceive the land and the spirits inhabiting it as channelling the people in some directions rather than others. By the 1920s, most of the population along the north-west coast identified with Catholicism. Church affiliations along the north-west coast have become slightly more diverse since the 1990s;[23] however, the majority of residents of Kakabona and all of the churches are Roman Catholic.

This widespread identification with Catholicism has been central to the emergence of particular patterns of legal plurality. Christian idioms are clearly relevant to understandings of land in Kakabona: Mary, cited at the outset of this chapter, expressly grounded her critique of gendered exclusion in the language of sin. However, in stark contrast to records of land claims in Marovo and other parts of the western islands (see Chapters 2 and 3), Christian idioms were not a prominent feature of the argumentative patterns I observed in court records for north-west Guadalcanal. I suggest that this is precisely because church membership has not provided a focus for territorialising projects or a salient marker of social difference among local lineages.

The cessation of raiding, the establishment of Catholic authority and the expansion of plantations along the north-west coast led to a significant reorganisation of space and social life as people moved from relatively small, mobile hamlets in the interior into larger, and more stable, villages on the coast. These were very new kinds of communities, and social networks expanded, contracted and shifted in multiple ways. People now gathered in coastal settlements comprising many different groups, and groups that had not historically engaged with each other or intermarried began to do so. At the same time, groups that had historically coexisted may have been able to

---

[22] Laracy, *Marists and Melanesians*, 45, 55, 83.

[23] The 2009 National Census records that Guadalcanal had the highest proportion of the population identifying with the Roman Catholic Church (38%) followed by the Anglican Church of Melanesia (24%). A recent assessment of Kakabona and inland areas found that approximately 50% of the population is Roman Catholic, and 30% is South Seas Evangelical Church: Patison and Ereinao, *Mamara New Capital City Development*.

disentangle themselves from each other as the new religion displaced the performance of rituals at 'paired', complementary shrines. New constraints on intermarriage also arose, as Marists emphasised monogamy and prohibited polygamy, discouraged cross-cousin marriage and banned Catholics from marrying Protestants – an enforcement of heteropatriarchal relationships that maintained Catholic land control and the relatively homogeneous denominational geography.[24]

Land use in coastal areas intensified and stabilised during this period. Villages became larger and more permanent, and the concept of a 'spear line' – a Pijin term for territorial boundary – emerged. According to Bathgate the term emerged as local lineages sought to prevent other Indigenous groups from encroaching on their traditional territories.[25] I suspect that more significant threats came from the expanding missions and plantations, and the European allegations of 'trespass' against locals who entered plantations seeking resources essential for their livelihoods. The term 'spear line', which is strikingly suggestive of warfare and the need to defend the land and its people against encroachment, probably also emerged in response to the preoccupation of colonial officials with the identification of outer boundaries. The close association between the establishment of these outer boundaries and colonial officials is perhaps exemplified by the fact that it was the nickname of Alexander Herbert 'Spearline' Wilson, who was initially a government surveyor in 1919 before rising to hold many of the most influential natural resource portfolios.

4.2.2 *Renegotiation of Paths to Prestige*

Existing scholarship tells us very little about the forms of authority or influence women may have held prior to colonial expansion on Guadalcanal, or the ways in which these forms may have been reconfigured during the early colonial period. When Guadalcanal women are mentioned in existing accounts, it is often as background rather than as key actors in a larger narrative.[26] Furthermore, whereas people in Marovo were quick to draw my attention to vuluvulu, residents of Kakabona were less explicit about the impacts of colonisation on gender relations. Women are, however, very prominent in the oral histories discussed throughout this chapter: they

---

[24] Bathgate, *Fight for the Dollar*; Bathgate, *Matriliny and Coconut Palms*.
[25] Bathgate, Fight for the Dollar, 761.
[26] DeLisle makes similar observations regarding the place of CHamoru women in existing histories and historiographies: DeLisle, *Placental Politics*, 1–2

frequently appear not only as named participants, but as key agentive ancestors in the gift exchanges that are now cited as the basis for contemporary land relations. People in Kakabona also sometimes refer to the daki taovia, 'a kind of big woman'. This title is also mentioned by Tarcisius Kabutaulaka for the Weather Coast[27] and Siona Koti for central Guadalcanal, and Koti concludes that it was held by 'the female chief of the reigning lineage' as well as 'the wife of a chief'.[28] Such women were often senior within their families, and they are remembered for their leadership in organising other people, as well as their skill in cultivating the gardens and pigs that were essential for the reciprocal feasts associated with status-earning activities and important events such as marriage or death. As we shall see in Section 4.2.3, these forms of influence remain highly visible during contemporary gift exchanges, and are exercised by women who are routinely referred to as 'big women' and 'leaders'.

Guadalcanal's precolonial polities have typically been discussed in existing scholarship in terms of three idealised models of masculinity: the taovia, often referred to in Pijin as jif (chief), malaghai (warrior) and vele (sorcerer). The malaghai typically appear in oral histories as younger men, who proved themselves by protecting their lineage as well as other people, and accumulating traditional valuables in return, before acquiring a reputation as a taovia. The prestige of the taovia appears to have been associated with older men, who were known for their ability to stabilise the multiple groups living on the land; their skill in managing social disruption associated with warfare or sorcery; and their ability to build prestige by mobilising and distributing wealth such as pigs and shell money. A taovia was never assured of their position – they were constantly required to compete with others, and as they became more successful they might marry more women, who could collectively maintain larger gardens and more pigs. The most influential taovia were those who could not only mobilise the food, shell valuables and pigs of their own household or village, but more expansive social networks. Larger villages were often associated with more influential taovia, as they could command widespread support, manage larger areas of land and often allowed people from elsewhere to settle on land in exchange for labour and valuables such as pigs and shell money.[29]

---

[27] Tarcisius Kabutaulaka, *Footprints in the Tasimauri Sea: A Biography of Dominiko Alebua* (Institute of Pacific Studies, University of the South Pacific, 2001), 64.

[28] Koti, 'A Historical Analysis on Gender Inequality in Solomon Islands', 26, citing pers. comm. with S. Rodie.

[29] HI Hogbin, 'Social Advancement in Guadalcanal, Solomon Islands' (1938) 8(3) *Oceania*, 290, 303ff; Bathgate, *Fight for the Dollar*, 34, 78, 184; Bathgate, *Matriliny and Coconut Palms*, 17; Lasaqa, 'Melanesians' Choice', 124ff.

The taovia seems to conform to images of 'big men' elsewhere in Melanesia, and as Ian Hogbin put it in the 1930s, their reputations were 'enhanced not by accumulating wealth in order to use it for one's self, but by giving it away'.[30] Oral histories are also clear that these idealised models of 'men of war' representing an aggressive model of masculinity associated with conflict, and 'men of peace' associated with cohesion, were not distinct institutions.[31] The generative and destructive forces of masculine power could coalesce, with the physical violence of the malaghai, the mysticism of the vele and the cohesive influence of the taovia finding expression not only in a single person but also a single act, such as instances of interpersonal and metaphysical violence that severed some relations while restoring others.[32]

As we have seen in previous chapters, these historically produced, idealised models of masculinity were destabilised during the nineteenth and twentieth centuries. On north-west Guadalcanal, the ability of men to demonstrate efficacy became constrained by the decline in polygyny and feasting, the cessation of Indigenous warfare and the rise of a new source of spiritual power, but new opportunities to exert influence were simultaneously opening up. The men who had the language skills (either plantation Pijin or English) necessary to communicate with foreigners were the first to engage in trade with Europeans, and were also those likely to be appointed district headmen in the government administration, and catechists in the Roman Catholic churches. It is also clear from the historical record that men who spoke Pijin or English – often acquired while labouring in Queensland – were among the first to sell land.[33]

None of this is to suggest that recognition from foreigners was all that was required to be accepted among locals as a 'big man'. As Isireli Lasaqa has demonstrated, many (but not all) of the men who rose to prominence during this period were known for their mastery of historical knowledge and magic,

---

[30] Hogbin, 'Social Advancement', 290. See also Lasaqa, 'Melanesians' Choice', 125.

[31] For discussion of these models within Melanesian anthropology see Michael W. Scott, 'Ignorance Is Cosmos; Knowledge Is Chaos: Articulating a Cosmological Polarity in the Solomon Islands' (2000) 44(2) *Social Analysis* 56.

[32] Some of the oral histories mobilised in land claims in Kakabona refer to one named man who is described in testimonies as 'a leader' immediately prior to colonisation. He is said to have killed an influential man associated with another group, before killing his own sister in order to atone for the death of his competitor and make peace between the lineages.

[33] For example in the 1970s a dispute arose with respect to land that had been sold, apparently by men from elsewhere, who had returned from Queensland and were therefore able to speak to Europeans when the local people could not: SINA: BSIP LAN 2/1/106: Letter to the District Commissioner from Ellison Hanivoti of Verahue Village, 21 August 1971

and their ability to sustain, protect and lead people.[34] European recognition was, however, central to the sedimentation of particular idealisations of masculine authority. Expatriate planters, foreign missionaries and colonial administrators repeatedly intervened in ways that shifted public authority over both land and people in favour of a relatively small number of men, namely those they perceived to be 'chiefs'. Furthermore, whereas the reputation of the taovia had historically been enhanced not by accumulating wealth, but by distributing it through competitive feasting, it was now often retained by individuals, particularly where cash was concerned.[35] As I explain further in the sections that follow, this not only enabled the accumulation of wealth, but left land transactions open to future debate.

4.2.3 *Gift Exchange and Migration in a Commodity Economy*

By the 1940s, numerous expatriate-run plantations – held by Burns Philp, Levers and a number of smaller enterprises – had been established along the north coast of Guadalcanal. A number of trading stations, missions and mission schools were also operating.[36] Growing numbers of people from across the island and the Protectorate were drawn into these projects, and while many returned home at the end of their employment contracts or training, some stayed and were incorporated into local villages. Often this occurred through adoption or marriage into a local group, thus access or attachment to land, and attachment to a local lineage, were mutually constitutive.[37] Gift exchange – which is often referred to as chupu in Pijin – was a salient feature of all of these arrangements, and is central to understanding the reconfiguration of understandings of landholding, community and belonging underway at this time.

Chupu is often translated as 'pile' or 'heap', referring to the piles of cooked food, garden produce, live pigs, betel nut (areca nut) and shell money that form the basis of gift exchange between groups. In this chapter I use the term as it is often used in Pijin, to refer to both the pile and to a diverse range of exchanges that have different names, purposes and implications. These exchanges may be grand occasions that reconcile differences between Members of Parliament, enthrone chiefs or commence major government

---

[34] Lasaqa, 'Melanesians' Choice', 125–132.

[35] Hogbin, 'Culture Change', 252.

[36] For detailed accounts see Bennett, *Wealth of the Solomons*; Lasaqa, 'Melanesians' Choice'.

[37] See e.g. *In re Estate of Kona*, concerning the estate of a man from West Kwara'ae, Malaita, who came to Guadalcanal prior to 1950, and was adopted and given a piece of land at Vilu: *In re Estate of Kona* [1998] SBHC 84; HCSI-CC 331 of 1995 (15 May 1998).

projects; they may also be relatively intimate, such as those that enable the sharing of knowledge regarding land among a small number of people.[38] In the context of landholding arrangements, a chupu may, as one chief told me, symbolise 'the land moving from the original person to another woman or man',[39] such as when a lineage that has no further descendants wishes to transfer custodianship to another group.[40] A chupu is often provided by children to their father's matrilineage, in order to enable them to continue using the trees and gardens he cultivated while simultaneously acknowledging the authority of his matrilineage on the land. These exchanges may occur at various times – before a death, or many years later – especially if people perceive their claim to be weakened or threatened in some way, and in need of affirmation.[41]

When people from Guadalcanal describe the ideal role of chupu in the context of migration, they typically sketch a process in which migrants request permission from chiefs; those men make the migrants' request known among the lineage who then discuss it; and the chiefs then report a decision back to the people wishing to settle. Many people emphasise that if permission is granted, migrants should not only provide a large pile of goods, but the landholding group should provide a smaller pile in return.[42] While cash may form part of these exchanges, a 'proper' chupu is said to require goods of ritual significance, such as pigs, shell money and betel nut. These norms are not always observed, and as we shall see, the absence or presence of these goods may become crucial to the interpretation of a chupu and the credibility of claims to land associated with it.

The chupu that I have observed have been held for various purposes. Goods are arranged in a prominent place in the village, people gather and senior men give speeches explaining the purpose of the chupu and the relationship between the parties. In the case of land, these speeches will recount aspects

---

[38] Gordon L. Nanau, *Oceanic Diplomacy: Popo and Supu Diplomacy in the Modern State of Solomon Islands* (No 2021/28, ANU, November 2021).

[39] See also Franklin Takutile, 'Mortuary Feast at Vatupilei' in P Larmour (ed.), *Land Tenure in Solomon Islands* (1979), 23–27; Commission of Inquiry Into Land Dealings and Abandoned Properties on Guadalcanal, *Consultation on Customary Land Issues in the Giana Region* per Xavier Betu, per Hilda Kii; Nanau, 'Theory of Insecure Globalisation', 147.

[40] This situation is frequently referred to in the transcripts of hearings before chiefs and courts, and in 2009 I attended one such chupu.

[41] Commission of Inquiry Into Land Dealings and Abandoned Properties on Guadalcanal, *Consultation on Customary Land Issues in the Giana Region* per Francis Repeka, per Hilda Kii. See also Bathgate, *Matriliny and Coconut Palms*, 17.

[42] Commission of Inquiry Into Land Dealings and Abandoned Properties on Guadalcanal, *Consultation on Customary Land Issues in the Giana Region* per Xavier Betu, per Hilda Kii.

of the history of the land, the lineages involved and the reciprocal obligations of different people.[43] People arrange the pigs, food and shell money into attractive piles, often under the direction of senior women; in some exchanges I have seen women standing in prominent places and dramatically holding the shell money as it passes from one group to another. On at least one occasion I have observed a knowledgeable woman quietly intervening to discuss and correct the details of speeches given by a male relative. A chupu usually closes with a prayer given by a church leader (usually a man), people shake hands and women then carefully divide, parcel and distribute the items in the chupu among the different social groups involved, sometimes through the creation of smaller piles labelled with names. The women who are most prominent in these processes are those frequently referred to as 'big women' and 'leaders', and they demonstrate characteristics similar to their men counterparts – they have exceptional knowledge of lineage histories, they are charismatic and able to represent the group and they have a capacity to mobilise people and resources. In many instances they are the eldest sister within a family, and some have a relatively high degree of formal education and/or employment in the cash economy.

Chupu practices are critical 'performances of property': they establish, make visible and affirm specific relations between people with respect to the land. A 'proper' chupu is also anything but an individual or private affair. It requires the collaboration of numerous people to gather and prepare pigs, shell money and other goods; share knowledge of ritual and lineage histories; and divide, allocate and consume the items exchanged. These material, corporeal processes all entail the articulation and affirmation of specific relationships between people and places. In particular, they make visible the privileged position of some people with respect to the land – that is, the group that is now commonly referred to as the 'landowners' – while enabling 'other' kinds of people to 'come into' the land to settle, build houses and cultivate gardens for the purpose of subsistence.

These exchanges are not generally understood to be a permanent 'transfer' of all entitlements, particularly when the landholders are still in existence. Rather, they are an assertion of the capacity to include, and to welcome people into the land, with incomers obliged to observe the claims of that privileged group. A migrant might be perceived to be breaching these norms if

---

[43] Debra McDougall provides detailed accounts of similar exchanges on Ranongga: McDougall, *Engaging with Strangers.*

they initiate a project that indicates an intention to permanently claim the land, for example by planting crops with a long lifespan, or if they purport to exercise the 'capacity to include' by permitting others to use the land. This authority to *include* remains with the earlier group on the land, even with respect to the descendants of incomers – according to widespread understandings of kastom, exchanges should be repeated by each generation of those who wish to stay on the land (hence the provision of chupu by the descendants of men who live with their wife's matrilineage).[44]

A chupu therefore makes socio-spatial distinctions visible, while also affirming mutual obligation, entanglement and inter-connectedness. As Debra McDougall explains for the comparable practice of pajuku on Ranongga, these exchanges involve an oscillation between the poles of estrangement or distinction on the one hand, and kinship on the other.[45] In this sense, the practice of chupu conforms to the image of gift exchange elsewhere in the Pacific, and may be distinguished from commodity exchange. A chupu provides for inclusion of 'other' people on the land and affirms the authority of the 'landowners', whereas commodity exchange is often associated with the right to exclude, and entails the transfer of an alienable commodity from one discrete person or group to another, a process that (ideally) severs the original owners' claims.[46] These distinctions are not complete but exist on a continuum, and as McDougall observes, gift exchanges have certainly been amenable to 'reworking traditional land tenure into more capitalist models'.[47] George Curry and Gina Koczberski have similarly noted that the boundary between gifts and commodities is not always clear to participants in exchanges in Papua New Guinea, with migrants interpreting them as an outright 'purchase', and landholders refuting this.[48] These dynamics are also prominent in struggles over land in Kakabona – the

---

[44] See also McDougall's discussion of the practice of *pajuku* on Ranongga: McDougall, 'The Unintended Consequences of Clarification', 88

[45] McDougall, *Engaging with Strangers*, 155–156.

[46] E.g. James G Carrier, 'The Gift in Theory and Practice in Melanesia: A Note on the Centrality of Gift Exchange' (1992) 31(2) *Ethnology* 185; Michael Goddard, 'Of Cabbages and Kin: The Value of an Analytic Distinction between Gifts and Commodities' (2016) 20(2) *Critique of Anthropology* 137; Margaret Jolly, 'Gifts, Commodities and Corporeality: Food and Gender in South Pentecost, Vanuatu' (1991) 14(1) *Canberra Anthropology* 45.

[47] McDougall, 'The Unintended Consequences of Clarification', 88.

[48] George N Curry and Gina Koczberski, 'Finding Common Ground: Relational Concepts of Land Tenure and Economy in the Oil Palm Frontier of Papua New Guinea' (2009) 175(2) *Geographical Journal* 98, 103, see also Gina Koczberski, George N Curry and Jesse Anjen 'Changing Land Tenure and Informal Markets in the Oil Palm Frontier of Papua New Guinea: The Challenge for Land Reform' (2012) 43(2) *Australian Geographer* 181.

practice of chupu has provided a vital mechanism by which migrants to Honiara may settle on land, but it has also become an increasingly contested subject.

4.3 WORLD WAR II AND THE DEVELOPMENT OF HONIARA

World War II transformed the geography of Guadalcanal in profound and enduring ways, laying the foundations for increased migration and rapid urban-isation of the north coast. The 1942 Battle of Guadalcanal was concentrated on the central and western parts of the north coast, and once the battle moved north, large numbers of foreign troops and a smaller number of local men flowed into Honiara and surrounding areas. Those areas then became a major transfer and supply base, and the Tandai Highway – the first well-established road along the north-west coast – was developed.[49] Once the war was over, the British sought to utilise this infrastructure and transferred the capital of both the Protectorate and the Western Pacific High Commission to Honiara.

The development of the new capital was associated with an increase in British aid, the establishment of further infrastructure and growing opportun-ities for education and employment. Honiara quickly became a hub for rural-urban migration, particularly by men: the town grew rapidly from approxi-mately 3,000 people in 1959, 76 per cent of whom were men, to almost 12,000 in 1970, 60 per cent of whom were men.[50] This suggests that women initially remained outside the geographical focus of the modern state, although it is also possible that the census focused on adult men and other people were under-counted.[51]

Urban development inevitably spilled out into areas outside the town boundary, such as Kakabona, and migrants from other islands and countries (the records highlight China and Fiji) increasingly sought to establish homes and businesses on customary land. Growing numbers of people from local lineages also moved down from the hills to coastal areas, where they could

---

[49] I owe much of my understanding of World War II to the late Bruno Nana, who was a local scout during the war, as well as his daughter Paula Aruhuri, who transcribed his wartime stories into a booklet. See also Bennett, *Natives and Exotics*; Kwai, *Solomon Islanders in World War II*.

[50] Bellam, 'The Colonial City'; Clive Moore, 'Honiara: Arrival City and Pacific Hybrid Living Space' (2015) 50(4) *Journal of Pacific History* 419; Nigel Oram, 'Land, Housing and Administration in Honiara: Towards a Concerted Policy' (1980) 1 *O'o: A Journal of Solomon Island Studies* 133.

[51] See discussion in Solomon Islands National Statistics Office, *Report on the 2009 Population and Housing Census – National Report (Volume 2)* Solomon Islands Government (2009), Appendix 1.

now utilise the highway to transport garden produce into the growing township. People from other parts of north-west Guadalcanal, such as Visale, Tangarare and the Weather Coast, arrived in Kakabona through the extensive kin and church-based networks that connect people across the island. People who had worked elsewhere, including a small but growing number of women, returned home to Guadalcanal with spouses from other islands, often from Catholic communities on nearby Malaita.

As rural-urban migration intensified and marriage networks widened, so too did the potential networks of people who could claim access to land held by local matrilineages. Claims to land and kinship were no longer confined to a close-knit network of cognatically and affinally linked groups, and whereas patrilocal residence had historically been predominant, residence patterns diversified as access to employment, education and transport became a critical factor in people's choice of where to live. The occupation and use of land in Kakabona was the subject of heated debate by the 1970s, with numerous disputes coming before the chiefs and courts, and residents writing letters of concern to government officials. One expatriate, Mrs IV Phillips of Ngautu Village, wrote to Protectorate officials warning them that 'the areas from Mataniko village to Kakabona, Poha, Vura, Tabkoko and Vatusi village areas are the most touchy...as far as land is concerned'.[52] Tensions arose within communities as the relatives of migrants who had married into local groups also sought to settle on land; there were disputes over the sale of land for a government housing scheme; and a number of Malaitan and Chinese settlers were chased out of the area after purchasing land.

Government records such as land titles and correspondence between administrators indicate that it was often senior men who were in the foreground of these land transactions and associated disputes, just as they had been in earlier arrangements with foreign traders, missionaries and planters. The names on government records are consistently those of men, such as Charlie Chilivi, the government-appointed headman for Visale District.[53] However, oral histories and the voluminous transcripts of court hearings often portray a more complex picture, and it is clear that at least some women

[52] SINA: BSIP LAND 1/1/1 Vol 1, 2: Land Legislation: Letter from Mrs I V Phillips, Ngautu Village c/o Guadalcanal Council, Honiara, 2 November 1974. See also G John B Muria, 'Guadalcanal' in Ian C Heath (ed.), *Land Research in Solomon Islands* (Land Research Project, Lands Division, Ministry of Agriculture and Lands, 1979), 41–46.

[53] SINA: BSIP LAN/2/167: Namoborunga (Kongulai); SINA: BSIP LAND 2/1/86: Land lease – Kakabona – Vatukola Cooperative Society; SINA: BSIP LAN 2/1/92: Kovuara, Kakabona; SINA: BSIP 7/III/F29/11 Vol II: Commission of Lands 1949–1954. Note Charlie Chilivi is also referred to as Charlie Tsilivi in the records.

played a significant role in managing land relations. For example, testimonies in land disputes concerning Kakabona contain numerous references to a named woman from a local lineage who is said to have frequently encouraged young men to chase migrants out of the area, and she is also remembered for uprooting gardens or trees planted without her permission.

It is also clear from court transcripts in particular that many aspects of chupu were becoming more contested during this period, and the practice modified into more capitalist forms in the context of urbanisation. As had historically been the case, migrants to Honiara continued to approach senior men for permission to settle on customary land, and when these men provided permission, they sometimes did so in return for cash, without consulting other members of their lineages, and without distributing the proceeds of transactions. The use of cash – which could easily exchange hands behind closed doors – enabled a degree of secrecy and individuation that had not previously been possible with the exchange by multiple groups of large, highly visible piles of pigs, shell valuables and other goods in a public place. Many of these transactions looked more like commodity exchange and less like the gift exchanges that had ensured that a larger number of people knew of arrangements and shared in their benefits.[54] As a result, the legitimacy and meaning of these transactions was often highly contested, and by the 1970s, the subject of chupu was one of the most prominent features of land disputes coming before the chiefs and courts. Land disputes frequently turned on details of a specific exchange, with claimants debating the precise name of an exchange, the details of speeches given, the exact goods provided and the people involved in order to establish their claims regarding the 'rights' that might flow from such exchanges.

These ongoing debates ultimately contributed to the grievances that underlay the Tension, discussed further in Chapter 5. In late 1998, residents of Kakabona and other areas around Honiara who were identified as Malaitan (many had genealogies connecting them to a number of places including Guadalcanal) were threatened, intimidated and sometimes evicted by people identified as being from Guadalcanal (who, equally, often had connections with multiple places). As the conflict escalated, armed groups established bunkers and checkpoints in the vicinity of the town boundary at White River, shoot-outs regularly occurred in the hills surrounding Kakabona and

---

[54] Koczberski et al. similarly emphasise the size and collectivity of exchanges as central to their legitimacy and public recognition of the claims of outsiders: Koczberski, Curry and Anjen 'Changing Land Tenure and Informal Markets in the Oil Palm Frontier of Papua New Guinea.

many residents fled the area.[55] In the aftermath of the conflict, the government established a Commission of Inquiry into land dealings as part of the Townsville Peace Agreement, and during the hearings in 2009, the 'proper' conduct and purpose of chupu became one of the most prominent and extensively discussed matters.[56]

4.4 URBANISATION AND UNSTABLE LEGAL GEOGRAPHIES: CONTESTING RIGHTS AND BOUNDARIES

Today Kakabona is densely populated, with most of the population living relatively close to the coastline. On the eastern side, much land has been registered under the Land and Titles Act, while land further west is generally unregistered, and widely understood to be divided into large 'blocks' or territories associated with different matrilineages. In this section I focus on a series of interlocking disputes concerning these blocks that came before the chiefs and courts throughout the 1980s and 1990s, largely as a result of attempts to register and then lease or sell land under Part V, Division 1 of the Land and Titles Act. These provisions establish a process whereby the Commissioner of Lands may acquire customary land (through lease or purchase) after a public hearing at which the 'owners' of the land are identified – in Kakabona, those 'owners' have typically been one or two named matrilineages. The land is then transferred back to the identified 'owners' through registration. Where land is held by a matrilineage, as is often the case, it may be registered in the names of up to five 'duly authorised representatives' on behalf of the landholding group, who are joint owners on a statutory trust.[57] To the best of my knowledge, land in the vicinity of Honiara has consistently been registered in the names of men, often as trustees for landholding lineages.

The processes set out by the Land and Titles Act, and the widespread understanding that land is held by lineages, necessarily require the identification and delineation of boundaries on the ground and between the many

---

[55] See e.g. the testimony of Claudette Liliau in the Solomon Islands Truth and Reconciliation Commission's Final Report, *Confronting the Truth for a Better Solomon Islands*, Vol IV, Annex I (2012), 1068–1073.

[56] See for example Commission of Inquiry Into Land Dealings and Abandoned Properties on Guadalcanal, *Consultation on Customary Land Issues in the Giana Region*, 9 April 2010. On the establishment of the Commission see Prime Minister Derek Sikua, 'Commission of Inquiry into Land Dealings and Abandoned Properties on Guadalcanal' in Solomon Islands', *Supplement to the Solomon Islands Gazette* No 13, 15 April 2009, 60. The commission held a number of hearings but was suspended indefinitely due to allegations of corruption.

[57] Land and Titles Act ss 60–70.

intermarrying groups that have historically moved through the landscapes of north-west Guadalcanal. They reproduce Euro-American understandings of land as comprising neat parcels held by distinct, bounded lineages, and they prompt claimants to define previously flexible social groups and territories in more precise terms. These processes are invariably extremely divisive, and give rise to protracted litigation in a variety of fora. Decisions of a land acquisition officer are nearly always appealed to the Magistrates Court, with a further and final right of appeal to the High Court.[58] The courts regularly refer matters of custom back to the chiefs, and decisions of the chiefs may be appealed to the Local Court, and then to the Customary Land Appeal Court, with a final right of appeal to the High Court on a question of law.[59] Disputes can therefore cycle repeatedly through the courts, and this is exactly what has occurred in the ongoing struggles over land I discuss further below, which relate to blocks that have not yet proceeded to registration.

The repeated rehearing of land claims creates space for extended debates. It delays the sedimentation of arrangements via registration, and provides a range of opportunities for claimants to press their claims. It would be very easy to emphasise the negotiability and even uncertainty of property here. However, these processes also involve the construction, reinscription, and stabilisation of socio-spatial categories that are marked by uneven power relations – specifically, hierarchies of 'leaders', 'owners' and 'users' of land.

4.4.1 *Constructing Hierarchies of Rights*

Court records for Kakabona provide vital insights into the ways in which specific 'truths' about land have been established and sedimented, and the files I draw upon here relate to a number of ongoing and intertwined disputes concerning two large blocks of land, referred to here as Parcel A and Parcel B.[60] The transcripts of hearings indicate that people do not typically bring claims for themselves only, but rather on behalf of a group they claim to be landholding matrilineage. In this sense, there has not been the shift towards individualisation and patriliny that Special Lands Commissioner Colin Allan predicted in the 1950s (Chapter 2). The representatives of these lineages are usually, although not exclusively, senior men, and typically those who are

---

[58] Land and Titles Act, s 66.

[59] Local Courts Act 1996 [Cap 19], ss 12–14, 28, Land and Titles Act, ss 254–257.

[60] The records that I draw upon are in a formal sense publicly available; however, I have anonymised material as the matters they discuss are not widely discussed and are often sensitive. See further Monson, 'Unsettled Explorations of Law's Archives'.

referred to as jifs (chiefs). Claims to land revolve around the genealogies of lineages and highly complex, fragmented and non-linear oral histories of ancestral origin and migration; interactions between ancestors and other beings that may be expressed in the form of snakes or rocks; the establishment of sacred sites; and instances of warfare, chupu and intermarriage between groups. In short, parties mobilise key aspects of tutungu – emplaced genealogical histories – in order to establish their lineage as the 'owners' of the land. These stories are embedded in the land and indexed to existing or abandoned villages or gardens, sacred sites, rivers and other features in the landscape.

When read closely, side by side and tracked over time, the narratives in land claims for Kakabona portray several interacting groups moving in and out of named areas at different times. From other details provided, this period often appears to stretch from the early 1800s until World War II – there are numerous references to chupu involving goods acquired through trade with Europeans, and many references to displacement due to warfare with neighbouring groups, as well as the expansion of plantations and confrontations with expatriate planters. Claimants and witnesses often describe processes of displacement as well as return to earlier sites. All of the narratives emphasise a unique connection between lineages and particular places; however, they also stress entanglement and incorporation, most obviously through intermarriage between the different lineages living on the land and the birth of their descendants. The image that emerges is one of numerous groups occupying overlapping and interwoven territories – while some scholars have described the landscape as a 'patchwork', this conveys a sense of neat, adjacent although connected parcels, and I find it more appropriate to think of a basket of interlaced and interdependent fibres holding and sustaining many people.[61]

In general terms, the records for Parcel A show that members of three matrilineages have sought to assert their ownership of the land by positioning their maternal forebears as either the original occupants of the land, or having received the land via chupu from the original occupants, a lineage that is said to have 'died out'. While the precise claims shifted over time, the histories recounted in court refer to two named matrilineages – which I refer to as Lineage A and Lineage B – moving through the land together. Having heard the claims of the parties to the dispute, the chiefs concluded that '[Lineage A] of which [Alpheus] is the leader are the true owners of the land', with Alpheus having the 'ultimate power' to control the sale or development of the land.

---

[61] For a similar use of the basket metaphor see Michelle Nayahamui Rooney, 'As *Basket* and *Papu*: Making Manus Social Fabric' (2021) 91(1) *Oceania* 86.

The chiefs then went on to explain that Lineage B and another group, Lineage C, were able to use the land for gardening, with the rights of Lineage B flowing from the long history of intermarriage between women from Lineage B and men from Lineage A. These findings were essentially upheld in subsequent appeals.

In reaching these conclusions, the chiefs and courts delineated a hierarchy of rights based on the narratives of origin, migration and intermarriage that were presented to them. Their findings are consistent with popular understandings of customary tenure, according to which the group who can demonstrate that they are the 'original occupants' of the land are also its 'owners' who may 'speak about' the land, while those who 'come into' the land through other means such as intermarriage may settle and cultivate the land for subsistence. This hierarchy is often expressed by locals and outsiders alike as 'primary' and 'secondary' rights, and is predicated on the assumption that land is collectively 'owned' by a bounded descent group with a senior man or jif (chief) at the helm, with other people holding second (or third) order entitlements.

It is not clear when these understandings of 'primary' and 'secondary' rights entered the Solomon Islands' lexicon. The 1920s Phillips Land Commission operated on the assumption that land was held in the first instance by an autochthonous lineage, which could die out, relinquish its claims or transfer entitlements to another lineage. As far as I can tell, the commission generally (if not consistently) identified just one group as the 'owners'. The language of primary and secondary rights – reflecting understandings of property as a hierarchically ordered 'bundle of rights' – seems to have emerged later, and was well established by the time of Special Lands Commissioner Colin Allan's inquiries in the 1950s.[62]

Today, the concept of 'primary' and 'secondary' rights is widely accepted and regularly reproduced in court judgments, the reports of aid donors and scholarship. Yet as feminist scholars of agrarian change and customary tenure have frequently observed, the perception of such hierarchies is largely grounded in Euro-American juridical categories which first, may not be appropriate for all customary systems and second, may in fact work to *produce* inequality. A well-known and paradigmatic example of this arises when men who are perceived by government authorities to be 'household heads' with 'control' over land are issued with land titles, while people with other claims

---

[62] See also Pei-yi Guo, 'Law as Discourse: Land Disputes and the Changing Imagination of Relations among the Langalanga, Solomon Islands' (2011) 34(2/3) *Pacific Studies* 223; Foukona, 'Land, Law and History', 194; Scales, 'The Social Forest', 109–110.

are not.[63] The dispute over Parcel A provides an illustrative example of the application of these concepts to more collective and largely undocumented forms of tenure – the chiefs and courts identified a hierarchy of 'leaders', 'owners' and 'users' holding different entitlements to delineated parcels of land, where historical socio-spatial relations might be better understood in terms of fluid, reciprocal and interdependent relations, with people woven together by marriage, birth, gift exchange and ritual, moving along 'paths' and attached to 'focal points' in landscapes.

The constitutive effects of such determinations are often uncertain, and should not be assumed. As Debra McDougall has observed on Ranongga, the social distinctions and hierarchies that are asserted in courtrooms may be ignored, smoothed over or subverted in other fora.[64] However, the instability or dynamism of these pluralistic legal geographies – by this I mean the coexistence of multiple, competing narratives delineating boundaries on the ground and between groups, and still others emphasising reciprocity, flow and socio-spatial focal points – does not remove their exclusionary elements. While no party ever asserted an exclusive claim in the courts, eviction notices were issued to all settlers within the area, and explicitly referred to the chiefs' determination. In at least one instance, a Malaitan man who had married a woman from Lineage B was evicted from the family home. The couple's sons also left the area, and the woman and her daughters were harassed, until a senior man recognised as a chief intervened to protect them.

The socio-spatial distinctions that were drawn here – with the husband and sons being associated with patrilineal Malaita and expelled, and the mother and daughters being associated with matrilineal Guadalcanal and permitted to stay – cannot be understood by reference to rights-based accounts of gender inequality that assume that men and women are distinct propertied subjects who have separate entitlements to land, with the former generally being stronger and more expansive than the latter. Rather, they call to mind critical legal scholar Sarah Keenan's argument that property should be understood in terms of space and networks of relations that revolve around belonging, between subjects and objects and parts and wholes – subjects do not merely exist in space but are constituted by it, 'such that they cannot be easily separated from it, conceptually or materially'.[65]

In the case discussed here, the territorialisation of matrilineal property clearly constituted the sons and daughters of the in-marrying matrilineage in

---

[63] See eg Whitehead and Tsikata, 'Policy Discourses', 75; Shahra Razavi, 'Introduction: Agrarian Change', 22; Yngstrom, 'Women, Wives and Land Rights', 25.

[64] McDougall, 'The Unintended Consequences of Clarification'.

[65] Keenan, *Subversive Property*, 151.

quite different ways; we see that a person's belonging to land is informed by relations and networks including gender, matriliny and ethnicity. The sons were deemed to be 'out of place' and 'belong elsewhere'. The daughters appear to have been more firmly associated with the kin group and the land, possibly because according to contemporary discourses of matriliny it would be their children, as compared to the descendants of the sons, who would continue to be the most firmly associated with the matrilineage and the land. Thus while 'exclusive' possession was never sought or awarded, the pursuit of claims in state courts contributed to the emergence of relatively more sedimented and hierarchical relationships between people than may have previously existed, and these intersected with other gendered, ethnicised and spatialised categories and networks so as to render some people more firmly attached to place, and others more vulnerable to dispossession – even if many people also intervened to efface and bridge such differences.

4.4.2 *Expanding and Contracting the Boundaries of Belonging*

The construction and assertion of hierarchies of rights to land requires a process of disentanglement, and the establishment of distinctions between people and places, subjects and objects, which can then be ordered in particular ways. This phenomena is not unique to Solomon Islands, although it occurs in situated and emplaced ways, with specific valences, and with constitutive effects that may not be encountered everywhere. It is now well recognised amongst progressive property scholars that dominant, Euro-American models of property often prompt claimants to 'cut' broader networks of relations in order to establish their own claims, render themselves (and their territories) visible and limit those of others.[66] As Marilyn Strathern famously observed, 'ownership' in a legal sense can be used to curtail social relations because 'owners can exclude those who do not belong'.[67] In Kakabona, we see that these processes are inherently ambivalent: the juridical construction and regulation of property may prompt people to *either* contract *or* expand the scope of their connections, both socially and spatially, and depending on the range of claims being made and the interests at stake. The formal legal recognition of kastom, and the assumption that kastom entails landholding by lineages, means that property disputes turn on competing versions of

---

[66] E.g. Margaret Davies, 'Feminist Appropriations: Law, Property and Personality' (1994) 3 *Social and Legal Studies* 365; Blomley, 'Performing Property'.

[67] Strathern, 'Cutting the Network'. See also Ruth Meinzen-Dick and Esther Mwangi, 'Cutting the Web of Interests: Pitfalls of Formalizing Property Rights' (2009) 26(1) *Land Use Policy* 36.

lineage histories. This in turn ensures that the poles of kinship and estrangement that McDougall identifies for gift exchange emerge in the courts, too.

These processes are particularly clear in claims to Parcel B. As is the case for Parcel A, claimants to Parcel B have not sought exclusive possession, but sought to establish clear hierarchies with respect to the land. Claims to Parcel B turn on debates about the precise implications of two chupu, one held in 1937 and another in 1986, during which the larger parcel was purportedly divided into smaller ones and allocated to various lineages. The dispute, which was also noted by the now pre-eminent jurist John Muria in the 1970s, can be traced back to the 1930s at least.[68] It entails long-running and intricate debates about the entitlements those chupu created or transferred, including the extent to which any of the chupu entailed a permanent 'transfer' of the land (more akin to commodity exchange) or simply 'permission' to use it (more akin to gift exchange). These debates have turned on still other disagreements that relate to the socio-spatial boundaries of particular blocks and landholding groups. A particularly significant debate has revolved around the question of whether specific blocks were allocated to a senior man's children, to his matrilineal subtraeb or to the larger traeb. One group argued that it was held by the subtraeb rather than the larger traeb they belonged to with their opponents, and in so doing, they emphasised their differences rather than the shared ancestry that was acknowledged by all parties. Another group adopted the opposite approach: they emphasised the common ancestry of the lineages and foregrounded the traeb over the subtraeb.

These assertions of group identity were very clearly spatialised: the claimants emphasising the traeb asserted claims across the larger area, while groups that sought to disentangle themselves socially also sought to disentangle a smaller territory from the larger one. Thus the delineation of different boundaries *on the ground* was directly and immediately linked to particular social networks being foregrounded or backgrounded. Furthermore, these debates were linked to disagreements about which particular man could be said to 'lead' the group and hold authority over the blocks. Legal contests over spatial and social boundaries were therefore simultaneously contests over the scope of specific men's authority over both land and people.

Adjustment of social and spatial boundaries may also occur via extending or contracting the *temporal* scale of the narrative. This is particularly clear in claims to Parcel A, which predominantly turned on competing claims

---

[68] During fieldwork in 1978/1979, Muria found that this area was 'under dispute' in the 1930s, and stated that 'the issue was resolved through custom', which I take to be a reference to the 1937 feast: Muria, 'Guadalcanal', 41.

regarding original occupation. However, most parties acknowledged that their lineage had moved in and out of the area at various times. Claimants also sought to position their lineage as the original occupants by reference to named male ancestors who clearly have the characteristics associated with the taovia, malaghai and vele. This means that the claim to being the landowning lineage is reciprocally indexed to the claim to leadership: the 'big man' and the 'landowning group' cannot in any meaningful sense exist apart from each other. However, given the historical mobility of lineages, the co-residence of different groups, and the unstable nature of leadership, claimants may foreground slightly different sets of places and political relationships by expanding or contracting the temporal scope of their narrative. That is to say, claims that initially appear to be 'incompatible' or 'competing' may in fact be entirely consistent and emerge from shifts in the temporal scale of the narrative.

Similar processes of socio-spatial-temporal expansion and contraction, prompted by peoples' attempts to render precise definitions of previously flexible boundaries between people and on the ground, have been observed by anthropologists working elsewhere in Solomon Islands and the wider region.[69] For example, Pei-yi Guo has examined land disputes among the Langalanga people of Malaita, and argues that legal discourse has changed the ways in which people represent their genealogies, encouraging them to 'lean towards the principle of precedence and downplay the importance of incorporation'.[70] Michael Scott cautions us against assuming that the deployment of lineage histories in this manner is invariably 'partial' or 'invented', explaining that the cosmogonies of the Arosi people of Makira do in fact assert forms of bounded social identification (rather than unbounded flow), so that when they affirm or deny aspects of their histories they do so in culturally persistent ways.[71] Debra McDougall finds that resource extraction and the creation of landowning groups on Ranongga has compelled people to 'retell their local histories in ways that exclude, rather than include, "others"',[72] but also rightly

[69] See e.g. James G. Carrier, 'Property and Social Relations in Melanesian Anthropology' in CM Hann (ed.), *Property Relations: Renewing the Anthropological Tradition* (Cambridge University Press, 1998), 85; Stuart Kirsch, 'Property Effects: Social Networks and Compensation Claims in Melanesia in Melanesia' (2001) 9(2) *Social Anthropology* 147; Nicholas A. Bainton, 'Keeping the Network Out of View' in L Kalinoe and J Leach (eds.), *Property Effects: Social Networks and Compensation Claims in Melanesia* (2004), 79–89.

[70] Guo, 'Law as Discourse'.

[71] Scott, 'Neither "New Melanesian History" nor "New Melanesian Ethnography"'; Scott, 'Ignorance Is Cosmos; Knowledge Is Chaos'.

[72] McDougall, *Engaging with Strangers*, 162; see also McDougall, 'The Unintended Consequences of Clarification'.

emphasises that the need to critically examine myths about the solidarity of 'traditional' and 'landowning' corporate groups should not distract us from the importance of these forms of community to their members.[73]

There are important distinctions between the narratives examined by these authors, and in the authors' analytical emphases.[74] However, what is critical here is that all of the narratives examined by these authors may be understood as socio-spatial histories that assert that particular lineages are uniquely attached to particular places, and simultaneously recount interaction and entanglement with other ontologically diverse people, notably through exogamous marriage, gift exchange and co-residence on land. The same is also true of the fragments of tutungu that are narrated for Kakabona. As both Scott and McDougall have extensively argued, these socio-spatial histories hinge on the need to maintain inter-lineage cooperation, as well as the need to maintain distinctions founded on narratives of original occupation or, at least, a unique and privileged attachment to the land. This gives rise to forces of stability, cohesion and kinship on the one hand, and forces of destruction, fragmentation and estrangement on the other.[75]

Legal and anthropological analyses of 'property effects' in Melanesia have often associated or 'bundled up' Western ownership strategies, socio-spatial fragmentation and court processes, and then contrasted them with 'Indigenous' or 'Melanesian' strategies that are assumed to be those relations and processes that occur 'outside' processes of state recognition and emphasise cohesion and inclusion (such as gift exchange). This approach tends to hold the categories of kastom and state law apart and treat them as distinct and irreconcilable regimes of moral-normative and institutional authority, rather than interlaced, mutually constitutive and generative of new legalities.[76] I suggest that disputes regarding Kakabona land demonstrate the extent to which the constant oscillation between poles of incorporation and estrangement, inclusion and exclusion, continues in the courtroom and in the judgments that sediment particular understandings of landholding – understandings that are simultaneously informed by Euro-American conceptions of land *and* ancestrally received ideas of people and place. State recognition of

---

[73] McDougall, *Engaging with Strangers*, 185–186.

[74] For example, Scott focuses on cosmogonies, and land disputes in Kakabona turn on far more recent histories.

[75] Scott, 'Ignorance is Cosmos; Knowledge is Chaos'; Scott, 'Neither "New Melanesian History" nor "New Melanesian Ethnography"'; McDougall, *Engaging with Strangers*.

[76] For a similar observation on kastom and law more generally, see Melissa Demian and Benedicta Rousseau, 'Owning the Law in Melanesia' in Eric Hirsch and Will Rollason (eds.), *The Melanesian World* (Taylor & Francis Group, 2019), 315, 326.

kastom may prompt its reconfiguration, but it cannot expunge these elements – indeed, it ensures they reverberate throughout, even when property rights have supposedly been 'found', clarified and sedimented. The centrality of 'entangled' lineage histories to contemporary land claims, the emphasis on collective landholding by lineages (rather than smaller family units or individuals) and the courts' tendency to acknowledge multiple (albeit hierarchical) claims to land, all work to ensure that dynamism persists even as courts simultaneously seek to impose 'order', and delineate and stabilise the subjects and objects of property.

It would, again, be easy to over-emphasise the instability or fragility of property here. However, when the oscillation inherent in lineage narratives meets with the juridical construction of a hierarchy of claims, those narratives do tend to become imbued with more exclusionary valences. This is apparent in the eviction of Malaitan and Chinese settlers as early as the 1970s, and is starkly revealed by the eviction of spouses and children of Guadalcanal landholders during the Tension. In the section that follows, I demonstrate that the oscillation between inclusion and exclusion is crucial for understanding, first, the sense of insecurity generated by land disputes and second, their gendered effects.

4.5 THE INSECURITY OF PROPERTY AND THE 'DANGER' OF LAND DISPUTES

Residents of Kakabona often refer to land disputes not only as 'sensitive' matters, but as 'dangerous' and entailing 'a struggle for survival'. Disputes are described as 'a battle' or 'warfare', language that invokes comparisons to precolonial headhunting raids. While much of the literature on urbanisation and land tenure in Melanesia foregrounds the material aspects of insecurity,[77] competition for access to land and other material resources provides only a partial explanation for this language, particularly given the large areas of unoccupied, uncultivated land in the hills immediately behind Kakabona. I suggest that these references to danger, struggle and warfare draw attention to the emotional and affective dimensions of land disputes, and the epistemological challenges posed by urbanisation and the juridical construction and

---

77 E.g. John Connell, 'Elephants in the Pacific? Pacific Urbanisation and Its Discontents' (2011) 52(2) *Asia Pacific Viewpoint* 121; Paul Jones, 'Pacific Urbanisation and the Rise of Informal Settlements: Trends and Implications from Port Moresby' (2012) 30(2) *Urban Policy and Research* 145; Darryn McEvoy, David Mitchell and Alexei Trundle, 'Land Tenure and Urban Climate Resilience in the South Pacific' (2020) 12(1) *Climate and Development* 1.

regulation of property. As a growing body of work by feminist political ecologists emphasizes,[78] it is essential to understand these dimensions if we are to understand the ways in which people struggle over access to and control over land, how and why particular visions of territory and authority become resonant or 'persuasive'[79] and how these visions enable or constrain different people.

As I have explained elsewhere, court records are 'publicly available' in a formal, legal sense, but they are regarded with anxiety and interest, and access is carefully managed, precisely because they contain information that is not widely discussed in public arenas.[80] Narratives concerning genealogies, ancestral activities and sacred sites are carefully protected; they are not freely available to everyone, and are only ever shared with discernment and usually following the observance of various protocols. Furthermore, like many family histories, tutungu may contain information that may be a source of embarrassment or insult to descendants, such as the infraction of widely held norms regarding sexual behaviour. When such knowledge is mobilised in public fora such as courts, and written down in court records, it is no longer subject to the restrictions that might ordinarily apply. Court records entail the conversion of fragments of tutungu that have historically been oral, fiercely guarded, replete with deeply valued and sometimes controversial information and intended for a relatively narrow and specific audience, into legal knowledge that is comprehensible and accessible to a much wider audience such as legal practitioners, government bureaucrats and foreign researchers.

Moreover, as we have seen, when these fragmentary oral histories are recited in court and recorded in court files, they entail the public assertion of genealogies and claims to land, and the delineation of boundaries on the ground and between the groups that occupy the land in dispute and surrounding areas. In many societies across Solomon Islands, this is considered rude, 'trouble making' and antithetical to 'right living' – people will often skirt around questions of ownership in public, although in private they may share

---

[78] Eg Andrea J Nightingale 'Beyond Design Principles: Subjectivity, Emotion and the (Ir) Rational Commons' (2011) 24(2) *Society and Natural Resources* 119, Farhana Sultana 'Suffering *for* water, suffering *from* water: emotional geographies of resource access, control and conflict' (2011) 42(2) *Geoforum* 163, Farhana Sultana 'Emotional Political Ecology' in RL Bryant (ed) *The International Handbook of Political Ecology* (Edward Elgar 2015), 633, Marien González-Hidalgo and Christos Zografos 'Emotions, Power and Political Conflict: Expanding the 'Emotional Turn' in Political Ecology' (2020) 44(2) *Progress in Human Geography* 235.

[79] Carol Rose, *Property and Persuasion*.

[80] Monson, 'Unsettled Explorations of Law's Archives'.

stories regarding ancestral origins, mystical events and landmarks that they regard as evidencing that they are uniquely attached to the land.[81]

When people confront each other with their different claims in public, this will initially occur within meeting places in villages, and senior men (and sometimes women) will draw on a variety of idioms and metaphors, invoking both humour and sorrow, as they attempt to persuade their audience of their claims. These speakers will invariably compete with the hustle and bustle of village life – the laughter of children, crowing roosters, waves lapping at nearby beaches. Furthermore, assertions of difference via speech are constantly mediated by the material and corporeal evidence that these differences may also be traversed – by the bunches of betel nut and cups of tea exchanging hands, by the churches that different lineages build and attend together and the children who embody connections to multiple lineages running through the village. By contrast, when oral histories are relayed in the relative quiet and order of courtrooms and recorded in court documents, they are stripped of much of this context and rendered static. The sensitive aspects of tutungu not only appear far more blunt and crude when transformed into stark, black script on white pages, but are brought into a new realm that may be accessible to a new audience, while simultaneously less accessible to those who previously enjoyed wider access to oral tutungu (such as those who do not know how to approach the courts and request copies of records). It is not surprising that I often felt quite uncomfortable when reading court transcripts, and aware that they provided me with access to information that might not, in other contexts, be shared with me.

The explicit and public articulation of lineage histories, and their 'sedimentation' in court records, is therefore 'dangerous' and akin to warfare in multiple, intersecting and mutually reinforcing ways. While kastom often entails the implicit articulation of differential claims – for example, in the distribution of food to socially distinct people – the legal processes and conceptions of property introduced by colonisers, which Solomon Islanders constantly seek to reconfigure to make their own, require the explicit, even brutal, delineation of such claims.

This creates a bind for land claimants: the articulation of lineage histories and the assertion of socio-spatial distinctions threatens to undermine the vital union of these distinct groups, yet restraint may be equally dangerous, because it may constitute a failure to assert the identity of the group in the context of

---

[81] For further discussion see also Scott, 'Ignorance is Cosmos; Knowledge is Chaos'; Scott 'Neither "New Melanesian History" Nor "New Melanesian Ethnography"'; McDougall, *Engaging with Strangers*, 157.

mounting threats to that identity.[82] When chiefs and courts record these narratives and their decisions, some interpretations of kastom are legitimated rather than others, with the effect that not all social actors are equally positioned to gain endorsement of their claims to land as property into the future. The loss of documents from the archives of courts and other government agencies is a direct result of Solomon Islanders' awareness that the power of their claims to persuade is directly linked to the textual and material production of the law. Moreover, land disputes are, quite literally, 'dangerous' matters that constitute a threat to material, epistemological and ontological survival – they confront people with profound questions of who they are, where and how they belong and how they relate to others. Rather than generating 'security of tenure', these processes all work to construct land disputes as threatening matters, and peri-urban areas as sites of instability and precarity in which people are engaged in 'a struggle for survival'.

4.6 FROM TAOVIA TO TRUSTEE

In previous chapters we have seen that violence, both threatened and realised, was central to the foundation and legitimation of the colonial property regime in Solomon Islands. Representations of Solomon Islanders as 'savage' head-hunters, occupying a space beyond law and without property were central to the violence of 'pacification', the imposition of British law over Indigenous people and places, the appropriation of Indigenous lands and the exclusion of Indigenous 'trespassers'.

The codes of access, belonging and exclusion that were introduced by the colonial state continue to be implicated in the violence of property today, a theme I extend in the next chapter, where I focus on the civil conflict. The violent enactment of boundaries – for example, through the eviction of Malaitans who had married into or been birthed by local lineages – needs to be understood in the context of these perceived, if not actual, threats to long-standing models of identification and relatedness. Moreover, I emphasise that the violence of property must be understood not only in terms of highly visible, material forms of physical violence involving guns, but also the more mundane, everyday epistemic violence of the law, including the privileging of particular kinds of knowledge and the silencing, misinterpretation and erasure of others.[83] This epistemic violence is brutally demonstrated by the Land and

---

[82] See also McDougall, 'Unintended Consequences of Clarification'.
[83] Discussed further in Monson, 'Unsettled Explorations of Law's Archives'. On epistemic violence, see for example Chandra Mohanty, 'Under Western Eyes: Feminist Scholarship and

Titles Act, which, as I explained in Chapter 1, readily privileges the claims of foreign academics over Indigenous knowledge-holders. These processes all endow long-standing models of place-making and relatedness with increased potential for social fragmentation; produce land disputes as not only a material threat but an epistemological (and possibly cosmological) one; and constitute peri-urban areas as sites of precarity, insecurity and uncertainty.

These processes are central to the sense of certainty or uncertainty in landholding arrangements, and to the meanings attached to land disputes and to land itself. They are also central to the production and reinscription of gendered norms and patterns of decision-making and disputing with respect to land. As we have seen, prior to colonisation, ideals of masculine leadership on Guadalcanal revolved around the unifying force of the taovia and the fracturing power of the malaghai and vele. Scott has suggested that among the Arosi of Makira, similar models of masculine prestige – 'men of peace' and 'men of war' – embodied the tension between cohesion and fragmentation that exists within lineage narratives. According to Scott, chiefs were responsible for uniting and stabilising the multiple lineages co-resident on the land, and if the unique claims of the original lineage were encroached upon, a 'remedial and even violent response could erupt in the form of a warrior or defender of the local lineage and its land'.[84]

I suggest that similar idealisations of masculinity are entangled with perceptions of land disputes as 'dangerous', and this animates land disputes as a masculine domain. When I asked people why women were less likely than men to appear as claimants or witnesses before chiefs and courts, they often drew on metaphors of warriors and warfare. As one influential woman explained, 'On Guadalcanal, the woman must stand behind the man – but this is for protection, *not* because she is secondary.' The ability to 'lead' and 'defend' the collective interests of the group by speaking on their behalf has now emerged as a critical means by which the oratorical power, and physical and metaphysical aggression, that was previously associated with the taovia, malaghai and vele may be performed, expressed and reproduced. In other words, the idealised models of 'men of peace' and 'men of war' find their coalesced expression in the ideal representative of the group in discussions, disputes and deals with respect to land. This constructs men who conform to

Colonial Discourses' (1988) 30 *Feminist Review* 61; Gayatri Chakravorty Spivak, 'Can the Subaltern Speak?' in Cary Nelson and Lawrence Grossberg (eds.), *Marxism and the Interpretation of Culture* (University of Illinois Press, 1988); Boaventura de Sousa Santos, *Epistemologies of the South: Justice Against Epistemicide* (Routledge, 2014).

[84] Scott, 'Ignorance is Cosmos; Knowledge is Chaos', 63–64.

these ideals, and certainly not women, as the ideal spokespersons for the group.

The reproduction of the authority of such 'big men' through land disputes occurs at a number of levels. When a group is defined by land acquisition officers, chiefs and courts as the 'landowning group', the land may be registered in the names of up to five 'duly authorised representatives' on behalf of that group. The names listed on existing land titles are, in most if not all cases, the names of those 'big men' and 'chiefs' who also appear in state forums on behalf of the successful group. People often explain that the men who were identified as trustees during land registration proceedings were nominated because they were 'big men' and skilled spokespersons who could 'fight for', defend and represent the interests of the group. Yet registration fixes their control over land and the wealth that flows from it, enhancing their authority over the land vis-à-vis other members of the landholding group even further – indeed today, the role of 'spokesperson', 'trustee' and 'chief' are so entwined as to be mutually constitutive.

The 'dangerous', socially fragmenting power of land disputes therefore has implications for the gendered construction of leadership, decision-making and disputing that appear to be inimical to increased participation by women. As one woman succinctly put it to me,

> Land goes through women, but men speak on behalf of the tribe. This has turned men into landowners, it privileges men who can claim 'that's mine' or 'the boundary is there'.

A man widely recognised as a paramount chief from another part of Guadalcanal similarly explained,

> Guadalcanal is matrilineal, and Guadalcanal people always say, 'the side of women, the side of women', but when development comes, they say 'I'm a trustee, I'm a trustee'...

4.7 CONCLUSION

There is a persistent tendency in global development discourse to assume that state recognition of property rights is both necessary and capable of providing 'security' of tenure. Yet in Kakabona, we see that state recognition of property has not only worked to promote the potential for fragmentation that already exists within long-standing, Indigenous models of place-making and relatedness, but imbue both land disputes and land itself with quite particular valences. The last seventy years have seen a range of developments that have destabilised landscapes and social relationships in the vicinity of Kakabona, and the state's legitimation of claims to land promotes a sense of insecurity by forcing sensitive tutungu into the public realm, recognising some groups and not others as the 'owners' of land, and sedimenting distinctions between strangers and kin. The juridical construction and regulation of property in the context of urbanisation constitutes a material threat, as well as a threat to long-standing forms of social identification and relatedness founded in land-scapes: these processes quite literally confront people with questions of who they are and where they belong. In this context, it is hardly surprising that many people experience urban areas as sites of instability, insecurity and precarity.

These processes have immense potential to deepen given Honiara's growth rates, Kakabona's location on the ocean front and growing concerns within Solomon Islander communities regarding the prospect of climate-induced sea level rise. They also have immense potential to consolidate particular forms of masculine authority over land. This is highlighted by the records of a number of meetings held in Kakabona during the mid-1980s, the stated purpose of which was to 'clarify our positions as *husbands* of the [Named Line] and as such *spokespersons* for their interests'.[85] Whereas historically, and in the cases discussed earlier, a man's authority to speak was reciprocally indexed with his belonging to the matrilineage of the land (that is, as a son, brother, uncle, nephew), here we see a very self-conscious reconsideration of kastom so as to enable men to assert their authority as husbands and fathers of the women and children of the dominant matrilineage. Residents of Kakabona are as keenly aware as property scholars that kastom is dynamic and political, and the minutes point to an explicit attempt to, as legal theorist Margaret Davies has argued we must, prefigure and test alternative conceptualisations that might lead to new 'performances' and 'facts on the ground'.[86]

The new performances and facts proposed in the minutes clearly reproduce rather than disrupt received ideas about gendered land control. However, they also demonstrate that residents of Kakabona are negotiating their 'struggle for survival' through active, self-conscious revaluation of kastom, and this creates immense space not only for anxiety and sedimentation of predominant models of property and authority, but also innovation and renewal. Narratives of danger, risk and uncertainty may certainly be drawn upon to constrain women – this is abundantly clear in the chapter that follows – but they might also provide an enabling environment in which 'new things' might be attempted. Mary Borgia clearly perceived the Tension in such terms. For

[85] Copies of Minutes on file with the author, emphasis added.
[86] Davies, 'Material Subjects', 39.

Mary, the conflict was a moment of rupture and a vital opportunity to reconsider property and authority, and she advocated reconfiguration to ensure greater inclusion in decision-making.

When Mary and I first began discussing land matters in 2008, it was common for me to hear people assert that 'women cannot be chiefs on Guadalcanal'. Yet since that time, the Tandai House of Chiefs, which covers a large area including Kakabona, has emerged and increasingly formalised. It has established a council, a headquarters and held regular elections for the paramount chief. Notably, the structure of the House of Chiefs requires the inclusion of daki taovia (which are clearly understood as 'women chiefs'), and provides for a Board of Trustees that must comprise two representatives from each of the member tribes, one man and one woman.[87] Even if these commitments are not fulfilled at present, they create scope for particular kinds of claims to be made, legitimated and made real on the ground in the future.

[87] Patison and Ereinao, *Mamara New Capital City Development Phase 1.*

5

'Land Is Our Mother'

Ethno-territorial Conflict and State Formation

From 1998 to 2003, Solomon Islands, the country that had been known as 'the Happy Isles', was plunged into a period of land-related conflict that involved an unknown number of deaths, the displacement of around 10 per cent of the country's population, the collapse of the economy and in many senses a general breakdown in law and order. The conflict, commonly referred to as the Tension, is one of the most significant that has occurred in the southwest Pacific since World War II, and has often been seen as exemplifying wider concerns about land tenure, economic development and political instability in the region. While episodic fighting occurred in many parts of the country, the conflict was overwhelmingly focused on Guadalcanal, including Honiara and surrounding areas such as Kakabona. By 2003, the country was routinely described locally and internationally as 'a failed state', and the Solomon Islands government repeatedly sought the assistance of other countries in the region. This eventually resulted in the mobilisation of the Regional Assistance Mission to Solomon Islands (RAMSI), which is widely critiqued for its emphasis on neoliberal statebuilding but also regarded as providing a critical circuit breaker to the fighting.

The root causes of the conflict are many and complex, but it is typically understood to have commenced when groups of Guadalcanal militants began evicting people they believed to be from other islands, pursuing an agenda that might be broadly described as ethno-territorial. It is therefore unsurprising that the 'ethnic' dimensions of the conflict have been the subject of significant scholarly attention, with most writers stressing that the militants' emphasis on ethnicity needs to be understood in the context of Solomon Islands' socio-economic and political history.[1] Tarcisius Kabutaulaka and Matthew Allen

---

[1] There are now four monographs on the conflict: Jon Fraenkel, *The Manipulation of Custom: From Uprising to Intervention in the Solomon Islands* (Victoria University Press, 2004); Clive

have both extensively argued that the grievances expressed during the conflict reflect a history of spatially-uneven development and long-standing concerns regarding social and economic deprivation that can be traced to Solomon Islands' earliest articulations with the global economy.[2] In this chapter I extend these accounts by foregrounding what has often been neglected in scholarship on land conflict, political authority and state-building in the southwest Pacific, namely gender.

My reference to 'gender' here is not confined to women, nor to people's different roles and experiences during the conflict. Rather, consistent with shifts in feminist political ecology over the last 15 years, I emphasise post-structuralist understandings of gender as a dynamic process or performance; social and material meanings as co-produced; and gendered cultural categories, discourses and power structures as intimately bound with ethnicity and territorialisation.[3] In this chapter I trace the territorialised categories of 'ethnic' solidarity and difference that were mobilised during the conflict to the profoundly gendered colonial geography of governance, wage labour and crucially, the construction and regulation of property. I then demonstrate that these long-standing narratives of gender, ethnicity, property and territory were mobilised during the conflict in a manner that hardened socio-spatial boundaries; obscured long histories of intermarriage and exchange; and entailed the violent physical division of couples and families with genealogies connecting them to both Malaita and Guadalcanal.

My emphasis on legal geographies and the co-production of the legal and the spatial enables me to expose the centrality of the state and 'formal' law to these processes. Debra McDougall has observed that both proponents and critics of RAMSI's neoliberal state-building have tended to situate the conflict within the context of a 'weak', 'failing' or 'distant' state, that is, as either eroding state institutions or exposing their fragility and limited influence,

---

Moore, *Happy Isles in Crisis: The Historical Causes for a Failing State in Solomon Islands*, 1998–2004 (Asia Pacific Press, 2004); John Braithwaite et al., *Pillars and Shadows: Statebuilding as Peacebuilding in Solomon Islands* (ANU Press, 2010); Allen, *Greed and Grievance*.

[2] See in particular Kabutaulaka, 'Beyond Ethnicity', Allen *Resource Extraction and Contentious States*, 82

[3] Eg Elmhirst 'Introducing New Feminist Political Ecologies', Yvonne Underhill-Sem 'Marked Bodies in Marginalised Places: Understanding Rationalities in Global Discourses' (2003) 46(2) *Development* 13, Andrea Nightingale 'The Nature of Gender: Work, Gender and Environment' (2006) 24 *Environment and Planning D: Society and Space* 165, Andrea Nightingale 'Bounding Difference: Intersectionality and the Material Production of Gender, Caste, Class and Environment in Nepal' (2011) 42(2) *Geoforum* 153, Mollett and Faria, 'Messing with Gender'. See also Teresia Teaiwa 'Articulated Cultures: Militarism and Masculinities in Fiji During the Mid 1990s' (2005) 3(2) *Fijian Studies: A Journal of Contemporary Fiji* 201.

particularly as compared to the strength or 'resilience' of informal or customary justice institutions.[4] By tracing the ways in which different social actors
navigated multiple legal or moral-normative regimes, I demonstrate that the
Tension must *also* be understood in terms of the *presence* of the state, including as
an attempt by various groups to receive recognition of their claims to territorial
authority and reconfigure the current (formal) political order. This means, as
Matthew Allen has argued, that the conflict must be situated in the deeper historical
processes of state formation[5] and the ongoing reconfiguration of legal pluralities.

In making these arguments I seek to contribute to the growing body of
scholarship on the relationship between land control and state formation, in
which gender continues to be relegated to the margins and/or perceived as
concerning women only.[6] I also contribute to ongoing debates in a variety of
contexts regarding the relationship between property and political representa-
tion, by demonstrating that understanding the highly gendered relationship
between property and political authority at the local level in Solomon Islands
is crucial for understanding the under-representation of women in the
national parliament. The Tension reveals the extent to which the seemingly
'local' struggles described in previous chapters 'scale up' to the provincial and
national level, with both ethno-territorial conflicts and seemingly intimate
property disputes emerging from, and reproducing, legal pluralities in which
Euro-American conceptions of land law and political order have functioned to
exclude far more than include. These processes are profoundly gendered –
indeed I argue that struggles over state-sanctioned property and provincial
authority provide a crucial site for the performance of masculine authority and
prestige, and simultaneously reproduce state norms and institutions not only
as a masculine, but as a hypermasculine domain.

5.1 MULTISCALAR STRUGGLES: SOCIAL DIFFERENTIATION, PROPERTY AND THE STRUCTURE OF THE STATE

5.1.1 Mobility and Ethnicity during the Protectorate Era

'The Tension has been the subject of significant scholarly interest, and there is
a relatively broad consensus that the structural causes of the conflict included

---

4   Debra McDougall 'Customary Authority or State Withdrawal in Solomon Islands: Resilience
    or Tenacity?' (2015) 50(4) *The Journal of Pacific History* 450
5   Allen, *Greed and Grievance*, 186.
6   Farhana Sultana similarly observes that feminism and decolonial approaches are ignored in
    political ecology generally: Farhana Sultana 'Political Ecology 1: From Margins to Centre'
    (2021) 45(1) *Progress in Human Geography* 156.

spatial inequalities in socio-economic development originating during the colonial period, and long-standing concerns among Guadalcanal people about the migration of people from Malaita to Honiara and surrounding areas.[7] There is also widespread agreement that the categories of ethnic difference mobilised by militants emerged from the context of plantation labour, the colonial geography of governance, profoundly uneven economic development and successive waves of hegemonic discourse regarding cultural difference in Solomon Islands.[8] I extend these arguments here, highlighting that these categories emerge from gendered discourses and a distinctly masculine experience of the forms of mobility and solidarity elicited by colonialism.

It is now axiomatic to note that prior to colonial rule, the islands in the Solomons were populated by relatively dispersed political communities that had alliances for various purposes including trade and warfare, but rarely fell within a wider form of political authority. During the Protectorate era, colonial authorities created new national, district and sub-district divisions that sometimes conflicted with, and did not displace, existing forms of kinship and socio-spatial identification. For example, the establishment of a border between German-controlled Papua New Guinea and British-controlled Solomon Islands drew boundaries between the closely related peoples of Bougainville and Shortland Islands. However, as we saw in Chapter 2, the colonial delineation of administrative units also contributed to the emergence of new places and regional identities which, for some purposes at least, united previously fragmented groups into political communities such as 'West', 'Malaita' and 'Guadalcanal'. The geography of colonial administration was therefore a vital constituent of regional identities that persist today.

The geography of the plantation economy, and socio-economic development generally, have also been crucial to the emergence of contemporary regional identities. When the British established the Protectorate, they did so on the basis that a plantation economy would be established to finance the new Protectorate. This required land and labour, and the acquisition of both was uneven. It is particularly important to highlight the absence of plantations on Malaita, by far the most populous island, and their concentration in the western islands and on north-east Guadalcanal. This meant that Malaitan men comprised the bulk of labour on plantations located elsewhere in the Solomons, and from 1913 to 1940, Malaitans made up 68 per cent of plantation labour across the Protectorate.[9]

---

[7] For a substantial discussion of this literature, see Allen, *Greed and Grievance*, Chapter 2.
[8] Dureau, 'Decreed Affinities'; Scales, 'The Coup Nobody Noticed'; Scott, 'The Matter of Makira'.
[9] Bennett, *Wealth of the Solomons*, 167–191.

Plantations and Christian missions promoted novel patterns of movement and sociality, with important implications for contemporary regional identities and political struggles. Prior to colonisation, people frequently visited other hamlets, notably for marriage, trade and attendance at feasts, but mobility was also constrained due to the fear of attack by raiding parties or sorcerers. It was the men now often referred to as 'chiefs', 'warriors' and 'priests' who travelled greater distances, while many other people remained in the vicinity of the hamlet.[10] In some respects people could move more freely following colonisation and 'pacification', and new forms of mobility emerged as a result of plantation labour and training with the missions. However as Margaret Jolly observes for Vanuatu, mobility continued to be heavily circumscribed by gender: it was generally (but certainly not always) men who were drawn away for work or training at plantations and missions, and women remained in the villages.[11] Migration to plantations and missions was also associated with a particular stage of the life cycle of men, as it was usually young and unmarried men who left their villages to work on other islands, or even abroad, with many returning home to marry.

It is well known that these novel patterns of mobility and sociality facilitated the formation of new identities and allegiances that stretched beyond the old grounds of hamlet, kin group or language, and were founded instead on islands and regions. Young men from large islands such as Malaita, who had not previously perceived themselves to share a common identity, began to identify shared cultural concepts and practices that they saw as distinguishing them from people from other parts of the Protectorate, from wider Oceania, and certainly from their white employers.[12] As numerous scholars have observed, plantation life provided young men with opportunities to learn about, utilise and resist the language and customs of the *waet man* (white man), but within Solomon Islands, this was generally expressed in terms of island-based identities rather than a sense of national solidarity.[13]

---

[10] Bathgate, 'Movement Processes'.

[11] Jolly, 'The Forgotten Women. There were certainly numerous women in Solomon Islands who travelled to missions, and smaller numbers who travelled to plantations – as mentioned in Chapter 4, a number of women who reside/resided in Kakabona married men from other islands who they met through mission activities and education. However, the women who travelled to other islands are vastly outnumbered by men.

[12] These processes occurred within the plantations in the Pacific colonies as well as among Pacific workers in Australia, see Banivanua Mar, *Violence and Colonial Dialogue* 119.

[13] Discussed in Keesing, 'Plantation Networks, 163–170; Bennett, *Wealth of the Solomons*, 167–190; Allen, 70–73.

The spatialised cultural or ethnic distinctions emerging in the context of plantation labour were entangled with the colonial geography of governance in multiple and profoundly gendered ways. The delineation of districts by colonial officials appears to have been based on European conceptions of ethnicity rooted in the colonial division of labour, and within this geography, Malaitans were masculinised as physically big, strong and hard workers and also ambitious, aggressive and competitive, while the populations of Isabel, Makira or Guadalcanal were feminised as physically small, weak and non-confrontational.[14] These stereotypes of people and their places were inextricably linked not only with labour and mission discourses, but also with early-twentieth-century descent theory and associated debates about social organisation and land tenure within British anthropology: British administrators and their foreign advisors understood Guadalcanal primarily in terms of matriliny and Malaita in terms of patriliny, while the western islands were often perceived to be undergoing a transition from matriliny to patriliny. These understandings of socio-territorial organisation were incorporated into the legal construction and regulation of property and colonial governance more broadly, and formed a crucial part of the context in which Solomon Islanders reproduced and reinterpreted culturally distinct idioms of alterity and formed new kinds of solidarity. It is critical to note that the gendered, spatially territorialised notions of culture and ethnicity that emerged during this period – notably that of 'patrilineal' Malaita as compared to 'matrilineal' Guadalcanal – have endured and are regularly reproduced by locals and outsiders alike.[15]

In previous chapters we have seen that Christian missions often provided new arenas for bridging long-standing or emerging socio-spatial distinctions, although in other instances they reinforced them. The establishment of Catholicism on north-west Guadalcanal, for example, was associated with an expansion of marriage networks beyond old kin-based alliances and extended to other islands including Malaita. In Marovo, the establishment of Methodist and Adventist missions provided people with new opportunities to assert pre-existing distinctions, notably in relation to territorial claims. The role of the churches with respect to ideal models of 'good' women and men was similarly mixed. Church teachings emphasised the heteropatriarchal family, entrenched 'private' caring and domestic work as feminised tasks, and

---

[14] Eg Corris, *Passage* 88; Keesing, 'Plantation Networks', 167.
[15] See also Scott's extensive discussion and Kabutaulaka's critique of the role of Western academic discourse in the creation of the myth of Malaitan aggressiveness: Scott, 'The Matter of Makira', 115; Kabutaulaka, 'Beyond Ethnicity', 12.

furthered the construction of some roles (such as public speech-giving) as masculine. It is also likely that missions in Solomon Islands, as elsewhere, reinforced pre-existing norms of sexual restraint that limited women's involvement in plantation life.[16] However the participation of women in local mission life was actively encouraged by Islanders and outsiders alike, and church-based schools, health clinics and women's groups provided women with a range of opportunities to engage with Europeans and people from other islands. It was therefore the churches, far more than plantation life or colonial administration, which provided scope for women to participate in the colonial flow of language, rituals and ideas; form new identities and alliances; and achieve new kinds of influence within their communities.

The flow of people, goods, technologies and ideas within and into Solomon Islands gathered pace during World War II, and as we saw in Chapter 2, encounters between Solomon Islanders and American troops challenged the existing dynamics between Islanders and foreigners and contributed to the emergence of a number of anti-colonial movements. Existing documentary sources tell us very little about the ways in which women experienced the war, and even less about their perceptions or involvement in these movements.[17] While Solomon Islander women clearly interacted with American servicemen, they may have done so in far smaller numbers than the men who made up the Solomon Islands Labour Corps, who often lived and worked in close proximity to Americans. If the ideologies and discourses of resistance and solidarity that were promulgated after the war were forged in this context, as numerous scholars have suggested they were,[18] it is likely that they reflected men's experiences and encounters with American soldiers far more than they did women's experiences and encounters. Furthermore, I suggest that these encounters during World War II forged an even deeper connection between hegemonic masculinities of warriorhood and struggles over territory and political ordering, which have continued to accumulate salience in the

---

[16] Margaret Jolly, 'Damming the Rivers of Milk? Fertility, Sexuality, and Modernity in Melanesia and Amazonia' in Thomas Gregor and Donald F Tuzin (eds.), *Gender in Amazonia and Melanesia: An Exploration of the Comparative Method* (University of California Press, 2001), 175.

[17] See however Judith A Bennett and Angela Wanhalla (eds.), *Mothers' Darlings of the South Pacific: The Children of Indigenous Women and U.S. Servicemen, World War II* (University of Hawai'i Press, 2016).

[18] See e.g. Keesing, 'Kastom and Anticolonialism'; Laracy, *Pacific Protest*; Geoffrey M White, 'Histories of Contact, Narratives of Self: Wartime Encounters in Santa Isabel' in Geoffrey M White and Lamont Lindstrom (eds.), *The Pacific Theater: Island Representations of World War II* (University of Hawai'i Press, 1989) 43. See also Jolly, 'The Forgotten Women'.

context of extractive industries and the profoundly uneven distribution of the costs and benefits of so-called development.

5.1.2 *Migration, Urbanisation and the Ambiguity of Property*

At the end of World War II, the British relocated the capital of the British Solomon Islands Protectorate as well as the capital of the Western Pacific High Commission to Honiara. Much of the land required for the new capital had already been taken out of Indigenous control, and was acquired from expatriate families and companies. The colonial administration also purchased land at Mataniko and Kakabona from people they regarded as 'landowners'.[19] Today, the legitimacy of those transactions is highly contested, and the exact location of the Honiara town boundary is unclear. However, there is relatively widespread agreement regarding the approximate location of that boundary, and general agreement that land inside that ambiguous boundary is 'alienated land', regulated by the state rather than custom.[20] As we shall see, this legal construction and political perception of land became crucial to the material expression of the conflict that occurred from 1998 onwards.

Honiara grew rapidly in the aftermath of the war – between 1959 and 1970 the population tripled, reaching almost 12,000 people.[21] This rapid urbanisation was driven largely by the disparities in economic opportunity between the north coast of Guadalcanal and many other parts of the country. The development of infrastructure and the cash economy were overwhelmingly focused in Honiara, but this also meant that north-central Guadalcanal bore the brunt of the social and ecological consequences of rapid urbanisation. People who migrated to Honiara often settled on government-owned land, and while some held Temporary Occupation Licences (TOLs), many settled informally. By the 1970s, the development of informal settlements inside the town boundary was regarded as an urgent and growing problem, and one with an ethnic dimension, since significant numbers of migrants came from densely populated and underdeveloped island of Malaita, which comprised roughly 30 per

---

[19] Oram, 'Land, Housing and Administration'; Joseph Foukona, 'Urban Land in Honiara: Strategies and Rights to the City' (2015) 50(4) *Journal of Pacific History* 504; Joseph Foukona and Matthew Allen, 'Urban Land in Solomon Islands: Powers of Exclusion and Counter-Exclusion' in Siobhan McDonnell, Matthew Allen and Colin Filer (eds.), *Kastom, Property and Ideology: Land Transformations in Melanesia* (ANU Press, 2017), 85.

[20] During the course of this research, 2008–2020, Guadalcanal people's claims regarding land inside the town boundary generally focused on the question of whether it should be managed by the central government or provincial authorities.

[21] Bellam, 'The Colonial City', 73.

cent of the country's entire population. Cabinet discussed the possibility of evicting people from the growing settlements, but this did not eventuate because it was seen as impractical, and a breach of human rights.[22]

Migrants also settled outside the town boundary, accessing land held by Guadalcanal landowners through a variety of mechanisms. Court records attest to the presence of Malaitan and Chinese settlers in Kakabona during the 1970s, and Nigel Oram observed a significant increase in the number of Malaitans living and gardening in areas southeast of the city during the same period.[23] Some Guadalcanal people were concerned by this development, and perceived migrants to be accessing land without the permission of Guadalcanal landholders. However, many migrants claim that they did in fact seek permission. Michael Kwa'ioloa, a Kwara'ae (Malaitan) man, asserts that he and his relatives had been invited into the area around Mount Austin by the rightful landholders:

> When I came to Honiara as a boy at the end of the 1960s, my relatives living in Kobito and Sahalu Tandai areas [around Honiara] had been invited in by the rightful landowners. They agreed for us to plant gardens in the forest for taro, sweet potato and tapioca, and to cut trees for building materials, to hunt pigs and take anything we needed. These landholders, by observing the tradition of sharing, showed that they alone could allow our fathers access to this land. Then when the Malaitan Christians at Kobito celebrated their church feasts, they had to invite the rightful landholders and give them a share to take home for their families. During national election campaigns they sought the Malaitans' assistance and we co-ordinated the chiefs from the various outlying settlements and ran the campaign. . .[24]

While aspects of Kwa'ioloa's account would probably be disputed by some people, similar arrangements were observed by Isireli Lasaqa, who noted several Malaitan families living on the Guadalcanal Plains after being invited or permitted to settle there by senior men within a local matrilineage.[25] There is a clear sense in the historical record that these arrangements were underpinned by notions of reciprocity and culturally persistent models of masculine authority comparable to Ian Hogbin's 'centre man' or Marshall Sahlin's 'big

---

[22] Sam Alasia, 'Population Movement' in Hugh Laracy and Sam Alasia (eds.), *Ples Blong Iumi: Solomon Islands, the Past Four Thousand Years* (University of the South Pacific, 1989), 112, 119.

[23] Oram, 'Land, Housing and Administration', 140.

[24] Michael Kwa'ioloa and Ben Burt, '"The Chiefs' Country"': A Malaitan View of the Conflict in Solomon Islands' (2007) 77(1) *Oceania* 111, 115.

[25] See Lasaqa, 'Melanesians' Choice', 164–180, 235–236; T Kama, 'Guadalcanal Plains' in Ian Heath (ed.), *Land Research in Solomon Islands* (Land Research Project, Lands Division, Ministry of Agriculture and Lands, 1979).

man', according to which men accumulated influence by building an ever-expanding network of people who were indebted to them.[26]

Increased migration was also associated with expanding marriage networks, and many migrants obtained access to customary land through intermarriage with a landholding group. Some people viewed intermarriage with caution, concerned that when men from the densely populated, patrilineal Malaita married women from matrilineal Guadalcanal where much of the country's infrastructure was based, they did so primarily for the purpose of settling on Guadalcanal land. Some also expressed concern that when a Guadalcanal woman married a Malaitan man, they would be joined by his relatives and a 'Malaitan' settlement would spring up in the vicinity of their house, without appropriate permission from the customary landholders.[27] These perceptions, coupled with the stereotyping of Malaitans as especially patriarchal, led some families to actively discourage young women from marrying Malaitan men.

The arrangements struck between migrants and landholding communities entailed various forms of exchange, at least some of which were understood as 'land sales'. Some migrants purchased land registered under the Land and Titles Act, others purchased customary land. Irrespective of the (formal) legal status of land, it was often sold by small groups of people, predominantly senior men, without consulting other members of the landholding group, and without distributing the proceeds of sale.[28] People living in the vicinity of Honiara can point to specific parcels of land that were 'sold' in return for cash, rather than the items that have historically been necessary for chupu, such as pigs, shell money and betel nut. These practices contravene the widely held customary ideal that land transactions should be discussed among the members of the landholding group, who should also be involved in the chupu. They reduce the transparency of transactions and accountability of senior men: when cash is provided in return for permission to settle, it often exchanges hands away from the public eye, and may be distributed among a small number of people. In at least one dispute coming before the courts, the reinterpretation of chupu enabled senior men to sell the same parcel of land multiple times, without purchasers realising that it had been sold to others too.[29]

---

[26] H Ian Hogbin, 'Native Councils and Courts in the Solomon Islands' (1943) 14 *Oceania* 258; Sahlins, 'Poor Man', 285.

[27] These concerns are detailed in court records and Guadalcanal Commission of Inquiry transcripts discussed in Chapter 4. See also Nanau, 'Theory of Insecure Globalisation', 147–150.

[28] For one example see *Loboi v Laugana, Botu, Saika, Ofasisili, Attorney-General (for the Commissioner of Lands) and Attorney-General (for Registrar of Titles)* [2010] SBHC 38; HCSI-CC 212 of 2008 (30 July 2010). See also Kabutaulaka, 'Beyond Ethnicity', 15.

[29] *Bishop Tuhenua v Laugana, Mavi, Kurilau, Kavuchavi and Visona (Trustees of Kolotoha Land)* [2004] SBHC 89; HC-CC 238 of 2003 (16 July 2004).

The reworking of old forms of gift exchange into more individualised forms contributed to the proliferation of the possible grounds for claims to land, different perceptions of place, and significant debate regarding landholding arrangements. Migrants often understood land transactions as an outright sale, involving the privatisation of space and the transfer of alienable rights that they could pass to their children. Customary landholders often contested this, and emphasised the inalienability of customary land, and the illegitimacy of commercial transactions entered into by individuals rather than a wider group. As George Curry and Gina Koczberski have observed for the oil palm frontier in Papua New Guinea, the public performance of gift exchange is vital to ensuring that there are witnesses to attest to the legitimacy of a settler's claims if they are challenged in the future.[30] In many societies in Solomon Islands, the ideal gift exchange is not only performed publicly, but repeated over successive generations, enabling social relationships and narratives about land to be reproduced and consensus built over time. Transactions that emphasise cash are easily contracted socially, spatially and temporally – they require fewer people; they may be organised far more quickly than exchanges involving pigs and crops; and they may occur in smaller and relatively 'private' places. This leaves them open to reinterpretation, even if the parties initially shared a common understanding. All of these processes worked to generate controversy and leave migrants vulnerable to the allegation that they have settled on land 'without proper permission'. Moreover, they fuelled perceptions that migrants were demonstrating a lack of respect for both the people and the customs of Guadalcanal.

As the population of Honiara grew, so too did the number of people seeking access to land and employment, and this contributed to growing debates about land ownership. In some instances, land disputes between landholders and migrants led to the eviction of settlers from land they believed that they had purchased. Disputes also frequently arose between and within landholding groups. Guadalcanal people regularly confronted each other in the courts, with disputes revolving around questions of which lineage and leader had the authority to sell or permit others to settle on the land. In an influential article on the structural causes of the Tension, Tarcisius Kabutaulaka refers to resentment amongst younger people regarding the sale of their 'birth right', particularly in the context of mounting concerns about possible future land shortages.[31]

---

[30] Curry and Koczberski, 'Finding Common Ground', Koczberski, Curry and Anjen 'Changing Land Tenure and Informal Land Markets in the Oil Palm Frontier Regions of Papua New Guinea'.

[31] Kabutaulaka, 'Beyond Ethnicity', 14.

These disputes, and the process of litigation in the courts in particular, all worked to reiterate and sediment distinctions between migrants and Indigenous landholders, and groups now defined as landowners as compared to mere users. These processes also deepened the ideal of chiefly authority over land, and the ability of those men who became known as chiefs and trustees to control and organise access to land. In other words, as Christian Lund has extensively argued, initially in relation to Ghana, as people competed to have their claims to land recognised as property by state institutions, they simultaneously recognised and imbued those institutions – and particular men – with a greater degree of authority.[32]

While this chapter and the preceding one focus on the intergenerational, internecine and ethnopolitical contests that were playing out in the vicinity of Honiara and Kakabona, similar conflicts were occurring elsewhere on Guadalcanal. The island was not only home to the national capital, but the source of the country's most valuable agricultural export commodity, palm oil. In the 1970s, a large oil palm plantation was established on the Guadalcanal Plains to the east of Honiara. Solomon Islands Plantation Limited (SIPL) occupied a vast tract of land, and the financial returns to customary landowners were minimal. Furthermore, although SIPL became the biggest private employer on Guadalcanal, many Guadalcanal people felt excluded from the employment opportunities offered by the operation, and noted the large numbers of Malaitans employed by the company. This deepened social division, with some Guadalcanal people expressing the view that Malaitans were uninvited and disrespectful guests on Guadalcanal land, and noting the growth of Malaitan settlements in the vicinity of developments such as SIPL. These concerns were anything but new: when Special Lands Commissioner Colin Allan toured Guadalcanal in the 1950s, he noted that 'the worst fear the Tasimboko people have is in regard to the immigration of Malaita people'.[33]

5.1.3 *Demands for Provincial Autonomy and Restricted Migration*

Concerns regarding uneven patterns of development, migration and land transactions were not confined to Guadalcanal, but were expressed in many

---

[32] Lund, *Local Politics*; Sikor and Lund, 'Access and Property', Lund, 'Rule and Rupture'
[33] Colin Hamilton Allan, *Solomons Safari, 1953–58* (Nag's Head Press, 1986) 79. In a similar vein, Bathgate perceived a 'deep distrust' of Malaitan labourers among the local men of the far north-west coast of Guadalcanal during the 1970s: Bathgate, 'Movement Processes', 91.

parts of the country. In Chapter 2 we saw that people in the Western district, where a significant portion of the country's plantation agriculture, forestry and fishing was located, also expressed frustration about bearing the costs of such development, while receiving little in the way of government services. This served to deepen the reproduction of essentialised, territorialised collective identities based on islands and regions, often referenced against a masculinised, patrilineal and patriarchal Malaitan 'Other'. These struggles over political authority, territoriality, community membership and natural resource rights were channelled into debates about the post-Independence Constitution's approach to decentralisation, provincial autonomy, revenue and internal migration. While these debates have often been cited as evidence of the tenacity of kastom and the limited reach of the state, I suggest that they *also* reveal the centrality of the state to struggles over property, territoriality and authority. When the people in the western islands asserted a 'Western' identity and threatened to 'break away' from the rest of Solomon Islands, they did not claim a return to supposedly primordial kastom. Rather, they drew on the colonial legal geography and sought to entrench an essentialised, territorialised version of ethnic identity in the pre-eminent form of state law – the constitution.

Demands for greater devolution of political authority influenced the establishment of seven provincial governments in 1981, which largely reproduced the colonial legal geography. This did not quell demands for increased regional autonomy, particularly in relation to control over locally generated revenue and migration within the archipelago. On Guadalcanal, expressions of resentment and distrust towards migrants were heard not only in Honiara, but also in rural areas, where many people felt that they had been neglected by successive governments. In 1980, Guadalcanal politician Paul Tovua called on parliament to control the migration of people from one province to another. Sam Alasia notes that a 'theoretically possible and philosophically preferable' response to internal migration would be to decentralise development, and create more employment opportunities across the country.[34] However, this did not occur and the population of Honiara continued to climb, doubling in size between 1976 and 1987 to just over 30,000 people.

In 1987 a Constitutional Review Committee was established to review the 1978 constitution. The committee's report again reflects an emphasis on spatially territorialised categories of difference, largely expressed through distinctions between 'local communities' and 'migrants'. It found that there was a

---

[34] Alasia, 'Population Movement', 119.

widespread view that the individual right to freedom of movement had been 'extensively abused by intruders moving in to settle on other people's land without the proper consent of the landowners'.[35] In its report, the committee highlighted two possible paths to reform. The first option recommended the establishment of a federal system of government, reflecting the widespread belief that federalism would meet demands for the more equitable distribution of development benefits, and increased provincial control over natural resources and migration. It emphasised the primacy of custom and Indigenous authorities, envisaged a significant role for customary tribunals and councils of chiefs and provided for the privileged treatment of 'Indigenous people'.[36] The second option suggested a unitary republic with an Indigenous president, and qualifications on the individual right to freedom of movement. Notably, whereas previous debates had been framed primarily in terms of kastom, they were now also framed in terms of indigeneity, a vocabulary that Miranda Johnson observes was also gaining traction in neighbouring countries and providing new ways for Indigenous claimants to press their claims in and against state institutions.[37] In the end, neither of the proposed models was adopted – the report was never tabled in parliament, and the government of the day did not respond to the recommendations.

The following year, in 1988, a document titled *Petition by the Indigenous People of Guadalcanal* was submitted to the national government. The 1988 Petition sets out allegations of violence against Guadalcanal people by Malaitans, as well as detailing grievances revolving around the use of Guadalcanal land for development and the inequitable distribution of the benefits of that development. It lists a series of demands that require the central government to take 'immediate steps' to repatriate all 'illegal squatters'; establish a federal system of government; and enact legislation to allow the Guadalcanal Province to take control of all alienated land in the province, including Honiara. This last demand suggests that at least some Guadalcanal people accepted that particular areas of land had been alienated, taken outside

---

[35] Solomon Islands Government, 1987 *Constitutional Review Committee Report* (1988), Vol II, 50. For example, the Moro Movement emphasised in its submission that '[p]eople from other islands should have the right to travel from one place to another [but they] should not have the right to reside or settle without permission of those in authority': Solomon Islands Government, 1987 *Constitutional Review Committee Report* (Solomon Islands Government, 1988), Vol 1, 607.

[36] See further Yash Ghai, 'Constitutional Reviews in Papua New Guinea and Solomon Islands' (1990) 2(2) *The Contemporary Pacific* 313.

[37] Miranda Johnson, *The Land Is Our History: Indigeneity, Law, and the Settler State* (Oxford University Press, 2016), 6.

the control of Indigenous landholding groups and were now legitimately managed by state authorities for the benefit of Solomon Islanders more broadly. However, it also reveals the assertion of a spatially territorialised notion of culture and ethnicity which, while bound up with the language of kastom, was also entwined with the idea of provincial (or state) government: the Petition accepts the claims of the state to land, but distinguishes between provincial and national authorities and demands that Guadalcanal land be managed by the latter. To some extent at least, the Guadalcanal provincial boundaries and institutions were not seen as antagonistic to Guadalcanal interests, but as *representing* them. Further, while the Moro Movement had similarly asserted an island-wide 'customary' identity in the aftermath of World War II, the 1988 Petition now expressly framed this identity in the vocabulary of indigeneity.

Shortly after the submission of the 1988 Petition to the national government, the premier of Western Province wrote to the prime minister to express the Western Province's support for the petition.[38] However, the central government, which was led by Guadalcanal man Ezekiel Alebua, was either unable or unwilling to respond to the demands made in the petition. This is despite the 1988 Petition's clear invocation of coups and ethno-political conflict in nearby Fiji, and threats of similar violence:

> We the indigenous peoples of Guadalcanal are but human beings. We have been pushed too far for too long already, and there is a limit to how far you could go on pushing us. Nothing is impossible.

> Sir, Did any one ever dream that Fiji was going to go the way it did? No, Never…The mixing of two diverse types of people, whose colour of skin was almost identical, was a time bomb. Solomon Islands is no exception.[39]

5.2 THE 'ETHNIC' TENSION

By late 1998, Ezekiel Alebua was the premier of Guadalcanal Province, and another major development had commenced in the form of a gold mine at Gold Ridge, about 30 kilometres south-east of Honiara. Processes similar to those documented in previous chapters were underway at Gold Ridge, and this added to the existing sources of tension on Guadalcanal. Gordon Nanau observed that the delineation of territories and identification of trustees

---

[38] Nanau, 'Theory of Insecure Globalisation', 89.
[39] *Petition by the Indigenous People of Guadalcanal*, 1988 reproduced in Fraenkel, *The Manipulation of Custom*, Appendix 1.

contributed to tensions within communities, and a small number of senior men controlled royalties while other people, notably women, were on the 'receiving end of the cycle'.[40] Furthermore, as with so many other developments, Malaitans made up the majority of the workforce and often settled in the local area, and many Guadalcanal people felt that they would bear the brunt of the ecological and social burdens associated with mining but enjoy few of the benefits.[41]

Oral histories suggest that young Guadalcanal people, including young women, had been collecting guns and ammunition for a number of years, and in late 1998 rumours began to circulate that the people of Guadalcanal were going to 'fight' the people of Malaita.[42] Premier Alebua made several speeches in which he made a number of demands on behalf of the province, including that the national government pay rent to Guadalcanal Province for the use of Honiara as the capital, that Guadalcanal land 'stolen from the people' be returned and that settlers from other islands show respect to the Guadalcanal people.[43] Shortly afterwards, groups of young Guadalcanal men, initially calling themselves the Guadalcanal Revolutionary Army (GRA) and later the Isatabu Freedom Movement (IFM), embarked upon a campaign of harassment aimed at chasing migrants off Guadalcanal. In January 1999, the Guadalcanal Provincial Assembly signed a petition, the *Demands of the Bona Fide and Indigenous People of Guadalcanal* and submitted it to the national government. This document, which became known as the 'Bona Fide Demands', largely reproduced the demands made in the 1988 petition.[44] In fact as noted by John Naitoro, these demands had been made long before independence, including through the Moro Movement.[45]

The evictions by Guadalcanal militants were primarily directed at Malaitan people, but many Guadalcanal people were also targeted. The Truth and Reconciliation Commission (TRC) heard many accounts of Guadalcanal people being displaced from their villages after being rounded up at gunpoint,

---

[40] Gordon Nanau 'Local Experiences with Mining Royalties, Company and the State in the Solomon Islands' (2014) 138 *Journal de la Société des Océanistes* 77, 90 and Nanau, 'Theory of Insecure Globalisation', 218.

[41] Braithwaite et al., *Pillars and Shadows*, 124; Daniel Evans, 'Tensions at the Gold Ridge Mine, Guadalcanal, Solomon Islands' (2010) 25(3) *Pacific Economic Bulletin*, Allen *Resource Extraction and Contentious States* 81ff.

[42] This is referred to repeatedly in the transcripts of the Truth and Reconciliation Commission hearings. See also Kabutaulaka, 'Beyond Ethnicity', 2.

[43] Kabutaulaka, 'Beyond Ethnicity'.

[44] *Demands by the Bona Fide and Indigenous People of Guadalcanal*, reproduced in Fraenkel, *The Manipulation of Custom*, Appendix 2.

[45] Naitoro, 'Solomon Islands Conflict'.

assaulted and sometimes killed; and having their belongings stolen and their homes burnt to the ground.[46] The TRC also heard many stories of Guadalcanal people intervening to protect Malaitans, for example by visiting them under cover of darkness to warn them of threats, or physically intervening to plead with militants.[47] Grace Bana described how her own family, from Malaita, had purchased land on the Guadalcanal Plains, and were cared for by a male leader:

> In 1998 we heard stories that the Guadalcanal militants were going to chase the Malaitans who had settled illegally in and around Guadalcanal...The Landowner whom we bought the land from came and said, you stay put I will tell the militants not to harm you. So he ran to the militants and told them not to kill us...[48]

By the time of the census in November 1999, more than 35,000 people had been displaced from their usual place of residence, most of them from rural north Guadalcanal. The land they were evicted from included customary land, as well as land that was alienated during the colonial period which remains the subject of Indigenous claims to date. In this sense, some of the evictions might be seen as a repudiation of illegitimate land usage. However, some people were evicted from land that is widely accepted as alienated and which they had accessed in accordance with the rules of the state legal system, while others were evicted from customary land they had settled on with the permission of members of local landholding groups.

Displaced Malaitans generally sought refuge in Honiara town, and many then sought to return to the villages in Malaita into which they were born, or to which they had claims through their parents or grandparents. However once there, they often felt as unwelcome as they had on Guadalcanal. Grace Bana told the Truth and Reconciliation Commission that once her family arrived in Malaita, 'my people did not welcome me and my family' and they suffered as they did on Guadalcanal.[49]

---

[46] Solomon Islands Truth and Reconciliation Commission, *Thematic Public Hearing for Women*, 25 November 2010; Solomon Islands Truth and Reconciliation Commission, *Visale Public Hearing*, 23 June, 24 June and 25 June 2010.

[47] These issues are discussed extensively in Solomon Islands Truth and Reconciliation Commission, *Confronting the Truth*.

[48] Solomon Islands Truth and Reconciliation Commission, *Thematic Public Hearing for Women* per Grace Bana.

[49] Ibid.

5.2.1 Ethnicity, Property and the Geography of Violence

International media coverage of the emerging crisis in Solomon Islands was quick to portray the violence in racialised terms, characterising it as the product of primordial hatred between fundamentally different and 'tribal' people belonging to two islands. However, such representations not only ignore profoundly 'modern' debates regarding federalism, but depend upon relatively recent island-based identities and obscure long histories of inter-action between Guadalcanal and Malaitan people. As John Naitoro observed during the conflict, many Malaitan genealogies are traceable to Guadalcanal, oral histories record long-standing marriage and trade relationships, and some Malaitan and Guadalcanal languages have linguistic similarities.[50] Many of the people who were targeted as 'settlers' and 'migrants' – that is, as 'people out of place' – were second- and third-generation residents of Guadalcanal. Indeed in many instances, evictions targeted individuals, couples and families with ties to both Malaitan and Guadalcanal people and places, and this had devastating consequences.[51] One woman told the Truth and Reconciliation Commission:

> My name is Anna Kikini, my mother is from Guadalcanal and my father is from North Malaita. I was born and brought up on Guadalcanal until the Ethnic Tension started. I am not interested to live in Malaita because I was not born there, I am more interested to live on Guadalcanal than Malaita.[52]

Militants asserted dualistic, socio-spatial distinctions that reified differences between 'Malaitans' and 'Guadalcanal' people, and outside commentary often interpreted this as 'tribal' politics, the product of 'Indigenous cultures' and even 'Africanisation'.[53] However as we have seen, the distinctions drawn by militants are in fact crucially linked to the ongoing influence of early-twenti-eth-century British descent theory and legal constructions of property on popular narratives of Indigenous territory and social organisation.

---

[50] Naitoro, 'Solomon Islands Conflict'.

[51] See in particular the testimonies in Solomon Islands Truth and Reconciliation, *Thematic Public Hearing for Women* from Guadalcanal women who married Malaitan men, Malaitan women who married Guadalcanal men and women with both Malaitan and Guadalcanal ancestry.

[52] Solomon Islands Truth and Reconciliation, *Thematic Public Hearing for Women* per per Anna Kikini.

[53] See David Chappell, '"Africanization" in the Pacific: Blaming Others for Disorder in the Periphery?' (2005) 47(2) *Comparative Studies in Society and History* 286; Teaiwa, 'On Analogies'.

In Solomon Islands as in other areas of island Melanesia, narratives of unilineal descent and inheritance circulate among locals and outsiders alike. When I first visited Solomon Islands in 2004, in the immediate aftermath of the conflict, Solomon Islanders frequently explained that children born to women from matrilineal Guadalcanal and men from patrilineal Malaita were 'lucky', as compared to those born of Malaitan women and Guadalcanal men, who 'do not have any rights to land'. These understandings are reproduced by scholars and development practitioners, with one study of the conflict stating that when people from Malaita and Guadalcanal married, 'the result was a marriage in which a claim to land may be inherited either through both partners or through neither'.[54] These accounts reproduce the essentialised and binary discourses of gender, kinship and inheritance that underpinned the conflict and legitimated enormous violence.

Land relations are, however, usually far more fluid than these essentialised accounts of matrilineal and patrilineal tenure suggest: the children of Guadalcanal men may, and frequently do, make claims through their fathers, just as people on Malaita frequently make claims to land through women. Furthermore, the binary accounts of socio-spatial relations mobilised by militants were very selectively applied to render people out of place and legitimate violence. As Kikini and many other people can attest, the fact that their mother was from Guadalcanal did not ensure their access to land or shield them from violence. Hearings before the TRC demonstrated that Guadalcanal women who married Malaitan men were often harassed, and in many instances their husbands and sons were targeted as 'enemies' and 'spies' and evicted from the family home. Guadalcanal men who married Malaitan women were also targeted, and some fled to Malaita.[55] Young people who were known to have genealogies connecting them to both Malaita and Guadalcanal, and perhaps young men in particular, were vulnerable to harassment and violence by Malaitan and Guadalcanal militants alike. While the essentialised, dualistic notions of ethnic homogeneity asserted by militants during the conflict are not widely followed during peace, they meant that any person who crossed those socio-spatial boundaries – most obviously by birth or marriage, but also by friendship – was likely to be targeted as 'a spy'.[56]

---

[54] Braithwaite et al., *Pillars and Shadows*, 19.

[55] For example Kamilio Teke, a Guadalcanal man who was married to a Malaitan woman, initially tried to take his family to his birthplace on west Guadalcanal, but was unable to do so due to the 'very tense situation' there. They sought refuge in his wife's village on Malaita instead: Solomon Islands Truth and Reconciliation, *Visale Public Hearing* per Kamilio Teke.

[56] Collin Vigorau, a man from Guadalcanal, was targeted by Guadalcanal militants as 'a spy', possibly due to his work with the Catholic Church and his friendships with Malaitans: Solomon Islands Truth and Reconciliation, *Visale Public Hearings* per Collin Vigorau.

By mid-1999, Malaitan vigilante groups had formed to 'secure' the outskirts of Honiara, and in 2000, an organised force calling itself the 'Malaita Eagle Force' (MEF) emerged. The group claimed to represent displaced Malaitans, and they too issued demands, notably for compensation for property damaged and destroyed by the IFM. The MEF established roadblocks and bunkers around the perimeter of the town, and beyond this lay a 'buffer zone' and then IFM bunkers facing towards Honiara.[57] The MEF took control of Honiara, which became a Malaitan enclave as settlers flowed into Honiara from rural areas, while Guadalcanal people fled from urban areas into the rural areas controlled by the IFM.[58] By early 2000, confrontations involving shootouts between the MEF and IFM were regularly occurring in the hills behind Honiara and Kakabona. Many of the houses in Kakabona were burned down by both Malaitan and Guadalcanal militants, and bridges and other infrastructure were also destroyed.[59]

The spatiality of the conflict is significant in a number of ways. Much of the violence on north Guadalcanal was concentrated in the areas where claims to land by Guadalcanal people and migrants alike were most contested, such as Kakabona. Furthermore, the establishment of bunkers at the town boundary, and the flow of migrants into Honiara with a simultaneous flow of Guadalcanal people out into rural areas, reveals particular perceptions of place. As Matthew Allen has shown, many members of the MEF framed their motives in terms of a concern to 'secure', 'defend' and 'protect' Honiara, both to protect Malaitans seeking refuge inside the city and because the maintenance of the city was seen as central to the maintenance of the nation as a whole.[60] Notably, although migrant claims to land outside the Honiara town boundary were (and are) fiercely contested by many Guadalcanal people, the legitimacy of migrant claims to land *inside* the town boundary were (and continue to be) far more widely accepted.

The material expression or distribution of the conflict therefore reveals and reiterates the political and juridical perception of space: while the location of the town boundaries is contested, there is a degree of acceptance among Solomon Islanders, including many Guadalcanal people, that Honiara is the

---

[57] Norman Arkwright, 'Restorative Justice in the Solomon Islands' in Sinclair Dinnen, Anna Jowitt and Tess Newton (eds.), *A Kind of Mending: Restorative Justice in the Pacific Islands* (ANU Press, 2010), 177, 184; Braithwaite et al., *Pillars and Shadows*, 31.

[58] See J Schoorl and W Friesen, 'Migration and Displacement' in B de Bruijn (ed.), *Report on the 1999 Population and Housing Census* (SI Statistics Office, 2002).

[59] See also Solomon Islands Truth and Reconciliation, *Thematic Public Hearing for Women* per Claudette Liliau.

[60] Allen, *Greed and Grievance*, Chapter 5.

focal point of the nation and relatively available for settlement by migrants. Equally, most Solomon Islanders accept Guadalcanal assertions of authority over land outside Honiara, even when this land is defined by the state legal system as 'alienated land' and formally outside the realm of custom. This legal geography remains visible today: while Malaitan spouses of Guadalcanal people have often returned to their homes on Guadalcanal, many Malaitan families who purchased registered or unregistered land outside the Honiara town boundary appear to have resigned themselves to the loss of access to that land. While this is explained with sadness, there is also a degree of acceptance of the moral legitimacy of Guadalcanal authority over land.

This highlights the vital distinction drawn by Jesse Ribot and Nancy Peluso, between the ability to *access* land and the recognition of claims to land *as property*, at least insofar as that recognition comes from the state.[61] It also reveals the contingency of access to land in Solomon Islands, and the inability of the state to monopolise the legitimation of claims to land as property. While the previous chapters have demonstrated that Solomon Islanders compete to elicit state recognition of their claims to land as property, the geography of violence underscores the fact that the state is not the sole source of institutional and normative forms sanctioning or enforcing claims to land as property, although it is an undeniably important one. While the state legal system labelled particular areas as 'registered land' and recognised Malaitan claims to such land, it could not guarantee access. Furthermore, there appears to be widespread acceptance amongst many Solomon Islanders of the moral legitimacy of Guadalcanal claims to land outside the Honiara town boundary, including land that is legally defined as alienated and thus supposedly outside the realm of custom.

5.2.2 Peacebuilding, Negotiations and Demands for Regional Autonomy

The conflict escalated in June 2000, when a self-declared 'Joint Operation' between the MEF and the Royal Solomon Islands Police took over the state armoury at the police headquarters in Honiara, and placed Prime Minister Bartholomew Ulufa'alu (MP for Aoke-Langalanga, Malaita) under house arrest. Andrew Nori, the lawyer and spokesperson for the MEF, announced on national radio that the MEF had 'declared war' against the IFM. Ulufa'alu subsequently resigned and Manasseh Sogavare was elected as caretaker prime minister. Several months of intense fighting followed, during which up to

---

[61]   Ribot and Peluso, 'A Theory of Access'.

100 people were killed when the Royal Solomon Islands Police Force patrol boat was used to shell the coastline east of Honiara.

As the conflict intensified, a number of groups formalised their peacebuilding efforts. In contrast to neighbouring Fiji, where religious affiliation and religious discourses have sometimes deepened ethnic divides,[62] church-based networks in Solomon Islands provided a crucial avenue for people to mobilise across territorialised ethnic distinctions. The Solomon Islands Christian Association (the peak ecumenical body) and the Melanesian Brotherhood (an Indigenous Anglican order) were particularly active, and several women's groups emerged with the express purpose of 'peacebuilding'. Notably, the most detailed accounts of peacebuilding are those written during the conflict by women within those movements, including Ruth Liloqula, Alice Pollard, Dalcy Tovosia Paina and Selina Boso.[63]

One of the best known peacebuilding groups was Honiara-based 'Women for Peace', whose goal was to enable women to contribute to the peace process 'in their capacity as mothers of the nation'.[64] A 'Guadalcanal Women for Peace' group was also formed in close collaboration with the Honiara-based group.[65] The activities of these groups included meeting with militants and their leaders to discuss issues including 'law and order, good governance, peace, and the consequences of the tension for the lives of children and mothers'.[66] They also met with police officers, and with political leaders including the governor general. Prayer, singing hymns and Bible readings were a major feature of many of these meetings. In the weeks following the June 2000 coup, the National Council of Women organised and held a

---

[62] Robert Norton, 'Reconciling Ethnicity and Nation: Contending Discourses in Fiji's Constitutional Reform' (2000) 12(1) *The Contemporary Pacific* 83.

[63] Ruth Liloqula, 'Understanding the Conflict in Solomon Islands as a Practical Means to Peacemaking' (2000) 53 *Development Bulletin* 41; Alice A Pollard, 'Resolving Conflict in Solomon Islands: The Women for Peace Approach' (2000) 53 *Development Bulletin* 44; Dalcy Tovosia Paina, 'Peacemaking in Solomon Islands: The Experience of the Guadalcanal Women for Peace Movement' (2000) 53 *Development Bulletin* 47; Ruth Liloqula and Alice Aruhe'eta Pollard, 'Understanding Conflict in Solomon Islands: A Practical Means to Peacemaking' (Discussion Paper No. 7, Coral Bell School of Asia Pacific Affairs, College of Asia and the Pacific, the Australian National University, 2000); Helen Leslie and Selina Boso, 'Gender-Related Violence in the Solomon Islands: The Work of Local Women's Organisations' (2003) 44(3) *Asia Pacific Viewpoint* 325. See also the collective account in Judith Fangalasuu, Ruth Maetala, Patricia Rodi, Anah Vota and Elsie Wickham *Herem Kam: Stori Blo Mifala Olketa Mere*, Women's Submission to the Solomon Islands Truth and Reconciliation Commission, 2011.

[64] Liloqula and Pollard, 'Understanding Conflict in Solomon Islands', 10.

[65] Dalcy Tovosia Paina, 'Peacemaking in Solomon Islands'.

[66] Liloqula and Pollard, 'Understanding Conflict in Solomon Islands', 11.

service at St Barnabas' Anglican Cathedral, which was attended by the governor general, the leader of the Opposition, diplomats and other leaders. During the service the women prayed for peace, reconciliation, good governance and democracy; and called for foreign assistance in ending the conflict,[67] explicitly weaving together the vocabularies of Christianity, the nation state and the global community. Funding for these activities came from members themselves, as well as from aid donors.[68]

In July 2000, Australia and New Zealand supported a series of peace talks on the HMAS Tobruk with militants, representatives of church and women's groups and chiefs and provincial leaders. This was followed by a National Peace Conference aboard the New Zealand frigate *Te Kaha* in August. This conference was attended by delegates from throughout Solomon Islands, including representatives of the Solomon Islands Christian Association and Women for Peace, and it resulted in a communiqué that called for greater participation by members of civil society in the peace process. The MEF opposed this, and civil society groups were largely excluded from subsequent peace talks.[69] As a result, participation in the Townsville peace talks in October 2000 was confined to men representing the national government, provincial assemblies and the militant groups.

The exclusion of civil society from the Townsville peace talks is central to understanding the ways in which the embodied performance of gender and other forms of social difference during the conflict reiterated particular ideas about participation in public life. Some scholars have emphasised that the Townville peace talks excluded women,[70] but it is critical to note that they excluded *all* civil society representatives. This meant that the talks were confined to members of parliament – many of whom were perceived to play a crucial role in inciting disorder – and heavily armed police and militants. Other key leaders – people who were regarded as representing the churches and civil society and active in building peace, such as the Melanesian Brothers – were excluded. I stress this point here because these processes of embodied, material inclusion and exclusion produced and

---

[67] C Weir, 'The Churches in Solomon Islands and Fiji: Responses to the Crises of 2000' (2000) 53 *Development Bulletin* 49.

[68] Alice Aruhe'eta Pollard, 'Women's Organizations, Voluntarism, and Self-Financing in Solomon Islands: A Participant Perspective' (2003) 74(1/2) *Oceania* 44, 52.

[69] Allen, *Greed and Grievance*, 50.

[70] Helen Leslie, 'Conceptualising and Addressing the Mental Health Impacts of Gender Roles in Conflict and Peacemaking' (2000) 53 *Development Bulletin* 65, 65; Hilary Charlesworth, 'Are Women Peaceful? Reflections on the Role of Women in Peace-Building' (2008) 16(3) *Feminist Legal Studies* 347.

reinscribed formal political negotiations not only as a masculine domain but a *hypermasculine* one.

The Townsville Peace Agreement led to a ceasefire and marked the end of much of the fighting; however, it also contributed to the splintering of the Guadalcanal and Malaitan militias into a number of factions. A particularly significant split emerged between the IFM and the Guadalcanal Liberation Front (GLF), which was linked with differences between the former's association with the kastom-oriented Moro Movement and the latter's emphasis on Christianity. This rift contributed to a cycle of retaliation on the Weather Coast. In April 2003, six tasius (Melanesian Brothers) who had travelled to the Weather Coast to broker peace were accused of spying and brutally murdered, and when I first travelled to the Weather Coast in 2004, numerous young women shared their own experiences of assault with me. As Allen notes, the violence on the Weather Coast is widely regarded as a conflict between well-known men with varying allegiances to kastom, lotu (church) and state institutions (notably the police).[71] In this sense it represents another manifestation of the plurality of church, government and traditional authority that has characterised politics since the colonial period.

While the conflict was largely concentrated on Guadalcanal, the flow of guns and people to other islands was associated with episodic violence in many parts of the country. According to Ian Scales, combatants from Bougainville in Papua New Guinea arrived in various parts of Western Province during 1998 and 1999, and announced that they would protect the province against incursions by the MEF.[72] Bougainville was emerging from its own decade-long 'resource conflict', and the young men who arrived in Western Province were informed by this experience and often asserting relational ties that pre-existed colonial borders.[73] Young people around Munda began burning down houses with the stated aim of driving Malaitan settlers out, and the premier of Western Province expressed negativity towards Malaitan migration in a radio interview. Western members of the National Parliament were concerned that this could provoke attacks on Western Province people in Honiara, and organised a parliamentary delegation to meet with the premier and executive of the Western Province. This led to the 1999 'Munda Accord', which expressed the desire of the province to 'restrict the movement' of unemployed youths, particularly if they came from

---

[71] Allen, *Greed and Grievance*, 130–132, see also Appendix 1.
[72] For a detailed account see Scales, 'The Coup Nobody Noticed'.
[73] For a discussion of the Bougainville Crisis, particularly with respect to its spatiality, see Allen, *Resource Extraction and Contentious States*, 29–50.

other provinces; and to establish 'stringent measures' to restrict the settlement of land in the western islands by outsiders.[74]

Demands for regional autonomy were frequently heard and became increasingly formalised. The Townsville Peace Agreement of 2000 prioritised a number of matters including a process of constitutional reform to give greater autonomy to the provinces, particularly with respect to land and natural resource governance. This issue also dominated a conference of the premiers (all men), held in Buala on Isabel the same year. The demands for autonomy expressed by the Western Breakaway Movement in the lead-up to independence resurfaced, and the provincial executives of Choiseul and Western Provinces announced their intention to form a joint state government. On National Independence Day, the Premier of Western Province Reuben Lilo gave a speech asserting the Western Province's desire to have 'autonomy', 'indigenised democracy', 'rule of law' and 'legislative power over [Western Province's] resources'.[75] While this was followed by calls of 'God bless the State of Solomon Islands' and 'God bless the sovereignty of Solomon Islands', a newly designed State of Western Solomons' flag was also raised. Other provinces also called for greater decentralisation, often by seizing the symbols of the central state: Temotu began to negotiate separate trade and shipping arrangements with Vanuatu, and Rennell and Bellona began preparing a constitution to become a state within a federal system.[76]

It became increasingly obvious to observers both inside and outside Solomon Islands that the government lacked both the will and the capacity to deal with the deteriorating situation. The Solomon Islands government made numerous requests for international assistance, and in 2003, the Australian government announced its intention to lead the Regional Assistance Mission to Solomon Islands (RAMSI). RAMSI was deployed in July 2003, and initially consisted of several hundred police and almost 2,000 regional military personnel from Pacific Island Forum member states, as well as civilian advisors working in government agencies as part of a longer state-building programme.[77]

74 Scales, 'The Coup Nobody Noticed'.
75 Speech delivered by the Premier of Western Province, Hon. Reuben Lilo, on the occasion of the declaration of the State Government in the region on 7 July 2000, (Pacific Manuscripts Bureau, PMB MS 1292-013).
76 Dinnen, 'Winners and Losers'; Scales, 'The Coup Nobody Noticed'; Moore, *Happy Isles in Crisis*, 156–160.
77 On RAMSI see e.g. Tarcisius Kabutaulaka, 'Australian Foreign Policy and the RAMSI Intervention in Solomon Islands' (2005) 17(2) *The Contemporary Pacific* 283; Sinclair Dinnen, 'A Comment on State-Building in Solomon Islands' (2007) 42(2) *Journal of Pacific History* 255;

5.3 ETHNO-POLITICAL STRUGGLES AND STATE (TRANS)FORMATION

Scholars of the Tension, as well as conflicts elsewhere in Melanesia, have often seen the rhetoric of ethnicity, indigeneity and inequality mobilised during conflict as linked with the limitations of the contemporary state. In one of the best known articles on the Tension, Tarcisius Kabutaulaka critiqued the portrayal of the crisis as the product of ancient tribal differences, and situated it in the context of poor development planning, the inequitable distribution of development benefits and 'weak and ineffective structures and systems of government'.[78] Sinclair Dinnen has emphasised the disparity between a homogeneous, centralised state and the cultural and linguistic diversity and fragmentation of its territory, noting that at independence, '[n]ot only did the government of the newly independent state have limited institutional capabilities, it also had little legitimacy amongst most of its inhabitants'.[79] Jennifer Corrin has portrayed the divide between Solomon Islanders and the centralised state in particularly stark terms, describing the state as 'weak and irrelevant', 'with no resonance for indigenous people and no accommodation of their social systems or values'.[80] The literature on the Tension is complex and nuanced, but there is a general sense that the conflict exposed the weaknesses of state institutions that have failed to unite fragmented polities, are at odds with other sources of power and legitimacy in Solomon Islander societies and have consistently failed to address the profoundly inequitable distribution of the costs and benefits of socio-economic development.

The Tension undeniably revealed and highlighted the many weaknesses of state institutions in Solomon Islands, and the deep-seated grievances regarding the inequitable distribution of not only the burdens of resource extraction but also the benefits of desirable infrastructure such as health clinics and schools.[81] However, if we approach the conflict *only* in terms of the weaknesses, absences and failures of the state – on the ways in which institutions

---

Shahar Hameiri, 'The Trouble with RAMSI: Re-examining the Roots of Conflict in Solomon Islands' (2007) 19(2) *The Contemporary Pacific* 409; John Braithwaite et al., *Pillars and Shadows: Statebuilding as Peacebuilding in Solomon Islands* (ANU Press, 2010); Matthew Allen and Sinclair Dinnen (eds.), *Statebuilding and State Formation in the Western Pacific* (Routledge, 2018) ('Statebuilding State Form. West. Pacific').

[78] Kabutaulaka, 'Beyond Ethnicity'.
[79] Dinnen, 'State-Building in Post-Colonial Society', 54.
[80] Jennifer Corrin, 'Ples Bilong Mere: Law, Gender and Peace-Building in Solomon Islands' (2008) 16(2) *Feminist Legal Studies* 169, 170, 187.
[81] Tarcisius Kabutaulaka, 'A Weak State and the Solomon Islands Peace Process' (East West Center and Center for Pacific Islands Studies, Pacific Islands Development Series No 14, 2002);

fall short of an ideal Weberian model of a rational state – we may overlook the ways in which concepts, understandings and practices of the state are profoundly 'present' in the everyday lives of people.[82] Christian Lund has argued that in the context of Bawku, in the Upper East Region of Ghana, '[e]thnicised political competition can be seen, at least partly, as an attempt by various groups to solicit the recognition of rights and status by national and other levels of government'.[83] Lund acknowledges that communal violence and ethnically based politics can be seen as a 'governance deficiency', but also emphasises that struggles over chieftaincies, land, markets and names of places have played out through political practices including legal procedures, party politics, administrative exclusions and receptions of dignitaries. As Lund puts it, 'the idea of the state is, if not entirely clear, quite powerful despite the incapacity of government institutions'.[84]

Comparisons between states in the Pacific and those in Africa have often been overdrawn and racialised,[85] and it is important to acknowledge that the histories and causes of conflict in Ghana are markedly different from those in Solomon Islands, particularly in terms of the degree of state involvement in authorising and recognising customary authorities. However, Lund's account draws our attention to the fact that first, conflict may overtly challenge the state while simultaneously being a form of recognition, and second, struggles over resource control and community membership are tied up with the production of authority of public institutions.[86] In the case of Solomon Islands, scholars and development practitioners have often interpreted the invocation of kastom and references to ethnicity and indigeneity as highlighting the weak influence of state-based norms and institutions, and even their 'irrelevance'. Yet the narratives and actions of Guadalcanal and Malaitan militants reveal a consistent recognition, and in many instances an appreciation, of state-based norms and institutions. Far from being 'absent', the state

---

Sinclair Dinnen and Matthew Allen, 'State Absence and State Formation in Solomon Islands: Reflections on Agency, Scale and Hybridity' (2016) 47(1) *Development and Change* 76.

[82] For further discussion in other contexts, see e.g. Christian Lund and Catherine Boone (eds.), 'Land Politics in Africa: Constituting Authority over Territory, Property and Persons' (2013) 83 (1) *Africa*; Lund, 'Rule and Rupture'.

[83] Lund, *Local Politics*, 109.

[84] Ibid.

[85] Scholars of Melanesia have quite rightly rejected the racialised hyperbole of the 'Africanisation of the Pacific' thesis; however, as Teresia Teaiwa has observed, there is an equal danger in employing a kind of 'Pacific exceptionalism' that ignores global connections: Teaiwa, 'On Analogies'.

[86] See in particular Christian Lund 'Rule and Rupture'

was not only profoundly present, but the central point of reference in the forms of socio-spatial differentiation and authority asserted by militants.

5.3.1 *Defending the Motherland and Saving the Solomons: The Centrality of the State*

As previous chapters have demonstrated, Solomon Islanders frequently draw upon and weave together multiple threads of legitimacy associated with kastom, the Christian churches and the state. Similar legal pluralities or constellations are evident in the narratives mobilised by militants during the conflict. Other scholars have addressed these narratives in more detail than I do here, but it is worth noting that these accounts have generally been written by men – including ex-militants, politicians and academics – and have emphasised the voices of men who were influential in the conflict.[87] The state features prominently in these narratives, particularly in the widespread perception that the conflict arose from the state's failure to respond to, adjudicate and sanction particular claims. As I explain further below, the claims made by militants, and the material and embodied enactment of those claims, clearly drew on culturally distinct constructions of land and people that we might associate with kastom, but they were also redolent with the language, signs and rituals of state law. As Matthew Allen argues, these strategies need to be understood in terms of ongoing processes of state formation,[88] and here I emphasise some of the gendered dimensions of these processes.

As we have seen, grounded, territorialised notions of culture have been critical to political struggles in Solomon Islands. Property and 'ethnic territories' were central to colonial rule and also informed the strategies of movements resisting and disrupting such rule. So too were they central to the conflict. Guadalcanal militants foregrounded the unique status of Guadalcanal people as the Indigenous people of Guadalcanal, emphasising their privileged relationship with the matrilineal motherland of Guadalcanal and their obligation to defend it. The failure of *the state* to adequately engage with these claims is repeated again and again throughout Guadalcanal discourses surrounding the conflict. In the first issue of *Isatabu Tavuli*, a periodic

---

[87] There is a striking gendered division of labour within existing scholarship on the conflict cited throughout this chapter, visible in the authorship of accounts of peacebuilding and the TRC as compared to authorship of accounts focusing on underlying grievances, political economy and law and order issues.

[88] Allen, *Greed and Grievance*, 185–186.

newsletter produced by the IFM and circulated online, one correspondent wrote:

> In the past 14 months, the government has neither addressed nor in the process of addressing even one single issue raised by the Guadalcanal Province. We have raised these issues during the colonial era, at the time of independence, after independence...how much longer should we wait for the government to go on luk long hem moa? [Trans: 'How much longer should we wait for the government to look at this again?']

> Let us take the issue of land, for example. In the past 14 months the government has not received or indicated that it is in the process of reviewing the land legislation as requested by the Guadalcanal province. Do it! Don't just say 'We'll do it!'[89]

This anonymous correspondent went on to describe in detail his frustration with the failure of the national government to respond to Guadalcanal demands. In a similar vein, one former militant told Allen:

> The main idea behind the IFM was to make the government recognise the rights of the Guadalcanal people...And also control of migration of people from other provinces who come and work in Guadalcanal, like a law or a permit...I think that's the main thing that the IFM was trying to tell the government, that it must control the migration of people who come and live in Guadalcanal because they just come without any permits or anything...[90]

The grievances expressed by Guadalcanal militants regularly invoked the idea that the national government was responsible for controlling migration, and for ensuring greater equity in the distribution of revenue associated with the extraction of resources on Guadalcanal. These demands were not only made to state institutions, but framed in terms of the symbolic language of the state. Furthermore, the problems identified and the solutions proposed were generally constructed in the language of the law: the problem of migration could be resolved with 'a law or permit', and the problem of inequitable development could be resolved through constitutional reform granting statehood to Guadalcanal.

In a similar manner, Malaitan militants drew on the language of kastom to assert the legitimacy of their cause, while simultaneously referring to the state's failure to defend Malaitan interests and the nation state more broadly. As

---

[89] Unknown, 'The Govt and the Guadalcanal Crisis' (2000) 1(1) *Isatabu Tavuli* (copy on file with author).

[90] Allen, *Greed and Grievance*, 120.

Allen demonstrates, the theme of 'saving the nation' is a dominant one in their narratives.[91] One former militant stated,

> During the hard times, big rains, thunderstorms, it was only the Malaita Eagle Force that secured this town. If it wasn't for the Malaita Eagle Force, Solomon Islands would not be a nation and Honiara would have burned down.[92]

Thus as Allen stresses, far from blaming the people of Guadalcanal for the conflict, Malaitan militants directed their attention towards the state – they emphasised that it was the state that had produced the conditions that led to the conflict, by neglecting Malaita and forcing Malaitans to migrate elsewhere for work.[93] This continues to be a widespread view among Malaitans today.

While the Tension highlighted many of the challenges facing state institutions in Solomon Islands, state norms and institutions were also central to the ways in which militants framed their claims, attributed responsibility and proposed solutions. Guadalcanal and Malaitan militants alike were particularly aggrieved by the state's failure to respond to their demands, and frequently referred to the fact that state institutions and processes would have been the preferable means by which to contest and settle the claims made by both Guadalcanal and Malaitan people. This has long antecedents, particularly in the emergence of the post–World War II movements examined in previous chapters. While these narratives all draw on kastom and resist the central government's assertion of legal hegemony, they simultaneously recognise and imbue the state with authority.

This is not to suggest that Solomon Islanders regard the state as the *only* source of authority – the Tension exposed the very widespread acceptance of the moral authority of customary tenure and customary authorities, and the long-standing inability of the state to monopolise the definition of boundaries between people and on the ground. However, the narratives mobilised by Guadalcanal and Malaitan militants, as with the political movements before them, stress the interplay of kastom and the state, reproducing both as central and interwoven organising political categories. In short, despite the reciprocal opposition of kastom and state law, Solomon Islanders – like Pacific peoples elsewhere – have not only deployed state law but endeavoured to redefine it to ground their claims to justice. They have mobilised, rearranged and, as Sally Engle Merry put it, 'vernacularised' multiple networks of legal orders,

---

[91] Ibid, Chapter 7.
[92] Ibid, 137.
[93] Ibid; Allen, 'Resisting RAMSI', 10.

conjoining Indigenous concepts with state law, Christianity, and globally circulating ideas of Indigenous rights.[94]

5.3.2 Gender Violence and Territoriality

In previous chapters we have seen that land disputes have become an important arena for the performance of masculine authority and prestige, providing opportunities for aspiring men to embody the oratorical prowess of the chief (taovia on Guadalcanal) as well as the potential for aggression and division previously associated with the warrior (malaghai). The conflict reanimated the salience of the latter, as Guadalcanal militants drew on culturally persistent models of malaghai and 'warriors' defending the land. While my analysis here focuses on the people and place-making narratives of Guadalcanal militants, it is important to emphasise that Malaitan militants drew on similarly hypermasculinised forms of male solidarity and identity, symbolised by the ramo (warrior).[95] These assertions of masculine identity and solidarity had devastating consequences not only for women and children, but also for other people who were perceived and sought to express themselves differently.

The narratives mobilised by militants were simultaneously global and grounded in specific places; both timeless and profoundly contemporary. Militants mobilised territorial narratives that were marked by the invocation of a timeless, objectified kastom, aspects of state law and globally circulating ideas of Indigeneity and ethno-territorial struggles. Tetevete, a correspondent of the IFM's newsletter, referred to the fact that

> Guale people are not British or Americans who can migrate and live anywhere so long as they satisfy the necessary residence formalities.[96]

The idea of the rootedness of Indigenous peoples as compared to the rootlessness of Europeans is a familiar trope in nationalist discourse elsewhere in the

---

94 Sally Engle Merry, 'Legal Vernacularization and Ka Ho'okolokolonui Kanaka Maoli, The People's International Tribunal, Hawai'i 1993' (1996) 19 PoLAR: Political and Legal Anthropology Review 67, see also Sally Engle Merry, Human Rights and Gender Violence: Translating International Law into Local Justice (University of Chicago Press, 2006). See also Matthew G Allen et al., The Rush for Oceania: Critical Perspectives on Contemporary Oceans Governance and Stewardship (Working Paper No. 9, School of Government, Development and International Affairs, University of the South Pacific, 1 December 2018).

95 Allen makes similar observations, noting that the ex-militants he interviewed depicted themselves 'as traditional warriors and protectors of their peoples – the malaghai of Guadalcanal and the ramo of Malaita': Allen, Greed and Grievance, 25.

96 F Tetevete, 'Letter to the Editor', Isatabu Tavuli (6 June 2000).

region,[97] and asserts an inseparability of people and place that is at once particular to the places and communities in which they arise, as well as linked to global discourses of Indigenous rights. Tetevete, for example, compared the Guadalcanal struggle to that of 'the Aboriginals of Australia, the Maoris of New Zealand, the American Indians and Indigenous Hawaiians' as well as the people of Fiji and Kosovo.[98] These comparisons rhetorically link the situation of Guadalcanal people to those of Indigenous people in settler colonies, and as Sina Emde has observed of very similar claims in Fiji, the clear implication is that if people do not stand up and assert themselves, they will face colonisation and dispossession.[99] Andrew Te'e, one of the commanders of the IFM, wrote a lengthy essay for the group's newsletter that referred to the indivisibility of Guadalcanal as a people and a place and then made this relationship legible to a global audience by linking it to the creator spirits from a variety of cultures:

> To us, the sons and daughters of Isatabu, land is ultimately our mother. She takes care of us all the time. In return we must take good care of her. She is God's greatest gift to us. She was given to us by papa God, Yahweh, Allah, Visahu, Bahaullah, Bhudha, Irogli etc. Land is our 'mummy' and nothing less.[100]

The idiom of land as Mother, as sacred and holy, is common in many parts of the Pacific, and as we see in the final chapter, may be expressed in diverse ways. When mediated through hypermasculine solidarity and the context of political violence, it takes on particular valences that it may not have in other contexts.

It has often been noted that the slogan adopted by Guadalcanal militants – 'Land is Our Mother, Land is Our Life, Land is Our Future' – was also used by combatants on Bougainville. When mobilised in this way, such idioms draw on the essentialised versions of social organisation and land tenure and land tenure previously discussed. According to these narratives, Guadalcanal (or Bougainville) is constructed as a feminised people and place, vulnerable to appropriation and colonisation, particularly by people from a place of patriliny and patriarchy (in the case of Solomon Islands, Malaita).[101] Anna-Karina

---

[97] Margaret Jolly, 'Another Time, Another Place' (1999) 69(4) *Oceania* 282.

[98] Tetevete, 'Letter to the Editor'.

[99] Sina Emde, 'Feared Rumours and Rumours of Fear: The Politicisation of Ethnicity During the Fiji Coup in May 2000' (2005) 75(4) *Oceania* 387, 396.

[100] Te'e, 'Land Is Sacred'.

[101] See also Michael Scott, who suggests that Malaita is mythologised as masculine, colonising and allochthonous as against the feminised, colonised and autochthonous people of islands such as Guadalcanal and Makira: Scott, 'The Matter of Makira', 134.

Hermkens points out in her analysis of the conflict on Bougainville that these slogans also turn on an essentialisation of women's roles as reproducers and custodians of the land, and create an expectation that men will defend and protect the holy land and its people.[102] It is hardly surprising, then, that the Tension appears to have entailed a reassertion of the hypermasculine qualities of the malaghai in defence of a feminine-gendered people and place against a despoiling other.

I have no doubt that the claims made by militants were supported in various ways by at least some women, for I have heard them repeated by women in the years since the Tension. However, I suggest that the discursive strategies used by militants were promulgated primarily by male ideologues and perhaps more importantly, both emerged from and were expressed through hypermasculine forms of solidarity. George Gray, one of the commanders of the IFM, wrote at length about how militants gathered at camps with names such as 'Bravo Brigade', where they underwent a period of initiation during which 'various traditional rituals and ceremonies were carried out to prepare the men for war':

> It was also at this time that sacrifices of pigs were offered to ancestral spirits who were believed to take care and defend the malaghai (warriors). Furthermore, special betel nut limes and clubs (*ghai tabu*) were blessed and used as weapons to weaken and confuse enemy soldiers.

> Not all the warriors in the camps were sent to the frontline. It was only those who passed the tests and conformed to the rules prescribed by the elders that were sent. They were believed to possess a certain degree of ancestral power and discipline that would boost them and enable them to fight fearlessly and overcome the enemy.[103]

Gray describes the use of 'traditional rituals and practices in the search for a common Guadalcanal identity', and the expression of masculinity and male solidarity through the wearing of kabilato (a traditional loin cloth) and 'torn camouflage collected from other people'.[104] Thus the territorial narratives of Guadalcanal militants not only drew on the rhetoric of kastom and a global

---

[102] Anna-Karina Hermkens, 'Mary, Motherhood and Nation: Religion and Gender Ideology in Bougainville's Secessionist Warfare' [2011] (25) *Intersections*.

[103] George Gray and James Tanis, 'In Between: Personal Experiences of the 9-Year Long Conflict on Bougainville and Habuna Momoruqu (The Blood of My Island): Violence and Guadalcanal Uprising in Solomon Islands (Working/Technical Paper No 02/4, State, Society and Governance in Melanesia Program, Australian National University, 2002).

[104] Ibid.

discourse of 'ethnic conflict', but were expressed through particular forms of masculinist solidarity that were also grounded in these discourses.

These idioms, discourses and expressions of male solidarity were not only highly gendered, but had profoundly gendered and corporeal effects, including a deepening of gender-based violence. It is now axiomatic to observe that gendered nationalist discourses frequently revive gender codes that are said to be more 'traditional',[105] and in Solomon Islands, the reassertion of kastom-oriented philosophies included increasingly restrictive, gendered dress codes. On Guadalcanal, militants required men in some areas to wear kabilato (bark loin cloth) and women to wear grass skirts. On the southern Weather Coast, these dress codes appear to have been reinterpreted and enforced in a progressively restrictive manner as violence escalated – while women were initially required to wear grass skirts, they were later prohibited from wearing T-shirts, and then from wearing underwear beneath their grass skirts. Older and younger women often told me that they initially resisted these demands, explaining that they were not used to wearing such clothing and saw it as contrary to their 'rights'.[106] Many perceived these dress codes to heighten their physical vulnerability in a context where they were already exposed to an increased risk of rape and other forms of sexual violence.[107]

Gender violence was not merely an effect of territorial claims; it constituted them. The enforcement of 'customary' dress codes, particularly against women, underscores the profoundly embodied and material ways in which gendered and ethnic categories of difference were produced, reinscribed, 'marked' and 'performed'.[108] Militants invoked ancestral ideals of the warrior

---

[105] See e.g. Wenona Giles and Jennifer Hyndman, 'Introduction: Gender and Conflict in a Global Context' in Wenona Mary Giles and Jennifer Hyndman (eds.), *Sites of Violence: Gender and Conflict Zones* (University of California Press, 2004), 3, 9.

[106] Women and children who gave their testimonies to the Truth and Reconciliation Commission repeatedly described their discomfort at having to wear *kabilato* and grass skirts, because they were 'not used to it'. Many of the women described how they 'stood up for their rights' and refused to wear grass skirts: Solomon Islands Truth and Reconciliation, *Thematic Public Hearing for Women*, 25 November 2010; and Solomon Islands Truth and Reconciliation, *Thematic Public Hearing for Youth*, 22 November 2010.

[107] When I visited Solomon Islands in 2004, many people discussed these issues openly with me, by the time the Truth and Reconciliation Commission was established, they were far more reluctant: see Louise Vella, 'Documenting Women's Experiences of Conflict and Sexual Violence: On the Ground with the Solomon Islands Truth and Reconciliation Commission' in Renée Jeffery (ed.), *Transitional Justice in Practice: Conflict, Justice, and Reconciliation in the Solomon Islands* (Palgrave Macmillan, 2017), 141. See also Judy Fangalasuu, Ruth Maetala, Patricia Rodi, Anah Vota and Elsie Wickham, *Herem Kam: Stori Blong Mifala Olketa Mere: Women's Submission to the Solomon Islands Truth and Reconciliation Commission* (Solomon Islands Truth and Reconciliation Commission, 2011).

[108] Underhill-Sem 'Marked Bodies in Marginalised Places'.

as the defender of both the people and the land, as well as the ideal of Land as Mother, in order to legitimise their violent enactment of territorial claims. This reproduced land disputes not only as masculine but as *hypermasculine*; as 'dangerous' sites best suited to 'warriors' that women participate in at their own peril. The Tension involved violent assertions of land tenure and leadership that privileged certain ways of knowing, being and acting; and these modes were harmful for Solomon Islander women as well as many other people who did not conform to the hegemonic models of masculinity foregrounded during the conflict. Malaitan husbands were targeted and evicted at least as often as Malaitan wives, and when I first visited Solomon Islands in 2004, a number of young Guadalcanal and Malaitan men recounted the torture they experienced when they resisted joining the conflict. Media and scholarly discourses surrounding the Tension often convey the impression that 'women bore the heaviest burden', but as Hilary Charlesworth has pointed out in relation to violent conflict generally, 'men's experience of war is not simply one of brotherhood and glory; it is much more the experience of death, suffering and mental illness'.[109] The gender violence during the Tension reaffirmed the 'naturalness' of men as warriors and women as peacemakers, with implications for the reproduction of gendered relations not only within families and communities, but in state institutions, that require much closer attention than they have received to date.

It is critical to acknowledge that the violence that occurred during the Tension was not merely an *effect* of territorial claims, or the outcome of a 'breakdown' in law and order. Rather, it constructed and reinscribed the very ethnic and gendered categories of difference that underlay the conflict, which have been hardened by, and constitutive of, state-centric and originally Euro-American conceptions of land law and political order. These forms of social differentiation are reproduced not only through violence, but also through ongoing, everyday contests over the terms of land tenure and membership of descent groups, debates about the commodification of land and its resources and struggles over local leadership and wider political authority. The processes by which claims to land are contested and legitimated at the local level are therefore bound up with contests over belonging and leadership, and part of broader processes of constituting identities and authority at multiple scales including 'the local', 'the provincial' and 'the national'. This means that disputes over property at the local level are far from parochial; they involve

---

[109] Charlesworth, 'Are Women Peaceful?'.

contests over boundaries between people and on the ground that are entangled with multiscalar processes of creating and restructuring the nation state.

5.3.3 *Big Men, Land Struggles and the Hypermasculine State*

For all the obvious weaknesses of the state in Solomon Islands, the narratives of militants reveal that the signs, rituals and vocabularies of the state are widely understood to be crucial to social differentiation. As we saw in Chapter 4, the 'dangerous', socially fragmenting power of struggles over land, particularly once they involve processes of recognition by the state, has significant implications for the gendered construction of leadership and political authority in Solomon Islands. These implications occur at multiple scales, and while they are often most visible at moments of rupture such as the Tension, they may also be discerned in the ongoing, everyday processes of political governance and state formation.

During the conflict, militants and politicians drew on a complex repertoire of kastom, religion and state law to assert boundaries between people, and on the ground. These territorialising strategies have marked similarities to the property narratives examined in previous chapters, and they turn on gendered understandings of socio-spatial relations and reconstitute them, often in ways that are not immediately obvious to outsiders. We have seen that once local disputes enter the arenas established by the state – such as chiefs' hearings, courts, timber rights hearings and land acquisition procedures – it is primarily senior men who perform, endorse and reject these claims to land as property. If we then turn to provincial assemblies or the national parliament, the absence of women in state-based arenas becomes particularly stark. Solomon Islands has one of the lowest rates of women's political participation in the world, currently standing at around 2 per cent participation in the national parliament, as compared to 8 per cent in the broader Pacific and a global average of around 24 per cent. Rates of women in provincial government are slightly better, with a regional average of 14.8 per cent – still significant lower than the global average.[110] I argue that an appreciation of the highly gendered relationship between property, territory and political authority is crucial in

---

[110] Inter-Parliamentary Union, *Women in Parliament in 2017: The Year in Review* (2018); Pacific Islands Forum Secretariat, 'Pacific Leaders Gender Equality Declaration Trend Assessment Report 2012–2016' (2016); Pacific Women, *Pacific Women Women in Leadership Synthesis Report: Informing Pacific Women Shaping Pacific Development Roadmap 2017–2022 – Pacific Women Shaping Pacific Development* (2017).

understanding the relative absence of women from state-based arenas such as courts and parliaments.

Since the earliest days of the Protectorate, Solomon Islands' economy has been almost entirely dependent on the extraction of natural resources – copra, oil palm, fishing, logging and mining – by a small number of large-scale, foreign-owned companies. Many of these operations are based on customary land, and the state bureaucracy acts as both the regulator and mediator between local communities and foreign companies. In this context, securing the state's recognition of claims to land and other natural resources has become a vital avenue to building economic and political power and prestige. The example of logging in Marovo reveals that contests over natural resources and the negotiation of leadership at the local level are mutually constitutive and I have similarly suggested that land disputes in Kakabona have provided a critical means by which to assert masculine authority. These processes must be understood not only as material struggles over the means of production, but also as struggles over the meanings of land and the people associated with it: as women and men, migrants and landowners and 'ordinary people' as compared to chiefs and trustees. While the state is undoubtedly 'weak' in many ways, it has very effectively constructed, recognised and sedimented a structure of entitlements for some people while eroding and submerging the claims of others.

Importantly, these processes are not confined to 'the local' level, but 'scale up' to the provincial and national level, with seemingly intimate struggles over property being bound up with a range of interlaced territorialising projects. Solomon Islands is characterised by an extractive economy, a small middle class and relatively modest civil administration, and in this sense, shares many commonalities with neighbouring Papua New Guinea and Vanuatu. Formal political organisation is highly unstable and fragmented, and political alliances are maintained through highly personalised patronage networks. The country's narrow economic base, coupled with its dependence on primary resources and foreign capital, means that the finances required to support these patronage networks overwhelmingly come from the state, from revenues from natural resource extraction by foreign corporations and from foreign donors. This has worked to maintain social fragmentation and disperse rather than centralise power.[111] It has also contributed to a situation that Edvard

---

[111] For extensive discussion of these matters see e.g. Tarcisius Kabutaulaka, 'Parties, Constitutional Engineering and Governance in the Solomon Islands' in Roland Rich, Luke Hambly and Michael G Morgan (eds.), *Political Parties in the Pacific Islands* (ANU Press, 2008), 229; Shahar Hameiri, 'Failed States or a Failed Paradigm? State Capacity and the Limits of Institutionalism'

Hviding has described as 'compressed globalisation',[112] in which a variety of actors such as multinational logging, fishing and mining companies, as well as conservation organisations, bypass the central government to negotiate directly with communities. As we have seen in previous chapters, control over negotiations with landholding groups is often concentrated in the hands of a relatively small number of people, primarily male leaders. This means that local struggles over land and leadership are entwined with broader processes of social differentiation and state formation in ways that are often extremely condensed in both space and time.

Securing state recognition of authority over land has now become an important means by which to establish political authority not only at the local level, but also at the provincial and national level. This has resulted in processes of gendered social differentiation in which the semantic and institutional structures of the state have been produced and reinscribed as masculine, even hypermasculine domains. It is generally senior men who mobilise the language of state law on behalf of the group before chiefs, courts, timber rights hearings and land acquisition officers; men who are constructed as warriors and defenders of the land against incursion; senior men who are constituted as 'trustees' of land and the signatories of logging licences; and therefore senior men who control the access to revenue so crucial for effective participation in provincial and national politics.

The relationship between resources rights and the predominance of men in formal political arenas has often been understood in terms of the economic influence necessary to succeed in parliamentary politics in Solomon Islands. As a number of researchers have previously noted, national and provincial politicians generally have substantial logging interests,[113] and equally, many prominent politicians have been extremely successful in establishing themselves as the 'owners' and 'trustees' of registered land. The dependence of political leaders on resource rents also makes them heavily dependent on

(2007) 10(2) *Journal of International Relations and Development* 122; Shahar Hameiri, 'State Building or Crisis Management? A Critical Analysis of the Social and Political Implications of the Regional Assistance Mission to Solomon Islands' (2009) 30(1) *Third World Quarterly* 35; Matthew Allen, 'Long-Term Engagement: The Future of the Regional Assistance Mission to Solomon Islands' [2011] *Strategic Insights*; Sinclair Dinnen, 'State-Building in a Post-Colonial Society: The Case of Solomon Islands' (2008) 9 *Chicago Journal of International Law* 51; Sinclair Dinnen, 'The Crisis of State in Solomon Islands' (2009) 21(1) *Peace Review* 70, 76, Allen, 'Long-Term Engagement'; Allen, 'The Political Economy of Logging in Solomon Islands'.

[112] Edvard Hviding, 'Contested Rainforests, NGOs, and Projects of Desire in Solomon Islands' (2003) 55(178) *International Social Science Journal* 539.

[113] E.g. Bennett, *Pacific Forest*; Hviding and Bayliss-Smith, *Islands of Rainforest*.

relations with logging companies, mining companies and other private sector interests, who are widely believed to have a significant influence on the formation of government, the election of prime minister and the general operation of government.

However as I have shown, struggles over property cannot be understood merely as contests over the means of production and a crucial source of revenue. They have been crucial to the reproduction of particular models of masculinity. Moreover, we have seen that the norms and institutions of the state, far more than those associated with kastom and Christianity, are associated with these multiple forms of violence – they prompt the severing of connections between people and place, and this makes state-based arenas particularly 'dangerous' sites, and produces and reinscribes state norms and institutions as a hypermasculine domain. This is repeatedly revealed when Solomon Islanders refer to Malaitan or Guadalcanal politicians as ramo or malaghai (warriors); or when Australian police officers prevent Solomon Islander women from entering the 'dangerous' parliament, as they did when women leaders tried to broker peace during political riots in 2006. As I wrote this in late 2021, people – and young men in particular – had once again taken to the streets, and protests against foreign exploitation of local resources and demanding greater provincial autonomy had rapidly degenerated into rioting and looting. These processes cannot be understood solely in terms of the unequal distribution of rents and royalties within families or communities, or as resource conflicts exposing the weaknesses of political institutions; nor can they be easily remedied by 'state-building', anti-corruption programmes or reserved seats for women in the national parliament. Rather, they involve profound and ongoing struggles and debates over non-material, moral issues, and the meanings attached to law, land and people.

5.4 CONCLUSION

The Tension casts the entwining of local-level contests over land with wider processes of socio-spatial differentiation and state formation into sharp relief. The narratives of militants undoubtedly highlighted the continuity and persuasiveness of kastom in political struggles over socio-spatial categories, particularly in respect of the boundaries delineated by the state. However if overplayed, narratives of 'fragile', 'weak' or 'irrelevant' state institutions can obscure the role that the state *does* play in the establishment of boundaries between people and on the ground. Moreover, such narratives amplify the assumption that social inequality and instability can be attributed to an *absence* of state law rather than its very active *presence*.

In Solomon Islands, the state has provided a crucial set of semantic and institutional structures for constructing space, and for structuring claims to belonging and authority within that space. The grievances expressed by militants; the assertions of territorialised allegiances congruent with provincial boundaries; and demands for provincial autonomy heard across the country were all directed towards *the state* as a source of authority capable of legitimating social boundaries. In other words, for all its limits and weaknesses, the state was still a key point of reference in struggles over social and physical spaces.

Seen from this perspective, it is not surprising that in the years since the conflict, Solomon Islanders have devoted significant attention to reconfiguring the political order through a process of constitutional reform. The 2000 Townsville Peace Agreement committed the Solomon Islands Government to a review of the 1978 constitution so as to give greater autonomy to the provinces, and this resulted in a 2004 Draft Constitution and a 2005 White Paper setting out a process for reform. Since that time, a number of drafts have been reviewed. The most recent draft, the 2014 Draft Constitution, has been the subject of particularly widespread public consultations over a number of years. A consistent theme in each draft is the establishment of a federal republic, and the devolution of control over land and marine resources (including rents) to the provincial (which would be state) and community level. The debate about federalism is one that some sections of the donor community have sought to stifle, apparently due to concerns about the cost of operating a federal system. However, as this chapter has demonstrated, the 1998–2003 conflict emerged from long-standing debates regarding the demarcation of territorial boundaries and the distribution of political authority within those spaces. Indeed, when rioting broke out in Honiara in late 2021, it occurred in the context of petitions from the Malaita and Guadalcanal provincial governments that reinvigorated the demands expressed in the Townsville Peace Agreement, including with respect to provincial autonomy. The debate about federalism is not one that can be stifled.

Constitutional reform is the subject of intense interest among Solomon Islanders, and many people appear to have immense confidence that the 'right' constitution will resolve a vast range of social, economic and political ills.[114] The 2014 Draft Constitution is immensely detailed, comprising

---

[114] Cf Jean Comaroff and John L Comaroff, 'Law and Disorder in the Postcolony: An Introduction' in Jean Comaroff and John L Comaroff (eds.), *Law and Disorder in the Postcolony* (University of Chicago Press, 2006), 1, 22.

249 articles and 14 lengthy schedules, significantly longer than any other constitution in the region. It opens with the interweaving of kastom, Christianity and state law that has long been a feature of political life in Solomon Islands: the preamble invokes 'the guidance and blessings of God the creator' and asserts 'the authority of our traditional clan and tribal systems and leadership'. The draft provides for the nine existing provinces to become states, and each would delegate part of their power to 'community governments' that would be based on 'the authority traditionally vested in the tribes, clans, lineages, families or any customary groups' that have existed 'since time immemorial, and which have evolved and been modified as necessary to meet changing circumstances'.[115] Control over land and marine resources would be highly decentralised, situated primarily at the level of state and community government.[116] The 2014 Draft Constitution, like other drafts before it, represents yet another attempt to mobilise state law to delineate space, and to fix, consolidate and institutionalise particular forms of land control and social differentiation.

In previous work I have observed that the interest in constitutional reform must be understood as an attempt to craft Indigenous legal geographies and thus should not be managed or directed by non-Indigenous 'outsiders'.[117] This does not preclude me from also expressing my doubts about the 'constitutional optimism' I have noted. We have seen that in Solomon Islands this optimism has a long history, and as Ambreena Manji has recently observed for Kenya, it may also be linked to the wider, global inclination towards the rule of law and constitutionalism.[118] My doubts are grounded in the fact that state law and institutions have often worked to construct binary oppositions and deepen inequality between men and women, and landowners and migrants; to generate contests over socio-spatial distinctions imbued with a sense of insecurity and danger; and to consolidate authority over both land and people in the hands of a relatively small number of influential men. However, the Tension also provides a reminder that socio-spatial differentiation is never fixed, even – or perhaps *particularly* – in the terms set out by the state system. Enactments of property and territoriality have ebbed and flowed over time, influenced by a variety of understandings, vocabularies and audiences, and shifting political, legal and economic circumstances. In the years since the conflict, people

---

[115] *Second 2014 Draft for Proposed Constitution of the Federal Democratic Republic of Solomon Islands*, section 188.
[116] See in particular Chapter Four and Schedule 7.
[117] Monson and Hoa'au, '(Em)placing Law'.
[118] Ambreena Manji, *The Struggle for Land and Justice in Kenya* (James Currey, 2020), 168.

from Malaita and other parts of the country have gradually returned to their homes on Guadalcanal. In many instances, their return has been associated with the public restoration and affirmation of social relations through the provision of chupu, and it is striking that many Malaitans have also been unwilling or unable to assert their claims in the terms provided by the state legal system. It has been kastom, far more than the state, which has provided the means for crossing frontiers of difference.

6

Women Speak for Land

Disrupting and Re-forming Property and Authority

In Solomon Islands, most people have a place to build a house, establish a garden, raise children, go to church and participate in the life of a community. Indeed, many people – including many of the most economically marginalised of people living in informal urban settlements – have 'the ability to benefit from things'[1] in numerous places. By employing a focus on processes of 'making' or 'forming' property, we see that rather than 'securing' such relationships, state legitimation of claims to land as property has often submerged particular forms of attachment to land, generated a sense of insecurity and precarity and fuelled the reproduction of particular visions and ideals of (hyper)masculine control over land. This has consolidated formal legal control over land, and the financial benefits that flow from its exploitation, in the hands of people who conform to these hegemonic masculinities. The embodiment not only of land control but state power is now emphatically masculine – women rarely appear in land matters before chiefs or courts, they rarely appear as land trustees or signatories to logging licences, they are rarely in direct receipt of resource royalties and they are only occasionally elected to parliament.

All of this tends to affirm the assertion that I have heard from people in many parts of Solomon Islands, that 'olketa woman no save tok lo saed lo land' – a phrase that may variously refer to the social norms that dictate that women should not generally speak about land matters in public arenas; to the fact that women do not typically speak in such arenas as a matter of common practice; or to the view that women cannot speak effectively about land matters in public arenas as they often lack the customary knowledge and oratorical prowess necessary to do so. Yet ideologies and practices of land,

---

[1] Ribot and Peluso, 'A Theory of Access'.

gender and political authority are also actively debated, contested and reconfigured, and throughout this book we have seen that at least some women have exerted significant influence and 'talked' about land – including as wives or mothers-in-law of traders discussing land deals with kin; as experts consulted by the men appearing before colonial land commissions; and as senior women encouraging young men to evict migrants from peri-urban settlements.

As postcolonial critiques of development and transnational feminism have long argued, failure to attend to these forms of influence is to reproduce the very forms of silencing, marginalisation and erasure this book has sought to expose and address.[2] I therefore close by turning my attention more fully to the ways in which women 'speak' within the plurality of coexisting and interwoven norms and institutions that comprise land tenure in Solomon Islands. I focus on key instances in which Solomon Islanders have collectively mobilised *as women* – that is, on instances in which the grounds for their gendered exclusion have also provided the basis for their collective mobilisation – and consider the strategies they have used to generate legitimacy for their claims and resist, appropriate and rearrange the gendered legal pluralities I have exposed throughout this book.

In order to situate these movements, their strategies and my understanding of them, I start by recapping my core arguments regarding the hypermasculinisation of property, territory and authority. I then focus on particular instances in which (some) women have collectively mobilised to contest, disrupt and erode these processes so as to prise open space for more diverse and expansive land relations and futures. I understand these strategies as consciously linking past, present and future: they reanimate Indigenous knowledges and practices that have been eroded or submerged by colonialism, while also constituting a kind of prefigurative politics that explores alternative legal strategies and relations. These strategies, which I suspect may resonate elsewhere in Oceania, suggest that when Solomon Islanders challenge inequality in land relations, it is not the forms we might associate with the state that they explicitly turn to and foreground, but rather kastom and Christianity. An approach to gendered land relations that is preoccupied with the norms, institutions and technologies of the state as the primary mechanism for addressing inequality will not only detract attention from the strategies

---

[2]   See for example Chandra Talpade Mohanty 'Under Western Eyes: Feminist Scholarship and Colonial Discourses' (1984) 12/3 *boundary* 2 333, Chandra Talpade Mohanty '"Under Western Eyes" Revisited: Feminist Solidarity through Anticapitalist Struggles'(2002) 28(2) *Signs* 499, Teresia Teaiwa 'Microwomen: US Colonialism and Micronesian Women Activists' in Katerina Teaiwa, April K Henderson and Terence Wesley-Smith (eds.), *Sweat and Salt Water: Selected Works* University of Hawai'i Press 2021, 87.

employed by these movements but potentially constrain them, undermining the efforts of Solomon Islanders to reconfigure land relations, political structures and legal pluralities.

6.1 THE (HYPER)MASCULINISATION OF THE STATE

Land tenure in Solomon Islands is dynamic and characterised by multiple, complex and interwoven spheres of kastom, state and Christianity. Contact with Europeans and articulation with the global political economy set in motion new kinds of negotiations, debates and contests over land, and within an unstable profusion of normative and institutional forms, people compete to have their claims to land recognised as property, and also for recognition of their political authority to organise access to the land. These struggles have been crucial to the formation and contestation of contemporary subjectivities and social distinctions, including between men and women; between members of the central government and the people who desire a more decentralised system of government; between the landowners and migrants who are said to belong in other places; and between chiefs and other members of landholding groups. Participation in and influence over these processes has been uneven, leading to new and more entrenched social distinctions and deeper power asymmetries than may have historically been the case. In particular, once claims to land have entered the arenas established by the state – such as timber rights hearings, land acquisition proceedings, chiefs' hearings and the negotiation of peace agreements – it has been men who conform to hegemonic models of 'men of peace' or 'men of war' who have made, endorsed and rejected those claims.

The dominance of such men in state-based arenas is often explained by locals in terms of 'hu nao save tok' (who may/can/does speak) – a reference to customary ideals regarding who may, can or does 'talk' about land matters, at least in public arenas. Different people certainly had different responsibilities and attachments to place prior to the arrival of Europeans, but I have argued that the consolidation of authority over land and people in the hands of a relatively small number of men, and the marginalisation of many other people, emerges from long-term processes of missionisation, the accretion of Euro-American conceptions and practices of property and the integration of Islanders and their places into labour markets and extractive industries. The consistent legitimation and reiteration of particular models of masculinity has worked to imbue some men with authority over both land and people, in a context in which relationships between people and places have been rapidly and profoundly destabilised. Land disputes have now emerged as a vital arena for performing particular models of masculine influence and prestige, and as a pre-eminently masculine domain.

These processes extend far beyond struggles over land and leadership within and between lineages and villages, for contemporary property disputes are inextricably entwined with multiscalar contests over political participation and leadership. The political economy of Solomon Islands is profoundly informed by extractive industries, and has provided a particularly potent setting for land disputes to emerge as a critical arena for the reproduction of masculine authority and prestige at multiple scales. The people who manage access to land, forests and minerals at the local level are those most likely to have the financial means necessary to enter parliament; and these processes have entrenched particular forms of authority and influence so that the role of 'spokesperson', 'chief', 'trustee' and 'Member of Parliament' have become so thoroughly entangled as to be mutually constitutive. This recursive constitution of property and authority primarily, although not exclusively, through the state has not only worked to consolidate control over land in the hands of a relatively tight network of men, but simultaneously reproduced and reinscribed the norms, institutions, practices and spaces associated with the state as a masculine, even hypermasculine, domain.

Gendered struggles over land must therefore be understood as operating at multiple scales that are themselves socially and politically constructed. Contests over land are grounded in specific places and communities, and legal pluralities are diverse – we might wonder, for example, what the pluralities of north-west Guadalcanal would look like today if the ancestral peak behind Visale mission had not collapsed, with the land itself seeming to channel people towards the Marist Mission. However, these diverse, 'local' contests are also productive of wider struggles and processes of state formation. Whereas high levels of land disputation are often perceived as a challenge to a pre-existing, albeit 'weak' or 'fragile' state, I have shown that they are bound up with its making: the state is not a pre-given outcome, but requires ongoing recognition from its people. It is therefore important to situate seemingly local struggles within wider political, economic and ecological conditions, as well as trace the ways in which those struggles 'scale up' to inform and reproduce wider conditions, including the nature of the state. Land relations not only flow from legal pluralities but constitute them, and disputes over land are bound up with debates about belonging, leadership and political participation in the broadest sense. In Solomon Islands, these processes have worked to reproduce the state as a source of material and epistemological precarity, inequality and exclusion, and as an inherently hypermasculine domain.

6.2 HOW DO WOMEN SPEAK?

Solomon Islander women do speak and always have, although the ways they have exerted influence have often been erased from the historical record. David Akin has suggested that the exclusion of women from the colonial records of Maasina Rule sustained representations of the movement as oppressive towards women,[3] and a similar 'forgetting' is often evident in contemporary development discourses. When I first visited Solomon Islands in 2004, it was very well known both locally and internationally that women's groups had played a crucial role in peacebuilding during the conflict, particularly through the formation of Women for Peace. By the time I returned to commence this project in 2008, international knowledge of these groups had declined to such an extent that Australian 'experts' responsible for gender equality projects, including campaigns to advance women's political leadership, had never heard of these groups.[4] Furthermore, while the role of Women for Peace is often mentioned in existing scholarship, relatively little attention has been paid to *how* women undertook this work and the strategies they employed; and even less attention has been paid to what those strategies might reveal about Solomon Islands' legal pluralities. This neglect of women's knowledge, influence and I suggest worlds works to reproduce representations of Solomon Islander women as silenced, as victims of their culture and in need of solutions and expertise emanating from 'outside' the epistemes, practices and spaces associated with kastom and even Solomon Islands generally.

In the sections that follow I take the work undertaken by Women for Peace during the conflict as a starting point for considering the modes of action employed by women as they navigate 'multiple networks of legal orders'[5] and engage in struggles over land. I suggest first, that there are marked similarities between the strategies employed by women peace-builders as they engaged in ethno-territorial contests, and those used by women who assert their claims to land to oppose the more socially and ecologically destructive forms of 'development' occurring on their territories. Second, I highlight that rights-based discourses – for example, explicit references to property law, or human rights – are markedly 'quiet' in these strategies, and that it is kastom and Christianity

---

[3] Akin, *Colonialism, Maasina Rule and the Origins of Malaitan Kastom*, 280.
[4] In previous work I noted that this was the case for young Australian volunteers; however, it was also prevalent among very established international development consultants: Rebecca Monson, 'Vernacularising Political Participation: Strategies of Women Peace-Builders in Solomon Islands' (2013) 33 *Intersections: Gender and Sexuality in Asia and the Pacific*.
[5] De Sousa Santos, 'Law: A Map of Misreading'.

that appear to provide the primary grounds for women's struggles. Third, whereas existing scholarship has tended to interpret these strategies as a product of women operating within culturally prescribed parameters of 'good' womanhood,[6] I argue that the strategies employed by women may *also* challenge and rupture the hypermasculinisation of property, territory and authority, generating new norms, practices and legal pluralities. While my focus here is on the emplaced discourses and practices of Solomon Islanders, I draw attention to the ways in which these strategies may resonate with struggles elsewhere in Oceania.

There is a risk that in focusing on women's collective action as peacemakers and as custodians of the land I obscure the multivocality of people's politics and strategies, and contribute to the reproduction of tired gendered tropes – in particular the construction of women as a physically vulnerable, anti-militaristic, peaceful and ecologically oriented 'Other' against which an equally homogeneous, violent, exploitative category of men is constructed.[7] My purpose here is to take some of the most prominent mobilisations of women and acknowledge that when people have mobilised *as women* – that is, as 'peacebuilders' and 'custodians' of the land, and also specifically as 'women' and as 'mothers' – they have done so deliberately and strategically. That is, they have mobilised collectively and as women not because it is natural or inevitable, or because they have homogeneous interests, but because first, they have at least some shared interests in combatting their gendered exclusion and second, it is efficacious in the environment in which they operate.

6.2.1 *Mothers of the Land, Mothers of the Nation*

Maternal idioms of the relationship between people and land are widespread in Oceania and have often been central to struggles over land, property and territory. In the preceding chapter we saw that Guadalcanal militants adopted

---

[6] See e.g. Michelle Dyer, 'Ungrounded Cosmopolitanism: Intersections of Moral Responsibility and Gender in Environmental Activism in Rural Solomon Islands' (2018) 67(March–April) *Women's Studies International Forum* 128.

[7] On the emphasis on women and peacebuilding see for example Jean Bethke Elshtain, *Women and War* (University of Chicago Press, 2nd ed, 2013); Charlesworth, 'Are Women Peaceful?'. Gender and nature/culture binaries have been critiqued and debated for even longer: see eg Sherry B Ortner, 'Is Female to Male as Nature Is to Culture?' (1972) 1(2) *Feminist Studies* 5; Carol MacCormack and Marilyn Strathern (eds.), *Nature, Culture and Gender* (Cambridge University Press, 1981); Val Plumwood *Feminism and the Mastery of Nature* (Routledge, 1993), Haripriya Rangan, *Of Myths and Movements: Rewriting Chipko into Himalayan History* (Verso, 2000).

the slogan, 'Land is Our Mother, Land is Our Life, Land is Our Future', a phrase notably reminiscent to that used by militants on Bougainville during a ten-year secessionist struggle fuelled by mining. In Marovo, land is 'the womb of life', and Cliff Bird explains that this relationship was historically enacted not only discursively but materially and corporeally, through the ritual burial of the placenta and umbilical cord in the ground.[8] Similar idioms and practices are known to many Pacific people, and it is important to note that these idioms are not confined to societies that emphasise matriliny, or to people who are biological mothers. Rather, they extend to the multiple generations of women who birth, nurture and sustain the people who belong to the land.[9] Some expressions also appear to disrupt the sex binary of male/ female – according to David Gegeo, the patrilineal Kwara'ae of Malaita understand land 'as the hermaphroditic "great mother" (Te'a 'Inota'a)...from whose womb we emerge and birth and into whose hands we return in death'.[10]

In Solomon Islands and Bougainville, these complex idioms were reinvigorated by peacebuilders as much as militants, underscoring the heterogeneous and contradictory ways in which they may be mobilised.[11] One of the best known groups in Solomon Islands was the Honiara-based Women for Peace, which had the stated goal of enabling women to contribute to the peace process 'in their capacity as mothers of the nation'.[12] Women for Peace engaged in diverse activities including prayer groups; the collection and distribution of food and other essential items to militants and the general population; and organising meetings with militants, police officers, political leaders and diplomats to discuss questions of law and order, good governance

---

[8]   Bird, 'Pepesa'.
[9]   See e.g. Naomi Simmonds, 'Mana Wahine: Decolonising Politics' (2011) 25(2) *Women's Studies Journal* 11; Myjolynne Marie Kim, 'Nesor Annim, Niteikapar (Good Morning, Cardinal Honeyeater): Indigenous Reflections on Micronesian Women and the Environment' (2020) 32(1) *The Contemporary Pacific* 147, 152.
[10] David W Gegeo, 'Tribes in Agony: Land , Development , and Politics in Solomon Islands' (1991) 19(2) *Cultural Survival Quarterly* 1.
[11] For discussions of Bougainville see Ruth Saovana-Spriggs, 'Bougainville Women's Role in Conflict Resolution in the Bougainville Peace Process' in Sinclair Dinnen, Anita Jowitt and Tess Newton Cain (eds.), *A Kind of Mending: Restorative Justice in the Pacific Islands* (ANU Press, 2010) 195; Josephine Tankunani Sirivi and Marilyn Taleo Havini, *As Mothers of the Land: The Birth of the Bougainville Women for Peace and Freedom* (Pandanus, 2004); Hermkens, 'Mary, Motherhood and Nation'. For a comparison of the strategies employed by women peace-builders and international interventions in Solomon Islands and Bougainville see Nicole George, 'Liberal-Local Peacebuilding in Solomon Islands and Bougainville: Advancing a Gender-Just Peace?' (2018) 94(6) *International Affairs* 1329.
[12] Liloqula and Pollard, 'Understanding Conflict in Solomon Islands'; Pollard, 'Women's Organizations, Voluntarism, and Self-Financing in Solomon Islands' (2003) 74(1/2) *Oceania* 44, 51.

and peace. They visited the bunkers of different militias and attempted to persuade them to lay down their weapons. Peacebuilders also baked cakes, broke them in half and shared them between the warring parties; they prayed with militants and hugged them as they wept.[13]

These strategies are saturated with feminised tropes of care, nurturance and duty, and women peacebuilders often linked them to the sacred. Writing in the midst of the conflict, Alice Pollard, a well-known Solomon Islander leader and scholar, suggested that shared 'Christianity and motherly instincts' not only motivated women peace-builders and informed their actions, but united them in spite of the divisions asserted at the time.[14] Thus in contrast to militants who invoked maternal idioms to assert rigid socio-spatial distinctions and legitimate the violent defence of land and people, women peace-builders emphasised women's customary and sacred status as nurturers and peace-builders to literally and figuratively blur and subvert such distinctions.

The subversion and crossing of the distinctions asserted by militants was not only discursive but material and embodied. Peacebuilders went to the frontlines and crossed the bunkers that distinguished alienated land in Honiara from the customary land beyond, and Sisters from the Anglican Church of Melanesian collaborated with other clergy to establish a camp *between* the bunkers of rival militias at Alligator Creek.[15] Peacebuilders were able to broker a deal with militants whereby women who were trapped inside Honiara and unable to cross checkpoints at the town boundary could interact with those on the Guadalcanal Plains, who were similarly prevented from accessing the city. These strategies enabled people and vital goods to move across the boundaries established by militants – the work of Women for Peace contributed to the establishment of a market where women in Honiara could exchange essential goods available in the city, such as salt, rice, soap and kerosene, for fresh fruits and vegetables grown by women on the plains.[16]

---

[13] Liloqula and Pollard, 'Understanding Conflict in Solomon Islands'; AA Pollard 'Women's Organisations, Voluntarism, and Self-Financing in Solomon Islands'; Pollard, 'Resolving Conflict in Solomon Islands'; Sharon Bhagwan Rolls, 'Women as Mediators in Pacific Conflict Zones' [2006] (2) *Women in Action* 29, 32–34; *Thematic Public Hearing for Women*, Solomon Islands Truth and Reconciliation Commission 25 November 2010 per Margaret Maelanga.

[14] Liloqula and Pollard, 'Understanding Conflict in Solomon Islands', 10.

[15] George, 'Liberal-Local Peacebuilding', 1340.

[16] See also Nicole George, '"Just Like Your Mother?" The Politics of Feminism and Maternity in the Pacific Islands' (2010) 32(1) *Australian Feminist Law Journal* 77, 89; Weir, 'The Churches in Solomon Islands and Fiji', 50; Jack Maebuta, Rebecca Spence, Iris Wielders and Michael O'Loughlin, *Attempts at Building Peace in the Solomon Islands: Disconnected Layers* (Collaborative for Development Action, 2009) 35.

These strategies have enormous potential to reproduce the constraints that women face in contesting the terms of land tenure and political leadership. As Indigenous and non-Indigenous scholars have noted, maternal idioms may overlook the burden of maternity, confine women to the domestic sphere rather than the public realm of parliamentary politics and reinforce hetero-normativity.[17] Pauline Soaki has argued that the emphasis on maternity is likely to reinforce women's subordinate position, ensuring that 'women can have influence publicly, [but only] if it involves actions and attitudes that are consistent with cultural stereotypes of women as gentle, motherly and ameliorative'.[18] Nicole George cautions that maternal idioms may reproduce security vernaculars that contribute to gender-based violence, including policing of women's reproductive autonomy.[19] These are important concerns and identify significant risks that require ongoing scrutiny and debate. Yet as I have noted elsewhere, the strategies employed by peacebuilders have often been considered in terms of these risks, rather than in terms of their capacity to challenge existing social practice and enact change. I argue that it is crucial to *also* acknowledge the extraordinary achievements of peacebuilders during a profoundly violent, unstable period, and furthermore, consider the generative possibilities of their strategies.[20]

Idioms of maternity in Solomon Islands and wider Oceania are multi-valenced and do not necessarily have the same meanings as in 'the West'. They are central to Indigenous, land-based knowledges and practices, and I argue that they have the potential to disrupt *as well as* reinforce culturally prescribed parameters of gendered action. While I do not question that maternal idioms can be deployed to confine women to the domestic sphere, I suggest that Women for Peace drew on them to reinstate their gendered political authority, insisting on their inclusion in the highly masculinised, national and global spaces of good governance, rule of law and state-building,

---

[17] Christine Dureau, 'Nobody Asked the Mother: Women and Maternity on Simbo, Western Solomon Islands' (1993) 64(1) *Oceania* 18; Bronwen Douglas, 'Christianity, Tradition, and Everyday Modernity: Towards an Anatomy of Women's Groupings in Melanesia' (2003) 74 (1–2) *Oceania* 6; Margaret Jolly, 'Beyond the Horizon? Nationalisms, Feminisms, and Globalization in the Pacific' (2005) 52(1) *Ethnohistory* 137; George, '"Just like Your Mother?"; Christine Taitano DeLisle, 'A History of Chamorro Nurse-Midwives in Guam and a "Placental Politics" for Indigenous Feminism' [2015] (37) *Intersections: Gender and Sexuality in Asia and the Pacific*.

[18] Pauline Soaki, 'Casting Her Vote: Women's Political Participation in Solomon Islands' in M Macintyre and C Spark (eds.), *Transformations of Gender in Melanesia* (ANU Press, 2017), 95, 102.

[19] Liberal Local Peace, 1346

[20] For further discussion see Monson, 'Vernacularising Political Participation'.

at a time when it was exceptionally risky to do so. For example, leaders such as Alice Pollard and Polini Boseto very clearly espoused the idea that as 'mothers of the nation' and 'mothers of democracy' women are responsible for 'driving' the 'good governance' and 'prosperity' of the nation.[21] I do not dispute the risks inherent in these strategies, and their potential to reinforce a restrictive gendered logics, but I wonder whether they might *also* fracture and shift these logics, by disrupting the masculinisation of public spaces; extending 'good governance' beyond securitised understandings; and reiterating conceptions of politics more imbued with notions of nurturance, care and social and ecological flourishing.

Once we understand resource struggles and knowledge production as multisited and multiscalar,[22] and the boundaries of islands, regions and states not as 'natural' but as co-produced with colonial expansion, capital accumulation and geopolitical competition,[23] our attention is drawn beyond the terrestrial boundaries of contemporary states to struggles occurring across a vast and interconnected Oceania. There is now a growing body of scholarship, particularly by Pacific women, that draws attention to the significance of maternal idioms in contesting the land dispossession, resource depletion and cultural loss associated with extractive industries, climate change and militarism. One of the most prominent examples of this is Kathy Jetñil-Kijiner's 2014 performance of her poem 'Dear Matafele Peinam', written to her daughter, at the United Nations Climate Summit in New York. As Angela Robinson observes in her detailed engagement with Jetñil-Kijiner's performance, the poem abounds with references to Indigenous mothers' embodied knowledges, authority, responsibilities and insights, including with respect to non-human entities. Jetñil-Kijiner's disruption of technocratic approaches to climate change, and insistence on familial relationships between all of humanity

[21] Liloqula and Pollard, 'Understanding Conflict in Solomon Islands'; Polini Boseto, 'Melanesian Women, Mothers of Democracy' in B Douglas (ed.), *Women and Governance from the Grassroots in Melanesia*, State, Society and Governance in Melanesia Discussion Paper 00/2, Canberra, 2000), 8.

[22] See for example Katerina Teaiwa's tracking of the 'multisited, multiscalar and multivocal history' of Banaba's 'material development, decimation, and global consumption as well as the changing sociopolitical landscapes created across the mining enterprise': Teaiwa, *Consuming Ocean Island*, 3.

[23] Eg Tarcisius Kabutaulaka 'Mapping the Blue Pacific in a Changing Regional Order' Graeme Smith and Terence Wesley-Smith (eds.), *The China Alternative: Changing Regional Order in the Pacific* (ANU Press, 2021) 41, Allen *Resource Extraction and Contentious States*.

and the planet received one of the few standing ovations recorded in UN history.[24]

Interventions during armed conflict and appearances before UN Climate Summits are relatively 'dramatic', high-profile instances of advocacy, and as feminist scholars of agrarian change such as Ritu Verma and Cecile Jackson have often emphasised, it is vital to pay attention to the more mundane 'micropolitics' and 'everyday business' of struggles over land.[25] Christine Taitano DeLisle draws our attention to the significance of the persistent, embodied assertions of stewardship of land and people by the pattera (CHamoru midwives) who bury the placenta in the soil in Guam. They do so in defiance of US orders, and in a context where not only this practice but matriliny itself has been abolished by American rule. For DeLisle, this work of stewarding land and bodies constitutes an Indigenous, feminist, 'placental politics' that materially and symbolically roots CHamoru in the soil; disrupts efforts to alienate CHamoru from their lands; and reanimates Indigenous epistemologies, ontologies and connections between the past, present and possible futures.[26]

We have seen that by reading both 'against' and 'along' the archival grain, and engaging with oral histories we might identify some of the forms of influence exerted by women during the early colonial period, for example as wives and mothers-in-law of European traders, or as the custodians of Indigenous knowledge crucial to disputes before colonial administrators.[27] Contemporary debates about logging licences and land sales occur not only in courtrooms, but also in kitchens and gardens, by roadside stalls and at church gatherings. Women may be relatively absent from the courts but they are active elsewhere, and maternal idioms are not easily disregarded. For

[24] Angela L Robinson, 'Of Monsters and Mothers: Affective Climates and Human-Nonhuman Sociality in Kathy Jetnil-Kijiner's "Dear Matafele Peinam"' (2020) 32(2) *The Contemporary Pacific* 311. See also Nicole George, 'Climate Change and "Architectures of Entitlement": Beyond Gendered Virtue and Vulnerability in the Pacific Islands?' in Catarina Kinnvall and Helle Rydstrom (eds.), *Climate Hazards, Disasters, and Gender Ramifications* (Routledge, 2019), 101.

[25] Jackson, 'Gender Analysis of Land', 461, Ritu Verma *Gender, Land and Livelihoods: Through Farmers Eyes* (International Development Research Centre, 2001).

[26] DeLisle, 'A History of Chamorro Nurse-Midwives'. Note that DeLisle's placental politics has been taken up and reinforced in Brandon J Reilly, 'Reproductive Anticolonialism: Placental Politics, Weaponised Wombs and the Power of Abjection in the Early Spanish Mariana Islands' [2020] (44) *Intersections*.

[27] Ann Laura Stoler, *Along the Archival Grain: Epistemic Anxieties and Colonial Common Sense* (Princeton University Press, 2009); Bronwen Douglas, 'Provocative Readings in Intransigent Archives: Finding Aneityumese Women' (1999) 70(2) *Oceania* 111; Monson, 'Unsettled Explorations of Law's Archives'.

example, David Livingston Ziru of Vella Lavella explained to anthropologist Cato Berg that his uncles had spent many years trying to persuade his mother, their sister, to agree to logging, without any success. Ziru explained, 'she would listen to me, but it is very hard for me to question her authority. *Mama nomoa hemi graon* ('only the mother/woman is *qoqono* [ground/earth/land]')!'[28]

These interventions all assert collective rather than individual responsibilities with respect to land, and foreground a relationality between the human and non-human worlds. This disrupts both ideologies of individualism and anthropocentric understandings of land, rocks, trees and entire ecosystems as objects that can be owned and utilised. Ruth Maetala recounts that when a group of men were considering selling land near Honiara to a businessman, one of them turned to his niece for advice, and she said:

> If you sell my land rights, you have sold my great, great grandmother, my great grandmother, my grandmother, my mother, and me to this business-man. If you respect my ancestors who are your ancestors also, then you will not sell my right to Kongulai water source.[29]

The niece not only invoked the authority of the matrilineage and multiple generations of women belonging to the land, but analogised the sale of land to the sale of their bodies. I have frequently heard land transactions, industrial logging and mining rhetorically linked to 'prostituting' mothers. The term 'prostitution' is apt here, since what is being referred to is exploitation, not voluntary work. These strategies are intended to be confronting. They collapse distinctions between more intimate and wider forms of violence, and draw attention to the collective suffering that arises from exclusionary decision-making and the exploitation of places and ecosystems as well as living people and ancestors. Rather than romanticising maternity, these narratives foreground the 'maternal burden' to emphasise the violence of extractive industries against the land and the multiple generations of people entangled with it.[30] As Myjolynne Kim explains, she similarly draws on her own experience of the 'maternal burden' to expose the relationship between 'the challenges

[28] Cato Berg, 'A Chief Is a Chief Wherever He Goes': Land and Lines of Power in Vella Lavella, Solomon Islands' (PhD thesis, University of Bergen, 2008), 143–144. Berg also refers to a 1992 meeting at which the toutou (similar to the kokolo or butubutu in Marovo) 'was split in half, with the female matrilineal head staunchly against logging': 151.

[29] Maetala, 'Matrilineal Land Tenure Systems', 35. Kongulai refers to the very valuable land in the catchment that provides the majority of Honiara's water, mentioned in Chapter 4.

[30] See also Kim, who states that in Chuuk, 'to contaminate and destroy the environment is to degrade women': Kim, 'Nesor Annim, Niteikapar', 159.

confronting matrilineal kinship' in Micronesia and 'the destruction of the environment brought forward by colonialism, militarism and capitalism'.[31]

Such claims disrupt understandings of land as commodity. They refuse what Nicole Graham refers to as the 'dephysicalisation' of land[32] and reassert embodied relationships between people and their environment. They re-establish kinship, reciprocity and care for the land that feeds, nurtures and sustains many different people. Maternal idioms thus contest hegemonic definitions of property that split subject from object and divide people from their environment and each other, and they re-centre and reinvigorate Indigenous relationships, concepts of self and obligations to land. When people in Marovo repeatedly drew my attention to vuluvulu, they did so precisely because they were seeking to disrupt the simplification of relation-ships with land and reinstate them – they sought to reinvigorate the entangle-ment of many people with the land, and the authority of at least some women. In this sense these strategies share much in common with the forms of resist-ance and refusal that J. Kēhaulani Kauanui has recently advocated for Hawai'i: they are founded in an insistence on modes of relationality to land and all entities grounded in Indigenous epistemes and spaces rather than state power.[33] Such strategies can also be highly persuasive and effective: according to Maetala, it was the niece's verbal intervention that prevented the matriline-age from losing their land.

6.2.2 *Embodied Authority*

Many of the strategies described above are profoundly material and corporeal, yet these are precisely the kinds of strategies that are easily overlooked if employing predominant legal methods that might start with an analysis of land titles, court records, or idealized statements of custom. Rights-based accounts of land relations that focus on identifying key gender norms and institutions can very easily elide the myriad ways in which women actively work to defend land, property and territory, highlighting instead the work of a small group of men who publicly represent collective interests. The impos-ition of increasingly restrictive dress codes during conflict reminds us that power is ascribed to bodies through discursive and material social practices

---

[31] Ibid 148–149.

[32] See eg Nicole Graham 'Dephysicalisation and Entitlement: Legal and Cultural Discourses of Place as Property' in Brad Jessup and Kim Rubenstein (eds.), *Environmental Discourses in Public and International Law* (Cambridge University Press, 2012), 96.

[33] J Kēhaulani Kauanui, *Paradoxes of Hawaiian Sovereignty: Land, Sex and the Colonial Politics of State Nationalism* (Duke University Press, 2018), 29–30.

and this can be immensely constraining – yet as Teresia Teaiwa insists it may also be liberating.[34]

From the earliest phases of the conflict in Solomon Islands women were on the frontlines, physically intervening to stem the violence and loss of life, as well as ameliorate the immediate conditions of those caught in the crossfire. These interventions were firmly grounded in customary idioms, such as offering tafuliae – strings of shell valuables produced in Malaita and used in chupu on Guadalcanal – to appease militants, quell tensions within communities and facilitate the release of hostages.[35] One such story was recounted by Elsie Talei when she appeared before the Truth and Reconciliation Commission. Talei explained that she is of Malaitan and Guadalcanal descent, and described how Guadalcanal militants arrived in her village and began rounding up people understood to be of Malaitan descent. According to Talei, her uncle's wife, a woman from the Duff Islands in Temotu Province, 'took one Tafuliae and gave it to the militants' in an effort to protect her kin and bridge the social divides that were opening up in the village.[36]

Interventions such as this draw on long-standing models of gendered bodily comportment, avoidance and influence, notably the prohibition on physical contact between close kin of different genders, and understandings that senior women, as much as senior 'men of peace' have the authority to mediate conflict and reinstate order and social harmony.[37] Both Alice Pollard and Dalcy Tovosia Paina situate the strategies they used as women peacebuilders in their own cultural contexts, explaining that on Malaita and Guadalcanal respectively, women may control warring parties by standing between them. Since touching or stepping over women's bodies is prohibited, the fighting should cease.[38] Ruth Saovana-Spriggs refers to very similar strategies on Bougainville, and again traces their persuasive power to kastom.[39] These are not romanticised accounts of women's embodied influence, but an explanation of a strategy that is frequently used, to great effect, in a range of political struggles in Solomon Islands.

---

[34] Teresia Teaiwa 'bikinis and other s/pacific n/ocean' (1994) 6(1) *The Contemporary Pacific* 87
[35] Pollard, *Givers of Wisdom*; Monson, 'Vernacularising Political Participation'; Fangalasuu, Maetala, Rodi, Vota and Wickham, *Herem Kam*.
[36] Solomon Islands Truth and Reconciliation Commission, *Thematic Public Hearing for Women* per Elsie Talei.
[37] Kate Higgins, 'Outside-In: A Volunteer's Reflections on a Solomon Islands Community Development Program' (SSGM Discussion Paper No. 2008/3, Research School of Pacific and Asian Studies, The Australian National University, 2008), 4; George, 'Liberal-Local Peacebuilding'.
[38] Pollard, 'Resolving Conflict in Solomon Islands'; Paina, 'Peacemaking in Solomon Islands'.
[39] Saovana-Spriggs, 'Bougainville Women's Role in Conflict Resolution', 206.

Legal scholar Jennifer Corrin rightly observes that the use of the body to intervene in conflict in Solomon Islands 'is not necessarily indicative of wider political power', and suggests that 'cross-culturally [it] appears to be by those who do not have an effective political voice'.[40] There are certainly many examples of embodied protest that are acts of desperation in the face of very effective silencing, such as the hunger strikes undertaken by asylum seekers held in Australian detention centres in Papua New Guinea and Nauru. However, it is equally important not to assume a hierarchy of political speech in which embodied expressions are indicative of a lack of power, and correspondingly, the capacity to 'speak' is indicative of wider political power.

The assumption that material or corporeal expressions of authority are necessarily 'lesser' or 'weaker' than speech assumes a hierarchy of political expression that privileges 'speech' over other forms of voice. Yet as legal geographers have long pointed out, property and territory are 'made' and 'performed' through a variety of discursive, material and corporeal means. In previous chapters we have seen this in the establishment (or removal) of church buildings, survey pegs and gardens; the creation of bunkers and the eviction of migrants; and the crossing of bunkers between 'town' and 'customary' land by peacebuilders. Claims to land may also involve blockading roads or removing keys from bulldozers, discussed further below. These are actions that may be undertaken by established political leaders as well as those struggling to be heard in other arenas. Rather than evidencing a lack of 'voice', the use of the body may form part of a diverse repertoire of effective political expression.

Further, while material and corporeal expressions of authority may be 'lesser' in *some* legal pluralities, this should not be assumed of all. Katerina Teaiwa, whose family was among those forcibly displaced by phosphate mining on Banaba in the Gilbert and Ellice Island Colony (now Kiribati and Tuvalu) explains that when the British Phosphate Commission came to the island, it was the women who clung to the trees and obstructed the land transfers and mining that would ultimately strip Banaba of 90 per cent of its surface.[41] It is clear from Resident Commissioner McClure's cables that although he perceived the 'young men' of Banaba to be the most visible and vocal in expressing opposition to land leases and the destruction of trees, he

---

[40] Jennifer Corrin, 'Ples Bilong Mere: Law, Gender and Peace-Building in Solomon Islands' (2008) 16(2) *Feminist Legal Studies* 169, 172.

[41] Teaiwa, *Consuming Ocean Island*, 133, drawing on Barrie Macdonald, *Cinderellas of Empire: Towards a History of Kiribati and Tuvalu* (Institute of Pacific Studies, University of the South Pacific, 2001), 107–108.

thought the real political authority lay in the background: 'behind them and the most formidable of all is the feminine influence on which everything depends and which is entirely reactionary'.[42]

The emphasis on speech, on oratory, over other forms of 'voice' is problematic not only because it *overlooks* other forms of political expression, but because it *reproduces* the very hierarchies of knowledge, expression, influence and authority that have constituted contemporary inequalities in property relations. As we have seen, white traders, missionaries and colonial administrators consistently recognised quite particular forms of socio-political authority and *voice* in Solomon Islands, privileging the men who spoke for land on behalf of the group, particularly if it was the language of the colonisers. In the Gilbert and Ellice Island Colony – which, as part of the British Western Pacific Territories formed part of the same colonial network as Solomon Islands – Resident Commissioner McClure could acknowledge the influence of 'young men' of Banaba, but he could not bring himself to acknowledge the expertise and authority of 'women': he reduced them to an abstract 'feminine influence' that he then dismissed as 'entirely reactionary'. These processes of highly selective recognition continue today, with the normative and institutional forms of the state privileging the forms of authority demonstrated through public speech-giving, transforming male 'spokespersons' for the group into 'trustees' and 'land owners'. The privileging of particular forms of 'voice' may, therefore, not only *misrepresent* land relations but *produce* and *reinforce* inequality in those relations, because the claims of those who assert influence through oratory are not only assumed to be *but remade as* the primary power-brokers, subsuming other forms of politico-legal expression.

When Solomon Islanders assert that 'women cannot speak', they are referring to specific forms of politico-legal expression, which are those forms that are readily legible to and 'seen' by the state.[43] A much larger repertoire of political expression is legible within kastom. In Chapter 4 I referred to the visibility of women in gift exchange – women are active in arranging the pigs, food and shell valuables into the heap that comprise the visual and spatial focus of the gift exchange; they may visually and bodily represent the matrilineage and hold the shell valuables as they pass from one lineage to another; and they often take the lead in distributing the pile of goods among the groups involved in the exchange. These are all processes that make socio-spatial

---

[42] McClure to Rodwell, 26 November 1923, WPHC 4, 3357/1924, cited in Macdonald, *Cinderellas of the Empire*, 107.

[43] James C Scott, *Seeing Like a State: How Certain Schemes to Improve the Human Condition Have Failed* (Yale Agrarian Studies, 1998).

relations explicit, they are performances that make property (and gender) real
'on the ground'. An approach to legal pluralism that privileges the state and
oratorical prowess, and fails to acknowledge these other, vital forms of politico-
legal expression, contributes to the kinds of 'gender myths' and 'feminist
fables' that serve to silence women and deny their means to assert
themselves.[44]

In Solomon Islands, these embodied assertions of authority can be an
extremely effective form of political voice, with the capacity to disrupt the
forms of property and authority asserted by corporate power and legitimated by
the state. When I commenced this work in 2008, I regularly heard of protests
that had occurred the previous year, on Vella Lavella.[45] This blockade,
discussed further below, is typical of many that occur across the country on
a regular basis, but it stands out for the level of local and international media
coverage it received, and the heavily gendered public discourse. While it
clearly involved local men, it was widely discussed and is still remembered
as a protest undertaken primarily by 'women landowners' from Leona
village.[46]

The protest commenced in early 2007, when a group of women camped
out in the bush in temporary shelters in order to prevent logging on areas of
rare and relatively pristine swamp rainforest by Omex Limited. Omex, backed
by Australian banking heavyweight Westpac as guarantor, had a licence to
carry out logging on land claimed by Bolopoe traeb, however this land also
included the Barakasi Forest Management Area claimed by Barakasi traeb.
People associated with Barakasi traeb and Leona village established the
blockade on the main logging road through that area, and camped on a
number of logging roads as well as in areas where trees were being felled.[47]

---

[44] Cf Jessica Chu, 'Gender and "Land Grabbing" in Sub-Saharan Africa: Women's Land Rights
     and Customary Land Tenure' (2011) 54(1) *Development* 35; Yngstrom, 'Women, Wives and
     Land Rights'.

[45] I am extremely grateful to staff of the World Wildlife Fund and National Resources
     Development Foundation who provided me with access to their own collection of press
     clippings regarding this protest. These clippings did not always contain full details of the
     newspaper they appeared in, dates or page numbers, although the formatting of the articles and
     other details mean that they are recognisable as published in the *Solomon Star*.

[46] E.g. 'Solomons Women Injured in Logging Protest' (*Radio New Zealand*, 30 July 2007),
     available at www.rnz.co.nz/international/pacific-news/171607/solomons-women-injured-in-
     anti-logging-protest ; 'Solomon Islands Government Called Upon to Reconsider Approach to
     Logging Companies' (*Radio New Zealand*, 30 July 2007), available at www.rnz.co.nz/
     international/pacific-news/171610/solomon-islands-government-called-on-to-reconsider-
     approach-to-logging-companies; 'Logging Blocked in Vella Lavella' (*Solomon Star*, n.d.) 1.

[47] Dalcy Kukiti, one of the women who instigated the protest, discussed her motivations and
     actions in detail at a forum organised by the Ministry of Women, Youth and Children's Affairs

In May 2007, Leona villagers prevented a company ship from landing and unloading logging machinery, by sitting in canoes and blockading both the reefs and the shoreline in the surrounding area. They also blockaded the roads and felling areas, and according to Omex, disrupted logging operations by confronting workers, and by taking and damaging company equipment. Several confrontations occurred between logging company personnel and the people in the blockade camps, and in late July, a particularly violent confrontation resulted in the hospitalisation of one woman after she was stabbed with a bush knife.[48]

Local and international media coverage of this event portrayed these confrontations in highly gendered terms, emphasising the violence committed by loggers and security workers (who in popular discourse were assumed to be men), against protesters who were consistently referred to as 'women'.[49] Environmental advocates Marlon Kuve and Wilko Bosma stressed 'the beating of harmless, demonstrating women', and concluded that because of the consolidation of control over logging in the hands of chiefs and 'big men', women had no alternative but to intervene with their bodies, 'standing for their rights and in front of their trees'.[50] The Western Province's Council of Women urged provincial and national authorities to reconsider the logging operator's licence 'because the company has not respected the women and mothers of the province'.[51] The *Solomon Star*, the country's leading newspaper, published a story that featured an evocative image of the woman who was hospitalised, with her bandaged arm on prominent display as she stared sadly into the camera, telling reporters that 'I pray for my people in Leona every day.'[52] The headline immediately below read 'Injuries to women outrage MP' referring to the member of parliament for North Vella Lavella, Milton Tozaka, who 'slammed' Omex logging staff; described the attacks as 'an

---

in 2010. I was engaged as a consultant by the International Women's Development Agency at that forum. See also Public Solicitors Office Landowners Advocacy and Legal Support Unit (n. d), *Case Studies for Conservation*, Rory Callinan, 'Westpac Backs Logging Project', *Sydney Morning Herald* (2012).

[48] Moffat Mamu (date obscured) 'Victim Tell It All' *Solomon Star* (copy on file with the author); Unknown (date obscured) 'Logging Blocked in Vella Lavella' *Solomon Star* (Honiara) 1 (copy on file with the author).

[49] See 'Logging Guards Injure 6 Women' *Solomon Star* (Honiara) (1 August 2007); 'Press Release' *Solomon Star* (Honiara) (1 August 2007); Callinan, 'Westpac Backs Logging Project'.

[50] Marlon Kuve and Wilko Bosma, 'Pro and Anti-Loggers in Vella Lavella' (*Solomon Star*, 22 August 2007), 8.

[51] Ender Rence, 'Women Call for Suspension of Logging Licence' (*Solomon Times Online*, 2 August 2007), www.solomontimes.com/news/women-call-for-suspension-of-logging-license/472.

[52] 'Clash Victim Taken to Munda' (*Solomon Star*, 6 August 2007), page unknown.

outrageous and disgraceful act of Omex Company and partner taking the law in [*sic*] their own hands'; and called for Omex to immediately withdraw from the area.[53]

How are we to understand the public outrage regarding this confrontation, given that available data demonstrates that women in Solomon Islands face a very high risk of violence from an intimate partner or male family member, and this receives a degree of social acceptance?[54] Indeed how are we to understand it given the reportedly widespread sexual exploitation associated with the logging industry?[55] I cannot fully answer that here, in part because (to borrow the words of Dianne Rocheleau) it needs to be 'thought and wrought differently' in order to avoid the pathologising discourses that plague work on gender based violence in Melanesia, and I am 'not yet ready'.[56] I am, however, confident that the protests can only be understood by reference to the culturally particular ways in which gendered bodies come to bear meaning, and gendered and embodied subjectivities are (re)produced through resource struggles.[57]

Despite references to the 'vulnerability' of women, the public condemnation of the violence arose precisely because it challenged the widely accepted authority of women grounded in the norms of bodily comportment and maternal idioms discussed previously. Given the blockade was part of a coordinated strategy by villagers collectively, I suspect that women were at the forefront precisely because they were employing the power of their gendered bodies. Importantly, the violence occurred in a socio-spatial arena that is regarded as 'public': the confrontation between Omex employees and Leona women emerged from a dispute over land ownership between two traebs (the Barakasi and Bolopoe) rather than more privatised matters between

---

[53] 'Injuries to Women Outrage MP' (*Solomon Star*, 6 August 2007), page unknown.

[54] See further Secretariat of the Pacific Community, *Solomon Islands Family Health and Safety Study: A Study on Violence against Women and Children* (SPC, 2009) Chapters 5 and 6; Anouk Ride and Pauline Soaki, *Women's Experiences of Family Violence Services in Solomon Islands* (26 November 2019).

[55] Tania Herbert *Commercial Exploitation of Children in the Solomon Islands: A Report Focusing on the Presence of the Logging Industry in a Remote Region* (Christian Care Centre of the Church of Melanesia, 2007), Allen, Dinnen, Evans and Monson, *Justice Delivered Locally* 2013, IOM *Community Health and Mobility in the Pacific: Solomon Islands Case Study* (International Organization for Migration, 2019).

[56] Dianne Rocheleau 'A Situated View of Feminist Political Ecology From My Networks, Roots and Territories' in Wendy Harcourt and Ingrid L Nelson (eds.), *Practising Feminist Political Ecologies: Moving Beyond the 'Green Economy'* (Zed Books, 2015), 29, 52.

[57] See eg Sultana, 'Fluid Lives', Yvonne Underhill-Sem 'Embodying Post-Development: Bodies in Places, Places in Bodies' (2002) 45(1) *Society for International Development* 54.

intimate partners or close kin.[58] The violence against women protesters therefore emerged as an attack not only on the individuals protesting, but on 'the mothers of our province', that is, the foundations of the communities associated with the land and the province more broadly. This highlights the need to pay close attention to the immensely varied ways in which gender-based violence and women's political advocacy are informed by cultural norms regarding the body and the land – that is, to the co-production of places and gender identities and subjectivities to shape who, and what behaviour, is 'in' or 'out' of place.

The protests by Leona women serve as a reminder that property is not only enacted through discursive means, such as speeches at gift exchanges or the mobilisation of oral histories in the courts, but in profoundly material and corporeal ways ranging from gardening to the establishment of blockades in defence of land and trees. The fact that state norms and processes fail to recognise, validate or 'see' such enactments does not necessarily render them any less effective. Indeed, in the case here, women put their claims to work 'on material spaces and real people' in ways that not only contradicted the property claims legitimated by the state legal system, but were ultimately more effective, for Omex eventually withdrew from the land that Leona villagers claimed as their own.[59]

6.2.3 *From Adam's Rib*

With the notable exception of work on Islamic property and inheritance regimes, global scholarship on gender, land and legal pluralities has not yet paid sustained attention to religious norms, practices and institutions, nor to the co-production of religious subjects and places.[60] Yet as we have seen,

---

[58] Some of the Omex employees were from nearby villages, and therefore likely to be closely related to the women. However, media reports and descriptions by Leona villagers consistently referred to the men as 'Omex employees' rather than 'kin'.

[59] Public Solicitors Office Landowners Advocacy and Legal Support Unit, *Case Studies for Conservation* (n.d.).

[60] Eg Beverly B Mack and Susan F Hirsch, *Pronouncing and Persevering: Gender and the Discourses of Disputing in an African Islamic Court*, vol 43 (University of Chicago Press, 2000); Beshara Doumani (ed.), *Family History in the Middle East: Household, Property, and Gender* (State University of New York Press, 2003); Rajendra Pradhan, 'Legal Pluralism in the Supreme Court: Law, Religion, and Culture Pertaining to Women's Rights in Nepal' in Franz von Benda-Beckmann et al. (eds.), *Religion in Disputes: Pervasiveness of Religious Normativity in Disputing Processes* (Palgrave Macmillan, 2013), 165. See however Lynne Muthoni Wanyeki, *Women and Land in Africa: Culture, Religion and Realizing Women's Rights* (Zed Books, 2003).

Christianity is central to Solomon Islands' legal pluralities. In fact, as Matt Tomlinson and Debra McDougall have argued, the resonance of Christianity in the Pacific generally is such that it is 'the ground and starting point for political action'.[61] This is certainly true of women's collective action with respect to land.

In Solomon Islands as anywhere, the ideologies, practices and institutional structures associated with the churches are heterogeneous, and their intersection with pre-existing understandings of people and place is immensely varied and requires ongoing rearticulation. Christianity has been woven with kastom and the state in diverse ways, sometimes to assert socio-spatial differences and power asymmetries, but also to subvert or transcend them.[62] Christianity was crucial to the colonisation of Solomon Islands, but in the emergence of the Christian Fellowship Church in the Western Solomons, we see that it has also been reconfigured and central to Indigenous movements resisting and disrupting the subjugation of Indigenous people by imperial powers.[63] The implications for gender relations have been similarly diverse. As Claire Slatter has observed, Christianity has been a 'double-edged sword', with some biblical texts mobilised to deepen gender asymmetries, while others provide a foundation for claims to equality and women's human rights.[64] The teachings and practices of missionaries and churches have normalised heteronormativity, the nuclear family form and masculine privilege within households, villages and the wider sphere, but Christianity has also provided an enabling environment with new vocabularies for people to make morally authoritative claims and critique heteropatriarchal structures of power.[65] One of the few generalised observations that can be made is that Islanders have contested, negotiated and reconfigured Christianity just as they have the state.

---

[61] Matt Tomlinson and Debra L McDougall (eds.), *Christian Politics in Oceania* (Berghahn Books, 2013), 3.

[62] Cf McDougall, *Engaging with Strangers*; Michael W Scott, '"I Was Like Abraham": Notes on the Anthropology of Christianity from the Solomon Islands' (2005) 70(1) *Ethnos* 101.

[63] Teaiwa highlights the role of the Pacific Conference on Churches in providing a counter-hegemonic or subaltern space in the region more broadly: Katerina Martina Teaiwa, 'Our Rising Sea of Islands: Pan-Pacific Regionalism in the Age of Climate Change' (2018) 41(1/2) *Pacific Studies*.

[64] Slatter, 'Gender and Custom', 95.

[65] There is a growing stream of work by Pacific theologians – people who are members of and influential within Pacific churches and theological colleges – emphasising and conjoining Indigenous, feminist, queer and grounded (or oceanic) approaches, emphasising fluidity and negotiability: see e.g. Jione Havea (ed.), *Sea of Readings: The Bible in the South Pacific* (SBL Press, 2018).

Christianity was crucial to women's peacebuilding during the conflict, providing idioms, texts, networks and infrastructure such as church buildings and trucks that were central to the sustenance and legitimation of women's involvement in the politically charged, public act of peacebuilding.[66] Many people saw kastom and Christianity as providing a shared set of values and a commitment to fostering unity, restorative justice and forgiveness,[67] and women's testimonies before the Truth and Reconciliation Commission underscore the significance of church-based social networks and infrastructure to women living in the vicinity of Honiara. Claudette Liliau, for example, explained in detail the role that the women's desk officer located inside the town boundary at Holy Cross Cathedral played in supporting women from Kakabona and the hills further inland, by organising transport into and out of town, and providing accommodation if they were stranded inside Honiara overnight.[68]

Churches in Solomon Islands have, as Debra McDougall emphasises, often promoted a 'radical vision of Christian unity',[69] and have not only facilitated forms of collective action in the face of the division wrought by resource conflicts, but enabled women to emerge as public social actors.[70] It is therefore unsurprising that when women confront existing 'property effects' and advocate greater inclusivity they often do so by drawing on idioms associated with Christianity. In 2008, during one of many conversations with Mary Borgia, previously mentioned in Chapter 4, she explained that her 'tribal board', which manages her lineage's land further west on Guadalcanal, includes a number of women. None of the logging contracts or land titles I had reviewed bore the names of women, so I asked Mary why her tribe

---

[66] See in particular Pollard, 'Resolving Conflict'; Monson, 'Vernacularising Political Participation'.

[67] Debra McDougall and Joy Kere, 'Christianity, Custom, and Law: Conflict and Peacemaking in the Postconflict Solomon Islands' in Roland Bleiker and Morgan Brigg (eds.), *Mediating across Difference: Oceanic and Asian Approaches to Conflict Resolution* (University of Hawai'i Press, 2011), 141, 143.

[68] *Thematic Public Hearing for Women*, Solomon Islands Truth and Reconciliation Commission (25 November 2010) per Claudette Liliau.

[69] McDougall, 'Fellowship and Citizenship', 77. For extensive discussion see McDougall, *Engaging with Strangers*. Margaret Jolly has similarly observed that expressions of faith-based notions of shared humanity, of a 'radical Christian unity' or of God creating both Adam and Eve, may have much in common with the secular and rights-based conceptions of universalism that many feminists draw upon: Margaret Jolly, '"Woman Ikat Raet Long Human Raet o No?" Women's Rights, Human Rights, and Domestic Violence in Vanuatu' in Anne-Marie Hilsdon et al. (eds.), *Human Rights and Gender Politics: Asia-Pacific Perspectives* (Routledge, 2000), 124, 132

[70] McDougall, 'Church, Company, Committee', 139.

thought it necessary to include women on this formalised decision-making body. She explained,

> This tribe is different to other tribes – we think gender balance is important. It is a Christian principle. If there is going to be any [commercial] planting, or logging, or other activity, [the board] must obtain the women's point of view and consider it. We are trying to be good Christians, not just follow custom. Justice and love are important.

In a later conversation we returned to this subject, and Mary expanded on her arguments for the inclusion of women in formal decision-making structures:

> First God created the universe, animals and plants. Then Adam was created to look after them. However Adam couldn't stay by himself, he needed someone. He couldn't look after creation by himself. If you value creation, you value women. You must not stand on women.

Mary's reference to not 'standing' on women invoked an interpretation of the creation story in Genesis 2 that I have heard from many people throughout Solomon Islands. This exegesis emphasises that since Eve was taken from Adam's rib rather than his head or feet, 'men and women must stand together', rather than in a hierarchical relationship.[71] Like so many narratives, this exegesis may be employed in a variety of ways,[72] but as we saw in Chapter 4, Mary clearly regarded the subordination of women in land relations as a 'sin', a breach of both kastom and Christianity, with consequences including poverty, social disruption and even nation-wide conflict.[73] By intertwining references to Christianity and kastom, two powerful and intersecting sites of moral authority in Solomon Islands, Mary responded forcefully to those who would claim that the 'Christian' and 'traditional' woman should accept a subordinate position.

While Mary's arguments are not necessarily widely accepted, they are not marginal either – some churches, such as the United Church of Solomon Islands, which is influential across the western islands, expressly embrace gender equality. These commitments are not always reflected in everyday practice (a situation hardly unique to Solomon Islands), but this should not

---

71 For example, I have also been told 'God made Eve from Adam's rib – not from his head, not from his feet, but from his *rib*. This means that men and women must stand together. The woman should not stand on the man, and the man should not stand on the woman. They must stand together.'

72 Cf Claire Cronin, 'Speaking Suffering: A Post-Colonial Analysis of Why the Solomon Islands Truth and Reconciliation Commission Failed to "Touch the Heart of the People"' (PhD thesis, Australian National University, 2019), 114.

73 See the quote from Mary Borgia provided in Chapter 4.

obscure their persuasive potential. John Cox suggests that 'men may experience personal religious convictions that impel them to reconcile the dissonance between their own behaviour and official church views of proper Christian conduct',[74] and notes the example of Lloyd Maepeza Gina, who refers to the positive influence of his mid-life evangelical reawakening on his relationships with his wife and family.[75] Several men politicians have shared similar stories of personal transformation with me and recounted their shifting understandings of masculinities and gendered power dynamics, and like Cox, I am optimistic that these accounts may be 'rearticulations of social norms' that make 'overt male dominance less morally respectable'.[76]

Despite the ubiquity of Christianity and its significance to Solomon Islanders – and many people across Oceania – the *details* of the relationship between Christianity and political and legal advocacy have often received very little attention. Development partners in Australia, New Zealand and elsewhere are increasingly engaged with religious organisations in the region, seeing them as new actors to be enrolled in development and 'gender agendas'.[77] Yet while the *influence* of church leaders, institutions and networks is recognised, there is often little interest in discussing specific Christian concepts, vocabularies and arguments, or even engaging with the Pacific scholarship on 're-weaving development' in which these concepts and vocabularies are prominent.[78]

Christian vocabularies and practices are crucial to understanding how people come to understand themselves and relate to others as well as their lands and ecosystems, yet detailed discussion of these matters often provoke discomfort, even derision, when they arise in academic settings or in NGO offices *outside* the region. On more than one occasion, I have attended public presentations or meetings held in Australia, at which Solomon Islander

---

[74] John Cox, 'Kindy and Grassroots Gender Transformations in Solomon Islands' M Macintyre and C Spark (eds.), *Transformations of Gender in Melanesia* (ANU Press, 2017), 69–93, 80.

[75] Lloyd Maepeza Gina, *Journeys in a Small Canoe: The Life and Times of a Solomon Islander* (Pandanus Press, Canberra, 2003).

[76] Cox, 'Kindy', 80.

[77] For example, the Australian Government, through the Department of Foreign Affairs and Trade, currently has a Pacific Churches Partnership Program, the stated goal of which is 'to build the leadership capacities of Pacific Island church leaders to contribute to development outcomes in the Pacific': www.dfat.gov.au/geo/pacific/people-connections/church-partnerships-in-the-pacific

[78] For recent examples see e.g.: James Bhagwan, Elise Huffer, Frances C. Koya-Vaka'uta and Aisake Casimira (eds.), *From the Deep: Pasifiki Voices for a New Story* (Pacific Theological College, 2020) and Cliff Bird, Arnie Saiki and Meretui Raunabuabua, *Reweaving the Ecological Mat Framework: Towards an Ecological Framework for Development* (Pacific Theological College, 2020).

women have explained the importance of prayer to women's organisations, only to be met with stifled laughter or rolled eyes.[79] Such responses are obviously belittling, and they fail to comprehend the centrality of Christianity to the (co)production of spaces, subjectivities and practices; to collective action and reconfiguring social norms and practices. Many Solomon Islander women regard prayer as a profoundly *practical* means to provide encouragement and comfort to others, and to build understanding and cohesion where there might be disagreement.[80] Moreover, as Solomon Islanders know, public prayer may provide a site for the assertion and re-articulation of diverse socio-spatial claims and practices, some politically conservative and others progressive (again, a phenomena that is not unique to Solomon Islands).[81] As Bronwen Douglas has observed, there is a persistent disdain towards the 'unfashionable conjunction of women with parochial Christianity', and this ensures that the vital roles played by Christian narratives, church groups and church leaders remain largely ignored, poorly understood and sometimes actively undermined by foreign human rights advocates, gender and development specialists and aid donors.[82]

6.3 CONCLUSION

In Solomon Islands and the wider Pacific, ideas of gender equality are often presented as foreign and incompatible with kastom, Christianity and 'the social'; and women's rights are frequently discursively opposed to

---

[79] Bronwen Douglas has observed similar reactions to sewing, for she comments that 'in Vanuatu and the Pacific generally, sewing and the art of sewing machine maintenance are evidently not to be despised, and yet reference to them in academic settings routinely provokes sniggers': Bronwen Douglas, *Traditional Individuals? Gendered Negotiations of Identity, Christianity and Citizenship in Vanuatu* (No 98/6, 1998).

[80] Cf McDougall, 'Fellowship and Citizenship'; Paina 'Peacemaking in Solomon Islands'; Anne Dickson-Waiko, 'The Missing Rib: Mobilizing Church Women for Change in Papua New Guinea' (2003) 74(1–2) *Oceania* 98, 110.

[81] When I commenced this research I was on the board of an inner-city, faith-based non-governmental organization. One meeting opened with a reflection on the 'wide' and 'narrow' gates discussed in Matthew 7: 13–14, with the person giving the reflection stressing the importance of 'exclusion'. The full implications of this reading only became clear to me later in the meeting, when discussion turned to an ongoing debate between older and younger community members regarding the installation of gates to prevent heroin-injecting in the alley behind the building.

[82] Bronwen Douglas, 'Christianity, Tradition, and Everyday Modernity: Towards an Anatomy of Women's Groupings in Melanesia' (2003) 74(1–2) *Oceania* 6, 14; Caroline Sweetman, 'Special Issue: Gender, Religion and Spirituality' (1999) 7(1) *Gender and Development*; Margaret Jolly, 'Beyond the Horizon? Nationalisms, Feminisms, and Globalization in the Pacific' (2005) 52(1) *Ethnohistory* 137, 149.

Indigenous culture not only by traditionalists but also by human rights advocates.[83] A number of scholars have shown that this leaves women who expressly draw on the language of human rights vulnerable to the charge that they are overly influenced by 'foreigners' or 'foreign ideas', rather than 'good' women who lead their lives in accordance with Indigenous values inherent in kastom and Christianity. This discursive opposition is crucially linked to the processes I have exposed in this book – it both emanates from and reproduces the state as a hypermasculine domain. Given this terrain, it is hardly surprising that when Solomon Islander women mobilise collectively to contest the terms of property, territory and authority – to rupture the socio-spatial distinctions that marginalise and exclude them and many others – they ground their claims most firmly in kastom and Christianity, rather than explicitly adopting the vocabularies of property rights or human rights.

None of this is to suggest that women, or Solomon Islanders generally, have given up on the state as an important realm in which to engage in struggles over land, indeed I have shown quite the opposite. Solomon Islanders are well aware that, as Franz von Benda-Beckmann and Keebet von Benda-Beckmann have put it, 'places come and go',[84] and many have sought recognition from the state in order to sediment their claims. I have also sought to highlight the diverse ways in which Solomon Islanders navigate variable, multiple and interlaced constellations of kastom, Christianity and state law. It is clear that the language of human rights has been enormously generative in many struggles such as those against gender-based violence, and equally, kastom and Christianity may be wielded so as to keep women and many other people in a subordinate position. Pacific women have long drawn attention to the immensely variable ways in which all of these regimes of authority may be mobilised against them, while also weaving their own claims grounded in these regimes.

My point is that many, if not most, Solomon Islanders find the vocabularies, stories, practices and institutional forms associated with kastom and Christianity persuasive, sustaining and essential for advancing Indigenous communities, worlds and futures in all their complexity and plurality. Like people across Oceania, Solomon Islanders know that the legal construction and regulation of property has constituted landscapes and ecosystems as

---

[83] For discussion see e.g. Margaret Jolly, '"Woman Ikat Raet Long Human Raet o No?"; Douglas, 'Christianity'; Monson, 'Vernacularising Political Participation'; McDougall, '"Tired for Nothing?"; George, 'Just Like Your Mother'; Hermkens, 'Mary, Motherhood and Nation'.

[84] Franz von Benda-Beckmann and Keebet von Benda-Beckmann 'Places That Come and Go: A Legal Anthropological Perspective on the Temporalities of Space in Plural Legal Orders' in Irus Braverman et al. (eds.), *The Expanding Spaces of Law: A Timely Legal Geography* (Stanford University Press, 2014), 30.

'things' rather than kin, and been central to resource extractivism and 'development' that now pushes planetary boundaries to their limits. If we assume that 'the problem' is an absence of law, and turn too quickly to the reform of state laws and institutions as the most likely site of 'solutions', we not only ignore the multitude of ways in which people pursue their claims, but occlude the potential for their strategies to contest, resist, disrupt and reconfigure legal pluralities and land relations in more sustaining, just and emancipatory ways.

Bibliography

BOOKS, ARTICLES, REPORTS

Agarwal, Bina, A *Field of One's Own: Gender and Land Rights in South Asia* (Cambridge University Press, 1994)

Aikau, Hōkūlani K, 'Mana Wahine and Mothering at the Lo'i: A Two-Spirit/Queer Analysis' (2021) *Australian Feminist Studies*, https://dx.doi.org/10.1080/08164649.2020.1902272

Akin, David W, 'Ancestral Vigilance and the Corrective Conscience: Kastom as Culture in a Melanesian Society' (2004) 4(3) *Anthropological Theory* 299

   Colonialism, Maasina Rule, and the Origins of Malaitan Kastom (University of Hawai'i Press, 2013)

Akter, Sonia, Pieter Rutsaert, Joyce Luis, Nyo Me Htwe, Su Su San, Budi Raharjo and Arlyna Pustika, 'Women's Empowerment and Gender Equity in Agriculture: A Different Perspective from Southeast Asia' (2017) 69 *Food Policy* 270

Alasia, Sam, 'Population Movement', in Hugh Laracy and Sam Alasia (eds), *Ples Blong Iumi: Solomon Islands, the Past Four Thousand Years* (University of the South Pacific, 1989) 112

   'Party Politics and Government in Solomon Islands' (State, Society and Governance in Melanesia Program Discussion Paper No 97/7, The Australian National University, 1997)

Allan, Colin H, *Customary Land Tenure in the British Solomon Islands Protectorate* (Western Pacific High Commission, 1957)

   Solomons Safari, 1953–58 (Nag's Head Press, 1986)

   'The Post-War Scene in the Western Solomons and Marching Rule: A Memoir' (1989) 24(1) *Journal of Pacific History* 89

Allen, Matthew G, and Sinclair Dinnen (eds), *Statebuilding and State Formation in the Western Pacific* (Routledge, 2018)

Allen, Matthew G, 'The Evidence for Sweet Potato in Island Melanesia', in C Ballard et al. (eds), *The Sweet Potato in Oceania: A Reappraisal* (Ethnology Monographs 19/ Oceania Monograph 56, University of Pittsburgh and University of Sydney, 2005) 99

   'Long-Term Engagement: The Future of the Regional Assistance Mission to Solomon Islands' (Strategic Insights No 51, Australian Strategic Policy Institute, 2011)

Greed and Grievance: Ex-Militants' Perspectives on the Conflict in Solomon Islands,
   1998–2003 (University of Hawaii Press, 2013)
'The Political Economy of Logging in Solomon Islands', in Ron Duncan (ed.), *The*
   Political Economy of Economic Reform in the Pacific (Asian Development Bank,
   2011) 277.
'Resisting RAMSI: Intervention, Identity and Symbolism in Solomon Islands' (2009)
   79(1) *Oceania* 1
Resource Extraction and Contentious States: Mining and the Politics of Scale in the
   Pacific Islands (Palgrave Pivot, 2018)
Allen, Matthew G, Sinclair Dinnen, Daniel Evans and Rebecca Monson, *Justice*
   Delivered Locally: Systems, Challenges, and Innovations in Solomon Islands
   (World Bank, 2013)
Allen, Matthew G, Katerina Teaiwa, Cresantia (Frances) Koya-Vaka'uta, Wesley
   Morgan, Rebecca Monson and Tammy Tabe, 'The Rush for Oceania: Critical
   Perspectives on Contemporary Oceans Governance and Stewardship' (Working
   Paper No. 9, School of Government, Development and International Affairs,
   University of the South Pacific, 2018)
Amherst, Lord William, and Basil Thomson, *The Discovery of the Solomon Islands by*
   Alvaro de Mendaña in 1568: Translated from the Original Spanish Manuscripts
   (Hakluyt Society, 1st ed., 1901)
Andrews, Eleanor and James McCarthy, 'Scale, Shale, and the State: Political
   Ecologies and Legal Geographies of Shale Gas Development in Pennsylvania'
   (2013) 4(1) *Journal of Environmental Studies and Sciences* 7
Anghie, Antony, *Imperialism, Sovereignty and the Making of International Law*
   (Cambridge University Press, 1st ed., 2004)
Aqorau, Transform, 'Solomon Islands' Foreign Policy Dilemma and the Switch from
   Taiwan to China', in Graeme Smith and Terence Wesley-Smith (eds) *The China*
   Alternative: Changing Regional Order in the Pacific Islands (ANU Press, 2021) 319.
Arkwright, Norman, 'Restorative Justice in the Solomon Islands', in Sinclair Dinnen,
   Anna Jowitt and Tess Newton (eds), *A Kind of Mending: Restorative Justice in the*
   Pacific Islands (ANU Press, 2010) 177
Aswani, Shankar, 'Forms of Leadership and Violence in Malaita and in the New
   Georgia Group, Solomon Islands', in Pamela J Stewart and Andrew Strathern
   (eds), *Exchange and Sacrifice* (Carolina Academic Press, 2008) 171
(ed.), 'Special Issue: Essays on Head-Hunting in the Western Solomon Islands'
   (2000) 109 *Journal of the Polynesian Society*
AusAID, *Making Land Work*, vols. 1 and 2 (Commonwealth of Australia, 2008)
Bainton, Nicholas A, 'Keeping the Network Out of View: Mining, Distinctions and
   Exclusion in Melanesia' (2009) 79(1) *Oceania* 18
Lihir Destiny: Cultural Responses to Mining in Melanesia (ANU Press, 2010)
Ballard, Chris and Glenn Banks, 'Resource Wars: The Anthropology of Mining' (2003)
   32 *Annual Review of Anthropology* 287
Banivanua Mar, Tracey, 'Consolidating Violence and Colonial Rule: Discipline and
   Protection in Colonial Queensland' (2005) 8(3) *Postcolonial Studies* 303
Decolonisation and the Pacific: Indigenous Globalisation and the Ends of Empire
   (Cambridge University Press, 2016)

'Frontier Space and the Reification of the Rule of Law: Colonial Negotiations in the Western Pacific' (2009) 30(1) *Australian Feminist Law Journal* 23

Violence and Colonial Dialogue: The Australian-Pacific Indentured Labor Trade (University of Hawai'i Press, 2007)

Barker, John, 'All Sides Now: The Postcolonial Triangle in Uiaku', in John Barker (ed.), *The Anthropology of Morality in Melanesia and Beyond* (Ashgate, 1st ed., 2008) 75

Bartel, Robyn and Nicole Graham, 'Property and Place Attachment: A Legal Geographical Analysis of Biodiversity Law Reform in New South Wales' (2016) 54(3) *Geographical Research* 267

Bartel, Robyn, Nicole Graham, Sue Jackson, Jason H Prior, Daniel F Robinson, Meg Sherval and Stewart Williams 'Special Issue: Legal Geography: An Australian Perspective' (2013) 51(4) *Geographical Research*

Bathgate, Murray A, *Fight for the Dollar: Economic and Social Change in Western Guadalcanal, Solomon Islands* (Alexander Enterprise, 1993)

Matriliny and Coconut Palms: The Control and Inheritance of a Major Capital Resource among the Ndi-Nggai Speakers of Western Guadalcanal in the Solomon Islands (Alexander Enterprise, 1993)

'Movement Processes from Precontact to Contemporary Times: The Ndi-Nggai, West Guadalcanal, Solomon Islands', in Murray Chapman and R Mansell Prothero (eds), *Circulation in Population Movement: Substance and Concepts from the Melanesian Case* (Routledge & Kegan Paul, 1985) 83

Bayliss-Smith, Tim and Edvard Hviding, 'Taro Terraces, Chiefdoms and Malaria: Explaining Landesque Capital Formation in Solomon Islands', in Thomas N Håkansson and Mats Widgren (eds), *Landesque Capital: The Historical Ecology of Enduring Landscape Modifications* (Routledge, 2014) 75

Bayliss-Smith, Tim, Edvard Hviding and Tim Whitmore, 'Rainforest Composition and Histories of Human Disturbance in Solomon Islands' (2003) 32(5) *Ambio* 346

Bayliss-Smith, Tim, Matthew Prebble and Stephen Manebosa, 'Saltwater and Bush in New Georgia, Solomon Islands: Exchange Relations, Agricultural Intensification and Limits to Social Complexity', in Mathieu Leclerc and James Flexner (eds), *Archaeologies of Island Melanesia: Current Approaches to Landscapes, Exchange and Practice* (ANU Press, 2019) 35

Benda-Beckmann, Franz von and Keebet von Benda-Beckmann, 'Places That Come and Go: A Legal Anthropological Perspective on the Temporalities of Space in Plural Legal Orders', in Irus Braverman et al. (eds). *The Expanding Spaces of Law: A Timely Legal Geography* (Stanford University Press, 2014), 30

Benda-Beckmann, Franz von, Keebet von Benda-Beckmann and Anne Griffiths (eds), *Spatializing Law: An Anthropological Geography of Law in Society* (Ashgate, 2009)

Bellam, MEP, 'The Colonial City: Honiara, a Pacific Islands' Case Study' (1970) 11(1) *Pacific Viewpoint* 66

Bellwood, Peter, James J Fox and Darrell Tryon, 'The Austronesians in History: Common Origins and Diverse Transformations', in Peter Bellwood, James J Fox and Darrell Tryon (eds), *The Austronesians: Historical and Comparative Perspectives* (ANU Press, 2006) 1

Belshaw, Cyril, 'Native Politics in the Solomon Islands' (1947) 20(2) *Pacific Affairs* 187

Bennett, Judith A, 'Forestry, Public Land, and the Colonial Legacy in Solomon Islands' (1995) 7(2) *The Contemporary Pacific* 243

Natives and Exotics: World War II and Environment in the Southern Pacific (University of Hawai'i Press, 2009)

Pacific Forest: A History of Resource Control and Contest in the Solomon Islands, c. 1800–1997 (Brill, 2000)

Wealth of the Solomons: A History of a Pacific Archipelago, 1800–1978 (University of Hawai'i Press, 1987)

Bennett, Judith A and Angela Wanhalla (eds), *Mothers' Darlings of the South Pacific: The Children of Indigenous Women and U.S. Servicemen, World War II* (University of Hawai'i Press, 2016)

Berg, Cato, 'A Chief Is a Chief Wherever He Goes': Land and Lines of Power in Vella Lavella, Solomon Islands' (PhD thesis, University of Bergen, 2008)

Berry, Sara, 'Debating the Land Question in Africa' (2002) 44(4) *Comparative Studies in Society and History* 638

'Hegemony on a Shoestring: Indirect Rule and Access to Agricultural Land' (1992) 62(3) *Africa* 327

No Condition Is Permanent: The Social Dynamics of Agrarian Change in Sub-Saharan Africa (University of Wisconsin Press, 1993)

'Property, Authority and Citizenship: Land Claims, Politics and the Dynamics of Social Division in West Africa' (2009) 40(1) *Development and Change* 23

Bhagwan, James, Elise Huffer, Frances C. Koya-Vaka'uta and Aisake Casimira (eds), *From the Deep: Pasifiki Voices for a New Story* (Pacific Theological College, 2020)

Bird, Cliff, 'Pepesa – The Household of Life: A Theological Exploration of Land in the Context of Change in Solomon Islands' (PhD thesis, Charles Sturt University, 2008)

Bird, Cliff, Arnie Saiki and Meretui Ratunabuabua, *Reweaving the Ecological Mat Framework: Towards an Ecological Framework for Development* (Pacific Theological College, 2020)

Blomley, Nicholas, 'The Boundaries of Property: Complexity, Relationality, and Spatiality' (2016) 50(1) *Law and Society Review* 224

'Cuts, Flows, and the Geographies of Property' (2010) 7(2) *Law, Culture and the Humanities* 203

'Law, Property, and the Geography of Violence: The Frontier, the Survey, and the Grid' (2003) 93(1) *Annals of the Association of American Geographers* 121

'Performing Property: Making the World' (2013) 26(1) *Canadian Journal of Law & Jurisprudence* 23

Blomley, Nicholas, David Delaney and Richard Thompson Ford (eds), *The Legal Geographies Reader: Law, Power and Space* (Wiley, 2001)

Bolabola, Cema, Dorothy Kenneth, Henlyn Silas, Mosikaka Moengangongo, Aiono Fana'afi and Margaret James, *Land Rights of Pacific Women* (Institute of Pacific Studies of the University of the South Pacific, 1985)

Bolton, Lissant, *Unfolding the Moon: Enacting Women's Kastom in Vanuatu* (University of Hawai'i Press, 2003)

Boone, Catherine, 'Legal Empowerment of the Poor through Property Rights Reform: Tensions and Trade-Offs of Land Registration and Titling in Sub-Saharan Africa' (2018) 55(3) *Journal of Development Studies* 384

Boseto, Polini 'Melanesian Women, Mothers of Democracy' in Bronwen Douglas (ed), *Women and Governance from the Grassroots in Melanesia* (State, Society and Governance in Melanesia Discussion Paper 00/2, Canberra, 2000)

Boutilier, James A, 'A Bibliographic Review of Solomon Islands History' (1979) 12 *Transactions and Proceedings* (Fiji Society, Suva) 25

Boydell, Spike, 'The "Pacific Way": Customary Land Use, Indigenous Values and Globalization in the South Pacific', in Alan Tidwell and Barry Scott Zellen (eds), *Land, Indigenous Peoples and Conflict* (Routledge, 2015) 108

Braithwaite, John, Sinclair Dinnen, Matthew Allen and Valerie Braithwaite, Hilary Charlesworth, *Pillars and Shadows: Statebuilding as Peacebuilding in Solomon Islands* (ANU Press, 2010)

Braverman, Irus, Nicholas Blomley, David Delaney and Alexandre Kedar (eds), *The Expanding Spaces of Law: A Timely Legal Geography* (Stanford University Press, 2014)

Brickell, Katherine and Dana Cuomo, 'Feminist Geolegality' (2017) 43(1) *Progress in Human Geography* 104

Brown, Paula and Anton Ploeg, 'Introduction: Change and Conflict in Papua New Guinea Land and Resource Rights' (1997) 7(4) *Anthropological Forum* 507

Brown, Terry 'The Solomon Islands 'Ethnic Tension' Conflict and the Solomon Islands Truth and Reconciliation Commission: A Personal Reflection', in David Webster (ed), *Flowers in the Wall: Truth and Reconciliation in Timor-Leste, Indonesia and Melanesia* (University of Calgary Press, 2018) 279

Burt, Ben, *Tradition and Christianity: The Colonial Transformation of a Solomon Islands Society* (Harwood Academic, 1994)

Butler, Judith, *Bodies That Matter: On the Discursive Limits of 'Sex'* (Routledge, 1993)

Carrier, James G, 'The Gift in Theory and Practice in Melanesia: A Note on the Centrality of Gift Exchange' (1992) 31(2) *Ethnology* 185

'Property and Social Relations in Melanesian Anthropology', in CM Hann (ed), *Property Relations: Renewing the Anthropological Tradition* (Cambridge University Press, 1998) 85

Carter, George G, *Tiè Varanè: Stories About People of Courage from Solomon Islands* (Unichurch, 1981)

Chapa, Prima, Michelle Taylor and Jennifer Wate, *Participatory Rural Appraisal Workshop* (2008)

Chapman, Murray and Peter Pirie, *Tasi Mauri: A Report on Population and Resources of the Guadalcanal Weather Coast* (East-West Population Institute, East-West Center and University of Hawaii, 1974)

Chappell, David, '"Africanization" in the Pacific: Blaming Others for Disorder in the Periphery?' (2005) 47(2) *Comparative Studies in Society and History* 286

Charlesworth, Hilary, 'Are Women Peaceful? Reflections on the Role of Women in Peace-Building' (2008) 16(3) *Feminist Legal Studies* 347

Chimhowu, Admos, 'The "New" African Customary Land Tenure: Characteristic, Features and Policy Implications of a New Paradigm' (2019) 81 *Land Use Policy* 897

Chu, Jessica, 'Gender and "Land Grabbing" in Sub-Saharan Africa: Women's Land Rights and Customary Land Tenure' (2011) 54(1) *Development* 35

Comaroff, John L, 'Governmentality, Materiality, Legality, Modernity: On the Colonial State in Africa', in Jan-Georg Deutsch, Heike Schmidt and Peter Probst (eds), *African Modernities: Entangled Meanings in Current Debate* (James Currey, 2002)

Connell, John, 'The Death of Taro: Local Response to a Change of Subsistence Crops in the Northern Solomon Islands' (1978) 11(4) *Mankind* 445

'Elephants in the Pacific? Pacific Urbanisation and Its Discontents' (2011) 52(2) *Asia Pacific Viewpoint* 121

Connell, RW and James W Messerschmidt, 'Hegemonic Masculinity: Rethinking the Concept' (2005) 19(6) *Gender and Society* 829

Cooper, Davina, *Everyday Utopias: The Conceptual Life of Promising Spaces* (Duke University Press, 2014)

'Opening Up Ownership: Community Belonging, Belongings, and the Productive Life of Property' (2007) 32(3) *Law & Social Inquiry* 625

Corrin, Jennifer 'Plurality and Punishment: Competition Between State and Customary Authorities in Solomon Islands' (2020) 51(1) *The Journal of Legal Pluralism and Unofficial Law* 29

'Ples Bilong Mere: Law, Gender and Peace-Building in Solomon Islands' (2008) 16 (2) *Feminist Legal Studies* 169

Corris, Peter, *Passage, Port and Plantation: A History of Solomon Islands Labour Migration, 1870–1914* (Melbourne University Press, 1973)

Cox, John, 'Kindy and Grassroots Gender Transformations in Solomon Islands', in Martha Macintyre and Ceridwen Spark (eds), *Transformations of Gender in Melanesia* (ANU Press, 2017) 69

'Israeli Technicians and the Post-Colonial Racial Triangle in Papua New Guinea' (2015) 85(3) *Oceania* 342

Cronin, Claire, 'Speaking Suffering: A Post-Colonial Analysis of Why the Solomon Islands Truth and Reconciliation Commission Failed to "Touch the Heart of the People"' (PhD thesis, Australian National University, 2019)

Cuomo, Dana and Katherine Brickell, 'Feminist Legal Geographies' (2019) 51(5) *Environment and Planning A: Economy and Space* 1043

Curry, George N and Gina Koczberski, 'Finding Common Ground: Relational Concepts of Land Tenure and Economy in the Oil Palm Frontier of Papua New Guinea' (2009) 175(2) *Geographical Journal* 98

Davenport, William and Gülbün Çoker, 'The Moro Movement of Guadalcanal, British Solomon Islands Protectorate' (1967) 76(2) *Journal of the Polynesian Society* 123

Davies, Margaret, 'Can Property Be Justified in an Entangled World?' (2020) 17(7) *Globalizations* 1104

'Feminist Appropriations: Law, Property and Personality' (1994) 3 *Social and Legal Studies* 365

'Material Subjects and Vital Objects: Prefiguring Property and Rights for an Entangled World' (2016) 22(2) *Australian Journal of Human Rights* 37

Davison, Jean, *Agriculture, Women, and Land: The African Experience* (Westview Press, 1988)

Deere, Carmen Diana, 'Women's Land Rights and Rural Social Movements in the Brazilian Agrarian Reform' (2003) 3(1–2) *Journal of Agrarian Change* 257

Deere, Carmen Diana and Magdalena León, *Empowering Women: Land and Property Rights in Latin America* (University of Pittsburgh Press, 2001)

Deininger, Klaus, *Land Policies for Growth and Poverty Reduction* (World Bank and Oxford University Press, 11 June 2003)

Delisle, Christine Taitano, 'A History of Chamorro Nurse-Midwives in Guam and a "Placental Politics" for Indigenous Feminism' (2015) (37) *Intersections: Gender and Sexuality in Asia and the Pacific*

DeLisle, Christine Taitano, *Placental Politics: CHamoru Women, White Womanhood, and Indigeneity under U.S. Colonialism in Guam* (University of North Carolina Press, 2021)

Demian, Melissa, 'Dislocating Custom' (2015) 38(1) *PoLAR: Political and Legal Anthropology Review* 91

"Land Doesn't Come From Your Mother, She Didn't Make It With Her Hands': Challenging Matriliny in Papua New Guinea', in Lim, Hilary and Anne Bottomley (eds), *Feminist Perspectives on Land Law* (Routledge-Cavendish, 2007) 150

Dickson-Waiko, Anne, 'Colonial Enclaves and Domestic Spaces in British New Guinea', in Kate Darian-Smith, Patricia Grimshaw and Stuart Macintyre (eds), *Britishness Abroad: Transnational Movements and Imperial Cultures* (Melbourne University Press, 2007)

'The Missing Rib: Mobilizing Church Women for Change in Papua New Guinea' (2003) 74(1–2) *Oceania* 98

'Women, Individual Human Rights, Community Rights: Tensions within the Papua New Guinea State', in Patricia Grimshaw, Katie Holmes and Marilyn Lake (eds), *Women's Rights and Human Rights* (Palgrave, 2001)

Dinnen, Sinclair, 'A Comment on State-Building in Solomon Islands' (2007) 42(2) *Journal of Pacific History* 255

'The Crisis of State in Solomon Islands' (2009) 21(1) *Peace Review* 70

'State-Building in a Post-Colonial Society: The Case of Solomon Islands' (2008) 9 *Chicago Journal of International Law* 51

'Winners and Losers: Politics and Disorder in the Solomon Islands 2000–2002' (2002) 37(3) *Journal of Pacific History* 285

Dinnen, Sinclair and Matthew Allen, 'State Absence and State Formation in Solomon Islands: Reflections on Agency, Scale and Hybridity' (2016) 47(1) *Development and Change* 76

Dinnen, Sinclair and Stewart Firth (eds), *Politics and State Building in Solomon Islands* (ANU Press, 2008)

Doss, Cheryl, Gale Summerfield and Dzodzi Tsikata, 'Land, Gender, and Food Security' (2014) 20(1) *Feminist Economics* 1

Douglas, Bronwen, 'Christianity, Tradition, and Everyday Modernity: Towards an Anatomy of Women's Groupings in Melanesia' (2003) 74(1–2) *Oceania* 6

'Provocative Readings in Intransigent Archives: Finding Aneityumese Women' (1999) 70(2) *Oceania* 111

Traditional Individuals? Gendered Negotiations of Identity, Christianity and Citizenship in Vanuatu (Discussion Paper No 98/6, State, Society and Governance in Melanesia Program, Australian National University, 1998)

Doumani, Beshara (ed.), *Family History in the Middle East: Household, Property, and Gender* (State University of New York Press, 2003)

Dureau, Christine, 'Decreed Affinities: Nationhood and the Western Solomon Islands' (1998) 33(2) *Journal of Pacific History* 197

'Nobody Asked the Mother: Women and Maternity on Simbo, Western Solomon Islands' (1993) 64(1) *Oceania* 18

'Skulls, Mana and Causality' (2000) 109(1) *Journal of the Polynesian Society* 71

Dyer, Michelle, 'Eating Money: Narratives of Equality on Customary Land in the Context of Natural Resource Extraction in the Solomon Islands' (2017) 28(1) *Australian Journal of Anthropology* 88

'Growing Down Like a Banana: Solomon Islands Village Women Changing Gender Norms' (2017) 18(3) *Asia Pacific Journal of Anthropology* 193, 198.

'Transforming Communicative Spaces: The Rhythm of Gender in Meetings in Rural Solomon Islands' (2018) 23(1) *Ecology and Society* 17

'Ungrounded Cosmopolitanism: Intersections of Moral Responsibility and Gender in Environmental Activism in Rural Solomon Islands' (2018) 67(March–April) *Women's Studies International Forum* 128

Elmhirst, Rebecca, 'Introducing New Feminist Political Ecologies' (2011) 42(2) *Geoforum* 129

Elshtain, Jean Bethke, *Women and War* (University of Chicago Press, 2nd ed, 2013)

Emberson-Bain, 'Atu (ed.), *Sustainable Development or Malignant Growth? Perspectives of Pacific Island Women* (Marama Press, 1994)

Emde, Sina, 'Feared Rumours and Rumours of Fear: The Politicisation of Ethnicity During the Fiji Coup in May 2000' (2005) 75(4) *Oceania* 387

Evans, Daniel, 'Tensions at the Gold Ridge Mine, Guadalcanal, Solomon Islands' (2010) 25(3) *Pacific Economic Bulletin* 121

Fangalasuu, Judith, Ruth Maetala, Patricia Rodi, Anah Vota and Elsie Wickham, *Herem Kam: Stori Blong Mifala Olketa Mere: Women's Submission to the Solomon Islands Truth and Reconciliation Commission* (Solomon Islands Truth and Reconciliation Commission, 2011)

Farran, Sue, 'Fragmenting Land and the Laws That Govern It' (2008) 40(58) *Journal of Legal Pluralism and Unofficial Law* 93

Farran, Susan, 'Land Rights and Gender Equality in the Pacific Region' (2005) 11 *Australian Property Law Journal* 131

Farran, Sue and Jennifer Corrin, 'Developing Legislation to Formalise Customary Land Management: Deep Legal Pluralism or a Shallow Veneer?' (2017) 10(1) *Law and Development Review* 1

Farran, Sue and Don Paterson, *South Pacific Property Law* (Cavendish, 2004)

Farrelly, Trisia and Unaisi Nabobo-Baba 'Talanoa As Empathic Apprenticeship' (2014) 55(3) *Asia Pacific Viewpoint* 319

Filer, Colin, 'Custom, Law and Ideology in Papua New Guinea' (2006) 7(1) *Asia Pacific Journal of Anthropology* 65

'Compensation, Rent and Power in Papua New Guinea', in Susan Toft (ed.), *Compensation for Resource Development in Papua New Guinea* (Law Reform Commission of Papua New Guinea, Monograph No. 6, Research School of Pacific and Asian Studies at The Australian National University, National Centre for Development Studies at The Australian National University, Pacific Policy Paper No. 24) 156

Fitzpatrick, Daniel, 'Evolution and Chaos in Property Rights Systems: The Third World Tragedy of Contested Access' (2005) 115(5) *Yale Law Journal* 996

'Ontologies of Property: Land Titling after the Indian Ocean Tsunami Disaster' (2018) 11(2) *Global Environment* 294

Fitzpatrick, Daniel, Caroline Compton and Joseph D Foukona, 'Property and the State or "The Folly of Torrens": A Comparative Perspective' (2019) 42(3) *University of New South Wales Law Journal* 953

Foale, Simon and Martha Macintyre, 'Dynamic and Flexible Aspects of Land and Marine Tenure at West Nggela: Implications for Marine Resource Management' (2000) 71(1) *Oceania* 30

Forsyth, Miranda, *A Bird That Flies With Two Wings: Kastom and State Justice Systems in Vanuatu* (ANU Press, 2009)

Forsyth, Miranda and Thomas Dick, 'Liquid Regulation: The (Men's) Business of Women's Water Music?' (2021) *International Journal of Law in Context*, https://dx .doi.org/10.1017/s1744552321000574

Foukona, Joseph D, 'Urban Land in Honiara: Strategies and Rights to the City' (2015) 50(4) *Journal of Pacific History* 504

'Land, Law and History: Actors, Networks and Land Reform in Solomon Islands' (PhD thesis, Australian National University, 2017)

'Legal Aspects of Customary Land Administration in Solomon Islands' (2007) 11(1) *Journal of South Pacific Law* 64

Foukona, Joseph and Matthew Allen, 'Urban Land in Solomon Islands: Powers of Exclusion and Counter-Exclusion', in Siobhan McDonnell, Matthew Allen and Colin Filer (eds), *Kastom, Property and Ideology: Land Transformations in Melanesia* (ANU Press, 2017) 85

Fox, Charles E, *The Story of the Solomons* (DOM Publications, 1967)

Fox, James J, *Austronesian Paths and Journeys* (ANU Press, 2021)

'Place and Landscape in Comparative Austronesian Perspective', in James J Fox (ed), *The Poetic Power of Place: Comparative Perspectives on Austronesian Ideas of Locality* (ANU Press, 2006) 1

Fraenkel, Jon, *The Manipulation of Custom: From Uprising to Intervention in the Solomon Islands* (Victoria University Press, 2004)

Frazer, Ian, 'The Struggle for Control of Solomon Island Forests' (1997) 9(1) *The Contemporary Pacific* 39

Fry, Greg, 'Political Legitimacy and the Post-Colonial State in the Pacific: Reflections on Some Common Threads in the Fiji and Solomon Islands Coups' (2000) 12(3) *Pacifica Review* 295

Garrett, John, *To Live Among the Stars: Christian Origins in Oceania* (World Council of Churches/University of the South Pacific, 1982)

Where Nets Were Cast: Christianity in Oceania since World War II (Institute of Pacific Studies in association with World Council of Churches, 1997)

Gegeo, David W, 'Tribes in Agony: Land , Development , and Politics in Solomon Islands' (1991) 19(2) *Cultural Survival Quarterly* 1

'Cultural Rupture and Indigeneity: The Challenge of (Re)visioning 'Place' in the Pacific' (2001) 13(2) *Contemporary Pacific* 491

George, Nicole, 'Climate Change and "Architectures of Entitlement": Beyond Gendered Virtue and Vulnerability in the Pacific Islands?' in Catarina Kinnvall and Helle Rydstrom (eds), *Climate Hazards, Disasters, and Gender Ramifications* (Routledge, 2019) 101

'"Just like Your Mother?" The Politics of Feminism and Maternity in the Pacific Islands' (2010) 32(1) *Australian Feminist Law Journal* 77

'Liberal-Local Peacebuilding in Solomon Islands and Bougainville: Advancing a Gender-Just Peace?' (2018) 94(6) *International Affairs* 1329

Ghai, Yash, 'Constitutional Reviews in Papua New Guinea and Solomon Islands' (1990) 2(2) *The Contemporary Pacific* 313

'The Making of the Independence Constitution' in Peter Larmour (ed.), *Solomon Islands Politics* (Institute of Pacific Studies of the University of the South Pacific, 1983)

Giles, Wenona and Jennifer Hyndman, 'Introduction: Gender and Conflict in a Global Context', in Wenona Mary Giles and Jennifer Hyndman (eds), *Sites of Violence: Gender and Conflict Zones* (University of California Press, 2004) 3

Gillespie, Josephine and Nicola Perry, 'Feminist Political Ecology and Legal Geography: A Case Study of the Tonle Sap Protected Wetlands of Cambodia' (2018) 51(5) *Environment and Planning A: Economy and Space* 1089

Gina, Lloyd Maepeza, *Journeys in a Small Canoe: The Life and Times of a Solomon Islander* (Pandanus Press, 2003)

Goddard, Michael, 'Of Cabbages and Kin: The Value of an Analytic Distinction between Gifts and Commodities' (2016) 20(2) *Critique of Anthropology* 137

Godelier, Maurice and Marilyn Strathern (eds), *Big Men and Great Men: Personifications of Power in Melanesia* (Cambridge University Press, 2008)

Golden, Graeme A, *The Early European Settlers of the Solomon Islands* (GA Golden, 1993)

Goldie, John F, 'The People of New Georgia, Their Manners and Customs and Religious Beliefs' (1909) 22 *Proceedings of the Royal Geographical Society* 23

González-Hidalgo, Marien and Christos Zografos, 'Emotions, Power and Political Conflict: Expanding the 'Emotional Turn' in Political Ecology' (2020) 44(2) *Progress in Human Geography* 235

Goodwin, Bryonny, '"Supposed Figure of a Woman?" Homosociality in the British Solomon Islands, 1880–1940' (MA thesis, University of Auckland, 2006)

Graham, Nicole, 'Dephysicalisation and Entitlement: Legal and Cultural Discourses of Place as Property', in Brad Jessup and Kim Rubenstein (eds) *Environmental Discourses in Public and International Law* (Cambridge University Press, 2012).

Lawscape: Property, Environment, Law (Routledge, 2011)

Gray, George and James Tanis, 'In Between: Personal Experiences of the 9-Year Long Conflict on Bougainville and Habuna Momoruqu (The Blood of My Island): Violence and Guadalcanal Uprising in Solomon Islands' (Working/Technical Paper No 02/4, State, Society and Governance in Melanesia Program, Australian National University, 2002)

Griffen, Vanessa 'The Pacific Islands: All It Requires Is Ourselves', in Robin Morgan (ed.) *Sisterhood is Global* (Anchor Press and Doubleday, 1984) 517

Guo, Pei-yi, 'Law as Discourse: Land Disputes and the Changing Imagination of Relations Among the Langalanga, Solomon Islands' (2011) 34(2/3) *Pacific Studies* 223

Hameiri, Shahar, 'Failed States or a Failed Paradigm? State Capacity and the Limits of Institutionalism' (2007) 10(2) *Journal of International Relations and Development* 122

'State Building or Crisis Management? A Critical Analysis of the Social and Political Implications of the Regional Assistance Mission to Solomon Islands' (2009) 30(1) *Third World Quarterly* 35

'The Trouble with RAMSI: Reexamining the Roots of Conflict in Solomon Islands' (2007) 19(2) *The Contemporary Pacific* 409

Hau'ofa, Epeli, 'Our Sea of Islands' (1994) 6(1) *The Contemporary Pacific* 148

Havea, Jione (ed), *Sea of Readings: The Bible in the South Pacific* (Society of Biblical Literature Press, 2018)

Healy, AM, 'Administration in the British Solomon Islands' (1966) 5 *Journal of Administration Overseas* 194

Heath, Ian C, 'Land Policy in Solomon Islands' (PhD thesis, LaTrobe University, 1979)

Herbert, Tania. *Commercial Exploitation of Children in the Solomon Islands: A Report Focusing on the Presence of the Logging Industry in a Remote Region* (Christian Care Centre of the Church of Melanesia, 2007)

Hermkens, Anna-Karina, 'Mary, Motherhood and Nation: Religion and Gender Ideology in Bougainville's Secessionist Warfare' (2011) (25) *Intersections: Gender and Sexuality in Asia and the Pacific*

Hess, Sabine C, *Person and Place: Ideas, Ideals and the Practice of Sociality on Vanua Lava, Vanuatu* (Berghahn Books, 2009)

Higgins, Kate, 'Outside-In: A Volunteer's Reflections on a Solomon Islands Community Development Program' (SSGM Discussion Paper No. 2008/3, Research School of Pacific and Asian Studies, The Australian National University, 2008)

Hilliard, David, 'The South Sea Evangelical Mission in the Solomon Islands: The Foundation Years' (1969) 4(1) *Journal of Pacific History* 41

Protestant Missions in the Solomon Islands 1849–1942 (ANU, 1966)

Hirschon, Renee (ed.), *Women and Property, Women as Property* (Croom Helm, 1984)

Hocart, AM, 'Warfare in Eddystone of the Solomon Islands' (1931) 61 *The Journal of the Royal Anthropological Institute of Great Britain and Ireland* 324

Hogbin, H Ian, *Experiments in Civilization: The Effects of European Culture on a Native Community of the Solomon Islands* (Routledge & Kegan Paul, 1969)

'Culture Change in the Solomon Islands: Report of Field Work in Guadalcanal and Malaita' (1934) 4(3) *Oceania* 233

'Native Councils and Courts in the Solomon Islands' (1943) 14 *Oceania* 258

A Guadalcanal Society: The Kaoka Speakers (Holt, Rinehart & Winston, 1964)

'The Hill People of North-Eastern Guadalcanal' (1937) 8(1) *Oceania* 62

'Social Advancement in Guadalcanal, Solomon Islands' (1938) 8(3) *Oceania* 289

Huie, Shirley Fenton, *Tiger Lilies: Women Adventurers in the South Pacific* (Angus & Robertson, 1990)

Hunt, Sarah and Cindy Holmes, 'Everyday Decolonization: Living a Decolonizing Queer Politics' (2015) 19(2) *Journal of Lesbian Studies* 154

Hviding, Edvard, 'Contested Rainforests, NGOs, and Projects of Desire in Solomon Islands' (2003) 55(178) *International Social Science Journal* 539

'Disentangling the Butubutu of New Georgia: Cognatic Kinship in Thought and Action', in Ingjerd Hoëm et al. (eds), *Oceanic Socialities and Cultural Forms: Ethnographies of Experience* (Berghahn Books, 2003) 71

Guardians of Marovo Lagoon: Practice, Place, and Politics in Maritime Melanesia (University of Hawai'i Press, 1996)

'Indigenous Essentialism? "Simplifying" Customary Land Ownership in New Georgia, Solomon Islands' (1993) 149 *Bijdragen tot de Taal-, Land- en Volkenkunde/Politics, Tradition and Change in the Pacific* 802

Hviding, Edvard and Tim Bayliss-Smith, *Islands of Rainforest: Agroforestry, Logging, and Eco-Tourism in Solomon Islands* (Ashgate, 1st ed, 2000)

Inter-Parliamentary Union, *Women in Parliament in 2017: The Year in Review* (2018)

International Organization for Migration, *Community Health and Mobility in the Pacific: Solomon Islands Case Study* (International Organization for Migration, 2019).

Isser, Deborah (ed.), *Customary Justice and the Rule of Law in War-Torn Societies* (United States Institute of Peace, 2011)

Ivens, Walter George, *The Island Builders of the Pacific: How and Why the People of Mala Construct Their Artificial Islands, the Antiquity and Doubtful Origin of the Practice, with a Description of the Social Organization, Magic and Religion of Their Inhabitants* (Seely, Service & Co, 1930)

Melanesians of the South-East Solomon Islands (Kegan Paul, Trench, Trubner, 1927)

Jackson, Cecile, 'Gender Analysis of Land: Beyond Land Rights for Women?' (2003) 3 (4) *Journal of Agrarian Change* 453

Jackson, Kim Byron, 'Tie Hokara, Tie Vaka: Black Man, White Man: A Study of the New Georgia Group to 1925' (PhD thesis, Australian National University, 1978)

Jacobs, Susie, 'Gender, Land and Sexuality: Exploring Connections' (2014) 27(2) *International Journal of Politics, Culture, and Society* 173

'Women and Land Resettlement in Zimbabwe' (1983) 27–28 *Review of African Political Economy* 33

Johnson, Miranda, *The Land Is Our History: Indigeneity, Law, and the Settler State* (Oxford University Press, 2016)

Johnson, Osa, *Bride in the Solomons* (Garden City, 1946)

Joireman, Sandra F, 'The Mystery of Capital Formation in Sub-Saharan Africa: Women, Property Rights and Customary Law' (2008) 36(7) *World Development* 1233

Jolly, Margaret, 'Another Time, Another Place' (1999) 69(4) *Oceania* 282

'Beyond the Horizon? Nationalisms, Feminisms, and Globalization in the Pacific' (2005) 52(1) *Ethnohistory* 137

'Custom and the Way of the Land: Past and Present in Vanuatu and Fiji' (1992) 62(4) *Oceania* 330

'Damming the Rivers of Milk? Fertility, Sexuality, and Modernity in Melanesia and Amazonia', in Thomas Gregor and Donald F Tuzin (eds), *Gender in Amazonia and Melanesia: An Exploration of the Comparative Method* (University of California Press, 2001) 175

'The Forgotten Women: A History of Migrant Labour and Gender Relations in Vanuatu' (1987) 58(2) *Oceania* 119

'Men of War, Men of Peace: Changing Masculinities in Vanuatu' (2016) 17(3–4) *Asia Pacific Journal of Anthropology* 305

'Specters of Inauthenticity' (1992) 4(1) *The Contemporary Pacific* 49

'"Woman Ikat Raet Long Human Raet o No?" Women's Rights, Human Rights, and Domestic Violence in Vanuatu', in Anne-Marie Hilsdon et al. (eds), *Human Rights and Gender Politics: Asia-Pacific Perspectives* (Routledge, 2000) 124

Jones, Paul, 'Pacific Urbanisation and the Rise of Informal Settlements: Trends and Implications from Port Moresby' (2012) 30(2) *Urban Policy and Research* 145

Juul, Kristine and Christian Lund (eds), *Negotiating Property in Africa* (Heinemann, 2002)

Kabutaulaka, Tarcisius, 'Australian Foreign Policy and the RAMSI Intervention in Solomon Islands' (2005) 17(2) *The Contemporary Pacific* 283

'Beyond Ethnicity: The Political Economy of the Guadalcanal Crisis in Solomon Islands' (State, Society and Governance in Melanesia, Australian National University, Working Paper No 01/1, 2001)

'Land Groups, Land Registration and Economic Development Projects on Guadalcanal, Solomon Islands' (2020) 42(3) *Pacific Studies* 107

'Failed State' and the War on Terror: Intervention in Solomon Islands (East-West Center, Asia Pacific Issues 72, East-West Center, 2003)

Footprints in the Tasimauri Sea: A Biography of Dominiko Alebua (Institute of Pacific Studies, University of the South Pacific, 2001)

'Global Capital and Local Ownership in Solomon Islands' Forestry Industry', in Stewart Firth (ed), *Globalisation and Governance in the Pacific Islands* (ANU Press, 2006)

'Mapping the Blue Pacific in a Changing Regional Order', in Graeme Smith and Terence Wesley-Smith (eds) *The China Alternative: Changing Regional Order in the Pacific* (ANU Press, 2021) 41

'Parties, Constitutional Engineering and Governance in the Solomon Islands', in Roland Rich, Luke Hambly and Michael G Morgan (eds), *Political Parties in the Pacific Islands* (ANU Press, 2008) 229

'Paths in the Jungle: Landowners and the Struggle for Control of Solomon Islands' Logging Industry' (PhD thesis, Australian National University, 2001)

'Re-Presenting Melanesia: Ignoble Savages and Melanesian Alter-Natives' (2015) 27 (1) *The Contemporary Pacific* 110

'Rumble in the Jungle: Land, Culture and (Un)Sustainable Logging in Solomon Islands', in Antony Hooper (ed.), *Culture and Sustainable Development in the Pacific* (ANU Press, 2000) 88

'A Weak State and the Solomon Islands Peace Process' (East-West Center and Center for Pacific Islands Studies, Pacific Islands Development Series No. 14, 2002)

'Westminster Meets Solomons in the Honiara Riots', in Sinclair Dinnen and Stewart Firth (eds), *Politics and State Building in Solomon Islands* (ANU Press, 2008) 96

Kalabamu, Faustin, 'Patriarchy and Women's Land Rights in Botswana' (2006) 23(3) *Land Use Policy* 237

Kalpagam, U, 'Colonial Governmentality and the Public Sphere in India' (2002) 15(1) *Journal of Historical Sociology* 35

Kama, T, 'Guadalcanal Plains', in Ian Heath (ed.), *Land Research in Solomon Islands* (Land Research Project, Lands Division, Ministry of Agriculture and Lands, 1979)

Kanngieser, Anja and Zoe Todd, 'From Environmental Case Study to Environmental Kin Study' (2020) 59(3) *History and Theory* 385

Karanja, Perpetua W, 'Women's Land Ownership Rights in Kenya' (1991) 1991 *Third World Legal Studies* 109

Kauanui, J Kēhaulani, *Paradoxes of Hawaiian Sovereignty: Land, Sex and the Colonial Politics of State Nationalism* (Duke University Press, 2018)

Keenan, Sarah, *Subversive Property: Law and the Production of Spaces of Belonging* (Routledge, 2015)

Keesing, Roger M, 'Creating the Past: Custom and Identity in the Contemporary Pacific' (1989) 1(1/2) *The Contemporary Pacific* 19

Custom and Confrontation: The Kwaio Struggle for Cultural Autonomy (University of Chicago Press, 1992)

Elota's Story: The Life and Times of a Solomon Islands Big Man (University of Queensland Press, 1978)

'Kastom and Anticolonialism on Malaita: "Culture" as Political Symbol' (1982) 13(4) *Mankind* 357

'Plantation Networks, Plantation Culture: The Hidden Side of Colonial Melanesia' (1986) 82–83 *Journal de la Société des Océanistes* 163

'Politico-Religious Movements and Anticolonialism on Malaita: Maasina Rule in Historical Perspective (Part I)' (1978) 48(4) *Oceania* 241

'Politico-Religious Movements and Anticolonialism on Malaita: Maasina Rule in Historical Perspective (Part II)' (1978) 49(1) *Oceania* 46

Kevane, Michael and Leslie C Gray, 'A Woman's Field Is Made At Night: Gendered Land Rights And Norms In Burkina Faso' (1999) 5(3) *Feminist Economics* 1

Kieran, Caitlin, Kathryn Sproule, Cheryl Doss, Agnes Quisumbing and Sung Mi Kim, 'Examining Gender Inequalities in Land Rights Indicators in Asia' (2015) 46(S1) *Agricultural Economics* 119

Kim, Myjolynne Marie, 'Nesor Annim, Niteikapar (Good Morning, Cardinal Honeyeater): Indigenous Reflections on Micronesian Women and the Environment' (2020) 32(1) *Contemporary Pacific* 147

Kirch, Patrick Vinton, *The Evolution of the Polynesian Chiefdoms* (Cambridge University Press, 1984)

Kirsch, Stuart, 'Keeping the Network in View: Compensation Claims, Property and Social Relations in Melanesia' in L Kalinoe and J Leach (eds), *Rationales of Ownership: Transactions and Claims to Ownership in Contemporary Papua New Guinea* (Sean Kingston, 2004) 79

'Property Effects: Social Networks and Compensation Claims in Melanesia in Melanesia' (2001) 9(2) *Social Anthropology* 147

Koczberski, Gina, George N Curry, and Jesse Anjen, 'Changing Land Tenure and Informal Markets in the Oil Palm Frontier of Papua New Guinea: The Challenge for Land Reform' (2012) 43(2) *Australian Geographer* 181

Kolshus, Thorgeir and Even Hovdhaugen, 'Reassessing the Death of Bishop John Coleridge Patteson' (2010) 45(3) *Journal of Pacific History* 331

Koti, Siona Diana, 'A Historical Analysis on Gender Inequality in Solomon Islands: Solomon Islands Women Under Pre-Colonial, Colonial and Post-Colonial State' (Masters thesis, Seoul National University, 2014)

Kwa'ioloa, Michael and Ben Burt, '"The Chiefs' Country": A Malaitan View of the Conflict in Solomon Islands' (2007) 77(1) *Oceania* 111

Kwai, Anna Annie, *Solomon Islanders in World War II: An Indigenous Perspective* (ANU Press, 2017)

Laracy, Hugh and Eugénie Laracy, 'Custom, Conjugality and Colonial Rule in the Solomon Islands' (1980) 51(2) *Oceania* 133

Laracy, Hugh, *Marists and Melanesians: A History of Catholic Missions in the Solomon Islands* (ANU Press, 1976)

Pacific Protest: The Maasina Rule Movement, Solomon Islands, 1944–1952 (University of the South Pacific, 1983)

Larmour, Peter, 'Alienated Land and Independence in Melanesia' (1984) 8(1) *Pacific Studies* 1

(ed.), *The Governance of Common Property in the Pacific Region* (ANU Press, 2nd ed, 2013)

'Land Policy and Decolonisation in Melanesia: A Comparative Study of Land Policymaking and Implementation Before and After Independence in Papua New Guinea, Solomon Islands and Vanuatu' (PhD thesis, Macquarie University, 1987)

'Policy Transfer and Reversal: Customary Land Registration from Africa to Melanesia' (2002) 22(2) *Public Administration and Development* 151

Lasaqa, Isireli Qalo, 'Melanesians' Choice: A Geographical Study of Tasimboko Participation in the Cash Economy, Guadalcanal, British Solomon Islands' (PhD thesis, Australian National University, 1968)

Lawrence, David Russell, *The Naturalist and His 'Beautiful Islands': Charles Morris Woodford in the Western Pacific* (ANU Press, 2014)

Leslie, Helen, 'Conceptualising and Addressing the Mental Health Impacts of Gender Roles in Conflict and Peacemaking' (2000) 53 *Development Bulletin* 65

Leslie, Helen and Selina Boso, 'Gender-Related Violence in the Solomon Islands: The Work of Local Women's Organisations' (2003) 44(3) *Asia Pacific Viewpoint* 325

Levien, Michael, 'Gender and Land Dispossession: A Comparative Analysis' (2017) 44(6) *Journal of Peasant Studies* 1113

Liligeto, Wilson Gia, *Babata: Our Land, Our Tribe, Our People: A Historical Account and Cultural Materials of Butubutu Babata, Morovo* (Institute of Pacific Studies, University of the South Pacific, 2006)

Liloqula, Ruth, 'Understanding the Conflict in Solomon Islands as a Practical Means to Peacemaking' (2000) 53 *Development Bulletin* 41

Liloqula, Ruth and Alice Aruhe'eta Pollard, 'Understanding Conflict in Solomon Islands: A Practical Means to Peacemaking' (Discussion Paper No. 7, State, Society and Governance in Melanesia, Australian National University, 2000)

Lindstrom, Lamont, 'Melanesian Kastom and Its Transformations' (2008) 18(2) *Anthropological Forum* 161

Lindstrom, Lamont and Geoffrey M White (ed), 'Special Issue: Custom Today' (1993) 6(4) *Anthropological Forum*

LiPuma, Edward, 'The Formation of Nation-States and National Cultures in Oceania', in Robert J Foster (ed.), *Nation Making: Emergent Identities in Postcolonial Melanesia* (University of Michigan Press, 1997) 33

London, Charmian Kittredge, *Voyaging in Wild Seas, Or a Woman Among the Head Hunters (a Narrative of the Voyage of the 'Snark' in the Years 1907–1909)* (Mills & Boon, 1915)

Loughlin, Neil and Sarah Milne, 'After the Grab? Land Control and Regime Survival in Cambodia since 2012' (2021) 51(3) *Journal of Contemporary Asia* 375

Lukere, Vicki, 'Conclusion: Wider Reflections and Survey of the Literature', in V Lukere and M Jolly (eds) *Birthing in the Pacific: Beyond Tradition and Modernity?* (University of Hawai'i Press, 2001) 178

Lukere, Vicki and Margaret Jolly (eds) *Birthing in the Pacific: Beyond Tradition and Modernity?* (University of Hawai'i Press, 2001)

Lund, Christian, *Local Politics and the Dynamics of Property in Africa* (Cambridge University Press, 2008)

'Rule and Rupture: State Formation through the Production of Property and Citizenship' (2016) 47(6) *Development and Change* 1199

'Twilight Institutions: Public Authority and Local Politics in Africa' (2006) 37(4) *Development and Change* 685

Lund, Christian and Catherine Boone, 'Land Politics in Africa: Constituting Authority over Territory, Property and Persons' (2013) 83(1) *Africa*

Luxton, CTJ, *Isles of Solomon: A Tale of Missionary Adventure* (Methodist Foreign Ministry, 2nd ed, 1955)

Macdonald, Barrie, *Cinderellas of Empire: Towards a History of Kiribati and Tuvalu* (Institute of Pacific Studies, University of the South Pacific, 2001)

Macintyre, Martha, 'Petztorme Women: Responding to Change in Lihir, Papua New Guinea' (2003) 74(1–2) *Oceania* 120

"Hear Us, Women of Papua New Guinea': Melanesian Women and Human Rights', in Anne-Marie Hilsdon, Martha Macintyre, Vera Mackie and Maila Stivens (eds), *Human Rights and Gender Politics: Asia-Pacific Perspectives* (Routledge, 2000) 143

Mack, Beverly B and Susan F Hirsch, *Pronouncing and Persevering: Gender and the Discourses of Disputing in an African Islamic Court*, vol 43 (University of Chicago Press, 2000)

Mackenzie, Fiona A, 'Gender, Land Tenure and Globalisation: Exploring the Conceptual Ground', in Dzodzi Tsikata and Pamela Golah (eds), *Land Tenure, Gedner and Globalisation: Research and Analysis from Africa, Asia and Latin America* (International Development Research Centre, 2010) 35

MacCormack, Carolyn and Marilyn Strathern (eds), *Nature, Culture and Gender* (Cambridge University Press, 1981)

Maebuta, Jack, Rebecca Spence, Iris Wielders and Michael O'Loughlin, *Attempts at Building Peace in the Solomon Islands: Disconnected Layers* (Collaborative for Development Action, 2009)

Maetala, Ruth, 'Matrilineal Land Tenure Systems in Solomon Islands: The Cases of Guadalcanal, Makira and Isabel Provinces', in Elise Huffer (ed.), *Land and Women: The Matrilineal Factor: The Cases of the Republic of the Marshall Islands, Solomon Islands and Vanuatu* (Pacific Islands Forum Secretariat, 2008) 35

Mamdani, Mahmood, *Citizen and Subject: Contemporary Africa and the Legacy of Late Colonialism* (Princeton University Press, 1996)

Manji, Ambreena, *The Politics of Land Reform in Africa: From Communal Tenure to Free Markets* (Zed Books, 2013)

'Gender and the Politics of the Land Reform Process in Tanzania' (1998) 36(4) *Journal of Modern African Studies* 645

'"Her Name Is Kamundage": Rethinking Women and Property among the Haya of Tanzania' (2000) 70(3) *Africa* 482

The Struggle for Land and Justice in Kenya (James Currey, 2020)

McDonnell, Siobhan, 'Exploring the Cultural Power of Land Law in Vanuatu: Law as a Performance That Creates Meaning and Identities' (2013) 33 *Intersections: Gender and Sexuality in Asia and the Pacific*

'Urban Land Grabbing by Political Elites: Exploring the Political Economy of Land and the Challenges of Regulation', in Siobhan McDonnell, Matthew G Allen and Colin Filer (eds), *Kastom, Property and Ideology: Land Transformations in Melanesia* (ANU Press, 2017) 283

McDougall, Debra, 'Church, Company, Committee, Chief: Emergent Collectivities in Rural Solomon Islands', in Mary Patterson and Martha Macintyre (eds), *Managing Modernity in the Western Pacific* (University of Queensland Press, 2011) 121

'Customary Authority or State Withdrawal in Solomon Islands: Resilience or Tenacity?' (2015) 50(4) *The Journal of Pacific History* 450

Engaging with Strangers: Love and Violence in the Rural Solomon Islands (Berghahn Books, 2016)

'Fellowship and Citizenship as Models of National Community: United Church Women's Fellowship in Ranongga, Solomon Islands' (2003) 74(1/2) *Oceania* 61

'Paths of Pinauzu: Captivity and Social Reproduction in Ranongga' (2000) 109(1) *Journal of the Polynesian Society* 99

'"Tired for Nothing?" Women, Chiefs, and the Domestication of Customary Authority in Solomon Islands', in Hyaeweol Choi and Margaret Jolly (eds), *Divine Domesticities: Christian Paradoxes in Asia and the Pacific* (ANU Press, 2014)

'The Unintended Consequences of Clarification: Development, Disputing, and the Dynamics of Community in Ranongga, Solomon Islands' (2005) 52(1) *Ethnohistory* 81

McDougall, Debra and Joy Kere, 'Christianity, Custom, and Law: Conflict and Peacemaking in the Postconflict Solomon Islands', in Roland Bleiker and Morgan Brigg (eds), *Mediating across Difference: Oceanic and Asian Approaches to Conflict Resolution* (University of Hawai'i Press, 2011) 141

McEvoy, Darryn, David Mitchell and Alexei Trundle, 'Land Tenure and Urban Climate Resilience in the South Pacific' (2020) 12(1) *Climate and Development* 1

McKinnon, JM, 'Tomahawks, Turtles and Traders' (1975) 45(4) *Oceania* 290

Meinzen-Dick, Ruth and Esther Mwangi, 'Cutting the Web of Interests: Pitfalls of Formalizing Property Rights' (2009) 26(1) *Land Use Policy* 36

Merry, Sally Engle, 'Legal Vernacularization and Ka Ho'okolokolonui Kanaka Maoli, The People's International Tribunal, Hawai'i 1993' (1996) 19 *PoLAR: Political and Legal Anthropology Review* 67

Human Rights and Gender Violence: Translating International Law into Local Justice (University of Chicago Press, 2006)

Merry, Sally Engle and Donald Brenneis, 'Introduction', in *Law and Empire in the Pacific* (School of American Research Press, 2004)

Minter, Tessa, Grace Orirana, Delvene Boso and Jan van der Ploeg, *From Happy Hour to Hungry Hour: Logging, Fisheries and Food Security in Malaita, Solomon Islands* (Worldfish, 2018)

Mohanty, Chandra, 'Under Western Eyes: Feminist Scholarship and Colonial Discourses' (1988) 30 *Feminist Review* 61

Mohanty, Chandra Talpade, '"Under Western Eyes" Revisited: Feminist Solidarity through Anticapitalist Struggles'(2002) 28(2) *Signs* 499

Mollett, Sharlene and Caroline Faria, 'Messing With Gender in Feminist Political Ecology' (2013) 45 *Geoforum* 116

Molyneux, Maxine and Shahra Razavi (eds), *Gender Justice, Development, and Rights* (Oxford University Press, 2002) 1

Monson, Rebecca, 'Negotiating Land Tenure: Women, Men and the Transformation of Land Tenure in Solomon Islands', in Janine Ubink and Thomas McInerney (eds), *Customary Justice: Perspectives on Legal Empowerment* (International Development Law Organization, 2011) 169

'Vernacularising Political Participation: Strategies of Women Peace-Builders in Solomon Islands' (2013) 33 *Intersections: Gender and Sexuality in Asia and the Pacific*

'Unsettled Explorations of Law's Archives: The Allure and Anxiety of Solomon Islands' Court Records' (2014) 40(1) *Australian Feminist Law Journal* 35

'From *Taovia* to Trustee: Urbanisation, Land Disputes and Social Differentiation in Kakabona' (2015) 4 *The Journal of Pacific History* 437–449

'The Politics of Property: Gender, Land and Political Authority in Solomon Islands', in Siobhan McDonnell, Matthew Allen and Colin Filer (eds), *Kastom, Property and Ideology: Land Transformations in Melanesia* (ANU Press, 2017) 383

Monson, Rebecca and George Hoa'au, '(Em)Placing Law: Migration, Belonging and Place in Solomon Islands', in Fiona Jenkins, Mark Nolan and Kim Rubenstein (eds), *Allegiance and Identity in a Globalised World* (Cambridge University Press, 2014) 117

Monson, Rebecca, Keith Camacho and Joseph Foukona, 'The Pacific', in Sundhya Pahuja, Luis Eslava and Ruth Buchanan (eds), *Oxford Handbook of International Law and Development* (Oxford University Press, forthcoming 2022)

Moore, Clive, *Happy Isles in Crisis: The Historical Causes for a Failing State in Solomon Islands, 1998–2004* (Asia Pacific Press, 2004)

'Honiara: Arrival City and Pacific Hybrid Living Space' (2015) 50(4) *Journal of Pacific History* 419

Kanaka: A History of Melanesian Mackay (Institute of Papua New Guinea Studies and University of Papua New Guinea Press, 1985)

Making Mala: Malaita in Solomon Islands, 1870s–1930s (ANU Press, 2017)

Moreton-Robinson, Aileen, *The White Possessive: Property, Power and Indigenous Sovereignty* (University of Minnesota Press, 2015)

Morrell, William P, *Britain in the Pacific Islands* (Clarendon Press, 1969)

Mugambwa, John, 'A Comparative Analysis of Land Tenure Law Reform in Uganda and Papua New Guinea' (2007) 11(1) *Journal of South Pacific Law* 39

Munro, Doug and Stewart Firth, 'German Labour Policy and the Partition of the Western Pacific: The View from Samoa' (2008) 25(1) *Journal of Pacific History* 85

Muria, G John B, 'Guadalcanal', in Ian C Heath (ed.), *Land Research in Solomon Islands* (Land Research Project, Lands Division, Ministry of Agriculture and Lands, 1979)

Mytinger, Caroline, *Headhunting in the Solomon Islands Around the Coral Sea* (Macmillan, 1942)

Nagarajan, Vijaya and Therese MacDermott, 'Empowering Women through Recognition of Rights to Land: Mechanisms to Strengthen Women's Rights in Vanuatu' (2013) 86(3) *Pacific Affairs* 471

Naitoro, John Houainamo R., 'Articulating Kin Groups and Mines: The Case of the Gold Ridge Mining Project in the Solomon Islands' (PhD thesis, Australian National University, 2002)

Naitoro, John Houainamo, 'Solomon Islands Conflict: Demands for Historical Rectification and Restorative Justice' (Paper presented at the Pacific Updates on Solomon Islands, Fiji and Vanuatu. Hosted by the National Centre for Development Studies, Asia Pacific School of Economics and Management, Australian National University, 2000)

Nanau, Gordon Leua, 'Can a Theory of Insecure Globalisation Provide Better Explanations for Instability in the South Pacific? The Case of Solomon Islands' (PhD thesis, University of East Anglia, 2008)

Nanau, Gordon, 'Local Experiences with Mining Royalties, Company and the State in the Solomon Islands' (2014) 138 *Journal de la Société des Océanistes* 77

Oceanic Diplomacy: Popo and Supu Diplomacy in the Modern State of Solomon Islands (Department of Pacific Affairs, Australian National University, InBrief No. 2021/28, 2021)

Naupa, Anna, 'Making the Invisible Seen: Putting Women's Rights on Vanuatu's Land Reform Agenda', in Siobhan McDonnell, Matthew G Allen and Colin Filer (eds), *Kastom, Property and Ideology: Land Transformations in Melanesia* (ANU Press, 2017) 305

Naupa, Anna and Joel Simo, 'Matrilineal Land Tenure in Vanuatu: "Hu i Kakae Long Basket?" Case Studies of Raga and Mele', in Kristina E Stege (ed.), *Land and Women: The Matrilineal Factor: The Cases of the Republic of the Marshall Islands, Solomon Islands and Vanuatu* (Pacific Islands Forum Secretariat, 2008) 74

Nightingale, Andrea, 'The Nature of Gender: Work, Gender and Environment' (2006) 24 *Environment and Planning D: Society and Space* 165

Nightingale, Andrea J, 'Beyond Design Principles: Subjectivity, Emotion and the (Ir)Rational Commons' (2011) 24(2) *Society and Natural Resources* 119

'Bounding Difference: Intersectionality and the Material Production of Gender, Caste, Class and Environment in Nepal' (2011) 42(2) *Geoforum* 153

Norton, Robert, 'Reconciling Ethnicity and Nation: Contending Discourses in Fiji's Constitutional Reform' (2000) 12(1) *The Contemporary Pacific* 83

O'Brien, Claire, *A Greater than Solomon Here: A Story of Catholic Church in Solomon Islands 1567–1967* (Catholic Church Solomon Islands, 1995)

Odgaard, Rie, 'Scrambling for Land in Tanzania: Process of Formalisation and Legitimisation of Land Rights' (2002) 14(2) *European Journal of Development Research* 71

Olsen, Wendy, *Moral Political Economy and Poverty: Four Theoretical Schools Compared* (Department of Economics, University of Oxford, Economics Working Paper Series No. GPRG-WPS-031, 2005)

Oram, Nigel, 'Land, Housing and Administration in Honiara: Towards a Concerted Policy' (1980) 1 *O'o: A Journal of Solomon Island Studies* 133

Ortner, Sherry B, 'Is Female to Male as Nature Is to Culture?' (1972) 1(2) *Feminist Studies* 5

Otto, Ton and Poul Pedersen (eds), *Tradition and Agency: Tracing Cultural Continuity and Invention* (Aarhus University Press, 2006)

Pacific Islands Forum Secretariat, *Improving Access to Customary Land and Maintaining Social Harmony in the Pacific* (2008)

Pacific Leaders Gender Equality Declaration Trend Assessment Report 2012–2016 (2016)

Pacific Women, *Pacific Women in Leadership Synthesis Report: Informing Pacific Women Shaping Pacific Development Roadmap 2017–2022 – Pacific Women Shaping Pacific Development* (2017)

Paina, Dalcy Tovosia, 'Peacemaking in Solomon Islands: The Experience of the Guadalcanal Women for Peace Movement' (2000) 53 *Development Bulletin* 47

Paravicini, Eugen, *Reisen in Den Britischen Salomonen* (Huber and Company, 1931)

Patison, Fred Siho and Steve Ereinao, *Mamara New Capital City Development Phase 1 Environment Impact Statement (EIS): Chapter 11: Social and Cultural Assessment Report* (Meropolis Pacific and Telios Corporate and Consultancy Services, 2020)

Pels, Peter, 'The Anthropology of Colonialism: Culture, History, and the Emergence of Western Governmentality' (1997) 26 *Annual Review of Anthropology* 163

Peluso, Nancy Lee and Christian Lund (eds), *New Frontiers of Land Control* (Routledge, 2013)

Pendeverana, Lincy, 'Pursuing Livelihoods and Re-Imagining Development in the Oil Palm Regions of the Guadalcanal Plains, Solomon Islands' (PhD thesis, Australian National University, 2021)

Peters, Pauline E, 'Inequality and Social Conflict Over Land in Africa' (2004) 4(3) *Journal of Agrarian Change* 314

Petrou, Kirstie, *If Everyone Returned, the Island Would Sink: Urbanisation and Migration in Vanuatu* (Berghahn Books, 2020)

Platteau, Jean-Philippe, 'The Evolutionary Theory of Land Rights as Applied to Sub-Saharan Africa: A Critical Assessment' (1996) 27(1) *Development and Change* 29

Plumwood, Val, *Feminism and the Mastery of Nature* (Routledge, 1993)

Pollard, Alice Aruhe'eta, *Givers of Wisdom, Labourers Without Gain: Essays on Women in the Solomon Islands*, edited by Anthony R Walker (Institute of Pacific Studies, University of the South Pacific, 2000)

'Painaha: Gender and Leadership in 'Are'Are Society, the South Sea Evangelical Church and Parliamentary Leadership – Solomon Islands' (PhD thesis, Victoria University of Wellington, 2006)

'Resolving Conflict in Solomon Islands: The Women for Peace Approach' (2000) 53 *Development Bulletin* 44

'Women's Organizations, Voluntarism, and Self-Financing in Solomon Islands: A Participant Perspective' (2003) 74(1/2) *Oceania* 44

Pottage, Alain, 'The Measure of Land' (1994) 57(3) *Modern Law Review* 361

Pradhan, Rajendra, 'Legal Pluralism in the Supreme Court: Law, Religion, and Culture Pertaining to Women's Rights in Nepal', in Franz von Benda-Beckmann et al. (eds.), *Religion in Disputes: Pervasiveness of Religious Normativity in Disputing Processes* (Palgrave Macmillan, 2013) 165

Premdas, Ralph R and Jeffrey S Steeves, 'The Solomon Islands: An Experiment in Decentralization' (Working Paper Series, Pacific Islands Studies Program, Center for Asian and Pacific Studies, University of Hawaii at Manoa, 1985)

'Decentralization and Development in Melanesia: Papua New Guinea and the Solomon Islands' (1985) 51(2) *International Review of Administrative Sciences* 120

'The Solomon Islands: First Elections after Independence' (1981) 16(4) *Journal of Pacific History* 190

Premdas, Ralph, Jeff Steeves and Peter Larmour, 'The Western Breakaway Movement in the Solomon Islands' (1984) 7(2) *Pacific Studies* 34

Public Solicitors Office Landowners Advocacy and Legal Support Unit, *Case Studies for Conservation* (n.d.)

Regional Assistance Mission to Solomon Islands, *2011 People's Survey: Full Report* (RAMSI, 2012)

Radcliffe, Sarah A, 'Gendered Frontiers of Land Control: Indigenous Territory, Women and Contests over Land in Latin America' (2014) 21(7) *Gender, Place and Culture* 854

Rao, Nitya, 'Custom and the Courts: Ensuring Women's Rights to Land, Jharkhand, India' (2007) 38(2) *Development and Change* 299

'*Good Women Do Not Inherit Land': Politics of Land and Gender in India* (Taylor & Frances Group, 2017)

Rangan, Haripriya, *Of Myths and Movements: Rewriting Chipko into Himalayan History* (Verso, 2000)

Rawlings, Greg, '"Once There Was a Garden, Now There Is a Swimming Pool": Inequality, Labour and Land in Pango, a Peri-Urban Village in Vanuatu' (PhD thesis, Australian National University, 2002)

Razavi, Shahra, 'Introduction: Agrarian Change, Gender and Land Rights' (2003) 3 (1–2) *Journal of Agrarian Change* 2

'Liberalisation and the Debates on Women's Access to Land' (2007) 28(8) *Third World Quarterly* 1479

Reilly, Brandon J, 'Reproductive Anticolonialism: Placental Politics, Weaponised Wombs and the Power of Abjection in the Early Spanish Mariana Islands' (2020) (44) *Intersections: Gender and Sexuality in Asia and the Pacific*

Ribot, Jesse C and Nancy Lee Peluso, 'A Theory of Access' (2003) 68(2) *Rural Sociology* 153

Ride, Anouk and Pauline Soaki, *Women's Experiences of Family Violence Services in Solomon Islands* (Australian Aid and Solomon Islands Government, 2019)

Riles, Annalise, 'Law as Object', in Donald Brenneis and Sally Engle Merry (eds), *Law and Empire in the Pacific: Fiji and Hawai'i* (School of American Research Press, 2004) 187

'Property as Legal Knowledge: Means and Ends' (2004) 10(4) *Journal of the Royal Anthropological Institute* 775

Robinson, Angela L, 'Of Monsters and Mothers: Affective Climates and Human-Nonhuman Sociality in Kathy Jetnil-Kijiner's "Dear Matafele Peinam"' (2020) 32(2) *The Contemporary Pacific* 311

Robinson, Daniel F and Nicole Graham, 'Legal Pluralisms, Justice and Spatial Conflicts: New Directions in Legal Geography' (2018) 184(1) *The Geographical Journal* 3

Rocheleau, Dianne and David Edmunds, 'Women, Men and Trees: Gender, Power and Property in Forest and Agrarian Landscapes' (1997) 25(8) *World Development* 1351

Rocheleau, Dianne, 'A Situated View of Feminist Political Ecology From My Networks, Roots and Territories', in Wendy Harcourt and Ingrid L Nelson (eds) *Practising Feminist Political Ecologies: Moving Beyond the 'Green Economy'* (Zed Books, 2015) 29

Rodman, Margaret C, *Masters of Tradition: Consequences of Customary Land Tenure in Longana, Vanuatu* (University of British Columbia Press, 1987)

Roe, David, 'Prehistory without Pots: Prehistoric Settlement and Economy of North-West Guadalcanal, Solomon Islands' (PhD thesis, Australian National University, 1993)

Rolls, Sharon Bhagwan, 'Women as Mediators in Pacific Conflict Zones' (2006) 2 *Women in Action* 29

Rooney, Michelle Nayahamui, 'As *Basket* and *Papu*: Making Manus Social Fabric' (2021) 91(1) *Oceania* 86

——'"There's Nothing Better than Land": A Migrant Group's Strategies for Accessing Informal Settlement Land in Port Moresby', in Siobhan McDonnell, Matthew Allen and Colin Filer (eds), *Kastom, Property and Ideology* (ANU Press, 2017) 111

Rose, Carol M, *Property and Persuasion: Essays on the History, Theory and Rhetoric of Ownership* (Westview Press, 1994)

Russell, T, 'The Culture of Marovo, British Solomon Islands' (1948) 57(4) *Journal of the Polynesian Society* 306

Sack, David Robert, *Human Territoriality: Its Theory and History* (Cambridge University Press, 1986)

Sahlins, Marshall D, 'Poor Man, Rich Man, Big-Man, Chief: Political Types in Melanesia and Polynesia' (1963) 5(3) *Comparative Studies in Society and History* 285

Sanga, Kabini, Martyn Reynolds, Irene Paulsen, Rebecca Spratt and Joash Maneipuri, 'A Tok Stori about Tok Stori: Melanesian Relationality in Action as Research, Leadership and Scholarship' (2018) 2(1) *Global Comparative Education* 3

Santos, Boaventura de Sousa, *Epistemologies of the South: Justice Against Epistemicide* (Routledge, 2014)

——'Law: A Map of Misreading: Toward a Postmodern Conception of Law' (1987) 14(3) *Journal of Law and Society* 279

Saovana-Spriggs, Ruth, 'Bougainville Women's Role in Conflict Resolution in the Bougainville Peace Process' in Sinclair Dinnen, Anita Jowitt and Tess Newton Cain (eds), *A Kind of Mending: Restorative Justice in the Pacific Islands* (ANU Press, 2010) 195

——'The Peace Process in Bougainville During the Cease-Fire Period: 1999–2000' (2000) 53 *Development Bulletin*

Scales, Ian, 'The Coup Nobody Noticed: The Solomon Islands Western State Movement in 2000' (2007) 42(2) *Journal of Pacific History* 187

——'The Social Forest: Landowners, Development Conflict and the State in Solomon Islands' (PhD thesis, ANU Press, 2003)

Scarr, Deryck, *Fragments of Empire: A History of the Western Pacific High Commission, 1877–1914* (ANU Press, 1967)

Scheyvens, Regina, 'Church Women's Groups and the Empowerment of Women in Solomon Islands' (2003) 74(1/2) *Oceania* 24

Schneider, Gerhard, 'Land Dispute and Tradition in Munda, Roviana Lagoon, New Georgia Island, Solomon Islands: From Headhunting to the Quest for Control of Land' (PhD thesis, University of Cambridge, 1996)

Schoorl, Jeannette and Ward Friesen, 'Migration and Displacement', in Bart de Bruijin (ed), *Report on the 1999 Population and Housing Census* (Solomon Islands Statistics Office, 2002)

Scott, James C, *Seeing Like a State: How Certain Schemes to Improve the Human Condition Have Failed* (Yale University Press, 1998)

Scott, Michael W, 'Ignorance Is Cosmos; Knowledge Is Chaos: Articulating a Cosmological Polarity in the Solomon Islands' (2000) 44(2) *Social Analysis* 56

'"I Was Like Abraham": Notes on the Anthropology of Christianity from the Solomon Islands' (2005) 70(1) *Ethnos* 101

'The Matter of Makira: Colonialism, Competition, and the Production of Gendered Peoples in Contemporary Solomon Islands and Medieval Britain' (2012) 23(1) *History and Anthropology* 115

'Neither "New Melanesian History" nor "New Melanesian Ethnography": Recovering Emplaced Matrilineages in Southeast Solomon Islands' (2007) 77(3) *Oceania* 337

The Severed Snake: Matrilineages, Making Place, and a Melanesian Christianity in Southeast Solomon Islands (Carolina Academic Press, 2007)

Secretariat of the Pacific Community, *Solomon Islands Family Health and Safety Study: A Study on Violence against Women and Children* (2009)

Stocktake of the Gender Mainstreaming Capacity of Pacific Island Governments: Kiribati (2015)

Sen, Amartya, *Development as Freedom* (Oxford University Press, 1999)

Sheppard, Peter, 'Four Hundred Years of Niche Construction in the Western Solomons', in Mathieu Leclerc and James Flexner (eds), *Archaeologies of Island Melanesia: Current Approaches to Landscapes, Exchange and Practice* (ANU Press, 2019) 117

Sieder, Rachel and John Andrew McNeish, 'Introduction', in John Andrew McNeish and Rachel Sieder (eds), *Gender Justice and Legal Pluralities: Latin American and African Perspectives* (Taylor & Francis Group, A GlassHouse Book, 2013) 1

Silva, Noenoe K, *Aloha Betrayed: Native Hawaiian Resistance to American Colonialism* (Duke University Press, 2004)

Sikor, Thomas and Christian Lund, 'Access and Property: A Question of Power and Authority' (2009) 40(1) *Development and Change* 1

Sikua, Derek, 'Commission of Inquiry into Land Dealings and Abandoned Properties on Guadalcanal' in Solomon Islands' *Supplement to the Solomon Islands Gazette* No 13, 15 April 2009, 60

Sillitoe, Paul, *Social Change in Melanesia: Development and History* (Cambridge University Press, 2000)

Simmonds, Naomi, 'Mana Wahine: Decolonising Politics' (2011) 25(2) *Women's Studies Journal* 11

Simpson, Audra, 'The Ruse of Consent and the Anatomy of "Refusal": Cases from Indigenous North America and Australia' (2017) 20(1) *Postcolonial Studies* 18

Sirivi, Josephine Tankunani and Marilyn Taleo Havini, *As Mothers of the Land: The Birth of the Bougainville Women for Peace and Freedom* (Pandanus, 2004)

Slatter, Claire, 'Gender and Custom in the South Pacific' (2012) 13–14 *Yearbook of New Zealand Jurisprudence* 89

Smith, Linda Tuhiwai, *Decolonizing Methodologies: Research and Indigenous Peoples* (Zed Books and University of Otago Press, 2006)

Soaki, Pauline, 'Casting Her Vote: Women's Political Participation in Solomon Islands', in M Macintyre and C Spark (eds), *Transformations of Gender in Melanesia* (ANU Press, 2017) 95

Solomon Islands Government, 1987 *Constitutional Review Committee Report* (Vols I & II, 1988)

Solomon Islands Law Reform Commission, *Review of the Law That Applies to Land below High Water Mark and Low Water Mark* (2012)

Solomon Islands Legislative Assembly, *Report of the Constitutional Committee, 1975* (1976)

Solomon Islands National Statistics Office, *Report on the 2009 Population and Housing Census: National Report (Volume 2)* (2009)

2019 *National Population and Housing Census Project: Provisional Count* (2020)

Solomon Islands Truth and Reconciliation Commission, *Confronting the Truth for a Better Solomon Islands* (2012)

Somerville, Boyle T, 'Ethnographical Notes in New Georgia, Solomon Islands' (1897) 26 *The Journal of the Anthropological Institute of Great Britain and Ireland* 412

Spivak, Gayatri Chakravorty, 'Can the Subaltern Speak?', in Cary Nelson and Lawrence Grossberg (eds), *Marxism and the Interpretation of Culture* (University of Illinois Press, 1988)

Spriggs, Matthew, 'Taro Irrigation Techniques in the Pacific', in Satish Chandra (ed.), *Edible Aroids* (Clarendon Press, 1984)

Stead, Victoria, 'Money Trees, Development Dreams and Colonial Legacies in Contemporary Pasifika Horticultural Labour', in Victoria Stead and Jon C Altman (eds), *Labour Lines and Colonial Power: Indigenous and Pacific Island Labour Mobility in Australia* (ANU Press, 2019) 312

Becoming Landowners: Entanglements of Custom and Modernity in Papua New Guinea and Timor-Leste (University of Hawai'i Press, 2017)

Stege, Kristina E, 'An Kōrā Aelōñ Kein (These Islands Belong to Women): A Study of Women and Land in the Republic of the Marshall Islands', in Elise Huffer (ed), *Land and Women: The Matrilineal Factor: The Cases of the Republic of the Marshall Islands, Solomon Islands and Vanuatu* (Pacific Islands Forum Secretariat, 2008) 1

Stege, Kristina E, Ruth Maetala, Anna Naupa, Joel Simo and Elise Huffer, *Land and Women: The Matrilineal Factor – The Cases of the Republic of the Marshall Islands, Solomon Islands and Vanuatu* (Pacific Islands Forum Secretariat, 2008)

Stoler, Ann Laura, *Along the Archival Grain: Epistemic Anxieties and Colonial Common Sense* (Princeton University Press, 2009)

Strathern, Marilyn, 'Cutting the Network' (1996) 2(3) *Journal of the Royal Anthropological Institute* 517

The Gender of the Gift: Problems with Women and Problems with Society in Melanesia (University of California Press, 1988)

Kinship, Law and the Unexpected: Relatives Are Always a Surprise (Cambridge University Press, 2005)

Sultana, Farhana, 'Emotional Political Ecology' in RL Bryant (ed) *The International Handbook of Political Ecology* (Edward Elgar, 2015) 633

'Fluid Lives: Subjectivities, Gender, and Water in Rural Bangladesh' (2009) 16(4) *Gender, Place and Culture* 427

'Political Ecology 1: From Margins to Centre' (2021) 45(1) *Progress in Human Geography* 156

'Suffering for Water, Suffering from Water: Emotional Geographies of Resource Access, Control and Conflict' (2011) 42(2) *Geoforum* 163

Sumeo, Karanina, 'Land Rights and Empowerment of Urban Women, Fa'afafine and Fakaleitī in Samoa and Tonga' (PhD thesis, Auckland University of Technology, 2016)

Sweetman, Caroline, 'Special Issue: Gender, Religion and Spirituality' (1999) 7(1) *Gender and Development*

Tabe, Tammy, 'Climate Migration and Displacement: Learning from Past Relocations in the Pacific' (2019) 8(7) *Social Sciences* 218

Tagini, Philip, 'The Search for King Solomon's Gold: An Examination of the Policy and Regulatory Framework for Mining in Solomon Islands' (PhD thesis, Monash University, 2007)

Takutile, Franklin, 'Mortuary Feast at Vatupilei' in P Larmour (ed), *Land Tenure in Solomon Islands* (1979) 2

Tamanaha, Brian Z, Caroline Sage and Michael Woolcodk (eds), *Legal Pluralism and Development: Scholars and Practitioners in Dialogue* (Cambridge University Press, 2012)

Talasasa, Francis M, 'Settlement of Disputes in Customary Land in British Solomon Islands Protectorate' (1970) 11 *Melanesian Law Journal*

TallBear, Kim, 'Identity Is a Poor Substitute for Relating: Genetic Ancestry, Critical Polyamory, Property, and Relations', in Brendan Hokowhitu et al. (eds), *Routledge Handbook of Critical Indigenous Studies* (Routledge, 2021)

Taylor, John Patrick, *The Other Side: Ways of Being and Place in Vanuatu* (University of Hawai'i Press, 2008)

Teaiwa, Katerina Martina, *Consuming Ocean Island: Stories of People and Phosphate from Banaba* (Indiana University Press, 2014)

'Our Rising Sea of Islands: Pan-Pacific Regionalism in the Age of Climate Change' (2018) 41(1/2) *Pacific Studies*

Teaiwa, Teresia, 'Articulated Cultures: Militarism and Masculinities in Fiji During the Mid 1990s' (2005) 3(2) *Fijian Studies: A Journal of Contemporary Fiji* 201

'bikinis and other s/pacific n/ocean' (1994) 6(1) *The Contemporary Pacific* 87

'On Analogies: Rethinking the Pacific in a Global Context' (2006) 18(1) *The Contemporary Pacific* 71

Teresia, Teaiwa, 'Microwomen: US Colonialism and Micronesian Women Activists', in Katerina Teaiwa, April K Henderson and Terence Wesley-Smith (eds) *Sweat and Salt Water: Selected Works* (University of Hawai'i Press, 2021), 87

'The Ancestors We Get to Choose: White Influences I Won't Deny', in Katerina Teaiwa, April K. Henderson and Terence Wesley-Smith (eds.) *Sweat and Salt Water: Selected Works* (University of Hawai'i Press, 2021), 223

Teaiwa, Teresia and Claire Slatter, 'Samting Nating: Pacific Waves at the Margins of Feminist Security Studies' (2013) 14(4) *International Studies Perspectives* 447

Tedder, Margaret M, 'Old Kusaghe' (1976) 4 *Journal of the Cultural Association of the Solomon Islands* 41

Thomas, Tim, 'Axes of Entanglement in the New Georgia Group, Solomon Islands' in M Leclerc and J Flexner (eds), *Archaeologies of Island Melanesia: Current Approaches to Landscapes, Exchange and Practice* (ANU Press, 2019) 103

Tiffany, Sharon W, 'Customary Land Disputes, Courts and African Models in the Solomon Islands' (1983) 53(3) *Oceania* 277

  'Disputing in Customary Land Courts: Case Studies from Solomon Islands' (1979) 7 *Melanesian Law Journal* 99

Tippett, Alan Richard, *Solomon Islands Christianity* (Lutterworth Press, 1967)

Tomlinson, Matt and Debra McDougall (eds), *Christian Politics in Oceania* (Berghahn Books, 2013)

Tripp, Aili Mari, 'Women's Movements, Customary Law, and Land Rights in Africa: The Case of Uganda' (2004) 7(4) *African Studies Quarterly* 1

Tuwere, Ilatia Sevati, *Vanua: Towards a Fijian Theology of Place* (Institute of Pacific Studies, University of the South Pacific, 2002)

Tuza, Esau, 'The Solomon Islands Response to the Gospel' (Paper presented to the South Pacific Regional Conference on the World Methodist Historical Society, Wesley College, Auckland, New Zealand, 18–23 May 1987).

Ubink, Janine M and Kojo S Amanor (eds), *Contesting Land and Custom in Ghana: State, Chief and the Citizen* (Leiden University Press, 2008)

Ubink, Janine M and Thomas McInerney (eds), *Customary Justice: Perspectives on Legal Empowerment* (International Development Law Organisation, 2011)

Underhill-Sem, Yvonne, 'Embodying Post-Development: Bodies in Places, Places in Bodies' (2002) 45(1) *Society for International Development* 54

  'Marked Bodies in Marginalised Places: Understanding Rationalities in Global Discourses' (2003) 46(2) *Development* 13

United Nations Development Programme, *Briefing Note for Countries on the 2020 Human Development Report: Solomon Islands* (UNDP, 2020)

  Project Identification Form: Integrating Global Environment Commitments in Investment and Development Decision-Making (UNDP, 2011)

  2018 Statistical Update: Human Development Indices and Indicators (2018)

United Nations General Assembly, *Transforming our World: The 2030 Agenda for Sustainable Development*, 70th sess, Agenda items 15 and 116, UN Doc A/RES/70/1 (21 October 2015)

Vandergeest, Peter and Nancy Lee Peluso, 'Territorialization and State Power in Thailand' (1995) 24(3) *Theory and Society* 385

Vella, Louise, 'Documenting Women's Experiences of Conflict and Sexual Violence: On the Ground with the Solomon Islands Truth and Reconciliation Commission', in Renée Jeffery (ed), *Transitional Justice in Practice: Conflict, Justice, and Reconciliation in the Solomon Islands* (Palgrave Macmillan, 2017) 141

  '"What Will You Do with Our Stories?" Truth and Reconciliation in the Solomon Islands' (2014) 8(1) *International Journal of Conflict and Violence* 91

Vella, Louise and Jack Maebuta, 'Building National Unity, Reconciliation and Peace in the Solomon Islands: The Missing Link', in Bert Jenkins, DB Subedi and Kathy Jenkins (eds), *Reconciliation in Conflict-Affected Communities: Practices and Insights from the Asia-Pacific* (Springer, 2018) 57

Verma, Ritu, *Gender, Land and Livelihoods in East Africa: Through Farmers' Eyes* (International Development Research Centre, 2001)

Vermeylen, Saskia, 'Special Issue: Environmental Justice and Epistemic Violence' (2019) 24(2) *Local Environment* 89

Wairiu, Morgan and Gordon Nanau, *Logging and Conflict in Birao Ward of Guadalcanal, Solomon Islands* (Islands Knowledge Institute, IKI Working Paper No. 1, 2010)

Wanyeki, Lynne Muthoni, *Women and Land in Africa: Culture, Religion and Realizing Women's Rights* (Zed Books, 2003)

Watson, Irene, 'Sovereign Spaces, Caring for Country, and the Homeless Position of Aboriginal Peoples' (2009) 108(1) *South Atlantic Quarterly* 27

Watts, Michael, 'Violent Environments: Petroleum Conflict and the Political Ecology of Rule in the Niger Delta, Nigeria', in Richard Peet and Michael Watts (eds), *Liberation Ecologies: Environment, Development and Social Movements* (Routledge, 2nd ed, 2004) 250

Watts, Michael and Nancy Lee Peluso (eds), *Violent Environments* (Cornell University Press, 2001)

Wehner, Monica and Ewan Maidment, 'Ancestral Voices: Aspects of Archives Administration in Oceania' (1999) 27(1) *Archives and Manuscripts* 23

Weiner, James F and Katie Glaskin, *Customary Land Tenure and Registration in Australia and Papua New Guinea: Anthropological Perspectives* (ANU Press, 2007)

Weir, C, 'The Churches in Solomon Islands and Fiji: Responses to the Crises of 2000' (2000) 53 *Development Bulletin* 49

West, Paige, *Dispossession and the Environment: Rhetoric and Inequality in Papua New Guinea* (Columbia University Press, 2016)

West, Paige and Martha MacIntyre, 'Special Issue: Melanesian Mining Modernities: Past, Present, and Future' (2006) 18(2) *The Contemporary Pacific*

White, Geoffrey M, 'Histories of Contact, Narratives of Self: Wartime Encounters in Santa Isabel' in Geoffrey M White and Lamont Lindstrom (eds), *The Pacific Theater: Island Representations of World War II* (University of Hawai'i Press, 1989) 43

Identity through History: Living Stories in a Solomon Islands Society (Cambridge University Press, 1991)

White, Geoffrey M and Lamont Lindstrom (eds), *The Pacific Theater: Island Representations of World War II* (University of Hawai'i Press, 1989)

White, Geoffrey M and Lamont Lindstrom, *Chiefs Today: Traditional Pacific Leadership and the Postcolonial State* (Stanford University Press, 1997)

Whitehead, Ann and Dzodzi Tsikata, 'Policy Discourses on Women's Land Rights in Sub–Saharan Africa: The Implications of the Re–Turn to the Customary' (2003) 3 (1–2) *Journal of Agrarian Change* 67

Whiteman, Darrell, 'Melanesians and Missionaries: An Ethnohistorical Study of Socio-Religious Change in the Southwest Pacific' (PhD thesis, Southern Illinois University, 1981)

Yngstrom, Ingrid, 'Women, Wives and Land Rights in Africa: Situating Gender Beyond the Household in the Debate Over Land Policy and Changing Tenure Systems' (2002) 30(1) *Oxford Development Studies* 21

SELECT MEDIA

Bartlet, G, 'Holy Mama Again', *Pacific Islands Monthly* (January 1979)

Callinan, Rory, 'Westpac Backs Logging Project', *Sydney Morning Herald* (13 August 2012), available at www.smh.com.au/environment/conservation/westpac-backs-logging-project-20120812-242wq.html, last accessed 10 January 2022

Ewart, Richard, 'Civil Society in Uproar over Proposed Land Law Changes in Vanuatu' (ABC News Australia, 2021), www.abc.net.au/radio-australia/programs/pacificbeat/vanuatu-government-land-reform-proposals-under-fire/13358172, last accessed 10 January 2022

Kuve Marlon and Wilko Bosma, 'Pro and Anti-Loggers in Vella Lavella' letter to the editor, *Solomon Star* 22 August 2007, 8

Melanesian Indigenous Land Defence Alliance, 'Declaration of the 3rd Meeting of the Melanesian Indigenous Land Defence Alliance (MILDA) Held at Natapao Village on the Island of Lelepa, Vanuatu, 10–11 March 2014' (2014), available at http://milda.aidwatch.org.au

Mamu, Moffat, (date unknown) 'Victim Tell It All' *Solomon Star*, 2007 (copy on file with the author)

Rence, Ender, 'Women Call for Suspension of Logging Licence' *Solomon Times Online* 2 August 2007

Rikimae, Joy A., (date unknown) 'Six charged over logging attack' *Solomon Star* 2007 (copy on file with the author)

RNZ, 'Solomons Women Injured in Anti-Logging Protest', *Radio New Zealand* (30 July 2007) https://rnz.co.nz/international/pacific-news/171607/solomons_women-injured-in-anti-logging-protest last accessed 12 December 2021

'Solomon Islands Government Called on to Reconsider Approach to Logging Companies', *Radio New Zealand* (30 July 2007), www.rnz.co.nz/international/pacific-news/171610/solomon-islands-government-called-on-to-reconsider-approach-to-logging-companies last accessed 12 December 2021

Te'e, Andrew, 'Land Is Sacred to Me', *Isatabu Tavuli* (2 March 2000)

Tetevete, F, 'Letter to the Editor', *Isatabu Tavuli* (6 June 2000)

Tuza, Esau, 'Paternal Acidity', *Pacific Islands Monthly* (January 1979)

Unknown, 'The Govt and the Guadalcanal Crisis' 1(1) *Isatabu Tavuli* (2000) (copy on file with the author)

'Logging Blocked in Vella Lavella' *Solomon Star* 1 (copy on file with the author)

'Injuries to Women Outrage MP' *Solomon Star* 6 August 2007 (copy on file with the author)

'Logging Guards Injure 6 Women', *Solomon Star* (Honiara) (1 August 2007) (copy on file with the author)

'Press Release', *Solomon Star* (Honiara) (1 August 2007) (copy on file with the author)

Wasuka, Evan, 'Push for Return to Indigenous Names for Honiara Streets and Landmarks', *Pacific Beat* (ABC Radio Australia, 2020), available at www.abc.net.au/radio-australia/programs/pacificbeat/push-for-return-to-indigenous-names-for-honiara-landmarks/12529132

TREATIES, STATUTES, BILLS

1st 2009 Draft Federal Constitution of Solomon Islands (Solomon Islands)

2nd 2014 Draft for Proposed Constitution of the Federal Democratic Republic of Solomon Islands (Solomon Islands)

The Constitution of Solomon Islands 1978 (UK)

Convention on the Elimination of All Forms of Discrimination Against Women, opened for signature 18 December 1979 (entry into force 3 September 1981), 1248 UNTS 13

Forest Resources and Timber Utilisation Act 1978 [Cap 40] (Solomon Islands)

Land and Titles Act 1996 [Cap 133] (Solomon Islands)

Lands (Amendment) Act 1972 [Cap 98] (Solomon Islands)

Local Courts Act 1996 [Cap 19] (Solomon Islands)

Native Administration (Solomons) Regulation 1922 (King's Regulation No 17 of 1922) (UK)

Native Administration Regulation 1953 (King's Regulation No 10 of 1953) (UK)

Native Courts Regulations (King's Regulation No. 2 of 1942) (UK)

Native Tax Regulation 1920 (King's Regulation No 10 of 1920) (UK)

Pacific Order in Council 1893 (UK)

Solomons and Gilbert and Ellice Islands (Commission of Inquiry) Regulation 1914 (King's Regulation No. 4 of 1914) (UK)

Solomons Labour Regulation 1921 (King's Regulation No 15 of 1921) (UK)

Solomons Labour Regulation 1922 (King's Regulation No 15 of 1922) (UK)

Solomons (Land) Regulation of 1896 (Queen's Regulation No 4. 1896) (UK)

Solomons Land Regulation 1914 (Kings Regulation No. 3 of 1914) (UK)

Solomons Land (Amendment) Regulation 1915 (King's Regulation No 4 of 1915) (UK)

Solomons Land (Amendment) Regulation 1920 (King's Regulation No 7 of 1920) (UK)

Solomons Land Registration Regulation 1918 (King's Regulation No 6 of 1918) (UK)

Solomons Land Registration (Amendment) Regulation 1921 (King's Regulation No 6 of 1921) (UK)

Solomons Land Registration (Amendment) Regulation 1922 (King's Regulation No 10 of 1922) (UK)

Solomons Land Registration (Amendment) Regulation (King's Regulations No 2 of 1919) (UK)

Solomons (Waste Lands) Regulation of 1900 (Queen's Regulation No. 3 of 1900) (UK)

Solomons (Waste Land) Regulation 1904 (King's Regulation No. 1 of 1904) (UK)

Townsville Peace Agreement, concluded 10 October 2000, UNSC S/2000/1088

Truth and Reconciliation Commission Act 2008 (Solomon Islands)

Western Pacific Order in Council 1877 (UK)

JUDICIAL DECISIONS, PUBLIC INQUIRIES

Allardyce Lumber Company Limited, Bisili, Roni, Sakiri, Hiele, Sasae, Poza, Zogabule, Daga, Pato and Zinghite v Attorney-General, Commission of Forest

Resources, Premier of Western Province and Paia [1989] SBHC 1; [1988–1989] SILR 78 (18 August 1989)

Bishop Tuhenua v Laugana, Mavi, Kurilau, Kavuchavi and Visona (Trustees of Kolotoha Land) [2004] SBHC 89; HC-CC 238 of 2003 (16 July 2004)

Clerk to Western Customary Land Appeal Court v Attorney-General [2003] SBHC 106; HC-CC 070 of 2003 (6 June 2003)

Concerning Luqa Land, Marovo Native Court Civil Case No 6/1974

Commission of Inquiry into Land Dealings and Abandoned Properties on Guadalcanal, *Consultation on Customary Land Issues in the Giana Region*, 9 April 2010

Deni v Metu, Local Court Land Case 2/2006

Estate of Oliver Jino v Majoria [2017] SBCA 1; SICOA-CAC 15 of 2016 (5 May 2017)

Gandley Simbe v East Choiseul Area Council, Eagon Resources Development Company Limited, Taki and Madana [1997] SBHC 67; HC-CC 033 of 1997 (17 July 1997)

In re Estate of Kona [1998] SBHC 84; HCSI-CC 331 of 1995 (15 May 1998)

Koina v Clerk to Local Court (Western) [2013] SBHC 69; HCSI-CC 155 of 2013 (21 June 2013)

Kasa v Biku [2004] SBHC 62; HC-CC 126 of 1999 (14 January 2000)

Lada v Majoria [2016] SBHC 65; HCSI-CC 134 of 2016 (17 May 2016)

Laugana (for Haubata Tribe) v Pukuvati, Kurilau, Keku, Botu and Roko (Trustees of PN-191-064-1) and Attorney-General (representing Commissioner of Lands) and Attorney General (representing Account General) [2009] SBHC 45; HCSI-CC 50 of 2008 (27 May 2009)

Letipiko v Ruben Ngatu, Marovo Native Court 3/1976

Loboi v Laugana, Botu, Saika, Ofasisili, Attorney-General (for the Commissioner of Lands) and Attorney-General (for Registrar of Titles) [2010] SBHC 38; HCSI-CC 212 of 2008 (30 July 2010)

Majoria v Jino [2003] SBHC 29, HC-CC 261-2002 (8 April 2003)

Majoria v Jino [2008] SBHC 54, HCSI-CC 225 of 2005 (16 May 2008)

Okeni v Ragoso WP 29/8/1950

Oreli of Telina v John Kera and Tuti of Rukutu, Marovo Local Court Case 8/1978

Patson Dioni v Miriam Achi Marovo Local Court, 7/1985

Perogolo v Laugana [2011] SBHC 103; HCSI-CC 162 of 2009 (3 October 2011)

Regina v Ome (2011) SBHC 27; HCSI-CRC 265 of 2006 (6 May 2011)

Report of the Lands Commission: Native Claim No 26 respecting land at Telina Island, Marovo Lagoon, claimed by the Australian Conference Association Ltd, 18 June 1924

Solomon Islands Truth and Reconciliation Commission, *Visale Public Hearing* Solomon Islands Truth and Reconciliation Commission 23, 24 and 25 June 2010

Solomon Islands Truth and Reconciliation Commission, *Thematic Public Hearing for Youth*, 22 November 2010

Solomon Islands Truth and Reconciliation Commission, *Thematic Public Hearing for Women* 25 November 2010

T Koni v J Repi High Court of the Western Pacific, Native Land Appeal No 5 of 1972

Timothi Koni v Rebi from New Michi Native Court, Marovo Civil Case No 4/1971

Timothy Koni of Gepae v Rebi of New Michi Native Court Civil Case 11/1969

ARCHIVAL SOURCES

Solomon Islands National Archives: BSIP I/III/49/19: Letter from the District Officer of Gizo to the Secretary of the Government re: Native Courts, October 1941.

Solomon Islands National Archives: BSIP I/III/F/14/23: Memorandum: Native Administration Officers, 14 October 1943.

Solomon Islands National Archives: BSIP I/III/F35/49: Lands Commission.

Solomon Islands National Archives: BSIP II/F3/9/1/1: Tour Report – Visale Subdistrict – April 1–5, 1957.

Solomon Islands National Archives: BSIP 7/III/33/4: Report on a Tour of Marovo Subdistrict by the District Commissioner, 1 June 1949

Solomon Islands National Archives: BSIP 7/III/F29/11 Vol II: *Commission of Lands 1949–1954.*

Solomon Islands National Archives: BSIP 7/VII/SS5/1: Policy on Leasing and Renting of Crown and Native Land.

Solomon Islands National Archives: BSIP 18/I/2 and 18/II/5: Lands Commission, Matanikau Claims by Lever's Pacific Plantation Ltd.

Solomon Islands National Archives: BSIP 18/I/41: Reports, Notes, Proceedings and Other Papers Relating to Land Claims. *Land Commissioner's Office, Lands Commission 1920–1924.*

Solomon Islands National Archives: BSIP 18/IV/25/24: Allen, Allen and Hemsley to F. Beaumont Phillips, 28 May 1921.

Solomon Islands National Archives: BSIP 18/IV/25/24: Petition from the Chiefs and Land-Owners of the Western Sols, 21 June 1921, J. F. Goldie to the Acting Commissioner of the British Solomon Islands, 19 November 1921.

Solomon Islands National Archives: BSIP 18/IV/25/24: Letter from the Resident Commissioner, 22 May 1922.

Solomon Islands National Archives: BSIP 18/IV/25/24: H. M. Blunden, Seventh Day Adventist "Islands Missions Secretary" to R. R. Kane Esquire, Resident Commissione of the British Solomon Islands, dated 12 July 1922.

Solomon Islands National Archives: BSIP 18/IV/25/24: Letter from the Resident Commissioner, 23 August 1922.

Solomon Islands National Archives: BSIP F3/12: Rev Fr de Klerk, 'A Few Observations on Native Relationship', *Tangarare Roman Catholic Mission* (1959).

Solomon Islands National Archives: BSIP LAN 2/1/67: Namoborunga (Kongulai).

Solomon Islands National Archives: BSIP LAN 2/1/86: Land Lease – Kakabona – Vatukola Cooperative Society.

Solomon Islands National Archives: BSIP LAN 2/1/92: Kovuara, Kakabona.

Solomon Islands National Archives: BSIP LAN 2/1/106: Letter to the District Commissioner from Ellison Hanivoti of Verahue Village, 21 August 1971.

Solomon Islands National Archives: BSIP LAND 1/1/1 Vol 1, 2: Land Legislation; Letter from Mrs I. V. Phillips, Ngautu Village c/o Guadalcanal Council, Honiara, 2 November 1974.

Solomon Islands National Ardchives: WPHC 2671 of 1922: Kane to High Commissioner, 26 August 1922.

Pacific Manuscripts Bureau: PMB 1109: Ishmael Ngatu, Diaries, 1927–1954 (English Translations and Some Originals).

Pacific Manuscripts Bureau: PMB 1189/15: Colin H Allan, Memoir of the Solomon
   Islands, 1948–1957, 300pp.

Pacific Manuscripts Bureau: PMB 1189/127: Colin H Allan, Special Lands
   Commission. Marovo: Draft Report.

Pacific Manuscripts Bureau: PMB 1292/013: Speech Delivered by the Premier of
   Western Province, Hon. Reuben Lilo, On the Occasion of the Declaration of
   State Government in the Region on July 7, 2000, Gizo, 8pp.

Index

Printed by Printforce, United Kingdom